Instead of presenting new research findings in entrepreneurship, this new book provides interesting stories about many of the luminary scholars in the field of entrepreneurship. Their intellectual and academic journeys are interesting and shed light on how entrepreneurship emerged as a genuine cross-disciplinary field of research.

Robert Fairlie, *Professor, University of California, Santa Cruz, USA*

The autobiographical chapters in this unique book reveal the passions and motivations of the scholars whose works created the surge in entrepreneurship research, and it provides an essential history of the thinkers and their thoughts.

John T. Scott, *Professor of Economics, Dartmouth College, USA*

The Routledge Companion to the Makers of Modern Entrepreneurship

Once relegated to the dusty shelves of ancient muses, research and scholarship on entrepreneurship has exploded as a field of research, with impactful additions from a range of disciplines rendering the field a tricky one to traverse. *The Routledge Companion to the Makers of Modern Entrepreneurship* offers a comprehensive guide to entrepreneurship, providing an authoritative exploration of the key people and their ideas. This book tells the stories of the scholars who have set the standard and tone for thinking and analysing entrepreneurship.

Edited by two of the world's leading entrepreneurship scholars, this comprehensive volume offers a platform for understanding and future research that is both state-of-the-art and authoritative. It expands on how modern entrepreneurship has developed, with a focus on the key "makers" of the field – including theories, such as social psychology; concepts, such as neuroeconomics; and types, such as political entrepreneurship.

The contributions to the collection are grouped into three sections:

* Emergence of Entrepreneurship Research
* Theories in Modern Entrepreneurship
* Concepts and Makers in Modern Entrepreneurship

This companion is essential reading for students and academics interested in entrepreneurship, entrepreneurial management and business management.

David B. Audretsch is a Distinguished Professor and Ameritech Chair of Economic Development at Indiana University, USA, where he also serves as Director of the Institute for Development Strategies. He is also an Honorary Professor of Industrial Economics and Entrepreneurship at the WHU–Otto Beisheim School of Management in Germany and a Research Fellow of the Centre for Economic Policy Research in London, UK.

Erik E. Lehmann is a Full Professor of Management and Organization at Augsburg University, Germany, and Director of the Global Business Management Program. He is also Adjunct Professor at Indiana University, USA, and Visiting Professor at University of Bergamo, Italy.

Routledge Companions in Business, Management and Accounting

Routledge Companions in Business, Management and Accounting are prestige reference works providing an overview of a whole subject area or sub-discipline. These books survey the state of the discipline including emerging and cutting-edge areas. Providing a comprehensive, up-to-date, definitive work of reference, Routledge Companions can be cited as an authoritative source on the subject.

A key aspect of these Routledge Companions is their international scope and relevance. Edited by an array of highly regarded scholars, these volumes also benefit from teams of contributors which reflect an international range of perspectives.

Individually, *Routledge Companions in Business, Management and Accounting* provide an impactful one-stop-shop resource for each theme covered. Collectively, they represent a comprehensive learning and research resource for researchers, postgraduate students and practitioners.

The Routledge Companion to the Makers of Modern Entrepreneurship

Edited by David B. Audretsch and Erik E. Lehmann

LONDON AND NEW YORK

First published 2017 by Routledge

2 Park Square, Milton Park, Abingdon, Oxfordshire OX14 4RN

52 Vanderbilt Avenue, New York, NY 10017

Routledge is an imprint of the Taylor & Francis Group, an informa business

First issued in paperback 2019

British Library Cataloguing in Publication Data
A catalogue record for this book is available from the British Library

Library of Congress Cataloging in Publication Data
Names: Audretsch, David B., editor. | Lehmann, Erik, editor.
Title: The Routledge companion to the makers of modern entrepreneurship / edited by David B Audretsch and Erik E. Lehmann.
Description: Abingdon, Oxon ; New York, NY : Routledge, 2017. | Includes bibliographical references and index.
Identifiers: LCCN 2016013724 | ISBN 9781138838109 (hardback) | ISBN 9781315734682 (ebook)
Subjects: LCSH: Entrepreneurship. | Small business. | Economic development.
Classification: LCC HB615 .R68354 2017 | DDC 338/.040922—dc23
LC record available at https://lccn.loc.gov/2016013724

ISBN: 978-1-138-83810-9 (hbk)
ISBN: 978-0-367-87156-7 (pbk)

Typeset in Bembo
by Apex CoVantage, LLC

Contents

Contents

Contents

1

Makers of modern entrepreneurship

David B. Audretsch and Erik E. Lehmann

Within the arc of a generation, entrepreneurship has come a remarkably long way. Business wants to harness it, policy wants to proliferate it, and students want to become it. The primacy of entrepreneurship has not escaped the attention of scholarship. Once relegated to the dusty shelves of ancient muses, research and scholarship on entrepreneurship have exploded into one of the most dynamic, lively fields of inquiry of our era.

This book is not about the phenomenon of entrepreneurship. By this point there is no paucity of analytical and critical works examining entrepreneurship from virtually every angle possible. Rather, this book is about the scholars who have studied entrepreneurship. Not just any scholars, but those who have set the standard and tone for thinking and analyzing entrepreneurship. It is a book, first and foremost, about people and their ideas.

The makers of entrepreneurship contributing to this volume may seem to be strikingly disparate. They span different scholarly disciplines, countries, cultural contexts, and modes of scholarship. Still, we find several salient themes and similarities uniting them. The first is that the makers of entrepreneurship typically did not study and were not trained in entrepreneurship research. Rather, they come from a myriad of academic backgrounds, disciplines, and fields, ranging from psychology to sociology, economics, geography, and political science.

The second observation is that, regardless of their starting point, their intellectual journey drew them off the path from known and familiar scholarly fields into the unknown terrain of what we today call entrepreneurship studies. A common feature of all of the authors and each of the chapters presented in this volume is that they resemble immigrants who have migrated to a new country and culture. Although they are now members of this new scholarly community, they still bear the traces and roots of the scholarly world of their intellectual origins. Each chapter reflects an author whose original research trajectory and scholarly methodologies, literature, and orientation were in some field other than entrepreneurship. Each one brings her or his own unique perspective, understanding, and academic and other experiences to the field, which in our view has richly embellished entrepreneurship studies.

A third common element among the authors and the chapters, which is impossible to miss when reading this book, is the high degree of passion and enthusiasm for their research topic, the overall field of entrepreneurship, and their own idiosyncratic journey that has taken them there.

These scholars love what they do, how they do it, and the people with whom they do it. Our experience is that such passion and commitment are rare and exceptional in the academy.

Our last observation is that it is best to let each scholar speak for herself or himself. We have found a plethora of insightful gems, not just in these common features among the makers of entrepreneurship, but in what each scholar has to say for herself or himself. We hope that you, the reader, will share this joy and reflection in reading what the makers of entrepreneurship have to say for themselves.

The godfather of entrepreneurship

Zoltan J. Acs

Introduction

In 1952 I found myself on a ship from Bremen, Germany, to New York City. The ship, the *USS General S. D. Sturgis*, was a WWII troop carrier that was shuttling displaced persons from war-torn Europe to destinations around the world. Of the 15 million or so displaced persons living in refugee camps after the war, about a million were now being relocated to the United States, Canada, and Australia.

One of my first memories in the new world is of my mother taking me to a diner on 89th Street and Buckeye Road in Cleveland, Ohio, where she bought me a hamburger. I loved it! On our second visit I asked for a hamburger again, but not knowing any English, I ended up with a ham sandwich. This was just the start of my long struggle in a new land. We yearned for our homeland, which, of course, we believed we would never see again.

I struggled on through my years as a young boy. Like any other youngster, I enjoyed climbing trees, playing baseball, and just running around the neighborhood. I played with a lot of kids, both black and white, who fought over everything and nothing. When I finished high school, I got busy climbing out of the world I had found myself in – that of a war refugee. With some luck and a lot of hard work, I navigated my way through college, earning a BA from Cleveland State University. I did not learn that much, but it was enough to spark my curiosity about my fate, which was like a burr under my saddle.

As a displaced person in the United States, two questions tore at me. First, what enabled the United States to offer unlimited opportunity to people from a faraway land? And second, what had failed in the world my family left behind? I felt lost and confused, and I wanted to know why and how the world turned out the way it did. I knew only that capitalism, fascism, and socialism had played some role in all of it.

So I did what most people do when life comes to a dead end – I went to graduate school. By some miracle I ended up at the New School for Social Research in New York City. This was a most curious place, full of members of the New Left and European intellectuals who were trying to explain the chaos in the world around us – the Vietnam War, poverty, capitalism, racism, democracy.

Over the next several years I earned a master's degree in political economy and, by the seat of my pants, managed to earn a PhD in economics. I accomplished this by working with Robert Heilbroner, Thomas Vietorisz, Edward Nell, Ross Thompson, and the late Stephen Hymer, who were the intellectual descendants of some of the greatest thinkers of our time: J. M. Keynes, John Hicks, Jürgen Habermas, Joseph Schumpeter, Paul Samuelson, Robert Solow, Hanna Arendt, and Levi Strauss.

The New School

My education at the New School taught me two things about the world. First, that industrial capitalism was about large firms and mass production on both sides of the Atlantic, and second, that the world was likely heading toward socialism, where state planning and nationalization would be the norm. It appeared that it was only a matter of time until capitalism would fail, as predicted by Marx (1867) and Schumpeter (1942). Put simply, overinvestment in industry would lead to a falling rate of profit, and without profit the capitalist world as we know it would cease to exist. However, my education included nothing about entrepreneurship or small firms.

And then fate stepped in. In my dissertation – by today's standards probably not a very good one – there was a small but important discovery. I had attempted to understand the evolution of capitalism through price theory and the study of industry. My discovery, the "two steels," showed that technical change can come from small firms, even in industries that have been dominated by large firms for a century or more. This curiosity was my first foray into the study of small firms and entrepreneurship, and it put me on the path to becoming a scholar of entrepreneurship.

I knew I had discovered something potentially significant, but was not sure what its relevance was at the time or what its full impact would be. However, I was not alone in my discovery: David Birch and Michael Piore, both at MIT, had independently and simultaneously found the same thing: that the capitalist model we had been studying no longer fit the facts, at least not as well as it should. Birch (1979) found that large enterprises in almost all metropolitan areas in the United States were no longer the main engines of job creation. Michael Piore and Charles Sable (1984) suggested in their book, *The Second Industrial Divide*, that after 200 years the organization of industry was again changing, this time away from mass production to flexible production.

My contribution, in *The Changing Structure of the U.S. Economy* (Acs, 1984), centered on technology, markets, and democracy, such as how small firms were both able to and allowed to innovate in industry after industry. And then, with the election of President Ronald Reagan in 1980, a set of institutional and social changes was unleashed upon the economy.

What did I know in 1980? Well, I put several issues on the table that would stand the test of time: If Schumpeter was wrong about the future of capitalism, who was right? If this new capitalism prevails, what might it look like? I also knew that economic growth had to be a piece of the puzzle, that we had to measure what was happening at the industry level, and that it had to be done in the tradition of existing studies on industrial organization.

At the policy level, I knew Keynesian economics was finished. As I wrote:

> Keynesian anticyclical policies cannot restore growth and eliminate unemployment. Planning would only make it worse. The conservative programs relying on small firms and markets, while going through a learning curve, appear to be moving in the "right" direction. The conclusion of this book is that the market today is a guiding light through the maze of economic uncertainty created by technological evolution.
>
> *(Acs, 1984 p. 223)*

These discoveries occurred from about 1976 to 1982. To understand what was happening, one only needed to read "The Coming Entrepreneurial Revolution: A Survey," an article by Norman Macrae that appeared in *The Economist* (1976, p. 41). *The Economist* had understood already that the world was going to change and that it was not moving toward more top-down management, central planning, and state ownership. The magazine's view was that we were approaching the end of big business, that state capitalism would not prevail, that it was the end of the "organization man," and that educated people would become more entrepreneurial. If any of this did prove true, then the field of small business and entrepreneurship was surely born out of a crisis in economics and the economic crisis of the 1970s.

Calling on a bit of economic theory at this point will be helpful in understanding a world in transition. For one thing, there are no entrepreneurs in general equilibrium theory. This means that, in a static world where all markets clear, the quantity supplied equals the quantity demanded – there is no role for the entrepreneur. General equilibrium theory had thus put the brakes on our understanding of the economy and on the development of economic theory in general.

One of the greatest developments in the field of economics was the Solow residual (Solow, 1957). Appearing in 1957, the concept had been years in the making. It shed light on where economic growth comes from and what causes it – that is, technical change. Solow pointed out that technical change was a term used for any kind of shift in the production function, and this calculation of his data was seen as an indication of where we needed to concentrate our attention – which was not on capital accumulated or hours worked. In fact, much economic growth (87%) remained unexplained, so it was now the turn of the explainers. What was in the residual?

Although the Solow story was interesting, an even more compelling story is that of Martin Weitzman (1970). In the Soviet Union, where technology was abundant, particularly in the military and space spheres, the Solow residual was only about 20%. In other words, capital accumulation and labor inputs explained the bulk of Soviet economic growth. However, the Soviet Union did not allow the substitution of capital and labor to create a new production function – in short, there was no economic freedom in the Soviet Union. Therefore, according to Weitzman (1970), the nation's economic growth would inevitably come to an end – which it did with the collapse of communism in 1989.

A second discovery that shed light on a world torn apart appeared in an essay by Harvey Leibenstein (1968). Leibenstein argued that entrepreneurs were needed to shift the production function and suggested that there are two kinds of entrepreneurs. The first is the replicative entrepreneur, who practices a kind of management that does not shift the production function but instead replicates an existing one, such as by opening another restaurant. The other is the novel or innovative entrepreneur, who shifts to a new production function, such as the cell phone. This creative destruction is what propels the capitalist system forward.

We now have the background for understanding the rebirth of entrepreneurship. The simultaneous discoveries made by Acs, Birch, and Piore and Sabel all revealed an empirical observation that did not fit with existing views of capitalism. In fact, their analyses predicted the entrepreneurial revolution, the fall of communism, and the rebirth of capitalism.

Now let's put some meat on the bones of this analytical skeleton. It was easy to study capitalism and socialism from an industrial perspective, as both systems had relatively few firms active in each industry. The West had more diversity in firm size, but not much more, than the Soviets in terms of what counts – innovative small firms. In the industrial organization literature, economists have at best studied a few hundred industries and the Fortune 500 firms. Small firms have long been thought to play a minimal role in job creation, innovation, and technical progress. Moreover, there was no perceived need for new firms, as the existing ones could do whatever was needed – even get man to the moon!

So this raises an obvious question: Why study small business? It may be helpful to start this discussion about the evolution of entrepreneurship with a story about small business. Small firms, which are smaller than big businesses no matter how measured, are at a disadvantage relative to larger firms – they have less money, less talent, etc. – which is common knowledge. However, we know very little about the history of small firms and, without an understanding of them vis-à-vis industry dynamics, it is almost impossible to understand entrepreneurship.

WZB and *Small Business Economics*

Over the decades, I have been part of five major research projects that have untangled the secrets of capitalist society and its evolution. After my discovery of innovative small firms in the steel industry, I started to examine industries in general, working with David Audretsch at the Wissenschaftszentrum Berlin fur Sozialforschung (WZB) in West Berlin. We looked at innovation in large and small firms in 247 industries and published the results in the *American Economic Review* (Acs and Audretsch, 1988). This was exciting work, and it had a major impact on the field of entrepreneurship, small business, innovation, and capitalist development. As Leonard W. Weiss wrote about our MIT Press book, *Innovation and Small Firms* (Acs and Audretsch, 1990):

> First, Acs and Audretsch establish quite convincingly the appropriateness of two data sets, one on small firms, industries, employment and output, and the other on thousands of innovations introduced in 1982 by firms of all sizes. Then they shake the earth. Every chapter knocks down many old beliefs and does so with a definitiveness that is uncommon in this line of study.

This piece of research changed the way people thought about the importance of small firms. To fully exploit our efforts in this emerging field, we started a new journal to disseminate our findings, which we called *Small Business Economics*.

The geography of innovation

After my stay in West Berlin I returned to the United States and took a job as an associate professor of economics at the University of Baltimore in Maryland. These were exciting times. Cities were in pursuit of high technology development, and Baltimore was no exception. I thereafter met Richard Florida, and my interests shifted from industries to cities.

The geography of innovation became an important research area just as the new economic geography was taking shape, influenced by the work of Paul Krugman. Research on cities, innovation, small firms, and entrepreneurship began to integrate the new economic geography, which helped shed light on the role of knowledge spillover and of agents and tolerance, which are forms of economic freedom. My second research project took what we learned from industry and applied it to cities. Our work was carried out at Carnegie Mellon University and a host of other institutions, including the Bureau of Economic Analysis at the U.S. Census Bureau. I published a book that integrated innovation into the growth of cities, *Innovation and the Growth of Cities* (Acs, 2002). A central premise of the book is that entrepreneurship is an important local activity that translates raw knowledge into ideas and start-ups that grow and underpin and sustain metropolitan growth. A second book with Catherine Armington (Acs and Armington, 2006) used longitudinally linked data from the Bureau of the Census to study the impact of human capital on regional employment growth. The fastest-growing regions are those that have the highest rates of new firm formation and that are not dominated by large businesses.

The Max Planck Institute of Economics

After a decade back in the United States, our research team shifted its center of gravity back to Germany. This time we set up a research unit at the Max Planck Institute of Economics in Jena, Germany, where David Audretsch made a great discovery: if all the firms we ever need already exist, then there is no need to explain how new firms emerge – firms are exogenous. What needs to be explained is how they endogenously created new knowledge that led to innovation. However, if this is not how the economy works, then we had to explain where new firms do come from. Knowledge, therefore, became exogenous, and starting innovative new firms became what needed explaining (Audretsch, 1995).

Our third project focused on the country level. Paul Romer's (1990) new growth theory had suggested an answer to the Solow puzzle, and it shed light on the entrepreneur (Acs and Sanders, 2013). This project was the first to look not only at U.S. data but also data from Organisation for Economic Co-operation and Development (OECD) countries. Our research led to theoretical insights about entrepreneurship – what I called the Knowledge Spillover Theory of Entrepreneurship (KSTE) – which offered an explanation of how economic agents create new firms and why new firms are important to an economy (Acs et al., 2009, 2010; Carlsson et al., 2009).

According to the KSTE, the context in which decision making is done can influence one's determination to become an entrepreneur. By commercializing ideas that evolved from an incumbent organization but were independent of the organization through the creation of a new firm, the entrepreneur serves not only as a conduit for the spillover of knowledge, but also for the ensuing innovative activity and enhanced economic performance. The KSTE is consistent with the Schumpeterian view of entrepreneurship, which sees the role of the entrepreneur as creating a new production function.

George Mason University

Following the fall of the Berlin Wall, all countries in the world abandoned central planning and the nationalization of industry and embraced free markets, capital markets, free trade, and entrepreneurship. We thus saw the merging of two fields of study: entrepreneurship and economic development. With its world-class scholars and cadre of bright graduate students, George Mason University provided a perfect place to pursue this new agenda.

Our fourth research project focused on the global economy, bringing entrepreneurship and small firms in developing countries to the forefront of economic development. The focus shifted to understanding how developing countries can use what has been learned in developed countries over the years. There was a race between research organizations to understand the subject and to move the world in the right direction. In 2000 the Global Entrepreneurship Monitor (GEM) was the first large global research project that provided an experiment in data measurement. In 1988 Laszlo Szerb and I created the Global Entrepreneurship and Development Index (GEDI), a tool for understanding entrepreneurial ecosystems. I was involved in the GEM project for a decade in several capacities and founded GEM Hungary. GEDI grew out of the GEM project because of the need for a global index (Acs, Autio and Szerb, 2014).

Building on institutional economics and entrepreneurship research, we developed a new index methodology that characterized national systems of entrepreneurship by recognizing interactions with various components such as entrepreneurial attitudes, entrepreneurial abilities, and entrepreneurial aspirations. In particular, GEDI identified bottleneck factors that hold back entrepreneurial performance. This systemic approach to national systems of entrepreneurship considers institutional arrangements beyond geographic proximity and location-specific endowments, thus portraying the phenomenon of country-level entrepreneurship more realistically. This approach also forces researchers and policy makers to think in systemic terms that widen their perspective when considering both individual-level and country-level indicators.

Finally, I returned to my original question of what the new capitalism looks like. It took a long time to figure out the answer. In 1995, when I was chief economist at the U.S. Small Business Administration, my boss asked me to develop an entrepreneurship policy for the United States and to have it ready in a week. Remember that this was a time of robust growth and innovation, and the U.S. economy was the envy of the world. Therefore the question of entrepreneurial policy was already in the air.

I pondered my new assignment for a few days. I knew small business policy was intended to help "disadvantaged businesses" (what they were called at the Defense Department). The tools also were rather well known – financial assistance, training, technical assistance, etc. But entrepreneurs were a different story. They certainly were not disadvantaged – I immediately thought of Bill Gates. What kind of help did he need to set up Microsoft? The next week I reported to my boss that I could not come up with an entrepreneurship policy that would make rich, white men richer – at least not one that the U.S. Congress would pass. He suggested that I create a policy for women.

A few weeks later I was at Yale University, where I told this story about creating policy to a friend who is an investment banker. He immediately suggested that I do not really understand American society. He said, "You study small firms and entrepreneurship," which I confirmed, and he responded, "That is only half the American story. What do you see around us?" I said, "Lots of buildings." He said, "Yes, and each one was donated by a rich guy." He was telling me that American capitalism is about both the creation of wealth and the reconstitution of capital.

I did not take this in right away, but it was in the back of my mind for a few weeks, and I finally decided to write a paper about it. I went to the library looking for books on entrepreneurship and philanthropy, and guess what? There weren't any. I found books on capitalism, entrepreneurship, philanthropy, wealth, and foundations, but nothing to suggest that any of it was connected. In fact, the whole issue of philanthropy was buried during most of the twentieth century, and the reason why is rather simple. Under socialism and communism, and to some extent under managerial capitalism, there is no need for entrepreneurship, entrepreneurs, small firms, philanthropy, or any of the above. The government is the prime actor in the system and directs most economic and social activity. It took me more than a decade to come up with an explanation of how the new capitalism worked. The reason it took so long was that we were all pushing against Schumpeter.

When I asked my publicist what makes best sellers, she replied, "Four factors: how well known the author is, how interesting the subject matter is, the book's scope and reach, and the 'X' factor." Applying these measures to Joseph A. Schumpeter's (1942) classic, *Capitalism, Socialism and Democracy* (hereafter CSD), the author was very well known, the subject was interesting, the book had great depth, and, most importantly, the X factor turned out to be huge. CSD went on to become an international sensation for half a century.

So what was the X factor that catapulted CSD to the best-seller list almost a century ago? Schumpeter's book fed into a growing global debate about economics, specifically the long-term evolution of capitalist society. In 1942, as World War II raged – the battles of Stalingrad and Midway, the carpet bombing of Axis cities – the world was concerned not so much with the individual battles as with what the world would look like after the bombs stopped falling.

Schumpeter provided a chilling and sober view of that great debate, posing and answering three questions. He first asked, "Can capitalism survive?" and responded, "I do not think so." He then asked, "Can socialism work?" and replied, "Of course." Finally, in response to his question, "Will socialism be democratic?" he punted – that is, he was not sure if socialism would or would not be democratic. Schumpeter was in fact wrong on all three counts. Whereas capitalism survived and flourished, socialism failed, and it also turned out to be authoritarian rather than democratic. The Age of Enlightenment (or simply the Enlightenment or the Age of Reason) is an era from the 1620s to the 1780s in which cultural and intellectual forces in Western Europe emphasized reason, analysis, and individualism rather than traditional lines of authority. In the twentieth century, as people lost patience with the enlightened ideal, communism and its variants spread throughout much of the world. Leaders who rejected capitalism, democracy, and philanthropy nationalized the means of production, replacing the free market with central planning and in many cases exchanging democracy for totalitarianism. There was widespread sympathy for the communists, even in the United States, especially during the Great Depression. A new world order was put in place, and only a few countries stood against it. But by the end of the twentieth century, communism had collapsed. It simply could not keep pace with the economic output of its democratic capitalist competitors.

The fall of the Berlin Wall and Fukuyama's (1989) book, *The End of History and the Last Man*, drove the final nail into the coffin of *Capitalism, Socialism, and Democracy* as an interpretation of the future. However, no new blueprint along the lines of CSD has emerged, not in this work by Fukuyama or in those by others who share this intellectual space. The removal of trade barriers and capital flows after 1990 continue to create efficient markets, and the results are what economists call a Zipf distribution: a few big winners and lots of losers, with economic opportunity tending to concentrate among a few and the losers becoming frustrated. To deal with this frustration, many in both the developed and the developing worlds have turned to religious fanaticism or some other realm for consolation. In fact, this was the subject of the final essay by the late Paul Samuelson (2008), who was the most important economist in the United States for fifty years.

My fifth research project was about understanding how the capitalist system works in the twenty-first century by focusing on altruism, or what I call the creation of opportunity. I focused on the entrepreneurship–philanthropy nexus (Acs and Phillips, 2002). The fact that Schumpeter was so wrong is interesting, but it is more interesting to understand why he was wrong. To do so, we needed to look at the building blocks of modern society: capitalism, philanthropy, and democracy. Although these pillars go back hundreds or thousands of years, their modern incarnation, which creates opportunity for the middle class, is new.

Before going on, I should define these terms a little better. By capitalism I do not mean Monopoly capitalism or corporatism, but a society that promotes entrepreneurship and innovation, with a focus on radical innovation. By philanthropy we mean that parts of society understand and support institutions that recycle capital so that private wealth can create public good. Finally, by democracy we mean a pluralistic society in which the goal is to create opportunity for all, including the pursuit of happiness.

However, only a few decades after the fall of the Berlin Wall there is a growing debate about the current state of economics, particularly the long-term evolution of capitalism, social inequality, the unequal concentration of wealth, and prospects for social stability. According to the international bestseller by Thomas Piketty (2014), *Capital in the Twenty-First Century*, the main driver of inequality is the tendency of returns on capital to exceed the rate of economic growth, which historically is close to 5% and the rate of economic growth is less than 2%, respectively. However, I believe the real X factor has been the policy prescription – a global tax on capital that was embraced by the Left and lamented by the Right.

Philanthropy matters in this debate because it offers an alternative solution to the Piketty conundrum without relying exclusively on a wealth tax or redistribution. So how does philanthropy resolve the conundrum? The answer is rather simple: the growth rate of the economy g should be increased so as to mitigate the difference between $r > g$ and reduce the share of income going to the owner of capital (*r* is the rate of return on capital). Philanthropy maintains the dynamism of the capitalist system and partially solves rising income inequality by increasing growth and reducing the share of capital income going to the wealthy. Like taxes, the focus is on the capital–income ratio, but it focuses on the stock of capital (wealth) rather than on the flow of income. Philanthropy does not affect the stock of capital and instead redirects the flow of income to activities that create opportunity. In other words, it turns a share of capital into moral capital, defined as the resources that sustain a moral community (Acs, 2016).

We would expect to find that moral capital has found its way into the universities, where opportunity is created for so many. In the United States, the top 1,000 schools are sitting on half a trillion dollars in university endowments; each has an average endowment of $500 million, with land and buildings of equal value. The second source of moral capital is the foundations. The largest 100 foundations in the United States have more than half a trillion dollars, with more than $30 billion held by the Gates Foundation alone; another half a trillion sits in smaller foundations. The third fund of moral capital is held by the churches, a sum close to 2 trillion dollars. A rough estimate of the total moral capital held in the United States is close to 5 trillion dollars, or 5% of the total capital stock – more than any other country in the world.

Philanthropy has long been a distinctive feature of American culture, but its crucial role in the economic well-being of the nation – and the world – has remained largely unexplored. Philanthropy addresses the question of what to do with capital: keep it, tax it, or give it away. Putting a portion of capital into a foundation that serves the public good helps to maintain the stock of capital and the capital–income ratio; the income in turn complements government efforts by flowing to a privately created public good. Philanthropy that focuses on education, science, and medicine has a particularly positive effect on long-term economic growth.

Many might ask how philanthropy can be a part of capitalism. Whereas capitalism is governed by the market system and democracy by the political process, philanthropy is to a large degree governed by laws outside the market. Nevertheless, it both reinforces and nourishes democracy and capitalism by relying on the better side of human nature.

Philanthropy lacks a set of laws to explain its ebb and flow; like royal patrons of the arts in centuries past, it is subject to the whims of the wealthy. Furthermore, philanthropy is largely ungoverned by economic principles and relatively free of the checks and balances found in a democracy. In short, philanthropy is governed by individual principles, such as altruism, whereas capitalism is governed by culture and institutions. As German sociologist, philosopher, and political economist Max Weber (1958) demonstrated, capitalism is a relatively orderly cultural system of institutions and incentives governed by the tractable logic of supply and demand.

However, philanthropy does not interfere with the dynamics of capitalism. In fact, I have argued in my Oxford lecture on philanthropy at Green Templeton College (Acs, 2015a) that philanthropy propels the basic machinery of capitalism as much as government and taxes. But whereas government reinforces the status quo, philanthropy changes it. Therefore, along with well-functioning markets, property rights, contract law, and the like, philanthropy provides a vital nonmonetary institutional force that spurs economic growth by supporting technological innovation, promoting economic equality, and cultivating economic security.

The London School of Economics

After the Mason years I took a position at the London School of Economics (LSE). I needed a perspective on exactly how entrepreneurship and philanthropy fit into the modern political economy of globalization, democracy, government, and advanced capitalism. At the LSE I had a chance to think this through from the perspective of an institution that is on the left and does not embrace either entrepreneurship or philanthropy. LSE students still want to change the world but do not necessarily want to be prime minister. The newly founded Marshall Institute for Philanthropy and Social Entrepreneurship at LSE will try and change all of this.

In the twenty-first century, capitalism and democracy are flourishing in both expected and unexpected countries across the globe. However, much of the global community does not yet fully appreciate that these two forces cannot survive and prosper without philanthropy. Whereas capitalism is a cultural phenomenon and democracy has institutional underpinnings, philanthropy is a natural force that has always existed in some form in all societies. The need to look after each other is part of humans' moral DNA, and philanthropy is the glue that holds the other social processes – capitalism and democracy – together (Acs, 2015a).

In "'Entrepreneurial Capitalism' in Capitalism Development: Toward a Synthesis of Capitalist Development and the Economy as a Whole" (Acs, 2008), I recast the theory of economic development as a synthesis of capitalism, development, and society as a whole. I interpret the founding of the United States as the product of a shift in human character and social roles that led to the Declaration of Independence and the Revolutionary War – and, ultimately, to modern American civilization. The paper argues that a new character type, the agent, had unprecedented powers of discretion and self-reliance, yet also was bound to collective ends by emerging forms of institutional authority and internal restraint. This newly emerged agent was responsible for the entrepreneurship–philanthropy nexus through which much world development has occurred.

My article "Defining Prosperity" (Acs and Auerswald, 2009) examines the subject of global prosperity from the perspective of the global financial crisis. In it I argue that the current crisis will pass, as such crises always do, and suggest that we think about the crisis calmly and carefully and ask critical questions: What exactly are we asking of our institutions? How did we come to care about economic growth in the first place? Capitalist growth succeeds because it creates wealth, which in turn generates economic opportunity through investments that seek the maximum private return. However, in this paper I argue that, without philanthropy, growth fueled by entrepreneurship in a capitalist economy will ultimately reach a dead end because of inequality.

The essence of advanced capitalism today is not a static "iron triangle" that balances the interests of large corporations and organized labor with the active intervention of government. Nor is it a free-for-all in which the interests of the many are readily subsumed by the acquisitive appetites of the few. Rather, American capitalism is a dynamic process that balances wealth and opportunity – the great seesaw of civilization. It follows that the success of advanced capitalism must turn not on its transient ability to generate macroeconomic growth but on its sustained ability to generate microeconomic opportunity (2009, p. 9 emphasis added).

Finally, in "The Great Seesaw of Civilization" (Acs, 2014), I restate the arguments made in my recent book, *Why Philanthropy Matters: How the Wealthy Give and What It Means for Our Economic Well-Being* (Acs, 2013). In order to invigorate the capitalist system, wealth needs to be kept in rotation, like the planets around the sun. I argue that philanthropy invigorates capitalism in two ways. The first is that it targets universities, research, and other productive efforts that lay the groundwork for new cycles of innovation and enterprise. The second is that – like creative destruction – it provides a mechanism to dismantle the accumulated wealth tied to the past and reinvests it in ways that strengthen future entrepreneurial potential.

Therefore, when philanthropy is absent, wealth remains concentrated, rent seeking flourishes, and innovation and entrepreneurship suffer. Although philanthropy is rarely understood as an entity intertwined with capitalism, it has both emanated from and continually nurtured the capitalist system. It is a nearly invisible and clearly underappreciated force for progress in American capitalism (Zunz, 2012).

I now know the answer to the question I raised earlier: If this new capitalism prevails, what might it look like? The answer is that twentieth-century capitalism, socialism and democracy gets replaced with twenty-first-century capitalism, philanthropy, and democracy. Converts to capitalism are won not so much by innovation (new consumer good) and entrepreneurship, but through the deeds of philanthropy. Philanthropy is natural, whereas capitalism is cultural. Nature always trumps nurture.

As I close this chapter, I have a much better understanding of my own two questions asked so long ago: What enabled the United States to offer unlimited opportunity to people from a faraway land? And what had failed in the world my family left behind? Entrepreneurship and philanthropy are part of the answer to both questions.

References

Acs, Z. J. (1984) The Changing Structure of the U.S. Economy: Lessons from the Steel Industry. New York: Praeger.

Acs, Z. J. (2002) Innovation and the Growth of Cities. Cheltenham: Edward Elgar.

Acs, Z. J. (2008) Entrepreneurship, Economic Growth and Public Policy: Prelude to a Knowledge Spillover Theory of Entrepreneurship. Cheltenham: Edward Elgar.

Acs, Z. J. (2013) Why Philanthropy Matters: How the Wealthy Give, and What It Means for Our Economic Well-Being. Princeton, NJ: Princeton University Press.

Acs, Z. J. (2014) The Great Seesaw of Civilization. Philanthropy Impact Magazine, 5(Spring), 15–18.

Acs, Z. J. (2015a) What is Philanthropy? And Why Does It Matter in the 21st Century? Inaugural Seminar Series Oxford Center for the Study of Philanthropy, Green Templeton College, Oxford University. www.youtube.com/watch?v=2fnO0OaCTuk

Acs, Z. J. (2015b) Global Entrepreneurship, Institutions and Incentives: The Mason Years. Cheltenham, UK: Edward Elgar Publishers.

Acs, Z. J. (2016) Moral Capital in the Twenty-first Century. CESIS Electronic Working Paper Series No. 418.

Acs, Z. J. and Armington, C. (2006) Entrepreneurship, Geography and American Economic Growth. Cambridge: Cambridge University Press.

Acs, Z. J. and Audretsch, D. B. (1988) Innovation in Large and Small Firms: An Empirical Analysis. American Economic Review, 78(September), 678–690.

Acs, Z. J. and Audretsch, D. B. (1990) Innovation and Small Firms. Cambridge: The MIT Press.

Acs, Z. J., Audretsch, D., Braunerhjelm, P., and Carlsson, B. (2010) The Missing Link: Knowledge Diffusion and Entrepreneurship in Endogenous Growth. Small Business Economics 2010, 43(1), 105–125.

Acs, Z. J., Audretsch, D. B., Lehmann, E. E., and Light, G. (2016) National Systems of Entrepreneurship. Small Business Economics, 46(4), 527–535.

Acs, Z. J. and Auerswald, P. (2009) Defining Prosperity. The American Interest, summer (May/June), 1–9.

Acs, Z. J., Autio, E., and Szerb, L. (2014) National Systems of Entrepreneurship: Measurement Issues and Policy Implications. Research Policy, 43(3), 476–494.

Acs, Z. J., Braunerhjelm, P., Audretsch, D. B., and Carlsson, B. (2009) The Knowledge Spillover Theory of Entrepreneurship. Small Business Economics, 32(1), 15–30. DOI: 10.1007/s11187–008–9157–3.

Acs, Z. J. and Phillips, R. (2002) Entrepreneurship and Philanthropy in American Capitalism. Small Business Economics, 19, 189–204.

Acs, Z. J. and Sanders, M. (2013) Knowledge Spillover Entrepreneurship in an Endogenous Growth Model. Small Business Economics, 41(4), 775–796.

Audretsch, D. B. (1995) Innovation and Industry Evolution. Cambridge: The MIT Press.

Birch, D. (1979) The Job Generation Process. Cambridge: MIT Program on Neighborhood and Regional Change.

Carlsson, B., Acs, Z. J., Audretsch, D. B., and Braunerhjelm, P. (2009) Knowledge Creation, Entrepreneurship and Economic Growth: A Historical Review. Industrial and Corporate Change, 2009, 18, 1193–1229.

Fukuyama, F. (1989) The End of History and the Last Man. Cambridge, MA: Harvard University Press.

Kirzner, I. M. (1973) Competition & Entrepreneurship. Chicago: University of Chicago Press.

Leibenstein, H. (1968) Entrepreneurship and Development. American Economic Review, 58, 72–83.

Marx, K. [(1876)1967] Capital: A Critical Analysis of Capitalist Production. New York, NY: Monthly Review Press.

Piketty, T. (2014) Capital in the 21st Century. Cambridge, MA: Harvard University Press.

Piore, M. and Sable, C. (1984) The Second Industrial Divide: Probabilities for Prosperity. New York: Basic Books.

Romer, P. (1990) Endogenous Technological Change. Journal of Political Economy, 98(October), 71–102.

Samuelson, P. (2008) "Innovation and Technician Change." In Z. J. Acs, D. B. Audretsch, and R. Strom, (eds.), Entrepreneurship, Growth and Public Policy. New York: Cambridge University Press, pp. 55–64.

Schumpeter, J. A. (1942) Capitalism, Socialism and Democracy. New York: Harper and Bros.

Solow, R. M. (1957) Technical Change and the Aggregate Production Function. Review of Economics and Statistics, 39(3), 312–320.

Weber, M. (1958) The Protestant Ethic and the Spirit of Capitalism, trans. Talcott Parsons. New York: Scribner.

Weitzman, M. L. (1970) Soviet Postwar Economic Growth and Capital-Labor Substitution. American Economic Review, 63(4), 676–692.

Zunz, O. (2012) Philanthropy in America: A History. Princeton, NJ: Princeton University Press.

3

Fifty years in the making
My career as a scholar of organizations and entrepreneurship

Howard E. Aldrich

Introduction

In this chapter, I describe my five-decades-long journey from sociology graduate student to small business researcher to, finally, a scholar of entrepreneurship. I begin with my four years at the University of Michigan, where I learned the craft of sociological research from the masters of the trade, and then cover briefly my early years as an assistant professor at Cornell University. My early work on studies of business succession in the United States and England heavily imprinted my subsequent work on organizational foundings and disbandings, and I describe how I got involved in that research. The 1970s were a critical era for organizational theory, and I review the major influences that shaped my thinking during that time, particularly with regard to the evolutionary perspective and resource dependence theory with which I came to be associated. My awakening as an entrepreneurship scholar occurred quite by accident, and I review the circumstances that catalyzed that identity. Collaboration with graduate students and like-minded colleagues has played a major role in all of my projects, and so I acknowledge some of these contributors as well. Finally, I conclude by offering a few words of advice to junior scholars still considering whether they want to make entrepreneurship research their life's work.

Academic beginnings

I graduated from Bowling Green State University in Ohio in 1965, majoring in sociology and minoring in psychology. (I came close to having minors in economics and English, as well.) After graduation, I took a few weeks off to get married and then entered graduate school at the University of Michigan. During my four years in Ann Arbor I felt I was on a constant learning journey. The social sciences were in their glory: the psychology, sociology, economics, history, and political science programs were all ranked in the top ten. An incredible infusion of federal money in the mid-1960s had invigorated the social sciences, particularly studies of urban environments, crime, and ethnic and race relations.

I was pursuing my PhD in sociology and also earned a minor in social psychology. I took courses in other departments, as well: mathematics, political science, and economics. For example, I took "consumer behavior" with George Katona (1964), one of the leading lights of the psychology of economic behavior, and two seminars with Phil Converse (1976), a leading political behaviorist. In Converse's seminar, I used three-wave panel data to study changes in voters' political identification. Writing that paper gave me my first taste of the value of panel study data, and many of the studies I subsequently carried out used that design.

During my graduate work, I was fascinated by the work of scholars such as Donald Campbell (1969), a psychologist who coined the term "evolutionary epistemology" and made pioneering contributions to many social science disciplines; Walter Buckley (1967), a sociologist who wrote about general systems theory; and social psychologists such as Daniel Katz and Robert Kahn. I took Katz's graduate course on organizations in which we used his book, *The Social Psychology of Organizations* (Katz & Kahn, 1978), in manuscript form. Katz gave me some advice about the theory building which I've never forgotten: "Design your theoretical framework so that other people's perspectives are a subset of yours." Readers familiar with the evolutionary perspective and its encompassing reach will appreciate how much I took Katz's recommendation to heart. I have always argued that the evolutionary perspective is a metatheory, an overarching framework that permits comparison and integration of other social scientific theories. It does not provide a set of law-like statements governing evolutionary processes, but rather takes what it needs from other pro approaches. It is purposefully eclectic.

Michigan offered excellent research opportunities, including an opportunity to run research projects through the Institute for Social Research (ISR). I was the study director for projects based on nationally representative samples, and through them I gained experience in designing surveys and working with interviewing and coding crews. In the summer of 1966, I began working on a project that would eventually become a natural experiment driven by the civil disorders of the late 1960s. Under the direction of my mentor Al Reiss, the director of the Center for Research on Social Organization, and with a grant from the US Crime Commission, some fellow graduate students and I began the first wave of interviews for a study of approximately 800 businesses and organizations in high-crime areas of three US cities: Boston, Chicago, and Washington, DC. We were looking at areas that were undergoing very rapid ethnic succession: Roxbury in Boston, the south and west sides of Chicago, and the Georgia/7th Avenue and 14th St. corridors in Washington, DC. All three cities were heavily affected by the civil disorders of 1967 and 1968.

Based on my work at ISR, by the time I was ready to begin my dissertation in 1968 I had the skills I needed to actually assemble my own research crew. My research questions were motivated by my interest in human ecology and population-level thinking. In my thesis, I tried to understand populations from an evolutionary point of view. I went back to the same high-crime areas we had studied in 1966 and did a second wave of interviews. I hired interviewers from Ann Arbor, flying them to the different cities, putting them up in YMCAs and cheap motels, and supervising their daily schedules. Also doing a lot of the interviewing myself, I spent the summer walking through decaying inner-city areas, interviewing business owners about their operations and asking how they coped with difficult business conditions. The experience of running my own study was incredibly instructive, compressing into those four years what many people spend five or six years in graduate school to accomplish – almost like an extended post doc.

I finished my thesis, *Organizations in a Hostile Environment*, in 1969. I was able to do my data collection and analysis and still finish in four years because I had full financial support from the National Science Foundation (NSF), as well as a Danforth Foundation Fellowship and a Woodrow Wilson Fellowship. I didn't use any of the Woodrow Wilson grant, but I did call upon the Danforth Foundation to support the production of my dissertation: I typed my first draft on an IBM Selectric typewriter and then passed the pages onto a professional service that used them to create masters, which in turn were used to produce multiple copies of the dissertation. It was a cumbersome procedure, and toward the end I spent almost a week in my office at the Perry

School Building, correcting the masters used to make the copies. When people talk about "the good old days," they tend not to write about misfortunes like that!

Finding a community of scholars at Cornell

I took my first job at the New York State School of Industrial and Labor Relations (ILR) at Cornell University in 1969. I wish I could say that I'd crafted a well-designed strategy that involved choosing Cornell as my first job, because it did work out so well, but I have to admit that it was a fortuitous choice. Cornell had several things going for it when I got here. Bill Starbuck left the year after I arrived, but there were other sociological colleagues in the ILR School in the Organizational Behavior Department, including William Foote Whyte, whose book on Street Corner Society (Whyte, 1943) I had read as an undergraduate. I shared an office suite with Gerry Gordon and began to realize that my research interests could be described not just as sociology and evolutionary thinking, but also in terms of organizational studies within sociology.

My writings in the early 1970s harkened back to a number of papers I had written in graduate school, where I was trying to apply evolutionary thinking to organizations. Back then, I had submitted one of my first attempts to Bill Starbuck at the *Administrative Science Quarterly* (ASQ). I knew about ASQ but I didn't know about its stellar reputation until much later, when I became its associate editor. Accordingly, I was very surprised when two weeks later, the manuscript came back, unreviewed, with a letter from Bill, saying something like, "Dear Sir, very sorry, but we are not going to review this paper because it is off the main line of interest of our journal." (When I became associate editor, I learned this was just "Form Letter 2a.")

I rewrote the paper, called it "Organizational Boundaries and Interorganizational Conflict," and sent it to Human Relations, where it was accepted with minor revisions (Aldrich, 1971). In that paper, I argued that we can't investigate organizations without paying attention to the environments they inhabit. In fact, no explanations are complete until they include the environments in which organizations acquire their resources. That paper became the foundation on which I built my subsequent papers and my 1979 book, *Organizations and Environments*. I went on to research other questions, but the response to my paper on population-level thinking made me realize that "evolution" was a very powerful perspective.

Early work on business succession in cities in the United States and England

My experience in working with multiwave panel studies at the University of Michigan gave me the confidence to conduct several panel studies of my own on ecological succession in inner-city neighborhoods. The first was a follow-up of my dissertation research, and the second extended my US research overseas.

The US project

In 1970 and 1972, I followed up with two more waves of the panel study I had begun in graduate school. Al Reiss and I were studying representative, random samples of businesses in environments that were incredibly challenging places to do business. Population composition was shifting as the suburbanization of these cities was under way, and ethnic succession was occurring as the white population was moving out and being replaced by African American and Hispanic residents (Aldrich, 1975). The business population was adapting to these changes, and our research design allowed us to relate the turnover in ownership to turnover in the population. We coded residential composition down to the level of census tracts, and because we had 1960 and 1970 US Census data, we knew the rate of residential population change at a very micro level.

Normally, when opportunities for new owners occurred because of turnover in business ownership, the next people in the queue to become owners would have been other whites. But because of the increasing proportion of African American residents in these neighborhoods, as well as relative neighborhood economic decline, whites no longer found this an attractive proposition. Over time in these areas – first in the most heavily African American neighborhoods and then gradually elsewhere – the white owners were replaced. This was a very orderly process, as the proportion of whites slowly decreased and the proportion of blacks who were becoming new owners slowly increased, occupying the vacancies that opened up as previous owners retired, moved on to other jobs, or passed away (Aldrich & Reiss, 1976).

The UK project

In 1975, when my wife and I were deciding where to take our upcoming sabbatical, I discovered that the Ford Foundation was funding scholars to study contemporary issues in England. I realized this could be an opportunity to test some of the business succession ideas I had developed in the American context. I applied for the grant, indicating that I was curious about the effect of civil disorders in English cities on their business populations. I had read about popular objections in the United Kingdom to the immigration from the New Commonwealth areas; many immigrants were Pakistani, Indian, or Caribbean. I said it would be really interesting to see whether the turnover in the residential population of UK cities was having an impact on the business population, in a process similar to what I had observed in the United States.

I proposed this to the Centre for Environmental Studies in London, which was running the grant program, and the first thing they said, in so many words, was, "This is preposterous. You can't make an assumption that relations between the races in the United Kingdom are anything like in the United States; we don't have your problems. This is a foolish endeavor, don't bother us." I thought they were wrong, and so I wrote back politely and said, "Look, give me a chance to prove who is right. Let me put this to an empirical test." So they relented, awarded me a grant, and I spent the fall of 1975 in London doing a pilot project.

I assembled a research small team and did about 250 interviews in a part of London called Wandsworth, which had sizable West Indian and Asian populations. I discovered that many of the concepts of succession that I'd used in my US work fit the United Kingdom beautifully. I learned some of these businesses had owners who no longer knew how to deal with their customers and that white owners seemed uninterested in buying shops in Wandsworth. That was sufficient evidence to convince a few scholars in social geography at Liverpool Polytechnic to join with me. We submitted a grant application to the Social Science Research Council, which awarded us funding to do a comparison study of the United States and the United Kingdom.

Working with three social geographers, we designed a four-wave panel study that followed hundreds of small firms, mostly retail and service establishments. We started planning the project in 1976 and went into the field for survey interviews in three cities in 1978, 1980, 1982, and 1984 (Aldrich, Cater, Jones, & McEvoy, 1983). Using voter registration lists, we were able to code down to the level of 100-meter by 100-meter square areas of residential composition and so we had incredible micro data, even better than I had used for the United States. The surveys lasted anywhere from 30 minutes to two hours and gave us richly detailed data.

The dynamics of ecological succession that I observed in the United States fit the pattern we found in England very well. As in the American context, business turnover rates were quite high, as one set of business owners, mainly white, was replaced by another set of business owners,

Table 3.1 Patterns of co-authorship over five decades (books and articles)

Authorship type	1970–79	1980–89	1990–99	2000–09	2010–15	Total N	Total %
Solo	15	5	8	10	11	49	25
Co-authored							
With current and former graduate students	4	18	17	19	21	79	40
With international scholars	1	13	12	5	1	32	16
Other co-authors	8	10	8	8	4	38	19
Total	28	46	45	42	37	198	100

mainly South Asian. We were ultimately able to put together a portfolio of about a dozen articles from the data we collected (Aldrich, Cater, Jones, McEvoy, & Velleman, 1985). My work with the Liverpool-based team was the beginning of extensive overseas collaboration, and I published more than two dozen papers with international scholars in the 1980s and 1990s, as shown in Table 3.1.

Lesson learned

My two small-business succession studies exemplify my general research strategy: I like to pick a project where I spend some time getting to know the lay of the land, explore ideas that might be testable, conduct a pilot project, and then build a comprehensive research design. I abhor cross-sectional research. It's anathema to me. I tell my students that if you want to study something, you have to watch it change (Aldrich, 1992). Such projects take a long time to design and bring to fruition. For example, the two small-business projects involved designing questionnaires, pretesting them in the field, selecting a representative sample, and conducting a four-wave panel study using face-to-face interviews. Many of my projects have taken a decade from the beginning to end, from setting up the design to writing for publication. In fact, in the case of the UK study, I was writing papers in the late 1980s from a project that began in the late 1970s. Later, in 1990, my colleagues and I did a book on ethnic entrepreneurs that came out of the UK project (Waldinger, Aldrich, & Ward, 1990). I like to use a long-term dynamic design that permits me to measure the same indicators over time and then be able to describe and explain analytically why things have changed (Aldrich, 2001).

A summer on the West Coast and many winters in Ithaca deepened my appreciation of evolutionary thinking. Although my education at the University of Michigan had laid the groundwork for my evolutionary views, these ideas were further refined by several opportunities that came my way in the 1970s, at Stanford and Cornell universities.

Stanford University

A summer spent at Stanford University in 1973 contributed significantly to my emerging perspective on organizations and ultimately generated the spark I needed to begin working on what eventually became *Organizations and Environments* (Aldrich, 1979). Dick Scott invited me to be a visiting scholar in the Stanford Research Training Program on Organizations and Mental Health, following my Cornell colleague, Karl Weick, who'd done it the year before. Dick was away in Europe, I believe, and so I spent a lot of time with his students. I taught an organizational theory course to a class that included Chuck Snow, Kaye Schoonhoven, and some of Mike Hannan and

John Meyers' students. In addition to studying the health care system, their students were working on a variety of "world systems" topics, and I found their projects fascinating.

Despite the mismatch between my empirical interests and those of the students, the Stanford experience rekindled my interest in a more comparative and political view of organizations, an interest that had lain dormant since I'd left Ann Arbor in 1969. I suspect that I learned as much over those three months as did the students in my course. Through these students, I also met Jane Weiss, and we began a collaboration that was cut short by her premature death in 1981. Jane challenged me to rise above the fairly empirical approach I was schooled in at Michigan and broadened my horizons, as reflected in the papers we published on class analysis (Aldrich & Weiss, 1981) and world systems theory (Weiss & Aldrich, 1977).

To put my Stanford experience into the context of the early 1970s, I would say that the type of organization theory popular in the 1960s emphasized structure at the expense of genesis and process. During the mid-1970s, additional approaches to organizational analysis were flowering in other parts of the world, and the paradigm shift challenged earlier approaches, as theorists on both US coasts developed distinctive ideas about organizational analysis. Curiously enough, I found that my Stanford experience was better preparation for understanding these new approaches than what I was exposed to on the East Coast, in Ivy League sociology. At Stanford and UC-Berkeley, three new views of organizational analysis had emerged: resource dependence (Pfeffer & Salancik, 1978), population ecology (Hannan & Freeman, 1989), and "new" institutional theory (Scott, 2008). My introduction to these schools of thought during my time at Stanford helped to shape the evolutionary approach to entrepreneurship that I ultimately became associated with and that I further developed throughout the course of my career at Cornell and UNC.

Developing an appreciation of evolutionary thinking

The evolutionary approach is a generic framework for understanding social change; the evolutionary approach to entrepreneurship is an overarching framework permitting comparison and integration of other social scientific theories. At the heart of evolutionary thinking, as applied to entrepreneurship, is the assumption that evolutionary processes are driven by entrepreneurs' and organizations' struggles to obtain scarce resources, both social and physical (Aldrich & Ruef, 2006a). Entrepreneurial activity creates the variation and diversity upon which selection forces operate, with selected forms being retained. The approach is applicable at multiple levels of analysis and directs our attention to the processes of variation, selection, retention, and struggle that jointly produce patterned change in evolving systems. In organizational communities, populations with different characteristics enter into relationships of competition and cooperation; those populations better able to deal with the environment are more likely to survive, and characteristics of the successful population may then be diffused to other populations in the same community.

During the 1970s, the thinking around such evolutionary models had more or less exploded, mainly as a result of the open-system revolution in organization theory and management studies. Scholars from different disciplines presented evolutionary theories, inspired by the seminal work of Donald T. Campbell (1969), to explain phenomena ranging from the micro to the macro levels of organization. When I was at Michigan, I had the good fortune to be exposed not only to the work of sociologists, but also people like Campbell, so I knew about the variation-selection-retention approach. I discovered as I began working on projects in the 1970s that this framework was a very powerful generic framework. It wasn't a detailed mechanism perspective, but once you understood the ideas of selective retention and variation, you could apply this to about anything – that was a real revelation to me.

For example, on the individual level, Karl Weick (1979) developed his landmark statement, *The Social Psychology of Organizing*, a social psychological theory of how individuals coordinate their actions, which drew on the variation, selection, and retention reasoning developed by Campbell. With Karl at Cornell, I had on campus another person who also appreciated an evolutionary approach, but at a micro level. Karl and I met regularly, mainly through our students, as I would be on committees he chaired and vice versa. Also, we shared people who enrolled in our courses. We didn't see eye to eye on everything, I discovered. But looking back, I realized we shared a common "home base," which was an appreciation for evolutionary thinking.

Michael Hannan and John Freeman (1977, 1984) also used a selection-based explanation in their work on the population ecology of organizations, in which they emphasized the founding and closure of organizations in populations, relative to the distribution of available environmental resources. On the macro level, Richard Nelson and Sidney Winter (1982) were pioneers in the application of evolutionary models of economic change. However, unlike me, they were more influenced by the Carnegie School of routine-based models of organizational action (Herbert Simon, James March, and Richard Cyert) as well as by Joseph Schumpeter, who was a prominent exponent of the idea that economic change could be conceptualized as an evolutionary process.

My interest in world systems theory that had been sparked at Stanford was further refined during my time at Cornell. Coincidentally, down the road in Binghamton, Immanuel Wallerstein (2004) had set up shop. I'd begun reading his work and I discovered that some of his disciples were on the Cornell campus. Accordingly, I decided to try offering a course on world systems theory. Looking back, I am shocked at my naïveté and boldness, as I had no formal training in world systems theory. I did it on a chance that there'd be people interested, and it turned out there were. Some of Wallerstein's students visited as guest lecturers, and Wallerstein himself drove up once from Binghamton to participate. The world systems perspective finally completed the levels of analysis that I was working toward: individual, organizational, population, and community/society.

It was thus in this intellectual context that I published *Organizations and Environments* (1979) in which I wrote about organizations and how they changed over time. It was arguably the first book-length statement of this perspective – not just thinking in evolutionary terms, but also on multiple levels, thinking about issues of selection. I argued that organizations flourish or fail because they are more or less suited to the particular environment in which they operate. My early work on evolutionary theory built on my ecological framework and emphasized how little control small-business owners had over their environments, and so my writings tended to privilege context as a driving force in organizational change. Later, as I drew more from resource dependence theory, I took more account of human agency and collective action.

The resource dependence perspective

Looking back, I realize that the other perspective I was working on but didn't emphasize enough was resource dependence. My book emphasized an evolutionary argument and using multiple levels of analysis, but I also discussed power, politics, dominance, governance, and the way in which two parties in a relationship strategically jockey for positions. The dynamics of that relationship are driven by resource dependence dynamics. Indeed, my papers in the early 1970s had drawn heavily upon the concept of resource dependence. For example, in our 1975 paper in ASQ, Sergio Mindlin and I wrote that "the major axiom of the resource dependence perspective on the study of organizational behavior is that organizations must be studied in the context of the population of organizations with which they are competing and sharing resources" (Mindlin & Aldrich, 1975: 382).

While at Stanford the summer of 1973, I began collaborating with Jeff Pfeffer on what became the first synthetic statement combining an evolutionary perspective and a resource dependence perspective. We laid out the premises of a resource dependence model, building on Stanford graduate Karen Cook's (1977) work and on work by Dick's mentor, Peter Blau (1964). Published in the *Annual Review of Sociology* (Aldrich & Pfeffer, 1976), it is one of my most cited papers. In that collaboration with Jeff, I was able to see that really it made no sense to talk about resource dependence or evolutionary theory as two separate ways of looking at the world. Even though the 1979 book and my subsequent work tend to be seen as evolutionary, the actual micro-mechanisms, the explanations of how things actually happen between people and organizations or between organizations, mostly concern power and exchange dynamics (Wry, Cobb, & Aldrich, 2013).

Jeff and Jerry Salancik (who was ultimately one of the associate editors with me at ASQ) went on to write *The External Control of Organizations* (Pfeffer & Salancik, 1978). Their book was published in 1978, and my book was published in 1979 – two statements that offered complementary views of the world of organization theory. Whereas Pfeffer and I combined the ideas of "populations" and "resource dependence" – and I tended to be seen as somebody who was associated with ecology (at that time it was called "population ecology") – Jeff and Jerry tended to downplay evolutionary thinking (though there's some selection logic in their book). Thus, I don't think people recognized that our two books were actually part of the same programmatic move in the organization studies' community to get away from the old simple contingency view, the old rational choice view, to a more dynamic, political evolutionary way of thinking.

All through the 1980s, I struggled to differentiate my evolutionary approach from the ecological approach. I didn't talk about "population ecology" until after Hannan and Freeman's article was published in 1977. Before that I called it the natural selection process or the population perspective. In *Organizations and Environments*, perhaps subtly influenced by the Stanford group's terminology, I rather carelessly used the label "population ecology" interchangeably with "natural selection." Looking back, I regret that I used the label "population ecology," because I think it confused people. Most of my work was rather different from population ecology reasoning, and my views would have been better described as a sociological approach, strongly informed by evolutionary principles. Therefore, in the book *Organizations Evolving* (1999) I adopted the label "evolutionary perspective" or "evolutionary approach."

Becoming an entrepreneurship scholar

Throughout the 1970s, I thought of myself as an organizational sociologist studying organizations from an evolutionary point of view. I discovered I was an "entrepreneurship scholar" totally by accident. Like Monsieur Jourdain in Moliere's *The Bourgeois Gentleman*, who discovered that he had "been speaking prose all my life, and didn't even know it," it was not until a fortuitous conjuncture of circumstances that I realized I was actually studying "entrepreneurship." Two events converged to change my self-identity: (1) an invitation to write a paper for a conference on social indicators, and (2) an invitation to attend a state-of-the-art conference on entrepreneurship.

First, in the early 1980s, I began working with several graduate students at Cornell University, studying the origins of organizational forms. I was invited to Washington, DC to give a paper at a conference and in preparation for the conference, I read David Birch's book, *The Job Generation Process*. I subsequently visited him on a very cold and snowy winter day at the Massachusetts Institute of Technology in Boston to learn more about the data set he had created, using the proprietary Dun & Bradstreet Market Indicators Database. After spending a day with him, I began to see the potential of integrating ideas from organizational ecology with those from evolutionary theory to understand business dynamics. One of my Cornell students, Ellen Auster, was then teaching at Columbia Business School and she joined with me in writing a paper about the problems facing new and small firms (Aldrich & Auster, 1986).

Second, in 1985, as Ellen and I were finishing our paper, I received an invitation from Don Sexton to attend his state-of-the-art conference on entrepreneurship in Austin, Texas. I was scheduled to comment on a paper presented by Al Shapero, but Al became ill and so Don called me on the Friday before the conference began (which was on a Monday!) and asked me if I would instead be willing to present an original paper. I had already been thinking about social networks because of my research on ethnic businesses and decided to accept his invitation. Over the weekend, I wrote a short paper called "Entrepreneurship through Social Networks" with one of my PhD students, Catherine Zimmer (Aldrich & Zimmer, 1986). Years later, I followed up some of these ideas with Phil Kim (Aldrich & Kim, 2007), showing how concepts from social network analysis shed light on entrepreneurial team formation.

The Texas conference was an eye-opening experience for me. The scholars I met – Neil Churchill, Alan Carsrud, Karl Vesper, Arnold Cooper, and others – were passionate about their work, energized about what they were finding, and cared deeply about the phenomena. Unlike the careerist and petty gossip that I heard at most professional meetings, the people studying entrepreneurship seemed to be genuinely interested in the research itself and eager to initiate new members into their group. The paper I presented struck a responsive chord in the entrepreneurship community, because it was a way of bridging networks and entrepreneurship and making the study of entrepreneurship more sociological. It is still widely cited today, and I still get requests for copies, 30 years later.

At that conference, I also discovered that there was a whole world out there of people studying entrepreneurship that I had been isolated from because I was in the organization studies community. Entrepreneurship was clearly not a central issue for organizations' people back in those days. The leading textbooks and highly cited papers, such as DiMaggio and Powell's (1983) paper on institutional isomorphism, contain no mention of entrepreneurs, the role of new organizations, new businesses, or where variation comes from. Suddenly discovering that there were dozens of people, mainly in business schools, studying entrepreneurship and associating my work with the concept was a revelation to me.

Because of contacts I made in Austin, I began attending the Babson College Entrepreneurship Conference and gave my first paper at the 1987 meeting at Pepperdine University. (The paper was on a study of social networks among entrepreneurs in the Research Triangle Area of North Carolina, carried out with Ben Rosen and the late Bill Woodward.) I have missed very few meetings since then and became a "lifetime member" of the Babson conference in 2013. Thus, starting in the mid-1980s, my research agenda shifted from talking about business and organizational change to talking about entrepreneurship, entrepreneurial strategies, activities, and variation.

Many of the phenomena that interested me as an organizational scholar were actually much easier to study in the entrepreneurial context, where things are fresh, new, and small and constituted an instant organizational laboratory with thousands of replications every day. I wrote several works on business formation and the role of networks in entrepreneurship. In this respect my collaboration with Marlena Fiol (Aldrich & Fiol, 1994) was really important for me. In the article "Fools Rush In? The Institutional Context of Industrial Creation," I started to describe my ideas in multilevel terms and saw more clearly that I could look at entirely new industries at the individual, group, organizational, and population levels. This multilevel approach became a key characteristic in my book *Organizations Evolving* (Aldrich, 1999) and in the revision I later published with Martin Ruef.

Beginning in the late 1980s, my involvement in evolutionary theory grew hand-in-hand with a series of large-scale entrepreneurship projects. With Pat Ray Reese, I conducted a panel study of several hundred potential and actual entrepreneurs in the Research Triangle area of North Carolina. My students Linda Renzulli and Amy Davis subsequently used that data set for their master's projects. Nancy Langton and I carried out a multiwave panel study of small firms in the Vancouver, British Columbia, region; in collaboration with Jennifer Cliff Jennings, I also wrote a number of papers from that project. In North Carolina, Arne Kalleberg, Peter Marsden, and I obtained an NSF grant to study different methods of sampling organizations, one part of which included an attempt to find newly founded firms in Durham County and the Research Triangle area.

When I realized that I was actually studying "entrepreneurship" rather than "small businesses," I reframed my research questions and began teaching seminars on the topic. I became associated in people's minds with entrepreneurship and received many invitations to teach courses and seminars internationally. Bocconi University in Milan hosted me for several month-long courses, and I visited the University of Economics in Vienna every spring for seven years in the 1990s to offer a course on entrepreneurship in their Institute for Small and Medium-Size Businesses. Spurred in part by my youngest son's interest in Japanese studies, I taught two short entrepreneurship courses at Keio University in Japan.

In the mid-1990s, Paul Reynolds began soliciting my participation in perhaps the most important US research project of the decade: the Entrepreneurship Research Consortium (ERC) project, which eventually became the Panel Study of Entrepreneurial Dynamics (PSED I). However, he had to drag me into it: I was reluctant to get involved, knowing how difficult it is to manage such diverse, multimember, collective action projects. To his credit, Paul never gave up, and I saw that he had really big plans; ultimately, the chance to do another four-wave panel study was just too good to pass up. And, of course, it wasn't coincidental that the earlier research projects that I had favored were four-wave panel studies. Although I did not join the executive committee of the first PSED, Paul always referred to me as his "overenthusiastic volunteer." That experience taught me that it was better to be on the inside of such projects, rather than criticizing from the outside, and so when he proposed PSED II, I signed up for the executive committee.

Organizations evolving

The impact of my shift from purely organization studies to entrepreneurship and organization studies is also evident in the first edition of *Organizations Evolving* (Aldrich, 1999). Even though it's sold as a trade book that's about organization theory, it's really about entrepreneurship. It starts with the creation of organizations and their internal dynamics, and moves through the building of organizational boundaries to the level of change at the organization and population levels, and ends at the community level. Many of the key ideas in the book date back to a paper I wrote in the early 1980s together with Bill McKelvey (McKelvey & Aldrich, 1983). In the article "Populations, Natural Selection and Applied Organizational Science," we argued that scholars could use the variation-selection-retention scheme to create a comprehensive understanding of organizational change: in populations of organizations in which there is great heterogeneity, no organization will represent the central tendency in the population – the organizations will differ from each other, and this variation paves the way for evolution due to selective elimination. The organizations that survive will be copied, thus diffusing a new form throughout the population. It was a breakthrough idea at the time, and I quarried that paper substantially for the 1999 book and then again with Martin Ruef for the 2006 edition (Aldrich & Ruef, 2006b), where we brought that argument up to date.

Graduate students' contributions

About half of what I publish is empirical and half is conceptual, and about 75% of my work is co-authored, as shown in Table 3.1. The only decade in which more than half my publications were sole authored was in the 1970s. Since the early 1970s, I've been able to find people to work with who've substantially enriched my understanding. Graduate students and people at other universities have been very important to my work. About 40% of my publications have been with current and former graduate students, and another 35% have been with international scholars and colleagues in my home department and at other universities. For example, Jennifer Cliff Jennings and I became acquainted when I was a visiting scholar at the University of British Columbia working with Nancy Langton (Aldrich, Renzulli, & Langton, 1998), and Jennifer and I subsequently wrote papers together on gender, family, and entrepreneurship (Aldrich & Cliff, 2003; Cliff, Langton, & Aldrich, 2005). My work relies heavily on teamwork with people whose skills are complementary to mine.

While I was at Cornell, I worked with a number of students on various aspects of organizational formation and change. David Whetten, my first doctoral student, is extremely interested in comparative approaches to organizational research. In 1973, Dave and I began a large study of interorganizational relationships in the manpower training program and published several papers using a resource dependence perspective (Aldrich & Whetten, 1981). Udo Staber did field research on trade associations, and we subsequently published a number of studies looking at the evolution of that industry over more than a century (Aldrich & Staber, 1988). Lance Kurke became interested in Henry Mintzberg's field study of managerial work, and we published one of the few empirical replications of that study (Kurke & Aldrich, 1983). Finally, Ellen Auster and I wrote several papers on ethnic businesses, but our best-known work was purely conceptual, with the title based on one of my favorite Werner Herzog movies, "Even Dwarfs Started Small" (Aldrich & Auster, 1986). It was one of the first papers to explicitly address the question of the complementarities between the liabilities facing small and new organizations and the liabilities facing old and well-established organizations. We argued that new small and nimble organizations often pioneered innovations but then were snapped up by larger established organizations, rather than continuing to grow organically. Steve Bradley (2011) recruited me to join with him, Dean Shepherd, and Johan Wiklund, in co-authoring a paper that tested the central proposition of Aldrich and Auster (Aldrich & Auster, 1986).

Over my years at UNC-Chapel Hill, I have been fortunate to find students interested in doing entrepreneurship research, sometimes in addition to another project for their dissertations. While preparing her dissertation on charter schools, Linda Renzulli also worked with Jim Moody and me on a study of social networks and entrepreneurship in the Research Triangle area of North Carolina. Using panel data that Pat Reese had collected with me, we found that an overabundance of family ties in someone's personal network inhibited their acting on entrepreneurial intentions (Renzulli, Aldrich, & Moody, 2000). Ted Baker came to graduate school after being involved in several entrepreneurial ventures of his own and worked on several projects with me, in addition to a dissertation on the consequences of entrepreneurs being beholden to "critical employees" (Aldrich & Baker, 1997; Aldrich & Baker, 2001; Baker, Aldrich, & Liou, 1997). Amy Kenworthy shared my fascination with the work of Donald Campbell, and together we wrote a paper applying his ideas to entrepreneurship (Aldrich & Kenworthy, 1999).

Amanda Elam was one of several students who earned a PhD in sociology but then eventually started her own company. She worked on several entrepreneurship projects with me at the University of North Carolina at Chapel Hill, including one on social networks with another student who became an entrepreneur, Pat Reese (Aldrich, Elam, & Reese, 1996). Courtney Hunt earned her PhD in the business school and while taking my organization theory seminar, saw the potential for the commercialization of the World Wide Web. In 1996, at the dawning of the dot com era, our collaboration resulted in the first paper ever presented on that topic at the annual meeting of the Academy of Management and then a subsequent paper two years later (Hunt & Aldrich, 1998). She also formed her own consulting firm.

With an undergraduate degree in management and then some business experience, Phil Kim turned his attention to entrepreneurship as a PhD student. Phil made good use of the PSED I for some research papers as well as his dissertation, focusing particularly on social networks (Kim & Aldrich, 2005; Kim, Aldrich, & Keister, 2006; Kim, Longest, & Aldrich, 2013). Amy Davis also joined with me in exploring the potential of the PSED data set, writing several papers on entrepreneurship and social networks (Davis, Renzulli, & Aldrich, 2006). Tiantian Yang worked with me on several projects using the PSED II data set (Aldrich & Yang, 2013; Yang & Aldrich, 2012; Yang & Aldrich, 2014) and then saw an opportunity to work with "big data," using the Swedish registry data called LISA. Her master's-level training in statistics came in handy for building state-of-the-art level models of entrepreneurial spawning, a skill I admired but did not possess.

Steve Lippmann and Martha Martinez are two former students who have continued to work with me on projects many years after they left graduate school. Steve's interest in historical analysis has led to a series of empirical and theoretical papers exploring the intersection of historiography and organization theory (Lippmann, 2005, 2007; Lippmann & Aldrich, 2014). Martha's eclectic interests have allowed us to contribute not only to the entrepreneurship literature (Aldrich & Martinez, 2001; Martinez, Yang, & Aldrich, 2011), but also to the family business (Martinez & Aldrich, 2014) and strategy and innovation (Aldrich & Martinez, 2015) literatures.

The importance of teamwork is particularly apparent in the development of the PSED II project. After leading the PSED I, Paul Reynolds raised money for a follow-on project with more cases and more waves of data collection, enriching the design and fixing some of the omissions in the earlier project. One paper in particular demonstrates the evolution of my thinking on a sociological approach to entrepreneurship: a project with Martin Ruef and Nancy Carter (Ruef, Aldrich, & Carter, 2003) showing that entrepreneurial teams are put together in a very homophilous way. Our results indicated that entrepreneurs' actions contradicted the old prescriptive argument that entrepreneurs should put together a team of people with diverse backgrounds. What we were able to show with this wonderful data set – a sample of people trying to start businesses – is that, in fact, the businesses that emerge from this process are very homophilous by age, sex, occupation, and race.

Current research on the maker movement

My good friend Jerry Davis, with his enthusiasm and optimism, drew me into studying the maker movement (Davis, 2013). He arranged a meeting for me with a near-neighbor of mine, Ted Hall, the founder of ShopBot and a leading voice in the maker movement. Jerry said to me, "There's this guy over in Durham who's doing some really interesting stuff, you ought to meet him." Jerry and I had talked a little bit about my interest in technology and technological revolution. My oldest son, Steven, is a serial entrepreneur whose work has been in high-tech and knowledge-intensive industries, and I've always been interested in high-tech. I looked up what Ted Hall was doing, and it turned out to be the portal into an amazing new movement. People mostly associate the term "hacker" with computer software, but it actually turns out to be a very powerful movement in open-source hardware as well.

What I discovered was that technological changes, such as 3D printing, numerically controlled machinery downsized to desktop size, and laser cutters were changing the way that people developed and experimented with prototypes. Traditional craft-based technologies were also involved: sewing, weaving, and other tools of the creative classes. I learned about a movement of people who say that the way things are made and distributed in modern societies doesn't tap into the inherent creativity of humans and that creativity could be unleashed if people were just given the tools to use that potential. Humans in the twenty-first century are accustomed to having goods just delivered to their door. They're told that this is just the way things are: "Don't open that computer, phone, or home appliance – you'll break it." In the maker movement, people reject that claim. They argue that humans can take something off the shelf made by manufacturers, open it up, look at its innards, figure out how it actually works, and make it better through hacking it by adding something to it or redesigning it. They can even put another program into its controller.

Starting in 2012, I began doing serious reading on the maker movement. I've now been to many of these spaces and have been able to give some presentations on the movement. I spent several days learning how to use a computer numerically controlled machine (CNC) machine. (I must admit that when my wife examined what I produced, she said to me something like, "Oh that's a lot better than I thought it would be.") What I've discovered is that the potential for a new industrial revolution seems to be emerging. This is what Jerry and I have been talking about, which is that the new technologies combined with this maker movement – which is a very powerful global movement to give people, in a sense, control over their own destiny – will make available the tools people can use to make things for themselves. These can be as simple as things that you play with or things that are functionally useful in the kitchen, the car, and the garage. It's an amazingly adaptable set of technologies.

What's important about the way this is developing is that makerspaces are being put together through contributed resources, like Kickstarter campaigns (Mollick, 2014). Over a thousand of these makerspaces exist throughout the world, and they're spreading. Makerspaces make available on an inclusive basis very flexible machines and often some kind of consulting help to inexperienced makers. Users sometimes pay nothing to use the equipment, or pay only for the materials, and get a chance to design things that will enrich their lives. What's interesting to me from an entrepreneurial point of view is that some of these projects do have commercial potential. There are two examples everyone knows about: one of them is the Pebble Watch, which was started with a Kickstarter campaign (a hacking of physical entities: the bracelet, with the microcontroller insider, and the sensors). It was put together by somebody who didn't go to a venture capitalist or an angel investor. Instead, he went to Kickstarter, a crowdfunding source, and raised the money. Square is another new venture that was put together from one of these campaigns.

The potential now exists for thousands of people working in makerspaces to engage in what Sonali Shah, Mary Tripsas, and Eric von Hippel have called user-driven innovation: they noted that people often discover innovations when they're working with an off-the-shelf design and spot ways to improve it (Shah & Tripsas, 2007; von Hippel, 2005). In makerspaces, you're not just stuck with a hammer and a screwdriver, you've got a CNC machine, a 3D printer, and computer software design programs that let you do craft work that was unthinkable fifteen or twenty years ago. Possibly the next revolution will emerge from these aggregated individual and collective efforts.

Another way to think about this is through a sort of anti-Schumpeter distorted lens: if the R&D labs of big firms were the only force in invention and innovation, we would be stuck with what the imaginations of those people can generate. In the hierarchies of big firms, people are assigned to work on projects, with varying degrees of autonomy in how they accomplish their goals. What if we take those same resources, downsize them, and make them available to people working in makerspaces? Instead of having corporate agendas driving the innovation, we would have users driving the innovation, based on recognizing local needs. Ithaca, New York, may have people who need goods and services that people in Binghamton or Elmira don't need. Alternatively, people in Binghamton or Elmira may collectively have needs that we wouldn't have in the Research Triangle Park. Who knows? The maker movement and the possibility that these people will come together and help one another means that the innovations and their variations that can be generated might well succeed in changing the world for those people locally. That's an unprecedented opening to the future.

Looking forward: advice to young scholars

I'm an evolutionary theorist, which means it's a violation of my credo if I claim clairvoyance and assert an ability to peer into the future. By definition, tomorrow is different than today, and we don't know what it will give us. I will only speculate about how to interpret the recent past and the immediate future.

"Entrepreneurship" used to be an area that people avoided because it wasn't sexy enough; it wasn't like studying big firms and their mergers and acquisitions (M&As) and initial public offerings (IPOs). But entrepreneurship actually is an amazingly attractive and interesting field. When you're studying big firms, such as the publicly held firms formerly favored by many entrepreneurship scholars, you will discover that there are perhaps 5000 publicly traded firms left in the United States. There are more than 5000 organizational scientists, right? We could, technically speaking, assign each one of the 5000 to one organization and have them all meet once a year to talk about their organizations and then go out for drinks afterward.

That's not true with entrepreneurship: there are millions of trials every year. There's lots of variation to study. Moreover, if you're trying to do a study of organizational change in big firms, you have to wait forever for interesting things to happen. Getting access to this means begging lots of people for permission and then having a lot of people to follow around. By contrast, consider startups: you have two or three people to follow. If something interesting is going to happen, it's going to happen right there in front of you. Immediately, people understand what's going on because the totality of what's happening is within your purview. New and small organizations thus constitute a great laboratory in which to study social processes such as social networks, power and resource dependence, and gender dynamics. All these things are visible in the micro laboratory of startups. I see several methodological challenges involving "big data" and "fieldwork/ethnography." Big data has given us the ability to discover patterns we were previously simply unable to recognize. The danger for a social scientist in using big data or archival data (for example, using patent data, data that comes from the census bureau, or using data from government registry–based projects, such as LISA in Sweden or IDEA in Denmark) is that you are an arms' length from the actual phenomenon. One of my arguments – going back to the first papers I wrote in the mid-1980s about entrepreneurship research methods – is that we don't have enough people doing the real field work: the ethnographic and observational field work (Aldrich, 2000). I would like to see more researchers venturing into entrepreneurial startups and new ventures – or into incubators and accelerators – and actually hanging out, spending days observing, taking notes, recording, doing mini-experiments if you're permitted to do so, collecting data in innovative ways: we don't have many people doing that.

I would like to see entrepreneurship researchers doing ethnographies that document in a typical day, week, or month what entrepreneurs actually do (Stewart & Aldrich, 2015). How do they spend their time? How much time are they spending in meetings? Are these people like Mintzberg's (1973) managers in *The Nature of Managerial Work* whose days are consumed with meetings and who spend very little time thinking about strategy? The managers in Mintzberg's study were mostly stuck answering memos or the phone and giving people orders. We have great articles in magazines like *Wired* and *Fast Company* that describe a very different world than the world described in cases on big companies. Some scholars are probably naturally gifted ethnographers who are good at watching people do things and interpreting what they see and then communicating to others the theoretical significance of what they observed. I'm hopeful that young scholars who are interested in entrepreneurship or organizations will think twice before beginning to use an archival data set – a data set handed to them by somebody, downloaded from the Web, from the Inter-University Consortium for Political and Social Research (ICPSR). I suggest that instead, they go out and spend a little time with the phenomenon.

I'm constantly amazed when I go to professional meetings and find how little people actually know about what they are studying. I meet with people in doctoral consortiums, talk with them about their proposals, and I'll ask them questions about their phenomenon. Something like, "You're studying people making gaming software. What's it like to be in one of their shops?" and they say, "I don't know, I've never actually watched them do this." Or I say, "What's it like to be in a biotech firm? What's it like in the lab? What's the interaction like between the scientist and the entrepreneurs?" "I don't know, I've never seen it." I'm astonished by investigators' inabilities to answer questions about basic descriptive characteristics of the phenomenon. They tell me what they've read in books or how the variables are described in a code book. But that's not enough. If you're going to convince me that you understand the phenomenon, I want a report from the field, as Watson (2011) has so forcefully argued. So I'm encouraging graduate student researchers who have the resources to maybe stay in grad school an extra year or find a mentor who is really interested in helping them. Let's get some reports from the field and perhaps transform our understanding of the entrepreneurial startup process.

Many of my projects have been planned and executed over many years. My study of small businesses in three American cities was designed in 1965, with data collection from 1966 until 1972. Coding and analyzing the data took more than a year and thus the first papers were not submitted until 1974. I continued publishing from that data set throughout the 1970s. Similarly, my study in England was conceptualized in 1975, designed in 1976, and data collection carried out from 1978 until 1984. In a third example, my project on trade associations was designed and funded in the early 1980s, with publications not appearing until the early 1990s. Many of my other projects were similarly measured in years, not months. My recommendation to young scholars is to realize that if you undertake large-scale long-term projects, you better have more than one project underway, and the other projects should have different beginning and ending times. Long-term planning for a portfolio of several projects needs to begin the moment your PhD advisor signs off on your thesis.

Closing thoughts

Over the past five decades, the world has changed and with it our understanding of organizations and how they operate has grown tremendously. I have been incredibly fortunate to have witnessed new perspectives taking shape and honored to have contributed to our understanding in some ways. By learning from excellent guides and mentors and their world-class research and theory-building strategies, the groundwork was laid for me to contribute to the growing realm of entrepreneurship research. I believe the current environment is ripe with opportunities for future scholars to build on these insights to study entrepreneurial efforts and outcomes and to take stock of the many new ways creators have to bring their ideas to life in the world.

Acknowledgements

Thanks to Nicole Bown for her help and to Ted Baker, Bill Gartner, Phil Kim, and Martin Ruef for their comments.

References

Aldrich, H. 1971. Organizational Boundaries and Inter-organizational Conflict. Human Relations, 24(4): 279–293.

Aldrich, H. 1975. Ecological Succession in Racially Changing Neighborhoods. Urban Affairs Review, 10(3): 327–348.

Aldrich. 1979. Organizations and Environments. Englewood Cliffs, NJ: Prentice-Hall.

Aldrich, H. 1999. Organizations Evolving. London: Sage.

Aldrich, H. E. 1992. Methods in Our Madness? Trends in Entrepreneurship Research. In D. L. Sexton, & J. D. Kasarda (Eds.), The State of the Art of Entrepreneurship: 191–213. Boston: PWS-Kent Publishing Company.

Aldrich, H. E. 2000. Learning Together: National Differences in Entrepreneurship Research. In D. L. Sexton, & H. Landström (Eds.), The Blackwell Handbook of Entrepreneurship: 5–25. Oxford, UK: Blackwell.

Aldrich, H. E. 2001. Who Wants to Be an Evolutionary Theorist? Remarks on the Occasion of the Year 2000 OMT Distinguished Scholarly Career Award Presentation. Journal of Management Inquiry, 10(2): 115–128.

Aldrich, H., & Auster, E. R. 1986. Even Dwarfs Started Small: Liabilities of Age and Size and Their Strategic Implications. In B. M. Staw, & L. L. Cummings (Eds.), Research in Organizational Behavior, Vol. 8: 165–198. Greenwich, CT: JAI Press.

Aldrich, H. E., & Baker, T. 1997. Blinded by The Cites? Has There been Progress in Entrepreneurship Research? In D. L. Sexton, & R. W. Smilor (Eds.), Entrepreneurship 2000: 377–400. Chicago: Upstart Publishing Company.

Aldrich, H. E., & Baker, T. 2001. Learning and Legitimacy: Entrepreneurial Responses to Constraints on the Emergence of New Populations. In C. B. Schoonhoven, & E. Romanelli (Eds.), The Entrepreneurship Dynamic: Origins of Entrepreneurship and the Evolution of Industries: 207–235. Stanford: Stanford University Press.

Aldrich, H. E., Cater, J., Jones, T., & McEvoy, D. 1983. From Periphery to Peripheral: The South Asian Petite Bourgeoisie in England. In I. H. Simpson, & R. Simpson (Eds.), Research in the Sociology of Work, Vol. 2: 1–32. Greenwich, CT: JAI Press.

Aldrich, H. E., Cater, J., Jones, T., McEvoy, D., & Velleman, P. 1985. Ethnic Residential Concentration and the Protected Market Hypothesis. Social Forces, 63(4): 996–1009.

Aldrich, H. E., & Cliff, J. E. 2003. The Pervasive Effects of Family on Entrepreneurship: Toward a Family Embeddedness Perspective. Journal of Business Venturing, 18(5): 573–596.

Aldrich, H. E., Elam, A., & Reese, P. R. 1996. Strong Ties, Weak Ties, and Strangers: Do Women Business Owners Differ from Men in Their Use of Networking to Obtain Assistance? In S. Birley, & I. C. Mac-Millan (Eds.), Entrepreneurship in a Global Context: 1–25. London: Routledge.

Aldrich, H. E., & Fiol, C. M. 1994. Fools Rush In? The Institutional Context of Industry Creation. Academy of Management Review, 19(4): 645–670.

Aldrich, H. E., & Kenworthy, A. 1999. The Accidental Entrepreneur: Campbellian Antinomies and Organizational Foundings. In J. A. C. Baum, & B. McKelvey (Eds.), Variations in Organization Science: In Honor of Donald T. Campbell: 19–33. Newbury Park, CA: Sage.

Aldrich, H. E., & Martinez, M. A. 2001. Many Are Called, but Few Are Chosen: An Evolutionary Perspective for the Study of Entrepreneurship. Entrepreneurship: Theory & Practice, 25(4): 41.

Aldrich, H. E., & Martinez, M. A. 2015. Why Aren't Entrepreneurs More Creative? Conditions Affecting Creativity and Innovation in Entrepreneurial Activity. In C. E. Shalley, M. A. Hitt, & J. Zhou (Eds.), The Oxford Handbook of Creativity, Innovation, and Entrepreneurship: Multilevel Linkages: 445–456. Oxford: Oxford University Press.

Aldrich, H. E., & Pfeffer, J. 1976. Environments and Organizations. Annual Review of Sociology, 2: 79–105.

Aldrich, H. E., & Philip, H. Kim 2007. Small Worlds, Infinite Possibilities. Strategic Entrepreneurship Journal, 1: 147–165.

Aldrich, H. E., & Reiss, A. J., Jr. 1976. Continuities in the Study of Ecological Succession: Changes in the Race Composition of Neighborhoods and Their Businesses. American Journal of Sociology, 81(4): 846–866.

Aldrich, H. E., Renzulli, L. A., & Langton, N. 1998. Passing on Privilege: Resources Provided by Self-Employed Parents to Their Self-Employed Children. In K. Leicht (Ed.), Research in Stratification and Mobility, Vol. 16: 291–317. Greenwich, CT: JAI Press.

Aldrich, H. E., & Ruef, M. 2006a. Organizations Evolving (2nd ed.). London: Sage Publications.

Aldrich, H. E., & Ruef, M. 2006b. Organizations Evolving (2nd ed.). London: Sage Publications.

Aldrich, H. E., & Staber, U. H. 1988. Organizing Business Interests: Patterns of Trade Association Foundings, Transformations, and Deaths. In G. R. Carroll (Ed.), Ecological Models of Organizations: 111–126. Cambridge, MA: Ballinger.

Aldrich, H. E., & Weiss, J. 1981. Differentiation Within the U.S. Capitalist Class: Workforce Size and Income Differences. American Sociological Review, 46(3): 279–289

Aldrich, H. E., & Whetten, D. A. 1981. Organization Sets, Action Sets, and Networks: Making the Most of Simplicity. In P. Nystrom, & W. H. Starbuck (Eds.), Handbook of Organizational Design: 385–408. New York: Oxford University Press.

Aldrich, H. E., & Yang, T. 2013. How Do Entrepreneurs Know What to Do? Learning and Organizing in New Ventures. Journal of Evolutionary Economics, 24(1): 59–82.

Aldrich, H. E., & Zimmer, C. 1986. Entrepreneurship through Social Networks. In D. Sexton, & R. Smilor (Eds.), The Art and Science of Entrepreneurship: 3–23. New York: Ballinger.

Baker, T., Aldrich, H. E., & Liou, N. 1997. Invisible Entrepreneurs: The Neglect of Women Business Owners by Mass Media and Scholarly Journals in the United States. Entrepreneurship and Regional Development, 9(3): 221–238.

Blau, Peter M. 1964. Exchange and Power in Social Life. New York: Wiley.

Bradley, S. W., Aldrich, H., Shepherd, D. A., & Wiklund, J. 2011. Resources, Environmental Change, and Survival: Asymmetric Paths of Young Independent and Subsidiary Organizations. Strategic Management Journal, 32(5): 486–509.

Buckley, Walter. 1967. Sociology and Modern System Theory. Englewood Cliffs, NJ: Prentice-Hall.

Campbell, D. T. 1969. Variation and Selective Retention in Socio-Cultural Evolution. General Systems, 14: 69–85.

Cliff, J. E., Langton, N., & Aldrich, H. E. 2005. Walking the Talk? Gendered Rhetoric vs. Action in Small Firms. Organization Studies, 26(1): 63–91.

Converse, P. E. 1976. The Dynamics of Party Support: Cohort Analyzing Party Identification. Beverly Hills, CA: Sage Publications.

Cook, Karen S. 1977. Exchange and Power in Networks of Interorganizational Relations. The Sociological Quarterly, 18(1): 62–82.

Davis, A. E., Renzulli, L. A., & Aldrich, H. E. 2006. Mixing or Matching?: The Influence of Voluntary Associations on the Occupational Diversity and Density of Small Business Owners' Networks. Work and Occupations, 33(1): 42–72.

Davis, G. F. 2013. How Affordable CNC Can Remake Industry: Thoughts on Technology and Business Structure. In T. Hall (Ed.), 100KGarages.com, Vol. 2015, 1–4. Durham, NC: Ted Hall.

DiMaggio, P. J., & Powell, W. W. 1983. The Iron Cage Revisited: Institutional Isomorphism and Collective Rationality in Organizational Fields. American Sociological Review, 48(2): 147–160.

Hannan, M. T., & Freeman, J. H. 1977. The Population Ecology of Organizations. American Journal of Sociology, 82(5): 929–164.

Hannan, M. T., & Freeman, J. H. 1984. Structural Inertia and Organizational Change. American Sociological Review, 49(1): 149–164.

Hannan, M. T., & Freeman, J. H. 1989. Organizational Ecology. Cambridge, MA: Harvard University Press.

Hunt, C. S., & Aldrich, H. E. 1998. The Second Ecology: The Creation and Evolution of Organizational Communities as Exemplified by the Commercialization of the World Wide Web. In B. Staw, & L. L. Cummings (Eds.), Research in Organizational Behavior, Vol. 20: 267–302. Greenwich, CT: JAI Press.

Ideological Capture in the Regulation of U.S. Broadcasting, 1920–1934. In H. Prechel (Ed.), Research in Political Sociology, Vol. 14: 111–150. Bingley UK: Emerald.

Katona, G. 1964. The Mass Consumption Society. New York: McGraw-Hill.

Katz, Daniel, & Kahn, Robert L. 1978. The Social Psychology of Organizations, Edited by R. L. Kahn. New York: Wiley.

Kim, P. H., & Aldrich, H. E. 2005. Social Capital and Entrepreneurship. Foundations and Trends in Entrepreneurship, 1(2): 1–52.

Kim, P. H., Aldrich, H. E., & Keister, L. A. 2006. Access (Not) Denied: The Impact of Financial, Human, and Cultural Capital on Entrepreneurial Entry in the United States. *Small Business Economics*, 27, 5–22.

Kim, P. H., Longest, K. C., & Aldrich, H. E. 2013. Can You Lend Me a Hand? Task-Role Alignment of Social Support for Aspiring Business Owners. Work and Occupations, 40(3): 211–247.

Kurke, L., & Aldrich, H. E. 1983. Mintzberg Was Right! A Replication and Extension of the Nature of Managerial Work. Management Science, 29(8): 975–984.

Lippmann, S. 2005. Public Airwaves, Private Interests: Competing Visions and Ideological Capture in the Regulation of U.S. Broadcasting, 1920-1934. In H. Prechel (Ed.), Research in Political Sociology, Vol. 14: 111–150. Bingley UK: Emerald.

Lippmann, S. 2007. The Institutional Context of Industry Consolidation: Radio Broadcasting in the United States, 1920–1934. Social Forces, 86(2): 467–495.

Lippmann, S., & Aldrich, H. E. 2014. History and Evolutionary Theory. In M. Bucheli, & R. D. Wadhwani (Eds.), Organizations in Time: History, Theory, Methods, 124–146. New York: Oxford University Press.

Martinez, M. A., & Aldrich, H. E. 2014. Sociological Theories Applied to Family Businesses. In L. Melin, M. Nordqvist, & P. Sharma (Eds.), The SAGE Handbook of Family Business: 83–99. London: Sage Publications.

Martinez, M. A., Yang, T., & Aldrich, H. 2011. Entrepreneurship as an Evolutionary Process: Research Progress and Challenges. Entrepreneurship Research Journal, 1(1), article 4.

McKelvey, B., & Aldrich, H. E. 1983. Populations, Natural Selection, and Applied Organizational Science. Administrative Science Quarterly, 28(1): 101–128.

Mindlin, S., & Aldrich, H. E. 1975. Interorganizational Dependence: A Review of the Concept and a Re-examination of the Findings of the Aston Group. Administrative Science Quarterly, 20(3): 382–392.

Mintzberg, H. 1973. The Nature of Managerial Work. New York: Harper & Row.

Mollick, E. 2014. The Dynamics of Crowdfunding: An Exploratory Study. Journal of Business Venturing, 29: 1–16.

Nelson, R., & Winter, S. 1982. An Evolutionary Theory of Economic Change. Cambridge, MA: Belknap.

Pfeffer, J., & Salancik, G. R. 1978. The External Control of Organizations: A Resource Dependence Perspective. New York: Harper & Row.

Renzulli, L. A., Aldrich, H., & Moody, J. 2000. Family Matters: Gender, Networks, and Entrepreneurial Outcomes. Social Forces, 79(2): 523–546.

Ruef, M., Aldrich, H. E., & Carter, N. M. 2003. The Structure of Founding Teams: Homophily, Strong Ties, and Isolation among U.S. Entrepreneurs. American Sociological Review, 68(2): 195–222.

Scott, W. Richard. 2008. Institutions and Organizations: Ideas and Interests. Newbury Park: Sage Publications.

Shah, S. K., & Tripsas, M. 2007. The Accidental Entrepreneur: The Emergence and Collective Process of User Entrepreneurship. Strategic Entrepreneurship Journal, 1: 123–140.

Stewart, Alex, & Aldrich, Howard. 2015. Collaboration between Management and Anthropology Researchers: Obstacles and Opportunities. The Academy of Management Perspectives, 29: 173–192.

von Hippel, E. 2005. Democratizing Innovation. Cambridge, MA: MIT Press.

Waldinger, R., Aldrich, H. E., & Ward, R. 1990. Ethnic Entrepreneurs: Immigrant Businesses in Industrial Societies. Beverly Hills, CA: Sage.

Wallerstein, I. M. 2004. World Systems Analysis: An Introduction. Durham: Duke University Press.

Watson, Tony J. 2011. Ethnography, Reality, and Truth: The Vital Need for Studies of "How Things Work" in Organizations and Management. Journal of Management Studies, 48: 202–217.

Weick, Karl E. 1979. The Social Psychology of Organizing. Reading, MA: Addison-Wesley.

Weiss, Jane, & Aldrich, H.E. 1977. The Supranational Organization of Production. Current Anthropology 18(4): 630–631.

Whyte, William Foote. 1943. Street Corner Society: The Social Structure of an Italian Slum. Chicago: University of Chicago Press.

Wry, T., Cobb, J. A., & Aldrich, H. E. 2013. More than a Metaphor: Assessing the Historical Legacy of Resource Dependence and Its Contemporary Promise as a Theory of Environmental Complexity. The Academy of Management Annals, 7(1): 441–488.

Yang, T., & Aldrich, H. E. 2012. Out Of Sight but Not Out Of Mind: Why Failure to Account for Left Truncation Biases Research on Failure Rates. Journal of Business Venturing, 27(4): 477–492.

Yang, T., & Aldrich, H. E. 2014. Who's the Boss? Explaining Gender Inequality in Entrepreneurial Teams. American Sociological Review, 79(2): 303–327.

4

Roots and wings

David B. Audretsch

The setting

When the doctoral student, Iris Beckman, rushed to my office at the Max Planck Institute of Economics in 2004, arms full of various volumes of the *Palgrave Dictionary of Economics*, wondering why only a handful of entries appeared under "Entrepreneurship," "Small Business" and even "Innovation," she was shocked (Beckmann, 2010). But I wasn't. After all, four years of graduate studies in economics at the University of Wisconsin, topping off a bachelor's degree in economics, had netted virtually no mention of entrepreneurship. At least small business had made an appearance in the industrial organization literature, under the topic of "sub-optimal capacity," and innovation was reserved as a special topic at the end of the semester, embedded in research and development, time permitting.

The scholarly discipline of economics had little use for concepts and phenomena such as entrepreneurship, small business and innovation. After all, the MIT scholar Robert Solow (1956) had been awarded the Nobel Prize in economics for explicitly identifying what mattered for the economic growth, employment and productivity that society so greatly coveted – investments in physical capital. The more, the better. The subdiscipline industrial organization quickly applied this to the units of analysis of the industry and the market and determined physical capital amassed at large-scale production bestowed the greatest levels of economic efficiency. The fields of management and strategy, led by scholars such as Alfred Chandler (1977 and 1990), analogously identified that the surest strategy to achieve dominance was made clear in the title of his best-selling book, *Scale and Scope*. The post–World War II economy seemed remarkably inhospitable, not just to small-scale production but also to new-firm startups or anything else smacking of entrepreneurship.

Thus, small business, entrepreneurship and innovation remained largely under the radar screens of economics and management, where scholars were busily absorbed analyzing the primacy of large-scale production and its benefits in terms of efficiency and productivity. It was hard to square the singular focus of what I was learning in Madison with what I actually observed when I visited my sister, who was living in Palo Alto at that time. She had started a small business producing instruction manuals for small companies producing personal computers and related electronics components. Because these were generally all small start-up companies, they simply lacked the resources and staff required to produce their own manuals. My sister brought together teams of self-employed people who would visit the company to write the text, take the photos, design the layout and do the actual printing. I couldn't help but notice that the structure of this industry, as well as the conduct of these individual businesses and self-employed, not only didn't conform to what was being taught in economics, it wasn't even on the radar screen.

Discovering small business

It was only after arriving at the International Institute of Management in Berlin, Germany, which subsequently would be renamed and reorganized as the Wissenschaftszentrum Berlin für Sozialforschung, or Berlin Centre for Social Science Research, that it actually occurred to me to focus on small business as a topic for research. The anomaly of what I had observed in Palo Alto could actually be subjected to systematic empirical scrutiny. In fact, I had been hired to research the competitive advantage of large corporations. But when Zoltan Acs and I got our hands on a brand-new data set created by the United States Small Business Administration, we could see that the issue of firm size wasn't so straightforward. Our first paper together (1988) questioned the pervasive assumption in economics that large companies had an innovative advantage as a result of their superior access to research and development. In what became widely referred to as the Schumpeterian paradox, our results suggested that in some industries small firms were actually more innovative than their larger counterparts. This inspired us to conduct a whole series of studies trying to uncover the role of small firms in industrial organization (Acs and Audretsch, 1990). The beauty of working in Berlin was that, thanks to the generosity of the Wissenschafts-zentrum Berlin für Sozialfoschung, we had direct access to the leading scholars in the field of industrial economics of that era, such as F.M. Scherer and my own PhD advisor, Leonard Weiss, who regularly visited our institute for extensive research visits. With their guidance we were able to begin to trace the contributions that small firms made in shaping the economic performance of industries.

Taking innovation seriously

In 1987 I attended one of the first Research in Entrepreneurship and Small Business (RENT) Conferences in Durham. The event was filled with management scholars presenting studies of why some people choose to start a new business whereas others don't. Although I could see their work was about small business, I couldn't figure out how it related to our own research. That was, until I returned to Berlin. At the conference showcasing the findings and results of the multi-country project organized and directed by the late Paul Geroski and Joachim Schwalbach (1991), *The Determinants of Entry: An International Comparison*, study after study, meticulously undertaken at the country level, dutifully reported which industry-specific characteristics were conducive to entry into a cross-section of (manufacturing) industries and which impeded entry. In the field of industrial organization, entry was of particular interest because it was the mechanism that equilibrated the industry and market by eroding excess profits or economic rents. If prices drifted above marginal cost and long-run average cost, enabling the producers to enjoy excess profits accruing from market power, it was the entry of firms into the market that would increase quantity and ultimately equilibrate the market. However, there was something glaringly absent from the analyses – people. To be more exact, the entrepreneur remained the invisible man in economics, certainly in industrial economics. Although excess profits combined with insufficient barriers to entry would induce firms into entering into the market, no one actually had any idea of what kinds of firms these new entrants actually were. But we did. Using the micro data files procured from Dunn & Bradstreet by the United States Small Business Administration, we could identify the entrants not just as some vague, undefined business entity, but most typically as either a new or small firm. The fact was, and remains, that most entry is in the form of a new business. But where did that new business come from? How did it come into existence? And why? In fact, what I had stumbled into was a gaping hole not just in the industrial organization literature but that was pervasive throughout economics. In its exclusive focus on firms and industries, the academic field of industrial organization had neglected people. The light bulb went off. Just as the great American novelist, Mark Twain, shared, "Sex was invented when I turned fourteen," I had discovered entrepreneurship around 10:30 a.m. on that cold, dark November morning in Berlin in 1989.

The standard of models of industrial organization at that time viewed the entry of new firms into an industry as responding to profit opportunities as a result of market supply resulting in prices above the long-run equilibrating level (Geroski, 1995; Caves, 1998). The entry of firms in an industry was about business as usual – the new entrants simply increased the quantity of that business. By contrast, we proposed the view that the entrants were typically new and small firms which were anything other than business as usual. In their efforts to generate innovations, new-firm startups were actually serving as agents of change. Rather than providing the equilibrating function so coveted and assumed in the models and thinking prevalent in industrial econom-ics, these new firms were actually disequilibrating the market through innovative activity. New firms were not necessarily about business as usual, just increasing the quantity supplied on the market, but in at least some cases, as an agent of change, which would ultimately disequilibrate the market and create entirely new products and industries. And we had the empirical evidence to back that up (Audretsch, 1995).

The Schumpeterian paradox

Small business did not seem a likely place to look for innovation. The thinking about innova-tion prevalent in economics at that time had been shaped by Zvi Griliches (1979), who had formalized the knowledge production function linking knowledge inputs, such as research and development and human capital, to innovative outputs. As Milton Friedman had famously quipped, "There's no such thing as a free lunch." And so it was with innovation. To generate the output of innovation, inputs were required, most obviously in the form of creating new knowledge and ideas.

The vast bulk of research and development in the United States was undertaken by the 500 largest corporations. Thus, a prediction of the knowledge production function obviously was that the large firms, who were investing in most of the research and development and employed most of the human capital, had the requisite knowledge inputs for generating innovative out-puts. Compelling empirical evidence supported the knowledge production function at the level of countries. Clearly the most important countries investing in research and development and with high levels of human capital, such as the United States, Japan and Switzerland, also exhib-ited considerably more innovative output than did developing countries with only a paucity of knowledge inputs. Similarly, at the level of the industry, high levels of research and development and human capital clearly contributed to greater innovative activity in computers, pharmaceuti-cals and electronics than did wood products and textiles.

Thus, the finding that small firms were actually more innovative in certain industries than their larger counterparts posed a startling contradiction to the prevalent thinking in economics at that time and became widely characterized as the *Schumpeterian paradox* (Acs and Audretsch, 1988 and 1990). If small business exhibited particularly robust innovative activity in certain industries, and in particular what seemed to be newly emerging industries such as biotechnology and software, where did they get the knowledge inputs?

Resolving the Schumpeterian paradox: entrepreneurship

The resolution of the Schumpeterian paradox came by rethinking and shifting Griliches' (1979) model of the knowledge production function. Griliches had assumed that the firm exists exogenously and then engages in strategic investments to generate the desired outputs and outcomes – innovation (Arrow, 1962). But when the light bulb suddenly turned on for me at that conference in Berlin in November 1989 by thinking first of people and individuals trying to do the best that they can with their knowledge, ideas and insights, and not just about firms and industries, as was prevalent in the field of industrial organization and technological change at that time, I could see the fallacy, or at least limitation, of that assumption. Of course firms exist, and of course they strategically invest to generate desired outcomes. But where did those firms come from in the first place? People, or someone, had started them. Why they would choose to start a new firm was clear from the accounts of famous entrepreneurs in Silicon Valley and elsewhere. When the organizers of that conference, and my colleagues at the International Institute of Management in Berlin, Paul Geroski and Joachim Schwalbach, invited me to contribute a chapter in their volume bringing together the different country studies on entry that they had commissioned, *Entry and Contestability: An International Comparison* (Geroski and Schwalbach, 1991), I wrote a chapter based on the now-famous *Stammbaum*, or family tree of spin-offs in Silicon Valley from Fairchild, "Innovation as a Means of Entry: An Overview" (Acs and Audretsch, 1991). The point of the chapter was that an employee or individual at an incumbent company unable to pursue her or his dreams and aspirations might start a new firm as a means of realizing those dreams and aspirations in generating innovative activity. It was only a trivial step to develop the *knowledge spillover theory of entrepreneurship*, which I introduced in *Innovation and Industry Evolution* (1995), suggesting that small firms are important and economically interesting because they are the result of an entrepreneur starting a new firm or organization, not to engage in business as usual, but rather to do something different that was not accepted by the incumbent organization (Audretsch, 1991).

Thus, resolving the Schumpeterian paradox started with inverting the basic assumption upon which Griliches' model of the knowledge production function of innovation rests – that the firm exists exogenously and then invests to create knowledge in order to endogenously generate innovative output. Instead, the starting point for the knowledge spillover theory of entrepreneurship is knowledge, which was already created by firms, universities and in other institutions. When an individual is not able to pursue her or his aspirations and dreams involved in new ideas, they may resort to creating a new business to innovate. Thus, according to the knowledge spillover theory of entrepreneurship, the knowledge exists exogenously and the new firm is endogenously created in an effort by the entrepreneur(s) to appropriate the value of their knowledge and ideas (Audretsch, 1995; Audretsch, Keilbach and Lehmann, 2006; Acs et al., 2009; and Ghio et al., 2015).

The missing W of economics

In the fall of 1990, Zoltan told me that a doctoral student, Maryann Feldman, at Carnegie Mellon University, had inquired about obtaining the geographic location of the innovating firms and establishments in the United States Small Business Administration database. I recalled that, in fact, a geographic locater for each record existed, but we had discarded it because it seemed irrelevant and extraneous. We had to have the original data tapes reread in order to send the data, including the geographic locator, to Maryann. Those were the days!

When the three of us sat down to work in 1991, Paul Krugman (1991) had just published his work on economic geography that would ultimately lead to the Nobel Prize in economics. Maryann explained to us that her goal was to do for innovation what Krugman had done for production – to decipher the missing W of economics! Whereas most of economics focused on what gets produced, who produces it and for whom is it produced, Maryann instead set out on a research agenda analyzing where it gets produced. For her, this opened up the door to a path-breaking PhD thesis, ultimately published as *The Geography of Innovation* (1994) and a career fueled as one of the pioneers exploring this missing W (Feldman, 2014; Lorenzen and Carlsson, 2014). For me, meeting and working with Maryann opened up an entirely new and unanticipated research direction – geography and economic space (Audretsch and Feldman, 1996; Audretsch and Stephan, 1996).

Maryann quickly pointed to Adam Jaffe's (1989) article showing that the knowledge production function holds across geographic space. Patents tend to be spatially concentrated within close geographic proximity to knowledge sources such as research and development and university research (Henderson, Jaffe and Trajtenberg, 1998). As Maryann put it, not only does knowledge spill over for use by other firms and individuals, but it is also spatially localized, in that the knowledge spillovers are geographically bounded within close geographic proximity to the knowledge source. We quickly set off to see how geography influences not just innovative activity, but also the innovative advantages of large and small firms (Acs, Audretsch and Feldman, 1992; Acs, Audretsch and Feldman, 1994; and Audretsch and Feldman, 1996).

Had Maryann, Zoltan and I not met up in Zoltan's office in 1991, I might have missed all this and remained oblivious to the missing W of economics, proving Maryann's important point in the first place – location matters.

Scaling up

Zoltan and I already had extensive experience with scaling up. He and I, along with the others, were academic refugees at the Wissenschaftszentrum Berlin für Sozialforschung, hidden away behind the Berlin Wall. As we stumbled into the new and uncertain terrain trying to decipher the role of small firms in industrial organization in general, and innovative activity in particular, we met largely with resistance, hostility and, what seemed preferable at that time, indifference. We knew that we couldn't get anywhere working alone. We had to scale up.

Zoltan had a knack for not just travelling across Europe and North America, but also for sniffing out scholars and policy makers who similarly suffered in the intellectual isolation inherent in working in a new and undeveloped area. Working at a great think tank like the Wissenschaftszentrum Berlin für Sozialforschung helped. Their commitment to us and our research agenda ensured ample resources for traveling to meet with like-minded scholars, inviting guest speakers for seminars and hosting workshops and conferences. We did all of that, in spades. The result was the emergence of a remarkably loose and informal, but still remarkable, network of young scholars who were discovering the same thing that we had – that small firms matter. Exactly how, why and in which ways were still up to us to determine. That was the great carrot at the end of the stick – the unknown answers.

We started a new journal, *Small Business Economics*, in 1988, to spur this emerging community of like-minded scholars, spanning quite different research fields and intellectual backgrounds, to coalesce. I doubt that without the backing, resources and visibility of the Wissenschaftszentrum Berlin für Sozialforschung, as well as the support and enthusiasm of our colleagues, who no doubt wondered in disbelief when we launched our new journal, including Joachim Schwalbach, Felix FitzRoy, Bob Hart, Harris Schlessinger, J. Matthias Graf von der Schulenburg, Talat Mahmood, and Hideki Yamawaki, that the journal would have lasted.

But lasted it has. Interest in *Small Business Economics* grew from a trickle to what today can safely be characterized as a flood of submissions from all around the world. Still, at some point, around the turn of the century, we could feel the momentum lapsing. Our original trajectory had been launched not just within economics, but largely within the subfields of industrial organization and labor economics within the discipline of economics. Industrial organization was exhibiting alarming signs of a declining field so that we seemed to be doomed to being a subfield within a declining field of economics. We couldn't help but notice that, like us, the authors were getting older and more senior.

It wasn't that young scholars lacked an interest in entrepreneurship. But the opportunities were elsewhere. I was stunned attending my first business meeting of the Entrepreneurship Division of the Academy of Management. Row after row of young, enthusiastic entrepreneurship scholars filled a spacious auditorium, as they applauded the annual best paper, best researcher and other awards. As Willie Sutton, the world-famous bank robber responded to the reporter who had asked why he keeps robbing banks as they led him off to prison for the fifth time, "That's where the money is." And that's where the opportunities were for young scholars – at least in North America – in management, in business schools. Locked away in a declining and stagnant subfield in economics, industrial organization, it seemed that we were doomed. Schumpeter's creative destruction was happening, and we were on the wrong side of the equation.

I accepted the offer to serve as a director of the Max Planck Institute of Economics in Jena by the president of the Max Planck Society, Professor Dr. Peter Gruss, a world-renowned biochemist, to scale up. After I signed the contract agreeing to serve as a director at the headquarters in Munich, Professor Gruss asked me, "So, what are you going to call your new division?" Fortunately, I had an answer: *Entrepreneurship, Growth and Public Policy*.

Scaling up also involved scaling out. A key part of the Max Planck vision was to integrate scholars across a broad spectrum of academic backgrounds, spanning economics, sociology, geography, psychology, and certainly management. Erik Lehmann and Max Keilbach signed on to serve as the assistant director and senior research fellow, blessing us with a formidable leadership team. As Max later reflected, "This could be the start of something Big" (Keilbach, 2010). When colleagues asked what our mission was at the Max Planck Institute of Economics, we boldly replied, "To create the field of entrepreneurship." It was meant to be a bona fide research and scholarly field, not merely a subfield in an established scholarly discipline. But it had to rely on those established scholarly disciplines, such as economics, sociology and psychology, for the most salient ideas, theories and methodologies. Still, our mandate was to spur the emergence of the field of entrepreneurship that had value per se and not simply because it contributed to the value proposition established by an incumbent scholarly discipline.

At this point, entrepreneurship scholars still suffered from an intellectual inferiority complex. After all, academic disciplines such as economics enjoyed a common theoretical basis, methodology and analytic approach. With troubling doubts about the lack of any singular theory or methodological approach, let alone definition or even conceptual understanding of what actually constitutes entrepreneurship apparent in entrepreneurship research, I took advantage of the annual meeting of the Max Planck Society directors to ask two colleagues serving as directors of Max Planck Institutes in chemistry and physics about what actually constitutes a bona fide research field. Their response was as rapid as it was full of the disdain that only natural scientists can have for their social science colleagues: "Ist doch Klar – Geld und Interesse!", or "It's obvious – money and interest". In the emerging hot areas of informatics and nanotechnology, colleagues didn't seem to get hung up or bogged down worrying about the existence of a singular methodology and common theoretical approaches and understandings. After all, these are inherently interdisciplinary or cross-disciplinary research fields drawing on a broad spectrum of basic traditional disciplines, including physics and chemistry.

Money and interest. Entrepreneurship had it in spades. It was not just the generosity of the Max Planck Society that was funding substantial research devoted to creating the field of entrepreneurship. The Ewing Marion Kauffman Foundation was investing large amounts of money to fund both research and teaching about entrepreneurship. The Netherlands soon developed its own HOPE program, just as chairs of entrepreneurship proliferated first across America and then quickly spread to Europe. As far as interest was concerned, one only had to look to the burgeoning enrollments in courses on entrepreneurship around the world, along with the explosion of participation in the Entrepreneurship Division, which was well on its way to ranking among the largest in the Academy of Management. The field was taking off.

At the Max Planck Institute of Economics, we felt it was crucial to integrate the different disciplines to make it clear how exactly and why entrepreneurship matters. Not just to those who are becoming or have become entrepreneurs, or to those firms fortunate enough to be entrepreneurial, but rather to everyone in society. Ultimately it is the stakeholders in society that benefit from entrepreneurship by enjoying a better economic performance in terms of what matters the most to most people – sustainable jobs, a high standard of living and viable communities. We had to make an explicit link between the most micro of phenomena – entrepreneurship – and the most macro – the economic performance of entire regions, states and countries. In *Entrepreneurship and Economic Growth*, the two colleagues who provided the foundation and cornerstone for the Division on Entrepreneurship, Growth and Public Policy at the Max Planck Institute of Economics – Erik Lehmann and Max Keilbach – teamed up to do exactly that (Audretsch, Lehmann and Keilbach, 2006). Erik served as the first assistant director, and Max provided a vital creative energy, helping sway some great and talented young scholars into coming to Jena and joining our team.

In making the link between one of the most micro phenomena in economics, the decision by an individual to start a new firm, and the overall macroeconomic performance of a country, we were able to show that entrepreneurship matters. Not just to those engaging in it or accruing the benefits from their own entrepreneurial activities. Rather, relying on the framework of the knowledge spillover theory of entrepreneurship, we provided not only a compelling explanation of why some people do it – decide to become an entrepreneur – but also why it is important in terms of generating the outcomes that society cares about – jobs, growth, innovation and competitiveness in a globalized economy. Those cities, states and regions exhibiting more entrepreneurship enjoy a stronger economic performance in terms of growth, jobs and competitiveness in global markets. By contrast, those places with a paucity of entrepreneurship tended to be burdened by economic stagnation.

The entrepreneurial society

Roy Thurik and I had spent several summers during the first half of the 1990s, locked away in his basement in Rotterdam, which he termed "The Dungeon", trying to make sense of why the United States had diverged so drastically from Europe. Whereas much of Western Europe continued to thrive with a manufacturing-driven economy based largely on the traditional industrial stalwarts that had served Europe so well throughout the postwar era, America had veered off into a bold, new direction. Rather than succumb to the misery that seemed inevitable with the loss of competitiveness in traditional manufacturing, a new set of high-technology companies, industries and services unexpectedly exploded onto the American economic scene, spearheaded by bold entrepreneurs such as Steve Jobs, Bill Gates and Mark Zuckerberg. With one of the fundamental tenets in economics, the law of comparative advantage, as our guiding star, we set to work on a paper, "The Managed and the Entrepreneurial Economies: Europe and the United States on Divergent Paths," to contrast the continuity of the managed economy in Europe with the emergence of the entrepreneurial economy in the United States.

However, Roy is a perfectionist. As we continued to meet summer after summer, laboring in Roy's dungeon through the minutiae of our paper, Europe slumped in the post–Berlin Wall globalization. At first we heard about the Swedish paradox. Then it was the European paradox. Our paradox was that we had a paper explaining that Europe had a decidedly different economic approach than the United States – only that no longer seemed to be true. In fact, the emerging bright spots of Europe, such as Bavaria and Randstadt, the region between Amsterdam and Rotterdam, were well on their way to abandoning the managed economy and embracing the entrepreneurial economy. Our resolution was to abandon the divergence thesis across the Atlantic, which had been the main point of our paper, and instead suggest "What's New about the New Economy? Sources of Growth in the Managed and Entrepreneurial Economies," (Audretsch and Thurik, 2001).

Even as *Entrepreneurship and Economic Growth* was in preparation, it was clear that the policy world was too impatient to wait for systematic econometric evidence. Policy makers everywhere wanted to know how to create an entrepreneurial economy. We defined an entrepreneurial economy as one where entrepreneurship serves as a driving force for economic performance. But how could policy makers achieve it?

The answer clearly had a lot to do with institutions and policy. *The Entrepreneurial Society* was my first attempt to write a book reaching out to thought leaders in business and policy, as well as the broader public, to explain not just why entrepreneurship matters for entrepreneurs, but why most places seemed desperate to foster and harness the fruits accruing from entrepreneurship. Entrepreneurship was no longer a topic just for entrepreneurship scholars, but had clearly become a priority in the policy community.

After countless policy presentations, it became clear that thought leaders lacked a systematic framework to understand why entrepreneurship matters. What the policy makers had at their disposal was a series of singular strategies, each which been fashionable in its own time, ranging from smokestack chasing during the postwar era when manufacturing ruled, to clusters, and more recently the creative class. Although each of these approaches surely contains considerable merit, the lack of any broader systematic framework seemingly left local policy makers with few choices. To show how and why entrepreneurship had emerged as one of the key strategies for enhancing the economic performance of a place, but also to provide such a fundamental systematic framework for formulating and implementing what might be termed the strategic management of place, I wrote *Everything in Its Place: Entrepreneurship and the Strategic Management of Cities, Regions and States* (2015). To provide an in-depth case study of a place that has transformed itself into an entrepreneurial society by dramatically turning around its economic performance from what had been characterized as the sick man of Europe at the end of the last century to the stunning economic, political and social success of today, Erik Lehmann and I teamed up for *The Seven Secrets of Germany* (2016). Although both of these books argue that there is no reason why a place, albeit a city, region, state or entire country, cannot transform into a high-performing, entrepreneurially driven society, recent research provides at least some grounds why this may be easier to implement in some places than in others. In Obschonka et al. (2015) and Stuetzer et al. (2015), we find compelling evidence that not all places have a culture that is equally conducive to entrepreneurship. Culture may yet prove to be the final frontier for both entrepreneurs and scholars of entrepreneurship.

Final thoughts

Some two centuries ago, the giant of a statesman, philosopher and scholar, Johann Wolfgang von Goethe, mused, "The greatest thing a father can give his son is roots. The second greatest thing is wings to escape those roots".[1] For me, those roots were cemented by the academic discipline of economics. It is entrepreneurship that has provided the wings to move beyond those roots. Goethe was, of course, right. Although the roots have been invaluable, it is the wings that have made all the difference.

Note

1 What Goethe actually wrote was "Zwei Dinge sollen Kinder von ihren Eltern bekommen: Wurzeln und Flügel" (Audretsch and Lehmann, 2016, p. 78).

References

Acs, Zoltan J. and David B. Audretsch, 1988, "Innovation in Large and Small Firms: An Empirical Analysis," American Economic Review, 78(4), 678–690.

Acs, Zoltan J. and David B. Audretsch, 1990, Innovation and Small Firms (Cambridge: MIT Press).

Acs, Zoltan J. and David B. Audretsch, 1991, "Innovation as a Means of Entry: An Overview," with Zoltan J. Acs in Paul Geroski and Joachim Schwalbach (eds.), Entry and Contestability: An International Comparison (Oxford: Basil Blackwell, pp. 222–243).

Acs, Zoltan J., David B. Audretsch and Maryann P. Feldman, 1992, "Real Effects of University Research," American Economic Review, 82(1), 363–367.

Acs, Zoltan J., David B. Audretsch and Maryann P. Feldman, 1994, "R&D Spillovers and Recipient Firm Size," Review of Economics and Statistics, 76(2), 336–340.

Acs, Zoltan J., David B. Audretsch, Pontus Braunerhjelm and Bo Carlsson, 2009, "The Knowledge Spillover Theory of Entrepreneurship," Small Business Economics, 32(1), 15–30.

Arrow, Kenneth, 1962, "Economic Welfare and the Allocation of Resources for Invention," in R.R. Nelson (ed.), The Rate and Direction of Inventive Activity (Princeton: Princeton University Press, pp. 609–626).

Audretsch, David B., 1991, "New-Firm Survival and the Technological Regime," Review of Economics and Statistics, 73(3), 441–450.

Audretsch, David B., 1995, Innovation and Industry Evolution (Cambridge: MIT Press).

Audretsch, David B., 2007, The Entrepreneurial Society (New York: Oxford University Press).

Audretsch, David B., 2015, Everything in Its Place: Entrepreneurship and the Strategic Management of Cities, Regions, and States (New York: Oxford University Press).

Audretsch, David B. and Erik E. Lehmann, 2016, The Seven Secrets of Germany (New York: Oxford University Press).

Audretsch, David B. and Maryann P. Feldman, 1996, "R&D Spillovers and the Geography of Innovation and Production," American Economic Review, 86(3), 630–640.

Audretsch, David B., Max Keilbach and Erik E. Lehmann, 2006, Entrepreneurship and Economic Growth (New York: Oxford University Press).

Audretsch, David B. and Paula E. Stephan, 1996, "Company-Scientist Locational Links: The Case of Biotechnology," with Paula E. Stephan, American Economic Review, 86(3), 641–652.

Audretsch, David B. and Roy Thurik, 2001, "What's New about the New Economy? Sources of Growth in the Managed and Entrepreneurial Economies," Industrial and Corporate Change, 10(1), 267–315.

Beckmann, Iris, 2010, "In the Right Place at the Right Time," in Zac Rolnik (ed.), Reflections: A Farewell to David (Boston: NOW Publishers, pp. 10–11).

Caves, Richard, 1998, "Industrial Organization and New Findings on the Turnover and Mobility of Firms," Journal of Economic Literature, 3, 1947–1982.

Chandler, Alfred, 1977, The Visible Hand: The Managerial Revolution in American Business (Cambridge: Belknap Press).

Chandler, Alfred, 1990, Scale and Scope: The Dynamics of Industrial Capitalism (Cambridge: Harvard University Press).

Feldman, Maryann P., 2014, "The Character of Innovative Places: Entrepreneurial Strategy, Economic Development and Prosperity," Small Business Economics, 43(1), 9–20.

Geroski, Paul, 1995, "What Do We Know about Entry?" International Journal of Industrial Organization, 13, 421–440.

Geroski, Paul and Joachim Schwalbach (eds.), 1991, Entry and Contestability: An International Comparison (Oxford: Basil Blackwell).

Ghio, Niccolo, Massimiliano Guerini, Erik E. Lehmann and Cristina Rossi-Lamastra, 2015, "The Emergence of the Knowledge Spillover Theory of Entrepreneurship," Small Business Economics, 44(1), 1–18.

Griliches, Zvi, 1979, "Issues in Assessing the Contribution of Research and Development to Productivity Growth," Bell Journal of Economics, 10, 92–116.

Henderson, Rebecca, Adam Jaffe and Manuel Trajtenberg, 1998, "Universities as a Source of Commercial Technology: A Detailed Analysis of University Patenting 1965–1988," Review of Economics and Statistics, 65, 119–127.

Jaffe, Adam B., 1989, "The Real Effects of Academic Research," American Economic Review, 79, 957–970.

Keilbach, Max, 2010, "Well, then Can I Walk Beside You?" in Zac Rolnik (ed.), Reflections: A Farewell to David (Boston: NOW Publishers, pp. 23–26).

Krugman, Paul, 1991, Geography and Trade (Cambridge: MIT Press).

Lorenzen, Mark and Bo Carlsson, 2014, "Maryann Feldman: Recipient of the 2014 Global Award for Entrepreneurship Research," Small Business Economics, 43(1), 1–8.

Obschonka, Martin, Michael Stuetzer, David B. Audretsch, Peter J. Rentfrow, Jeff Potter and Samuel D. Gosling, 2016, "Macropsychological Factors Predict Regional Economic Resilience During a Major Economic Crisis," Social Psychological and Personality Science, 7(2), 95–104.

Solow, Robert, 1956, "A Contribution to the Theory of Economic Growth," Quarterly Journal of Economics, 39, 312–320.

Stuetzer, Michael, Martin Obschonka, David B. Audretsch, Michael Wyrwich, Peter J. Rentfrow, Mike Coombes, Leigh Shaw-Taylor and Max Satchell, 2016, "Industry Structure, Entrepreneurship, and Culture: An Empirical Analysis Using Historical Coalfields," European Economic Review, 86, 52-72.

5

The effects of business ownership on people's lives

Sara Carter

Getting into entrepreneurship research

I grew up the middle child of émigré Scottish and Welsh parents who sold their house in London to start a business in the Kent countryside in the 1970s. Within a few years the business failed catastrophically, and the effects of bankruptcy plagued my parents and, therefore us children, for years. Following a BA degree at Lancaster (political and social science), I applied for a post as an assistant in the Scottish Enterprise Foundation, a newly created centre at the University of Stirling set up by Tom Cannon and later managed by Mike Scott. Tasked with pulling together a resource centre of books and papers about entrepreneurship, I became fascinated reading the accounts of small business ownership, but curious about the rather normative descriptions – so different from my own family's experience – and the narrow range of individuals who dominated the literature.

A few months after I started, Tom Cannon invited me to join him in tendering for a research contract issued by the UK Department of Employment to undertake a study of female entrepreneurs. This project was my first experience of doing research and allowed me to spend a year interviewing seventy women who had started businesses. Meeting these women in their businesses or their homes, listening to their experiences, the reasons they had started up, the challenges and the triumphs they had faced, hearing stories of persistence, sometimes leading to success and sometimes failure, was a formative experience and helped lay to rest the ghosts of my own family's business failure. The subsequent monograph 'Women as Entrepreneurs' (Carter & Cannon, 1992) was one of the first published studies on this subject. Despite being young and unqualified, the experience of successfully managing an academic research project from inception through to final publication, and my fascination with listening to individual accounts of business ownership, encouraged me to pursue further work.

Shortly after this project had finished, Peter Rosa joined the Scottish Enterprise Foundation as research director. Peter, an anthropologist by training, brought research expertise and disciplinary rigour to the new domain of entrepreneurship. Seeing untapped potential in the study of female entrepreneurship, we successfully applied for a large-scale research contract from the UK Economic and Social Research Council to undertake a more rigorous analysis of 600 (300 male owned and 300 female owned) British businesses in order to investigate the impact of gender and small business management. This study allowed us to move beyond descriptive accounts to systematically analyse the effects of gender on small business performance (Rosa, Hamilton & Carter, 1996) and gender differences in venture financing (Carter & Rosa, 1998).

Although gender and performance had been linked, only a small number of studies of any substance had been undertaken, and most shied away from direct examination of quantitative performance measures, employment creation or annual growth, tending to concentrate on qualitative measures of success or failure. Our study showed the complexities of the relationship between gender and small business performance, but found gender to be a significant determinant even after other key factors were controlled for. To a large degree, we found that gender differences in business performance were a consequence of initial resource decisions. Men and women use similar sources of finance, but women used less overall start-up capital – about one third of the starting capital used by men. Interestingly, for the small number of men whose starting capital was as low as that typically used by women, the performance of their firms was closer to that of women–owned firms. Gender differences in the volume of initial capital used to start a business – with women using about a third of that used by men – has been a consistent finding of UK studies that have used matched samples. Although there is now a well-rehearsed debate about gender, finance and entrepreneurial performance, the idea that gender differences are a function of variations in resource inputs – rather than differences in motivations or abilities – is fundamental and incontrovertible.

Getting on in entrepreneurship research

One of the tensions associated with being a woman engaged in research about women–owned business is that it pigeon-holes you into a particular category, where intellectual contributions can be easily overlooked. It was obvious that if I wanted to pursue a longer-term academic career, I would need to both broaden my subject focus and deepen my expertise. I applied for a position at Strathclyde University, working as an assistant on a research project investigating the British food trade deficit and spent the next three years (1992–95) with farmers and produce growers, corporate retailers and food manufacturers, examining supply chain linkages in key food industry sectors. In three years I gained two major insights. First, farmers behaved like every other small business owner I had ever met (which, by this point, was a great many). Second, I realised how much I loathed working as someone else's research assistant.

Reading the emerging literature on rural entrepreneurship provided little help in my day job. Major studies by scholars as eminent as David Keeble (Keeble et al., 1992), Jim Curran and David Storey (1993) deliberately excluded farm businesses. The idea of rural economic growth as a function of inward migrants moving to pretty locations to start businesses to me seemed to overstate the impact of newcomers and overlook the economic contribution of farms and their role in rural economic development. It was an obvious next step for me to undertake a PhD, and I chose to focus on understanding this conundrum. At this point, I believe I made two smart choices. First, I made a deliberate choice not to do a PhD in gender, an obvious topic for me but an equally obvious career cul-de-sac, instead opting for a curiosity-based study with the potential for intellectual depth and novelty. Second, I asked Peter Rosa to become my supervisor. Peter is one of the best academics, a scholar who would push me to produce the highest-quality thesis but would give me the latitude to get on with the work without unnecessary interference; I trusted him to step in only if I were going off track.

Giving up a job to do a PhD – without a scholarship and paying fees – is not a decision open to all. Fortunately, my husband Tom agreed to cover our living costs, and parents and friends helped with child care. But it was also a very convenient decision, because our son was transitioning from full-time day care to primary school where short hours and a lack of wraparound child care would have made full-time work very difficult. I gave myself two years to see what I could do with the project, expecting that I would have at least completed a good chunk before going back to work. What I didn't bargain for was that I would fall in love with my subject and find joy in my work. I felt the privilege of a rich intellectual life coupled with an easy family life, developed the good habits of working without interruption during school hours (and after-school children's TV) and completed my thesis by spring 1997.

I had often been embarrassed about spending so many years doing contract research before doing a PhD; it's certainly not the normal sequence of an academic career. In retrospect, I can see that years of interviewing small business owners had given me an understanding that could not be acquired through reading alone. Prior experience of contract research gave me a definite advantage over most PhD students: I was clear about the goals of the project, knew how I wanted to approach the fieldwork and analysis, understood what I needed to learn to fill the gaps in my knowledge, approached my thesis as a project with a clear end point and focused on writing an excellent and elegant thesis. I was also grateful for the luxury of being in charge of my own project and able to build a PhD based on curiosity.

Entrepreneurship and agricultural restructuring

The thesis led to five peer-reviewed articles. The first conceptual paper (Carter, 1996) directly addressed the historical and theoretical antecedents of the separation of agriculture and industry, not only within the contemporary small business literature, but also in the wider disciplines of economics and sociology, and in national and international regulatory frameworks. The reason farms commanded so little attention from small business researchers was largely because of the broad environment within which farmers operate. Economic development had reduced the relative importance of the sector, and widespread protection differentiated farms from other small businesses and added complexity to sectoral analysis. Although entrepreneurship scholars explained the exclusion of agriculture as a consequence of sectoral decline, this was clearly erroneous. Not only was agricultural decline overemphasised in the small business literature, there are also inherent difficulties in linking sectoral decline with academic indifference. The two main characteristics of agriculture are its complexity and its diversity. These, together with scholarly specialisation, were the real reasons why entrepreneurship researchers excluded the sector.

The exclusion of agriculture meant that entrepreneurship scholars had missed the profound changes that were taking place within the sector. Policy reform had pushed some farmers into seeking alternative sources of business income, whereas demand-side changes had pulled others into more entrepreneurial strategies. Farms faced a strategic choice to specialise in food production or to combine food with nonfood activities. For farmers focused on food production but unable to compete on a cost basis, three strategic responses were evident: value-added production; the exploitation of quality and delivery advantages; and specialized crop production, often accompanied by strategic alliances with retail multiples and food manufacturers. Farmers who chose to combine food production with nonfood activities had a much wider set of alternatives, influenced by the local environment and market and the resources available at the enterprise level. For farmers using their resources for nonfood production, broad choices involved developing new uses for farm resources, including converting redundant buildings as new business incubators and starting new businesses either on or off the farm. Of the 300 Cambridgeshire farmers participating in the study, about a third engaged in some form of off-farm business activity, on a spectrum from diversification to fully pluriactive. Most importantly, their multiple business ownership activities ensured that farms were significant contributors to new businesses and new job creation in rural areas (Carter, 1998; 1999).

Two ideas crystallised through this project. The first was the ability to draw parallels between the multiple business ownership activities of farmers with activities unfolding in other sectors. Studies showing the prevalence of serial and portfolio entrepreneurship had started to reveal this little understood phenomenon which, as Peter Rosa and Mike Scott (1995) demonstrated, had been hidden by the use of the firm, rather than the individual owner–manager, as the main unit of analysis in entrepreneurship studies. Data from the farm-based study were able to contribute to the contemporaneous debates about portfolio entrepreneurship (Carter, 1998), and a later paper with Monder Ram argued for a more processual approach to understanding the different contexts in which portfolio entrepreneurship occurs, the different contents that determine the form portfolio entrepreneurship takes and the different processes that are used to bring it about (Carter & Ram, 2003).

The second idea was that the role of the farm household went beyond the provision of a flexible labour resource and encompassed an important role in the strategic decision making of the enterprise. Within agricultural sociology the unit of analysis had evolved from the farm business to the farmer (owner–manager) and had started to focus on the farm household. Although it would be several years before I was able to focus on entrepreneurial households, my farm-based study instilled a belief in the household as a missing element within entrepreneurship studies.

Although my interests in entrepreneurship and farming were an unusual combination, I found a kindred spirit in Gry Alsos, who was completing her PhD at Nordland Research Centre in Norway, studying multiple business ownership in the Norwegian farming sector and developing very similar insights about multiple business ownership and the centrality of the household. I met both Gry and Elisabet Ljunggren on my first visit to the Nordland Research Institute in 2002; both became close friends and long-term collaborators who shared my research interests. Our first joint paper focused on the extent of resource transfer between farms and their newly created ventures and the subsequent effects on the performance of these new ventures (Alsos & Carter, 2006). We showed that substantial resource transfer takes place, mediated both by the resource richness of the farm and the degree of similarity in the activities of the farm and the new venture. The results showed a complex relationship between resource transfer and the performance (profitability) of the new venture. The transfer of physical resources tended to enhance, whereas the transfer of organisational and knowledge-based resources tended to reduce new venture performance.

Gry and I both regarded our interest in agriculture and rural economic development as a small niche within the entrepreneurship canon, a consistent sideline to more mainstream projects that were easier to pursue in terms of funding, publications and impact. Although this sector will never be at the fashionable end of the entrepreneurship research agenda, we were encouraged and a little flattered by the fact that an edited collection of research studies on entrepreneurship in agriculture and rural development attracted contributions from 46 contributors from across four continents (Alsos et al., 2011).

The lived experiences of the small business owner

In 1999 I was approached by the Federation of Small Business (FSB), one of the largest business associations in the United Kingdom, to undertake a survey of their membership. Unlike most research funders that optimise efficiencies by using sampling strategies, they were eager to ensure that all of their members had the opportunity to voice their opinions. Hence the questionnaire, relating mostly to the demographic characteristics of the membership, their attitudes towards business growth and their opinions of topical policy issues, was mailed to all of their 175,000 members. Given the size of the sampling frame, the survey garnered a large number of responses (circa 19,000), and the resulting reports were widely disseminated to policy makers nationally and across the UK regions. The survey was repeated three more times at roughly two-year intervals, each following the same format and garnering a similar volume of responses. In the pre-Internet days of postal responses, the FSB biennial surveys were the largest business surveys undertaken in the United Kingdom.

If we had known in advance that this survey would be commissioned four times over a period of eight years, we would – of course – have insisted on designing a very different (panel) study, but we didn't know and could not have predicted the longevity of the relationship with the FSB. We learned other valuable lessons on the way. First, the importance of ensuring that each survey led to academic outputs – several different people worked with me on these surveys over the eight years, but Colin Mason and Stephen Tagg were the core team who helped manage the project and co-authored the subsequent papers. Second, we became skilled in maintaining academic independence while still building a strong relationship with the research funders – a small business lobby organisation led by activists and vigorous campaigners. The strength of this relationship was tested by survey results that demonstrated that the membership as a whole did not always hold the expected views about issues on which the organisation had collectively campaigned. Finally, we became adept at demonstrating the independence of the research team from the research funders when giving joint briefings to civil servants and politicians, maintaining a clear distance between the data and the funding organisation's views.

Four of the most important papers that emerged from these studies focused on issues of contemporary policy interest, including small business owners' attitudes towards new employment legislation and the introduction of the national minimum wage, as well as small business owners' need for external finance and the scale of financial discouragement within the sector. A further two papers provided contemporary descriptions of the experience of entrepreneurship, including the prevalence of multiple income sources and the growing use of the home as a business location. Collectively these papers helped reveal the real world of the small business owner and illustrate the lived experience of business ownership.

The view that excessive employment regulation constrains small business growth has been a persistent theme within business and policy communities, and a particular focus for many small business lobby organisations. A radically different view of the effects of employment regulation was presented by Edwards, Ram and Black (2004) who drew on case study data collected from eighteen small firms to propose four reasons why employment legislation did "not damage" small firms. The FSB survey ($n = 16,779$) was an ideal vehicle to assess the robustness of their propositions. Our results provided empirical support for three of their four propositions (Carter, Mason & Tagg, 2009). First, we found that perceived dissatisfaction masks actual effects – small firms may grumble, but in reality very few had been affected by the new legislation; indeed a number of small firms actively welcomed the new legislation. Second, as Edwards et al. (2004) had proposed, regulatory effects are mediated by competitive conditions; although our results went further – we demonstrated that even resource-constrained firms reported few negative effects. Third, we confirmed that regulatory impact on small firms is eased by informality and typically close working relationships between managers and employees within small firms. Where our findings dramatically deviated from Edwards et al. (2004) was in their proposition that older laws, such as maternity provision, are 'routinized' and therefore do not affect small firms. In contrast, our large-scale survey found that length of time as a business owner was more influential than the age of the legislation. Owners who had been in business for many years had experienced a longer 'window of exposure', and length of time in business increased their likelihood of experiencing both negative and positive effects. A second paper exploring the impact of the recently introduced national minimum wage similarly found that affected businesses were able to absorb the costs, although in some cases at the expense of a slight decline in profitability (Mason, Carter & Tagg, 2006). Whereas the small business sector had been traditionally portrayed as politically conservative and resistant to change, these surveys helped reveal the vibrancy of the sector, a general willingness to implement change and more diverse and nuanced political views that both understood and often embraced the idea of small firms as socially responsible employers.

The FSB surveys also allowed us to explore the nature and extent of credit constraints in small firms. Supplementing our data set ($n = 15,750$) with one from the United States ($n = 3239$), we showed that small and medium enterprise (SME) financial behaviour exhibits substantial financial contentment (Vos, Jia-Yuh Yeh, Carter & Tagg, 2007). In contrast to the prevailing wisdom that characterised small firms as credit constrained, we found that only 1.32% of firms reported a shortage of capital other than working capital as a problem. Financial performance indicators, such as growth, return on assets and profit margin, were not found to be determinants of SME financing activities, as might be expected in a 'rational' risk–return environment. The studies found that younger and less educated SME owners more actively used external financing, whereas older and more educated ('wiser') SME owners were less likely to seek or use external financing. High-growth firms also exhibited contentment, in that they participate more in the loan markets than do low-growth firms. A later paper explored a different facet of credit constraints, focusing on discouraged borrowers – firms that fail to apply for external finance because of fear of rejection (Freel et al., 2012). We found twice as many businesses were discouraged from applying for a bank loan than had their loan request denied and observed a number of distinguishing characteristics among discouraged borrowers, including firm strategy, sector, prior entrepreneurial experience and banking relationships.

A further two papers from the FSB surveys provided insights into the economic and spatial conditions among small business owners. An analysis of multiple income sources among small business owners demonstrated that the economic activities of entrepreneurs are not confined to the ownership of a single firm, but encompass income generation from a variety of sources, including wage labour and nonearned income – including social transfers and share dividends – as well as profits from secondary business ventures and property rental (Carter, Tagg & Dimitratos, 2004). Modelling multiple income sources using latent class analysis revealed seven different groups of entrepreneurs differentiated by their degree of engagement in enterprise ownership and income generation ($n = 18,561$). We demonstrated the importance of multiple income sources in smaller firms and challenged prevailing assumptions that portfolio activities are expedited solely as a profit maximization strategy by growth-seeking entrepreneurs. Some used portfolio activities for wealth accumulation, but for others they are a survival mechanism. Similarly, whereas some new business owners retain employment only until the business becomes fully fledged and capable of replacing earnings, others retain their employment alongside running a business as a long-term strategy. A later paper explored the extent and characteristics of home-based businesses, a growing but largely invisible proportion of the small business sector (Mason, Carter & Tagg, 2011). Again challenging prevailing assumptions that their economic significance is minor, we found the majority of home-based business to be full-time businesses, with one in ten achieving significant scale.

Although the FSB surveys provided a vehicle for large-scale survey data, case study data provide more detailed and richer insights into the lived experiences of entrepreneurs. Working with my Norwegian colleagues, Elisabet Ljunggren and Gry Alsos, we went back into the field to collect detailed information from four (farm) case companies located in some of the most remote and rural regions of Norway and Scotland. In contrast to previous studies that focused on the individual or the firm, we explored the role of the entrepreneurial household in the process of business creation, development and growth (Alsos, Carter & Ljunggren, 2014). Whereas entrepreneurship studies typically view entrepreneurial growth as an outcome of personal ambition and business strategy, we revealed the importance of the entrepreneurial household and the household strategy in determining business growth activities. This was evidenced through the tightly interwoven connections between the business and the household, the use of family and kinship relations as a business resource base and the ways in which entrepreneurial households mitigate risk and uncertainty through self-imposed growth controls.

Women entrepreneurs: still not accessing finance

Early in 2002, one of the major UK banks approached me to explore the reasons why so few funding propositions came from women. Promised access to bank personnel for data collection, Eleanor Shaw and I secured Economic and Social Research Council funding to explore in more depth the reason why women use less finance than men when starting a business. This study, which took place over the next two years, built on prior work showing that women typically start businesses with lower levels of overall capitalisation, lower ratios of debt finance, rely more on personal savings and informal finance sources and make virtually no use of venture capital or angel investment. Gender differences in finance usage were most commonly explained as resulting from structural dissimilarities between male- and female-owned businesses. But this explanation was not entirely satisfactory; several studies reported residual gender differences even after structural factors had been controlled. Researchers had started to consider whether differences in patterns of finance usage could be explained by supply-side practices which inadvertently disadvantage women business owners. Others suggested that demand-side risk aversion constrained women from applying for funding. We sought to bring some clarity by examining both demand-side and supply-side perspectives, focusing on both the sex of the loan applicant and the sex of the bank loan officer as key elements of the gender, entrepreneurship and bank lending nexus. Using experimental and qualitative methodologies, we collected data from thirty-five bank loan officers (nineteen female, sixteen male) employed by the bank. We replicated the experimental protocol originally used by Fay and Williams (1993) to investigate whether the loan assessment criteria used by male and female bank loan officers differed either by the sex of the bank loan officer or the sex of the loan applicant. Repertory grids were then used to draw out personal constructs, and single-sex focus groups with bank loan officers allowed us to compare the loan application processes used by male and female bank loan officers presented with applications from male and female entrepreneurs.

We found no evidence of systematic bank discrimination; but a focus on the 'character' of loan applicants, which is integral to the lending process, allows subtle, engrained and unconscious gender differences in lending decisions (Carter et al., 2007). Female bank loan officers were as likely as male bank loan officers to draw gender distinctions between business owners (Wilson et al., 2007). We concluded that supply-side and demand-side factors interact to co-produce the lending decision. The aspirations and expectations of women business owners and the perceptions held by bank loan officers of women business owners and 'female-type' businesses both affect the loan decision. Quite unexpectedly, gender differences emerged between male and female bank loan officers. Female bank loan officers had less effective personal networks for introducing new business loan applications and connections that were not as strong with bank credit controllers who sanctioned deals – they followed bank rules but failed to bring in deals. We recommended changes in the training of bank loan officers, but also showed the need to ensure women business owners have sufficient capital to start and sustain their business.

This study attracted substantial attention from policy makers and banks, and we worked with the UK national and devolved governments and internationally with the EU, helping to hone

the economic case to support women entrepreneurs. The importance of women business owners in economic development and growth has been widely accepted in policy circles, as has the
need to develop innovative solutions to improve their relative access to finance. Eleanor and I
were invited to write the evidence base for the UK government's Women's Enterprise Taskforce
(2007–2009), and I was invited to join the taskforce. The need for a specific focus on women's
enterprise, particularly finance arrangements, was seen within the UK Enterprise Strategy (2008)
and Women's Enterprise Taskforce Report (2009). In Scotland, I chaired a series of workshops
for the Scottish government, which culminated in the publication of the Scottish government's
Women's Enterprise Draft Framework and Action Plan (2013), the first government strategy of
its type, and later joined the Council of Economic Advisers to the first minister, Nicola Stur-
geon. Among banks and finance providers this work led to a greater awareness of women's access
to business finance. The role of government in correcting this 'market failure' was seen in the
creation of a government-backed £12 million co-investment fund for women, introduced to
help support high-growth, women-owned ventures following the Women's Enterprise Taskforce
Final Report.

Economic well-being in the entrepreneurial household

One of the questions that entrepreneurship scholars have failed to address is an understanding
of what an individual can expect in the form of financial rewards when starting a business. In
a similar vein, and similarly unknown to entrepreneurship scholars, how does an entrepreneur
manage to pay a mortgage without a regular monthly income? If the answer to the first question
is 'very little' and the answer to the second question is 'their spouse pays', then it seems to me
that the entire subject domain of entrepreneurship has been built on sand. Rather than valoris-
ing the heroic entrepreneur (mostly men), we should start paying a bit more attention to the
spouse who pays the bills and, in doing so, subsidises their partner's entrepreneurial activities.
Is it coincidental that the growing number of entrepreneurs (mostly men) seen in practically
all developed economies over the past few decades has occurred at the same time as women's
growing and sustained participation in employment? If so, it has been fantastically convenient for
large numbers of households that combine business ownership and waged work. Entrepreneurship scholars do not know the answer to these questions because firm-level and individual-level
analyses fail to see the entrepreneur as contextualised within a (family) household and strategic
business decisions as arising from household priorities and preferences. Neither, in my view, are
entrepreneurship scholars sufficiently interested in the effects of business ownership on the lives
of entrepreneurs and their families.

Labour economists have tried to address the question of how much entrepreneurs earn with
some sophisticated studies of self-employed incomes. These show low median earnings and highlight the financial irrationality of entrepreneurship compensated by nonpecuniary factors, such as
autonomy and satisfaction. For entrepreneurship scholars to accept these results unquestioningly
is to admit that the entire subject domain is simply a collection of studies of people fiddling about,
earning nothing, but being very happy (Scott Shane, are you reading this?). More importantly,
these results don't explain at a fundamental level how entrepreneurial households manage to
survive and, often, prosper given their uncertain and irregular financial rewards.

Increasingly curious about these questions, it seemed to me that we could only start to address
these issues if we move away from using narrow measures (such as incomes) and instead focus on
a broad set of indicators that collectively contribute to overall economic well-being. Entrepreneurial rewards are multifaceted and include different types and amounts of rewards at different
stages of the business life cycle. These are determined not just by business rationality, but are

influenced by household needs that evolve over time. In Carter (2011), I argued that the analysis of entrepreneurial rewards requires an approach that captures the processes of reward decision making over the business life cycle while contextualising reward decisions within the entrepreneurial household.

Over the past couple of years, as part of the UK Enterprise Research Centre, I have had the opportunity to examine entrepreneurial rewards through a different lens. Rather than focus on incomes derived from business ownership, a highly problematic measure that is prone to under-reporting and mismeasurement, we have focused on household wealth, looking at the stock of economic resources in the form of accumulated personal assets. Mining the UK Wealth & Assets Survey, a large-scale panel survey of approximately 20,000 households, we found that entrepreneurial households own twice the wealth of employee households and that the household wealth of business owners with employees is greater than the household wealth of the self-employed with no employees (Mwaura & Carter, 2015). Although this work is at an early stage, the idea that entrepreneurs may be 'income poor but asset rich' makes more sense than the prevailing view that entrepreneurs are 'income poor but very happy'. Working with Samuel Mwaura and my PhD student, Aniela Kuhl, we are undertaking detailed case studies of thirty diverse households to explore how they manage to construct and sustain a sense of economic well-being over the long term. In doing so, we are also able to explore the effects of business ownership on the lives of the immediate family living within the household. These are the questions that I believe require research attention, and it is my intention to spend the next few years focusing solely on understanding these issues.

Looking backward and forward: advice to young scholars

In the years since I started my career, academic research has become increasingly professionalised and credentialised. It is no longer possible to start an academic career in the same haphazard and unqualified way that I did. Clearly, this is progress. But it's also a disadvantage, as I now see that the years spent in the field before my PhD gave me a deeper level of understanding than is generally possible today. My advice to young scholars is to invest time in the field and get to know and understand the real lives of small business owners. You will see practices that are not written about in academic papers, which may prompt you to develop new lines of enquiry, and this experience will provide a 'pole star' that will keep you grounded in real lives and sustain you over a career. Similarly, the growing pressures on young academics to produce papers in very high-quality journals has not been helpful to academic endeavour. Social science requires that you are a human being, not a robot. Developing a sense of intellectual independence and bringing in your own research contracts can help protect you from the worst excesses of university managers.

Academic careers are built over the long term. Overnight success is for popstars and celebrities; academics play the long game. I am constantly amazed at the age of some of our top researchers, despite their youthful good looks (it's true – working in universities keeps you young). Glory and success that comes to a sixty-year-old is based on a career and expertise built over forty years. Although it is great to be a specialist, doing the same thing for forty years is boring and hard to sustain. Be prepared to develop over the course of a career two or three areas of expertise that you can work on at different times. I started by studying women entrepreneurs and lost interest after a few years, but have periodically – usually when someone gives me large grants – revisited gender-related themes. It's a strategy that works well over the course of a career, as one theme becomes popular and in demand as another theme dips in popularity, and helps maintain your own interest levels.

For women, I offer special advice: avoid the trap of studying subjects – specifically gender – that will make it easy for colleagues and tenure committees to dismiss your work. As a younger woman, I knew that there was nothing my male colleagues liked more than seeing me doing gender-based studies – they knew it kept me out of competition. Unless you intend becoming a gender specialist working within a gender studies department, it is my belief that studying gender is a fast way into a dead-end career. If you choose to ignore this advice (as I myself have done), at least be prepared to develop a few more strings to your bow so that your expertise cannot be so easily dismissed. In other words, be smart about the choices you make. As a woman, you may also worry that you cannot have children and make career progress. Of course you can. Check out the careers of other successful academics. The philosopher Baroness Mary Warnock has five children – now in her eighties, she's still working in the House of Lords. Play the long game.

Increasingly I see that entrepreneurship academics are encouraged to provide policy implications and advice and to work closely with policy makers. The United Kingdom's Research Excellence Framework (REF), the quinquennial review of academic research in British universities, has introduced policy and practitioner impact as a new measure of research quality. This has led many university administrators to encourage young academics to actively seek policy impact. On several occasions in recent years at conferences and academic symposia, young academics have asked me how to go about influencing policy makers. If this is a route that you find interesting or attractive, I would advocate caution. I have worked on many policy-relevant projects, have given policy advice on numerous occasions and continue to work with policy makers at quite senior levels. In my view, chasing policy impact is a fool's errand. Policy impact (whatever this is) is arbitrary and unpredictable, and the ability to influence policy makers is as likely to occur standing at a bar at the right time as it is from spending years in academic specialisation. My advice is to focus on relevant and high-quality research. If they are interested, they will find you; there is no need to court them.

Finally, a word about methodology. As this chapter shows, I have spent time both on small-scale case studies and on developing and mining large-scale survey data. I started my career with the idea of a researcher as a craftsperson and methodologies as tools of our trade. To be a master craftsperson requires that we understand which tool is appropriate for the job in hand. Increasingly, researchers have become methodological specialists, and I see this generally as an important development. However, there is nothing morally superior about particular methodological approaches; the only judgement to be made is in the quality of the work. The methodological development that I am most excited about is the growth of evidence-based research, especially where researchers have been able to undertake meta-analyses that provide accurate insights into causal mechanisms. The work of Nina Rosenbusch and her colleagues has been particularly exciting. Evidence-based research, built on systematic review and 'gold standard' research trials, is a particular challenge for social science, but where it is possible to undertake evidence-based work there is potential for fundamental advances in the study of entrepreneurship.

References

Alsos, G., and Carter, S. (2006) Multiple Business Ownership in the Norwegian Farm Sector: Resource Transfer and Performance Consequences. Journal of Rural Studies. Vol.22, No.2, pp. 313–322.

Alsos, G., Carter, S. and Ljunggren, E. (2014) Kinship and Business: How Entrepreneurial Households Facilitate Business Growth. Entrepreneurship & Regional Development. Vol.26, No.1–2, pp. 97–122.

Alsos, G., Carter, S., Ljunggren, E. and Welter, F. (eds.) (2011) The Handbook of Research on Entrepreneurship in Agriculture and Rural Development (Cheltenham: Edward Elgar Publishing, ISBN 9781848446250, 320 pages).

Carter, S. (1996) The Indigenous Rural Enterprise: Characteristics and Change in the British Farm Sector. Entrepreneurship and Regional Development. Vol.8, No.4, pp. 345–358.

Carter, S. (1998) Portfolio Entrepreneurship in the Farm Sector: Indigenous Growth in Rural Areas? Entrepreneurship and Regional Development. Vol.10, No.1, pp. 17–32.

Carter, S. (1999) Multiple Business Ownership in the Farm Sector: Enterprise and Employment Contributions of Farmers in Cambridgeshire. Journal of Rural Studies. Vol.15, pp. 417–429.

Carter, S. (2011) The Rewards of Entrepreneurship: Exploring Entrepreneurial Incomes, Wealth and Economic Well-being. Entrepreneurship Theory and Practice. Vol.35, No.1, pp. 39–55.

Carter, S. and Cannon, T. (1992) Women as Entrepreneurs. London: Academic Press,

Carter, S., Mason, C. and Tagg, S. (2009) Perceptions and Experience of Employment Regulation in UK Small Firms. Environment and Planning C: Government and Policy. Vol.27, pp. 263–278.

Carter, S. and Ram, M. (2003) Reassessing Portfolio Entrepreneurship: Towards a Multi-disciplinary Approach. Small Business Economics. Vol.21, No.4, pp. 371–380.

Carter, S. and Rosa, P. (1998) Indigenous Rural Firms: Farm Enterprises in the UK. International Small Business Journal. Vol.16, No.4, pp. 15–27.

Carter, S., Shaw, E., Wilson, F. and Lam, W. (2007) Gender, Entrepreneurship and Bank Lending: The Criteria and Processes Used By Bank Loan Officers in Assessing Applications. Entrepreneurship Theory and Practice. Vol.31, No.3, pp. 427–444.

Carter, S., Tagg, S. and Dimitratos, P. (2004) Beyond Portfolio Entrepreneurship: Multiple Income Sources in Small Firms. Entrepreneurship and Regional Development. Vol.16, No.6, pp. 481–500.

Curran, J. and Storey, D. (eds) (1993) Small Firm in Urban and Rural Locations (London: Routledge).

Edwards, P., Ram, M. and Black, J. (2004). Why Does Employment Legislation Not Damage Small Firms? Journal of Law and Society. Vol.31, No.2, pp. 245–265.

Fay, M. and Williams, L. (1993). Gender Bias and the Availability of Business Loans, Journal of Business Venturing. Vol.8, No.4, pp. 363–376.

Freel, M., Carter, S., Mason, C. and Tagg, S. (2012) The Latent Demand for Bank Debt: Characterizing 'Discouraged Borrowers'. Small Business Economics. Vol.38, No.4, pp. 399–418.

Keeble, D., Tyler, P., Broom, G. and Lewis, J. (1992) Business Success in the Countryside (London: HMSO).

Mason, C., Carter, S. and Tagg, S. (2006) The Effect of the National Minimum Wage on the UK Small Business Sector: A Geographical Analysis. Environment and Planning C: Government and Policy. Vol.24, pp. 99–116.

Mason, C., Carter, S. and Tagg, S. (2011) Invisible Businesses: The Characteristics of Home-Based Businesses in the United Kingdom. Regional Studies. Vol.45, No.5, pp. 625–639.

Mwaura, S. and Carter, S. (2015) Does Entrepreneurship Make You Wealthy? Insights from the UK Wealth and Assets Survey. Enterprise Research Centre Research Paper No. 25 www.enterpriseresearch.ac.uk/wp-content/uploads/2015/03/Does-Entrepreneurship-Make-You-Wealthy.pdf

Rosa, P., Hamilton, D. and Carter, S. (1996) Gender and Small Business Performance. Small Business Economics. Vol.8, No.6, pp. 463–478.

Rosa, P. and Scott, M. G. (1995), Some Comments on the Unit of Analysis in Entrepreneurship Research on Growth and Start-up. Recent Research in Entrepreneurship (RENT IX), Piacenza, Italy.

Vos, E., Jia-Yuh Yeh, A., Carter, S. and Tagg, S. (2007) The Happy Story of Small Business Financing. Journal of Banking and Finance. Vol.31, No.9, pp. 2648–2672.

Wilson, F., Carter, S., Tagg, S., Shaw, E. and Lam, W. (2007) Bank Loan Officers' Perceptions of Business Owners: The Role of Gender. British Journal of Management. Vol.18, No.2, pp. 154–171.

6

Back to the roots

Marc Cowling

Academic provenance

I deliberately used the word provenance because it is a word that captures a more deeply rooted impact of my personal family history than potential alternatives. When I say 'family' I actually mean my father, Professor Keith Cowling, an industrial economist of some considerable note. My childhood years were often spent in the company of very famous economists at home and abroad in Berlin, St. Louis, and Philadelphia, to name but a few. I am without doubt the only living person who (with some help from my sister) broke Oliver E. Williamson's basketball net and his kitchen window in a matter of days and witnessed Richard (Dick) Easterlin catch a baseball in the stands at a National League game. He received a signed certificate and an invite to meet the players. I also had the honour of sitting next to James Mirrlees at a reception on a boat in Japan to celebrate his Nobel Prize for Economics after he spotted me walking up the gangplank and recognised my family name. This was most upsetting for his Japanese hosts. Not only a brilliant economist, but a lovely man too.

So what did this early exposure to the world of economics and great scholars mean for me? First, it gave me a huge appetite for history and a desire to understand the way the world is as we see it now and how and why it ended up like this. Economic history in particular has so much to tell us about how cities, regions, and countries develop (or not). More importantly, it teaches us how difficult it is to change the fundamentals. And this is particularly relevant to those who think creating an entrepreneurial culture is an easy task. People, cultures, and institutions change slowly, even when there is a desire for change.

To return to my academic provenance, despite this early informal immersion in economics, I initially chose to pursue a different path at college and spent five years studying construction. Aside from a great understanding of how buildings are designed and the properties of a multitude of building materials, it was during these studies that I began to appreciate the fundamentals of economics and business management, as well as significantly upgrading my mathematical capability through some tough courses on structural mechanics. The construction industry is hugely interesting, in part due to its general volatility, but also due to the composition of its labour force (large firms, small firms, self-employed, and unique configurations of all of them) and the fast pace at which technology changes. It is also an industry which is irrevocably linked to capital markets and macroeconomic elements; the latter are both features which remain at the forefront of my research to this day.

I made the transition to economics on my UG degree, a BA Honours in Industrial Economics. This gave me a thorough grounding in the nature and power of markets and the relevance of imperfect competition in shaping the behaviour of firms and, in particular, in restricting the actions of smaller firms. It also firmly established in my mind the nature of real-world trade-offs that firms and people face and how imperfect information meant that many decisions are made without the full set of information that one would like in order to make the best, and most informed, decisions. I was also, am still am, quite taken by the notion of satisficing rather than maximisation. Courses in labour economics also left me with a good understanding of how labour markets operate and how individuals make choices about, or are forced to as a second-best option, whether to participate in the labour market at all, and if so, as a waged or salaried employee or in a self-employed capacity. And, of course, I became very familiar with the relevance of formal and informal human capital in wage and income determination and, more importantly, the relative returns to different types of human capital in alternative labour market states.

My master's (MSc) in Economics was in many ways a more traditional run through the history of many of the greatest political economy theories, including Ricardo, Keynes, Smith, Mill, Hicks, etc., up to one of my particular favourites, William J. Baumol. My master's degree thesis was a very standard piece of macroeconomic research on US dollar to Japanese yen exchange rate determination. The results were very uninspiring, but it tested and expanded my econometrics skill set significantly and shaped what I was able to achieve with quantitative data going forward. Notable faculty members at that time included Professor David Miles, who became a member of the Bank of England's Monetary Policy Committee and a financial economics scholar of great repute.

Building a research career

So armed with a good background in economics and a fairly strong econometric tool kit, I was able to secure my first academic post as a lowly temporary research assistant at Warwick Business School in the United Kingdom. The specific project was to estimate the potential impacts of the UK recession of 1990 on the earned income of the university. The project manager was Professor David Storey, a man who inspired and shaped my career and thinking from that day onwards. Aside from developing a great understanding of how large universities are financed and the diversity of their income streams, the project taught me a great deal about the value of using multiple methods to triangulate research and gather information and data from different sources and constituencies. From telephone interviews with directors of arts centres, to analysing the different assumptions of the core UK macroeconomic forecasting models, to evaluating trends in the corporate conference market, and finally to assessing future UK government expenditure on core (academic) research funding, this project was vast in its scope and, of course, importance to the future well-being of the university.

My next step was away from Warwick to the Research Centre for Industrial Strategy at the University of Birmingham. This was my first permanent research post, and one which set me off down the small business path. In this sense, I gained first-hand knowledge of how unique, exogenous factors and events can have a long-lasting influence on future outcomes. I would have accepted this job regardless of the specific duties or the precise research topic under investigation, within the broad parameters of something with an economics aspect to it. I actually think I was very lucky in the sense that the United Kingdom was struggling with a deep economic recession at that time (lucky for me, not the UK population at large) and banks were tightening their credit terms and lending conditions to small businesses particularly severely. And the small business associations and representative bodies wanted to build an evidence base to lobby for government intervention in the market for small business finance.

The specific project was to design a small and medium enterprise (SME) finance survey and collect evidence on the nature of SME–bank relationships and the specifics of credit demand and supply. The desired output was a full report with a detailed evidence base backed up by robust empirical analysis. My learning outcomes from this specific project were significant. First, I learnt how to do a literature review and distinguish between different types and 'qualities' of published outputs. Second, I began to develop a good understanding of the seminal theories on credit rationing, including Stiglitz and Weiss (1981), but also other competing theories which make different assumptions about the nature of information – the body of work by David De Meza, (De Meza and Webb, 1997, 2001), exogenous shocks, and the role of collateral (the works of Helmut Bester (1985), Arnoud Boot (1977), and Arnie Thakor (1996) featured prominently.

On a more practical level, I learned how to design a survey instrument and how to draw a sample from the (biased and unrepresentative) population of Association of British Chambers of Commerce member list. I also learned how to use address and mailing software, stuff envelopes, and lick stamps. But the coding of returned surveys was my least favourite bit. In those days we used graph paper and hand-coded each survey return onto the graph paper, question response by question response. We then hand-typed each question response (with unique ID code) into an SPSS data sheet. Then the fun began. I had my first primary data set and a client desperate for a report.

Again I was lucky that I had one-to-one mentoring from a wonderful medical statistician, Dr Paul Hackett, who gave me helpful guidance into the importance of looking at response distributions and reshaping and recategorising data prior to even attempting more sophisticated analysis. Understanding the basics of the data and cleaning them up are fundamental to good-quality empirical research. This is still an issue that young and early career researchers struggle to comprehend. We make it too easy for students with beautifully crafted and cleaned secondary data sets that they can just launch into a battery of high-order econometric regression models with. And I even had a conversation recently with my university post-graduate director who had designed a master's of research programme which had no lessons on collecting primary data or cleaning up messy data. I still believe it to be true that if you look at distributions and general patterns in the data then you develop a deeper understanding of what types of questions your data can answer and what they are capable of doing. For contract researchers in particular, this is of critical importance.

Anyway, the report was well received and garnered a lot of public attention. More importantly for me personally, it raised my profile in academic and government circles. Arguably, it was the major contributory factor to being offered a research fellowship by Professor David Storey back at Warwick University in the SME Centre. I also published several academic journal papers from the data set. What did we find? Perhaps the major finding was that the general SME–bank relationship was characterised by mutual distrust and that this contributed to more severe information-based problems than were required for an efficient market outcome. It also found that access to finance, particularly longer-term capital, was more of an issue than the actual cost of finance. These two findings have always intrigued me, the former in particular because I have always held the general view that I would rather lend my cash-poor friend a £100 and ask him to pay me back at £10 per week over 10 weeks (affordability), than ask him to give me the whole £100 back next week (no chance). Something strange with the way banks discount revenues earned in the future.

I also hold the general view that SME credit is, on average, too cheap when adjusted for risk. Margins over base are largely within a 1.5% to 4.5% range. This suggests that banks operate on a pooling basis rather than a separating equilibrium. What this means in practical terms is that the best small businesses pay more than they should for credit and the worst small businesses pay less. On a broader level, it taught me how ill informed the public debate is on topical issues of the day. So many vested interests pursuing personal agendas whose arguments and articulations have no basis in evidence, only a large dose of anecdote. I am writing my Brighton Inaugural Professorial Lecture at the moment and have given it the title "Entrepreneurial Myths and Legends" to reflect this. Rather disappointingly, many of the mistruths and legends are perpetuated by academics who also have other agendas. For example, fewer than one in five venture capital (VC) funds make an above-market return (and many lose cash in absolute terms for the investor), but the largest element of the academic debate perpetuates the myth that VCs are 'special' people and we need to encourage more of them. Perhaps fewer of them might be a better option!

The halcyon days

Moving to the SME Centre at Warwick was a career-defining moment for me and the start of a personal golden age. David Storey was the director, and we had arguably the best entrepreneurship scholar who has not won the Global Award for Entrepreneurship to date, Paul Westhead. We also had Robert Cressy, who did some important work which unravelled several of the mysteries of the real-world small business performance effects of financial and human capital and the dependency of one on the other. More widely, the business school was packed full of great scholars across the board and led by a dynamic, but very human, dean.

What was apparent at that time was that I was surrounded by very talented people and that created a positive dynamic, albeit a very competitive one. There was a thirst for new knowledge and a desire to challenge prevailing orthodoxy. At that time entrepreneurship in academia had largely been a teaching subject and research was in its infancy. The subject, being naturally multidisciplinary, did not sit well with the typical business school disciplinary silos (accountancy, finance, HR, strategic management, operations research, marketing, etc.), and many academics were still arguing about definitions. What is a small business? What is an entrepreneur? What gave the SME Centre its core strength was the fact that virtually all the research we did, individually and collectively, had a direct and explicit policy focus. David Storey was quite clear that our key role was to shape government thinking and debates by developing a strong evidence base to inform their decision making. This would contribute to a stronger entrepreneurial business sector and more efficient utilisation of government resources. In this sense we followed the European tradition at this time which was underpinned by a strong economic base and a more questioning approach to entrepreneurship. I have to include Zoltan Acs and David Audretsch here, both of whom have European heritage, as honorary Europeans. Fundamentally, Europeans were more sceptical about whether all entrepreneurship per se is a good thing (Burke, Fitzroy, and Nolan, 2000; Cowling, Taylor, and Mitchell, 2004). Equally, we are more questioning about whether all government interventions to promote and support entrepreneurship are justified, particularly with respect to venture capital and business start-up programmes. This is probably still true today, although the recent predominance of psychologists in the field has shifted the general focus of entrepreneurship towards the 'special people' tradition to the detriment of the discipline in my opinion. How many of us 'older' scholars raise an eyebrow when we see multiple interaction terms as they desperately search for a significant psychological effect?

I was also very fortunate to develop some strong personal, mentoring, and working relationships with many academics in the world-class Economics Department at Warwick. Pete

Mitchell, a member of the Macroeconomic Modelling Bureau, became one of my long-standing co-researchers, but also the person who taught me state-of-the-art econometrics at a very high level. I became proficient in programming LIMDEP, SAS, SPSS (mainframe), and more generally in Microfit, E-Views, and Stata. Pete was that good, he even found an error in the LIMDEP manual and corrected it. Anyone who estimates the Inverse Mills Ratio today has him to thank. Although I was living in a co-integration heaven at this moment and learning new, increasingly complex, estimators on a weekly basis, perhaps the most important lessons I learned were that (1) there is always another test that can be done, but there are strongly diminishing marginal returns to doing them; and (2) if you clean your data properly and understand the underlying distributions and relationships, then a very basic, well-specified regression will arrive at roughly the same results as the most sophisticated and complex modelling technique. Unfortunately, I learned this lesson the hard way. On the former, Pete was not aware that I had already published one of our papers in a nice journal while he was still conducting more econometric tests on our data a year later. But it is also true that a thorough knowledge of the core econometric and statistical techniques is so important to the successful investigation of quantitative data. I know of a paper that got past a famous editor of a top-ranking management journal that has a selection model estimated the wrong way round.

My biggest breakthrough in terms of profile and credibility arose in strange circumstances to say the least. The UK Labour Party, under its newly elected leader, Tony Blair, were performing well in the polls a year before the 1997 national election and were seeking to end a twenty-year losing streak to the right of centre Conservative Party. But they had not really kept pace with the changing nature of the electorate in the sense that there has been a virtually unchecked rise in self-employment and small business activity since 1972. And these entrepreneurs had specific demands. In their totality they represented around 10% of the voting public. So it's 1996, twelve months out from the election, and the Labour Party has no small business policy. This isn't too strange to the initiated because its roots come from defending workers against the capitalist owners of the means of production.

The Institute for Public Policy Research, a centre left–leaning think tank, was tasked with this monumental job: effectively to write a complete small business policy from scratch in twelve months. This is where I stepped in to help out. In reality it was myself and another Mancunian (born in Manchester, England), Andrea Westall, who wrote the lion's share of the policy document that ultimately became published in book form as *The Entrepreneurial Society* (Gavron, Cowling, and Westall, 1998). The rest of the project team was composed of Gerry Holtham, chief economist, who took an oversight role; an editor on loan from Lord (Bob) Gavron's publishing empire; and the late Bob Gavron (the owner of St. Ives Press and The Folio Society) himself. Anyway, we managed to write a book with detailed policy recommendations across all spheres of small business activity in twelve months flat. As luck would have it, the Labour Party with Tony Blair at its head won the election. I say luck because we were invited to a seminar at 10 Downing Street, the prime minister's house, to present and discuss our findings. But more importantly, one of our key recommendations was enacted. Within three years the United Kingdom had its first dedicated Small Business Service (comparable to the US Small Business Administration). The SBS aimed at being a single organisation within government dedicated to helping small firms and representing their interests. Its broader aim was to help create an entrepreneurial society. For me personally, it put me right in the middle of the upper echelons of UK government and policy formulation. From that day on I had regular briefings with ministers and top civil servants. I saw my role as not only providing policy ideas to address barriers to entrepreneurship and the growth of entrepreneurial businesses, but of providing a robust evidence base to feed into policy deliberations. In short I have always favoured evidence-based policy making over policy-based evidence making.

In parallel with this exciting interlude into the world of policy making, I was also completing my PhD under the excellent supervision of Professor Martin Conyon. The irony was that Martin's PhD supervisor was none other than my dad. Martin was ahead of the game in terms of his knowledge of STATA and micro-econometric techniques, and I am eternally grateful to him for sharing some of this with me throughout the course of my thesis, as well as a much wider knowledge of the industrial organisation literature. The title of my thesis was "The Entrepreneur and the Smaller Firm" and was stimulated by earlier work carried out under the research leadership of Professor Paul Westhead into the importance of family business. A second irony is that one of my core thesis chapters, estimating an entrepreneurial production function, was the same as one of my dad's, as he had a chapter in his thesis using similar production function models, but for farm efficiency. I recollect that the fixed effect of the founding entrepreneur was £250,000 (around £425,000 in today's terms) indicating that once the original founder had exited, the typical small business struggled to replace him or her. Special thanks also go to Professors Gavin Reid and Mark Casson, both of whom read my thesis and provided valuable comments and direction. Both are extremely clever and deep thinkers about entrepreneurship.

Breaking the apron strings

So after an eventful, exciting, and highly productive (by the standards of those days) time at the SME Centre I decided I needed to move on to a new challenge. That took the form of the director of the Research Centre for Industrial Strategy at the University of Birmingham. I had my very own research team, staffed by clever, young, and keen people, but also the responsibility of generating enough research income to pay their wages. I was lucky in that David Storey had taught me the tricks of the funding game, and I managed to generate the required funding each year. This period was one where I became heavily involved in evaluating government interventions in the small business arena. Again I was drawn back to the European question. Is all entrepreneurship good? Is all policy directed at entrepreneurs good? The answers to both are clearly no, but it is also clear that with robust evidence to identify genuine market failures, good corrective policies can be designed and well targeted. And this generally, although not always, leads to positive outcomes. This period also highlighted to me how few people genuinely understand what market failure is. Too many academics and policy makers confuse someone not getting something as prima facie evidence of a market failure. The market might be far from perfect, but it is not completely stupid.

This period also marked my first foray into Competition Commission enquiries, in this case a large-scale investigation into competition in SME banking. I am currently finishing the background evidence to determine whether or not we should have a new full enquiry in 2016 on broadly the same terms. This type of enquiry was, and always will be, a political hot potato. You had the big four UK banks lined up against the powerful small business lobby groups, with Her Majesty's Treasury and the Bank of England stuck in the middle. Many of the serving UK ministers and lords were also board members at big financial institutions. One thing I do love about being involved in these things is being a neutral, but relatively well-informed, island in the middle of very powerful political manoeuvring and vested interests. Truly fascinating. As an amusing aside, I recently wrote a paper on big bank loan price discrimination, testing whether or not big banks exerted their market power against small firms when pricing loans. This is textbook competition stuff that any industrial economics second-year undergraduate would understand. A noted accountancy professor, who happened to be an editor of a journal I submitted this paper to, said (very explicitly) he couldn't understand why big banks would want to charge higher prices to small businesses. I guess he won't be invited to take part in any forthcoming competition enquiries.

But the big learning outcome for me was understanding how critical it is to define what the relevant market is. Is it spatial? Is it related to the presence of substitute goods or services as viewed by the consumer? Or a multitude of other criteria? The power of large firms in imperfectly competitive markets and their effects on smaller firms has unfortunately become an increasingly ignored aspect of our subject area as the disciplinary balance has shifted dramatically in favour of psychologists and away from economists. The notion that simply having a 'growth orientation' can overcome physical barriers to market entry, innovation, and access to customers is, at best, questionable!

The middle years

I enjoyed my first taste of running a research centre and began to appreciate why David Storey took great pleasure, and still does, in seeing his people go on to build successful careers. I had a very young team of eager and talented researchers at RCIS, but that created its own inevitability. Good people get good job offers and leave if you can't match those offers. My team was decimated, and for me it was difficult to envisage rebuilding every three years or so from scratch. That prompted my decision to seek a new challenge, and that came in the form of the Global Entrepreneurship Monitor (GEM).

However, on a personal level that time had been good. I had been, and still am, publishing a lot of loan guarantee schemes, and this led to the quirky truth that at that moment in time I had published 53% of total world output on loan guarantees. This was facilitated by a series of UK government evaluations of our long-standing Small Firms Loan Guarantee Scheme and a broader willingness of our Department for Trade and Industry (now the Department for Business Innovation and Skills) to support my general research in this area with access to data and advisory support. I also began a longer-term involvement with several supranational agencies – including the World Bank, United Nations, and OECD – around this body of work as loan guarantee schemes are the most prevalent SME intervention across the developed and developing world.

My involvement with the Global Entrepreneurship Monitor was interesting, and I am still in awe of the sheer scale of the undertaking. To organise and conduct surveys in that many countries is a phenomenal achievement. I still believe its greater value is as a social attitudes survey rather than capturing definitive measures of entrepreneurial activity. London Business School is a great institution, and I enjoyed my time there. The GEM project led me to The Work Foundation as the UK side of things shifted there with Dr Rebecca Harding. This working relationship was a match made in heaven. Rebecca was a real ideas person, and I think I am correct in saying that we produced the first formal categorisation of different types of social enterprise (based on core funding streams, income generation capacity, and relationship to profit [surplus] and its distribution) and the first-ever report on this exciting new area of entrepreneurship in 2004.

The Work Foundation was a research institution that viewed its primary role as generating new policy ideas and solutions to improve the general welfare of the United Kingdom, particularly with respect to labour markets. Its focus was very much on cutting-edge thinking and tackling the most pressing problems the United Kingdom faced at any given moment in time. As senior, then chief, economist my task was to conduct research that underpinned, and gave direction and credence to, policy recommendations. Our CEO at that time was Will Hutton, a political economist of note, former editor in chief of *The Observer* newspaper, and currently principal of Hertford College, Oxford University. Will was the most networked individual I have ever met, and this meant that my research got very quickly to the heart of government.

One of the largest research projects we conducted that was published in a report, "Cracking the Performance Code: How Firms Succeed" in 2005, set out to isolate unique and complementary strategic bundles that differentiated between the highest- and lowest-performing firms. The results show that in terms of added value, the top third of firms out-perform the bottom two-thirds by £1,600 per worker per annum. This means that if just 10% of the United Kingdom's lower-performing firms moved to the performance levels of the top third of UK firms, the United Kingdom's productivity growth rate would increase by 0.25% per annum. For me the key findings were (1) that firms do too much on a strategic level (too many strategies) given that nearly 90% of strategic choices have zero impact on overall business performance and (2) most strategic choices are not complementary to one another, particularly when we go across operating units or functional departments. That is to say that given the overall goals and objectives of the firm, most of the strategies to achieve them have no effect, and most individual strategies prevent another strategy from being successful. This has a strong theoretical basis in the body of work on strategic fit and complementarities from Paul Robert Milgrom and John Roberts. What followed on from that work was a forecasting model I developed to predict underlying business performance based on their adoption of a unique bundle of strategies. When applied to the FTSE 250, my model did pretty well in picking winners, and average medium-term stock price performance (growth) was 25% compared to the all-share average of 15% over the period investigated. Returning to the issue of overstrategising, anyone who has worked in a university will have observed this in their human resource department: new strategies and codes of conduct every month, no review of what works and what doesn't, and little underpinning evidence that we needed it in the first place.

More generally, this focus on the 'best' and 'worst' raised an interesting issue for future work. What are we really interested in finding out? Do we want to know the 'on average if this happens then that will happen' (the standard econometric regression model)? Or do we want to know whether the same things have the same effects across the whole distribution of firms (the quantile regression model)? Increasingly, in my policy-related work in particular, I am favouring the latter approach. This accords with current restrictions in government finance and forces us to focus on what firms or people would benefit most from a particular policy change or intervention. And anyone who has run quantile regressions will know that, in general, the results are quite different at the low and high ends of the relevant distribution. My friend and co-author Alex Coad is at the forefront of this approach and has produced many important insights around the growth of firms using these methods.

After my move to the Institute for Employment Studies, as chief economist, I spent around four years heavily involved in government evaluations of small business programmes. And the insights gained from this body of research were quite broad and shaped my thinking about entrepreneurs and smaller firms quite a lot. What is apparent is that fairly low-cost interventions aimed at a broad base of small firms can have very large, and positive, aggregate effects on jobs and productivity. At the firm level, my PhD work showed that the average small firm is operating at around two thirds of its potential efficiency. We know there are good reasons for this because most entrepreneurs are not the mythical profit maximisers found in textbooks, but have multiple objectives and are willing to trade profit for independence, flexibility of hours, and a host of other things. So, given this starting point, it is relatively easy to effect some tangible improvement. Examples of government interventions that have generated a net positive economic benefit to the United Kingdom include the Small Firms Loan Guarantee Scheme (renamed the Enterprise Finance Guarantee in 2009) and the Business Link Health Check. The former addresses credit gaps for young firms with no track record and/or no assets to securitise a bank loan.

The loan guarantee is one of the most popular schemes worldwide and also one of the most basic. It only has four parameters: the maximum loan size, the maximum loan term, the level of guarantee, and the interest rate premium. It is easy to understand and administer, but also, even with four basic parameters, the potential to be very flexible. This, I feel, is why loan guarantee schemes work relatively well and why they are able to address a specific issue around credit rationing. One thing that always intrigued me was why commercial banks would want to get involved in a loan guarantee scheme. Schemes are typically quite marginal in terms of their scale, representing a few percentage points of total bank lending to the SME sector. I originally thought that this was simply political expediency – banks wanting to be seen to be nice to government. So in the last few months I have been estimating the banks' profit function from the government-guaranteed lending using UK micro scheme data. The results are interesting and show that banks make a modest, but positive, surplus from this form of lending. But it makes sense in terms of the overall small firm–bank relationship because lending locks in small business customers and enables banks to extract supranormal profits from nonlending-related services. Note that banks typically earn two-thirds of their profit from nonlending-related services.

The UK Business Link Health Check was initiated in response to the global financial crisis (GFC). In basic terms an experienced business advisor assessed the managerial, functional, and strategic capabilities of the small firm and made recommendations for improvement – a bit like the sort of health check that men over fifty are encouraged to undertake by the UK health authorities. Again, this was a basic form of intervention targeted at a genuine, and specific, problem. The evaluation findings showed that even very modest changes that arose from the Health Check assessment could have a beneficial impact on treated firms.

Compare these basic forms of intervention with those in the area of venture capital. Methodologically, at an evaluation level, they are problematic. What is the relevant control group of untreated firms? VC is a unique source of finance, and the data show that typically less than 1% to 2% of all firms ever get it. But this is only part of the story. Most small firms do not want VC or any external ownership or involvement in their business operations. And most small firms are not VC relevant because they don't grow very quickly, if at all. In my opinion, too much is done in this space by governments, and by scholars. It is a 'sexy' subject, but largely irrelevant. Note that informal equity and business angel activity dwarfs that of formal VC. And VC schemes do not, on average, generate a positive economic effect of any note. Nor do private VC funds, but that is another story. In fact, three-fourths of private VC funds return less capital to their investors than they put in, but take out between 10% and 35% of the total capital invested in management fees. In economic terms this does not make sense, and is simply a transfer of wealth from productive individuals to less productive individuals. It is a difficult policy area, despite the theoretical benefits that might arise. One potential explanation is that governments are too concerned about 'fairness' when designing policies in this area. It is precisely the wrong policy instrument to be widely available at a spatial level particularly, but even at a firm level. Most geographic regions do not have the infrastructure, capabilities, innovation ecosystems, or talented entrepreneurs to make VC a viable policy instrument.

My next move was back into the world of academe full-time as a professor (full professor in US terminology) at Exeter University Business School, where I headed up the Entrepreneurship Group, and quite quickly became head of the Department for Management Studies. Aside from the onerous duties of running a department of around 50 academics with a total budget of £13m per annum, I continued my international activities on several levels, first, with the European Union, World Bank, and Inter-American Development Bank on the design and effectiveness of loan guarantee schemes, and second with the Australian government through an evaluation of their Innovation Investment Fund (an equity-based financial instrument) with my old friend

Professor Gordon Murray, and for the Australian Chambers of Commerce an assessment of the potential need for a loan guarantee programme to support lending to SMEs. This is where I began to get involved in the more practical aspects of scheme design and building an evidence base that feeds into operational scheme design. At this time I developed a checklist of ten criteria that would provide prima facie evidence of credit rationing as justification for intervention in the form of a loan guarantee programme. I also designed a loan guarantee scheme template for Australia based on a rigorous analysis of the nature of the SME stock and the current state of loan provision. The nature of the terms of engagement with relevant ministries of government also changes when you are dealing with practical scheme design. Largely, if you have prepared your evidence and case well, they trust your judgements on the scheme parameters and target group of SMEs. But the big question is always what are the contingent liabilities going to be? That is an articulate way of the Treasury asking, if it all goes wrong, how much will we have at risk? Their glass is always half empty. One thing about this vertical integration into scheme design was the potential for egg on my face, not to mention the real-world prospect of losing tens of millions of taxpayers' money if I got it wrong. A genuine test of my knowledge and skill.

Finally, I arrived in my current post at Brighton University Business School as Professor of Entrepreneurship and Director of Research. Aside from continuing my normal research activities, I am also tasked with helping support my younger colleagues to get on a research pathway. This is a difficult but potentially hugely rewarding task. And it reminds me of the role David Storey played in shaping my early research career in such a helpful and supportive manner. I hope to achieve similar results in the future and will take great pleasure in the success of my young colleagues as they build their careers.

My future research

So where is my research heading now? I am going to return to my roots and, to some degree, swim against the prevailing tide in entrepreneurship, which is largely psychology based. My focus will be on empirical research with a clear and rigorous theoretical basis drawn from economics. More specifically, I want to look at how financial agents generate income and profit from their interactions with smaller firms and the extent to which economic returns are unequally distributed between the entrepreneur and the financier. I will also be looking at how imperfect competition and the market power of larger firms distort what smaller entrepreneurial firms are able to achieve. This line of research will question many of the widely held assumptions that entrepreneurs create unique products and services through their talent and innovative capabilities, and this leads to the generation of supranormal profit (the returns to entrepreneurial talent). My starting point will be that in many cases large incumbent firms will not allow this to happen, regardless of whether an entrepreneur is a 'special' person or has a growth orientation.

Suggestions for young researchers

I was lucky in that I met David Storey and throughout my fledgling career had a series of wonderful mentors. So my first suggestion is that if you get stuck with one of those 'great' people who doesn't want anyone else to achieve 'greatness' then move jobs if you can. Starting off on the right track in a supportive environment is critical. My second piece of advice is to imagine the world of entrepreneurship as a gigantic jigsaw. No one person can solve all the unknowns and get all the answers. Focus on a single piece of the jigsaw, understand the key questions, and find the relevant theories and frameworks to set your research in. My third piece of advice is when you are dealing with empirical data, spend a lot of time getting a basic understanding of the fundamentals of your data. Look at the sample descriptives, draw the distributions, look at the simple correlations. Draw a simple picture of what you think the causal chain is based on what the seminal theories predict. And only then move on to more sophisticated analytical models. And when you get a contrary result, ask why. Is it because you did something wrong? Or is it because the world has changed and relationships between your variables of interest have changed? And there is absolutely no problem, despite what the editors of management journals think, of replicating previous empirical studies. Your time, sample firms, country, or any number of other things will be different. Economics was built upon testing theory, replicating these tests, revising theories, and only then concluding that there is a strong relationship between X and Y. This is what underpins its core rigour. And when you get a negative response from a journal editor or referee, remember there are good and bad editors and referees. Again, look at what they say and consider whether any of it has traction. Then choose whether to revise your work.

References

Bester, H. (1985), Screening vs. rationing in credit markets with imperfect information, The American Economic Review, 75(4), 850–855.

Boot, A.W.A. (1977), Relationship banking: what do we know?, Journal of Financial Intermediation, 9(1), 7–25.

Burke, A., Fitzroy, F.R. and Nolan, M.A. (2000), When less is more: distinguishing between entrepreneurial choice and performance, Oxford Bulletin of Economics and Statistics, 62(5), 565–587.

Cowling, M., Taylor, M. and Mitchell, P. (2004), Job creators, Manchester School, University of Manchester, 72(5), 601–617.

De Meza, D. and Webb, D.C. (1997), Too much investment: a problem of asymmetric information, The Quarterly Journal of Economics, 102(2), 281–292.

De Meza, D. and Webb, D.C. (2001), Advantageous selection in insurance markets, The RAND Journal of Economics, 32(2), 249–262.

Gavron, R., Cowling, M., Westall, A. and Holtham, G. (1998), The Entrepreneurial Society, Institute for Public Research. Available at: www.ippr.org/publications/the-entrepreneurial-society.

Stiglitz, J.E. and Weiss, A. (1981), Credit rationing in markets with imperfect information, The American Economic Review, 71(3), 393–410.

Thakor, A.V. (1996), Capital requirements, monetary policy, and aggregate bank lending: theory and empirical evidence, The Journal of Finance, 51(1), 279–324.

7

A research journey into entrepreneurial finance

Douglas J. Cumming and Silvio Vismara

Introduction

Finance scholars have historically considered entrepreneurship as a separate field (Audretsch et al. 2016). The implicit idea was that the issues in entrepreneurial finance are different from those faced by public corporations so as to limit the applicability of traditional finance theory. On the one hand, entrepreneurial finance primarily refers to early-stage financing mechanisms, often supplied by the entrepreneur's personal network as a consequence of his or her inability to access the public market. On the other hand, corporate finance literature tends to focus on publicly traded firms as the main unit of analysis. However, the evolution of both the real economy and academic research has clarified that this is no longer the case. Financial scholars have recognized that agency problems and information asymmetries, the basis of corporate finance and financial economics theory, are actually two fundamental issues of entrepreneurial finance. Information asymmetry (and related adverse selection problems) in the entrepreneurial setting is particularly pronounced due to the difficulty faced by entrepreneurs in conveying the quality of their new ventures to firm outsiders, resulting in potentially severe agency issues (and moral hazard problems). Contractual solutions adopted to prevent these issues are imperfect, more so in entrepreneurial ventures than in large established corporations.

The ultimate goal of entrepreneurial finance is to help managers make better investment and financing decisions in entrepreneurial settings. The starting point is, essentially, that in a world in which writing, issuing, and enforcing contracts consumes resources, and in which information is asymmetric and its acquisition costly, properly functioning financial systems can reduce these information and transaction costs. Research questions are coherently centered around the role and impact of legal and market infrastructures on the nature and availability of capital to entrepreneurial firms. This recognition leads to a plethora of studies on entrepreneurial finance issues, such as initial public offerings (IPOs) and venture capitalists (VCs), which are grounded both in financial economics and in entrepreneurship.[1]

The aim of this chapter is to discuss entrepreneurial finance in the realm of modern entrepreneurship. The editors of the *Routledge Companion to Makers in Modern Entrepreneurship*, David B. Audretsch and Erik E. Lehmann, asked us to discuss our personal research and, more broadly, our academic experience in the field. Accordingly, we dedicate the next section to articulate our 'academic journey' thus far. Although our experiences reflect our personal biases, we nevertheless hope they are helpful for others in the future. Therefore, the second section is essentially biographical. Silvio Vismara is an associate professor of entrepreneurial finance at the University of Bergamo, Italy. Though fully aware of being at what could at first be considered a peripheral university in a peripheral country, he will describe how he began to perform research in Italy. Audretsch and Lehmann would indeed like their companion to mix stories from top researchers from top business schools with examples of paths away from the 'mainstream'. The mentor during Silvio's first steps into academia was Stefano Paleari, who currently serves as president of the Cisalpino Institute for Comparative Studies in Europe (CCSE). The very idea of the establishment of the CCSE was shared by Erik and Stefano.[2] Among the initiatives of the CCSE, each year, David, Erik, and Silvio organize a summer school where students from Indiana University (United States), Augsburg University (Germany), and the University of Bergamo (Italy) meet to address a policy issue from a comparative perspective (Audretsch et al. 2015a). The adjective 'comparative' refers to both cross-country and cross-disciplinary methods, as students come from not only different universities but also different schools and fields. The CCSE, by fostering comparative studies between countries, aims to contribute to improve our understanding of why and how regions differ and how we can learn from each other to shape our common future in the best way (Audretsch and Lehmann 2016). This is hopefully an example of academic engagement that substantiates cooperation on a broad level, from research to teaching, involving a multifaceted set of stakeholders.

If you are interested in research in entrepreneurial finance, you surely have heard of Jay R. Ritter. Jay, also known in the media as 'Mr. IPO', is a professor of finance at the University of Florida. As a 'maker of modern entrepreneurial finance', his research directly contributed to the development of research on IPOs and indirectly contributed through his service to the profession as reviewer and conference chair; most importantly, he is a role model for many young scholars. The last two sections of this chapter are dedicated to two forms of public entrepreneurial finance: IPOs and crowdfunding. The third section explains the evolution of IPO research, and in the fourth section, this chapter is concluded by identifying how research on crowdfunding might evolve. We describe the evolution of IPO research essentially by summarizing some of Jay's articles, and his influence in the field, through international comparisons and replication of his original results. Our perspective with regard to crowdfunding is that of a parallel between this equity crowdfunding and IPOs, as research on the former might draw models and intuitions from that on the latter.

Toward research in entrepreneurial finance

Silvio was a student in management engineering at the University of Bergamo, fascinated by the academic profession, but considering a managerial career in the private sector. Facing the decision on how to approach his final dissertation, he contacted his former business economics professor. On 15 September 2000, Silvio entered Stefano Paleari's office for the first time. Stefano, who at the time was serving as associate professor at the Politecnico di Milano, proposed that he create a research thesis on IPOs, with an internship at the Italian Stock Exchange. It was a 'hot period' for IPOs, with people queuing outside banks to subscribe to IPO shares (with Silvio queuing to get hard copies of IPO-offering prospectuses). This is how Silvio's journey in IPOs started and how Stefano and Silvio started collaborating. Later, this cooperation led to a number of coauthored papers and to the establishment of an academic spin-off in 2006, Universoft, which is still profitable after ten years, although neither Stefano nor Silvio currently have a position in the company.[3] Stefano, as a PhD supervisor, guided Silvio's research, and especially propelled him on an international path, which was not the common academic practice of the day. Silvio was supported from the onset and stimulated to join the international research arena through conferences and visiting periods, including those spent as an EU Marie Curie fellow at the Manchester Business School with Arif Khurshed, who now feels like a member of the family due to his frequent travels to the University of Bergamo.[4] Later, in his position as rector of the University of Bergamo, Stefano pushed for internationalization, making the university more attractive for foreign students and visiting professors. Silvio, thanks to this university's mission, had the opportunity to mingle with top researchers. For instance, during Stefano, Silvio, and Michele Meoli's institutional visit at the Massachusetts Institute of Technology, and thanks to Jay Ritter's 'intermediation', he began to work with Thomas Chemmanur. Similarly, the decision to candidate the University of Bergamo to host the Technology Transfer Society's 2013 annual conference was a part of such an internationalization strategy, which eventually led to stronger cooperation with Al Link, Don Siegel, and the community of the *Journal of Technology Transfer* (Audretsch et al. 2014, 2015b). This, together with the CCSE initiative with Augsburg and the annual summer school with Indiana University, has been crucial in positioning the University of Bergamo on the map of entrepreneurial finance.

Working in finance with Stefano, who is a nuclear engineer, has involved a series of 'meetings' with different approaches. The two 'meetings' that are perhaps of broader interest are that of science with engineering, and science with policy. Two kinds of financial economists exist: those who understand the field as a type of engineering, and those who would prefer it to be more of a science. Stefano's guidance is a unique mix of the two approaches, where the real-world problem-solver attitude of engineers meets the scientist's goal to understand how the world works. Inevitably, this combination is policy oriented. It is enough to Google 'Stefano Paleari' to have an idea of how successful he is policy-wise. The example that we would like to mention here, however, is different. There is another place where educational policy influences the future – the classroom. 'Like policymakers, undergraduates typically have little interest in theory for theory's sake. Instead, they are interested in understanding how the real world works and how public policy can improve economic performance' (Mankiw 2006, 43). Stefano definitely prioritizes this in his mission to 'produce' citizens informed about good policy principles. The message that we as academics derive here is about delivering a role model of participatory citizenship, which is a value critical to our future.

Thanks to Stefano, during his PhD, Silvio worked on a number of projects with the Italian Stock Exchange, coauthoring research papers with people from Borsa Italiana (e.g., Paleari, Pellizzoni, and Vismara 2008).[5] The Italian Stock Exchange organized an 'IPO day', which offered the opportunity to invite Jay as the keynote speaker. Stefano Paleari and Jay Ritter addressed entrepreneurs and investment bankers on the IPO market's evolution on 1 March 2007. The following day, Silvio introduced Jay to the University of Bergamo, where he eventually returned multiple times, and with a formal position as visiting scholar in May 2010. After meeting Jay at various conferences, including first an invitation to Milan in October 2000 by Francesco Brioschi, professor of finance at Politecnico di Milano, Silvio started working with Jay. Silvio, meanwhile, was awarded the 2007 Morelli-Rotary Award, a prestigious grant that allowed him to visit the Warrington College of Business at the University of Florida in 2008. It was during that period that Jay, Stefano, and Silvio started working on a paper regarding Europe's second markets for small companies, which eventually won the European Financial Management 2012 Reader's Choice for Best Paper (Vismara, Paleari, and Ritter 2012). It was also during that period that Silvio photographed Jay next to an alligator at Paynes Prairie, a photograph that is often displayed by Jay at the beginning of his conference keynote speeches. A Google search for 'Jay Ritter alligator images' reveals this photo.[6]

Since then, Jay and Silvio have performed some of their research together. Needless to say, Silvio has benefited from this, especially with regard to the imperative of having a real understanding of the topics of research. This parallels what Howard Aldrich (2016) writes in his chapter of this book: 'I'm constantly amazed when I go to professional meetings and find how little they actually know about what they are studying.' If Jay is queried regarding IPO markets around the world, even with regard to information from decades ago, his mind clearly recollects what is or was occurring; it is virtually impossible to find corporate finance research published in a top journal that he is unfamiliar with. Aldrich (2016) says, 'I'm constantly struck by when I ask them questions about basic descriptive characteristics of the phenomenon and they can't tell me this.' If Jay is sent a table with descriptive statistics about a sample of IPOs, there is a high probability that he can spot a possible error in the data just by looking at the variables' statistics.

Douglas got started in research in venture capital as a JD/PhD student at the University of Toronto in 1996. He was fortunate to have Jeff MacIntosh, Toronto Stock Exchange Professor of Capital Markets at the University of Toronto Law School, as both mentor and friend. Jeff foresaw the importance of research in venture capital and entrepreneurship, particularly with the rise of the Internet boom at that time, and encouraged Douglas to start studying venture capitalists and the entrepreneurial firms that they finance. There was ample opportunity at that time, as scant others were performing venture capital research, and those few were based in the United States. There was, in fact, copious data regarding the Canadian venture capital industry that had not been considered.

Starting in mid-1996, Douglas benefited from the generosity of Mary McDonald, of MacDonald and Associates, Ltd., for sharing data on Canada's venture capital market. The data were quite striking: they indicated that unlike venture capitalists in the United States, who typically financed their companies with convertible preferred equity, venture capitalists in Canada frequently used securities other than convertible preferred equity. The academic literature at that time demonstrated that dozens of papers were written regarding the optimality of convertible preferred equity, but not a single paper on the use of securities in venture capital transactions, other than convertible preferred. This realization significantly inspired Douglas concerning the puzzle of security design and piqued a genuine curiosity about performing research to better understand such a puzzle. Were it not for that discovery, it is unlikely that Douglas would have pursued a career in academics and instead would have most likely pursued a career in law or finance.

Douglas' experience in discovering this puzzle turned out to be harder to convert into a publication than ever imaginable. Douglas had notable mentors guiding him on his substantive work as a graduate student at the University of Toronto, including Jeff MacIntosh and Ralph Winter. In his work, 'Publishing in Finance versus Entrepreneurship/Management Journals,' (Cumming 2016), he compares his experiences publishing in finance versus entrepreneurship/management journals and offers a number of insights on publishing entrepreneurial finance papers in different fields.

Cumming and Vismara (2016) argue that entrepreneurial finance literature has become massively segmented, partly due to differences in the referees that control different journals, which has unfortunate consequences for citation patterns and the development and dissemination of ideas, and even what topics younger scholars pursue with a perspective of likely publication. Cumming (2016) notes that, based on his convertible preferred equity experience, an inherent problem exists in some disciplines, as those that are pioneers for a topic and become references for others can distort the evolution of an area to favor their own interests, possibly even after their views have been discredited. This is definitely not the instance with Jay, who is interested in theories and approaches that contrast his research, and also accepts those papers that express different views; this can be easily checked, as finance journals often disclose the names of reviewers for accepted papers. Moreover, he is an international person. Top finance journals typically prefer studies based in the United States; Jay acts as an unbiased reviewer even in this regard. We believe he has reviewed a high percentage of studies based outside of the United States and published in top finance journals. Jay, aside from acting as a constructive reviewer, is also an outstanding researcher. Literature on IPOs is reviewed in the next section by essentially following the evolution of the topics studied in his papers.

How research on IPOs evolved

'Much of the initial public offering (IPO) literature can be summarized as fitting square pegs into round holes' (Ritter 2011), as noted in the abstract of Jay's work, 'Equilibrium in the IPO Market,' in which he criticizes the ability of asymmetric information-based theories to explain the magnitude of IPO underpricing. Most papers explain the recurrence of IPO underpricing with these kinds of theories that, as Jay argues, would be plausible if the average first-day return was low or even up to 5%. The average underpricing in almost all countries is noticeably higher than this. It is difficult to reconcile the extremely high averages in underpricing during the dotcom bubble, for instance, with traditional asymmetric information-based IPO underpricing theories. In his review Jay discusses the limit of these academic theories. Most papers, he argues, focus on only the demand for underwriting, without modeling the supply conditions that determine the equilibrium degree of underpricing. Issuing firms often hire underwriters with a history of excessively underpricing IPOs so that the certification hypothesis, which states that prestigious underwriters should be able to limit underpricing, does not hold (Beatty and Ritter 1986).[7] Loughran and Ritter (2002) explain why issuers do not become upset about 'leaving money on the table' in IPOs; Loughran and Ritter (2004) explain why issuing companies would hire an underwriter that is expected to leave more money on the table than necessary.

In the 1980s and 1990s, Jay's research explained underpricing using an information asymmetry framework. Since then, he has largely rejected this framework, focusing on explanations based on agency problems between issuers and underwriters. He has also focused on both the supply and demand sides of the market for underwriting services. To explain the severe underpricing in the Internet bubble period, he has focused on what he calls the CLAS controversies: excessive Commissions (soft dollars), Laddering, Analyst conflicts of interest, and Spinning (Liu and Ritter 2010). The baseline of these hypotheses is that there is limited competition between underwriters and that issuers focus on services bundled with underwriting rather than maximizing the offer's proceeds. First, underwriters use their discretion in allocating shares to recoup part of the money lost by giving preference to allocations from rent-seeking investors (Nimalendran, Ritter, and Zhang 2007). Consequently, Ritter and Zhang (2007) find evidence suggesting that there is a close relationship between the underwriting and asset management businesses among major investment banks. Second, related to this commission explanation, laddering is the practice of allocating shares, with the condition that the investor buy additional shares in the immediate aftermarket. Third, because sell-side analysts are partially paid by investment banking revenue, they have an incentive to give favorable 'buy' recommendations to underwriting clients.[8] Fourth, spinning is the practice of allocating underpriced IPOs to corporate executives' personal brokerage accounts to influence the executives in their choice of corporate investment banking decisions.

Underpricing is an opportunity cost for a firm going public; Jay has also studied the direct costs involved with going public (Ritter 1987). A well-known paper regarding this concept is that of Chen and Ritter (2000), 'The 7 Percent Solution,' in which they document that for moderate-size US IPOs, investment banking fees are almost always 7% of the proceeds. This parallels the underwriting markets as a series of local underwriter oligopolies, as later modeled by Liu and Ritter (2011). Underwriters with market power will vary across industries, with some industry specialization. Migliorati and Vismara (2014) apply this line of thought to European IPO underwriters, providing a ranking of investment banks by stock markets.

Jay, in addition to his work on IPO underpricing, has examined IPO volumes and why they fluctuate. Ritter's (1984) paper on the 1980 hot-issue market is perhaps one of the most well known on this topic. Gao et al. (2013) explain instead why the number of US IPOs has recently decreased. Loughran, Ritter, and Rydqvist (1994) demonstrate how the annual number of IPOs changes for multiple countries. This is perhaps the first paper on IPOs with data from several countries. Later examples of cross-country comparative perspectives include the work of Ritter (2003), Ritter, Signori, and Vismara (2013), and Vismara, Paleari, and Ritter (2012).[9]

Ritter and Welch (2002) note that 'the most common method for valuing firms going public is the use of comparable firm multiples.' Almost all sell-side analyst research reports contain peer firms and their multiples. Many finance textbooks, in spite of this widespread use of comparable firms, have zero to little analysis of the use of comps for valuation purposes. Only a few academic articles address the choice of comparable firms, and few papers in the literature explore the valuation of IPOs. The most notable exception is the work of Kim and Ritter (1999) and Purnanandam and Swaminathan (2004), which compares the valuation of IPO firms with that of peers selected using alternative procedures. Cassia, Paleari, and Vismara (2004), Cogliati, Paleari, and Vismara (2011), Paleari, Signori, and Vismara (2014), and Vismara, Signori, and Paleari (2015) extend this research stream.

Finally, we conclude our review of the IPO literature with IPO long-run performance. The first author on the topic, Ritter (1991), published 'The Long-Run Performance of Initial Public Offerings'. This paper and the Loughran and Ritter (1995) paper on the new issues puzzle, with more than 3,000 Google Scholar citations each, can be considered the standard in literature and have inspired countless articles regarding the dangers of investing in IPOs. They suggest that investors may systematically be too optimistic about the prospects of firms going public. Other researchers have shown that underperformance extends to other countries, as well as to seasoned equity offerings.

How research on crowdfunding might evolve

Ritter (2013), in a policy-oriented paper, proposed to the Securities and Exchange Commission (SEC) that the costs of going public can be lowered by encouraging the use of auctions rather than IPO book building. He posited that the SEC should achieve this by requiring the disclosure of soft-dollar commission revenue, generated when underwriters use book building. Jay believes that this would lead to a decrease in underpricing, as well as lower the direct costs of going public. However, despite its higher efficiency with respect to book building (Ritter 2013), online auction IPOs have never spread. Only one investment bank, W.R. Hambrecht, has developed a platform for online public offerings, and only twenty US companies have gone public with online auctions, including Google.[10] More recently, equity crowdfunding platforms have offered the opportunity to raise public equity through the Internet. Crowdfunding, albeit a relatively new phenomenon, is growing rapidly around the world. Ahlers et al. (2015) and Cumming and Johan (2013) believe that this growth will continue as crowdfunding markets become more open over time.

The crowdfunding phenomenon is now spreading globally, but academic research in this area is still in its infancy despite its rapid growth. Special issues have and will be dedicated to the topic as proof of academia's increasing interest, including those edited by Block, Colombo, Cumming, and Vismara for *Small Business Economics*; and from Block, Cumming, and Vismara for the *Journal of Industrial and Business Economics*. Crowdfunding platforms allow fundraising from a pool of online backers and will need to cope with collective-action problems because crowd-investors have neither the ability nor the incentive, due to the small investments, to devote substantial resources to due diligence. Therefore, a parallel with the IPO markets exists. Crowdfunding investors cannot rely on reports issued by financial analysts or on formal intermediaries, such as IPO underwriters. Signals delivered by other investors, or the 'crowd,' become essential, as certifications from third-party endorsements are unavailable (Vismara 2016b). With the exception of the work of Ahlers et al. (2015) and Vismara (2016a), little research has been performed on signaling in the context of equity crowdfunding. We believe that this is a promising research avenue.

Similarly, new research is due on platforms that trade pre-IPO shares, such as SecondMarket, the main platform for trading pre-IPO shares of Facebook, or SharesPost. These platforms provide alternative venues to investors and employees for cashing out. The JOBS Act clarified several legal uncertainties regarding the operation of these secondary markets that have reduced the benefits of going public in traditional stock exchanges. Whether these and crowdfunding platforms will be successful will ultimately depend on their ability to avoid listing 'lemons' on their markets. Jay's opinion in this regard is that 'it is unlikely that investors will earn high average returns on crowdfunding investments, although the returns may be higher than the -30% earned on purchases of state lottery tickets' (Ritter 2013).

Acknowledgments

We warmly thank Mattia Cattaneo, Sofia Johan, Paolo Malighetti, Michele Meoli, Renato Redondi, and Andrea Signori for helping us edit this chapter, as well as sharing a part of this journey. We also owe our gratitude to the editors, David B. Audretsch and Erik E. Lehmann, for their helpful comments and suggestions.

Notes

1 See, for instance, Levis and Vismara (2013) for a collection of papers on IPOs, Cumming and Johan (2013b) for work on venture capital, Cumming (2008) for work that connects venture capital to IPOs and acquisitions, and Cumming (2013) for a more general collection of work on entrepreneurial finance. Ritter (2015) defines growth capital investing as the financing of growing businesses that are investing in tangible assets and the acquisition of other companies. Growth capital is common in retailing, restaurant chains, and health care management and represents 12% of all VC-backed IPOs.
2 The original contact between Erik Lehmann and the research group in entrepreneurial finance came as Erik, serving as associate editor of *Small Business Economics*, appointed Stefano as the reviewer of an IPO paper. Erik also published papers, among other topics, on IPOs (e.g., Audretsch and Lehmann 2008; Lehmann, Braun, and Krispin 2012).
3 Universoft publishes an Academic IPO Factbook that reports a number of statistics about IPOs (see also, for example, Paleari et al. 2014).
4 Two examples of articles with Arif Khurshed are Khurshed et al. (2003, 2014).
5 See Cattaneo, Meoli, and Vismara (2015) for the history of IPOs in Italy.
6 One of those occasions was at the 2011 Annual Meetings of the European Financial Management Association in Braga, Portugal. Silvio and Douglas were introduced to each other by Jay in that conference.
7 As a reviewer, Jay is amenable to papers' different perspectives. Like many others, we had this experience with the paper by Migliorati and Vismara (2014), which explicitly refers to the certification hypothesis.
8 Bradley, Jordan, and Ritter (2008) report that 98% of US IPOs from 1999–2000 had analyst coverage from a bookrunner within one year of the IPO. In the work of Gao, Ritter, and Zhu (2013), analyst coverage by lead underwriters has been the norm, at least since 1993.

9 Other cross-country studies using EURIPO data are Bonardo, Paleari, and Vismara (2010, 2011), Meoli, Paleari, and Vismara (2013), Bertoni, Meoli, and Vismara (2014), and Akyol et al. (2014).
10 The full list of IPO auctions in the United States is available on Jay Ritter's website.

References

Ahlers, Gerrit K. C., Douglas J. Cumming, Christina Guenther, and Denis Schweizer. 2015. "Signaling in Equity Crowdfunding." *Entrepreneurship Theory and Practice* 39, 955–980.

Akyol, Ali, Tommy Cooper, Michele Meoli, and Silvio Vismara. 2014. "Do Regulatory Changes Affect the Underpricing of European IPOs?" *Journal of Banking and Finance* 45, 43–58.

Aldrich, H. 2016. "Fifty Years in the Making: My Career as a Scholar of Organizations and Entrepreneurship." In *The Routledge Companion to the Makers of Modern Entrepreneurship*, edited by David B. Audretsch and Erik E. Lehmann, 14–31. London: Routledge.

Audretsch, D. and E. Lehmann. 2008. "The Neuer Markt as an Institution of Creation and Destruction." *International Entrepreneurship and Management Journal* 4, 419–429.

Audretsch, D. and E. Lehmann. 2016. *The Seven Secrets of Germany: Economic Resilience in an Era of Global Turbulence*, Oxford: Oxford University Press.

Audretsch, D., E. Lehmann, A. Richardson, and S. Vismara. (Eds.) 2015a. *Globalization and Public Policy: A European Perspective,* New York: Springer.

Audretsch, D., E. Lehmann, and M. Wright. 2014. "Technology Transfer in a Global Economy." *Journal of Technology Transfer* 39(3), 301–312.

Audretsch, D., E. Lehmann, M.S. Meoli, and S. Vismara. (Eds.) 2015b. *University Evolution, Entrepreneurial Activity and Regional Competitiveness*, New York: Springer.

Audretsch, D., E. Lehmann, S. Paleari, and S. Vismara. 2016. "Entrepreneurial Finance and Technology Transfer." *Journal of Technology Transfer* 41(1), 1–9.

Beatty, Randolph P. and Jay R. Ritter. 1986. "Investment Banking, Reputation, and the Underpricing of Initial Public Offerings." *Journal of Financial Economics* 15, 213–232.

Bertoni, Fabio, Michele Meoli, and Silvio Vismara. 2014. "Board Independence, Ownership Structure, and the Valuation of IPOs in Continental Europe." *Corporate Governance: An International Review* 22, 116–131.

Bonardo, Damiano, Stefano Paleari, and Silvio Vismara. 2010. "The M&A Dynamics of European Science Based Entrepreneurial Firms." *Journal of Technology Transfer* 35(1), 141–180.

Bonardo, Damiano, Stefano Paleari, and Silvio Vismara. 2011. "Valuing University-based Firms: The Effects of Academic Affiliation on IPO Performance." *Entrepreneurship Theory and Practice* 35(4), 755–776.

Bradley, Daniel J., Bradford D. Jordan, and Jay R. Ritter. 2008. "Analyst Behavior Following the IPO: The 'Bubble Period' Evidence." *Review of Financial Studies* 21, 101–133.

Cassia, Lucio, Stefano Paleari, and Silvio Vismara. 2004. "The Valuation of Firms Listed on the Nuovo Mercato: The Peer Comparables Approach." *Advances in Financial Economics* 10, 113–129.

Cattaneo, Mattia, Michele Meoli, and Silvio Vismara. 2015. "Financial Regulation and IPO Survival: Evidence from the History of the Italian Capital Market." *Journal of Corporate Finance* 31, 116–131.

Chen, Hsuan-Chi and Jay R. Ritter. 2000. "The Seven Percent Solution." *Journal of Finance* 55, 1105–1131.

Cogliati, Giordano M., Stefano Paleari, and Silvio Vismara. 2011. "IPO Pricing: Growth Rates Implied in Offer Prices." *Annals of Finance* 7(1), 53–82.

Cumming, Douglas J. 2008. "Contracts and Exits in Venture Capital Finance." *Review of Financial Studies* 21, 1947–1982.

Cumming, Douglas J. 2013. *Oxford Handbook of Entrepreneurial Finance*, New York/Oxford: Oxford University Press.

Cumming, D. J. 2016. "Publishing in Finance Versus Entrepreneurship/Management Journals." In *How to Get Published in Top Management Journals*, edited by T. Clark, M. Wright, and D. Ketchen, New York: Wiley, forthcoming.

Cumming, Douglas J. and Silvio Vismara. 2016. "De-segmenting Research in Entrepreneurial Finance." *Venture Capital: An International Journal of Entrepreneurial Finance*, forthcoming.

Cumming, Douglas J. and Sofia A. Johan. 2013. *Venture Capital and Private Equity Contracting: An International Perspective*, 2nd ed, Amsterdam, The Netherlands: Elsevier Science Academic Press.

Gao, Xiaohui, Jay R. Ritter, and Zhongyan Zhu. 2013. "Where Have All the IPOs Gone?" *Journal of Financial and Quantitative Analysis* 48, 1663–1692.

Khurshed, Arif, Stefano Paleari, Alok Pandè, and Silvio Vismara. 2014. "Transparent Bookbuilding, Certification and Initial Public Offerings." *Journal of Financial Markets* 19, 154–159.

Khurshed, Arif, Stefano Paleari, and Silvio Vismara. 2003. "The Operating Performance of Initial Public Offerings: The UK Experience." SSRN Working Paper.

Kim, M. and J. Ritter. 1999. "Valuing IPOs." *Journal of Financials Economics* 53, 409–437.

Lehmann, E. B., T. V. Braun, and S. Krispin. 2012. "Entrepreneurial Human Capital, Complementary Assets, and Takeover Probability." *Journal of Technology Transfer* 37(5), 589–608.

Levis, M. and S. Vismara. (Eds.) 2013. *Handbook of Research on IPOs*, Cheltenham, UK: Edward Elgar.

Liu, Xiaoding and Jay R. Ritter. 2010. "The Economic Consequences of IPO Spinning." *Review of Financial Studies* 23, 2024–2059.

Liu, Xiaoding and Jay R. Ritter. 2011. "Local Underwriter Oligopolies and IPO Underpricing." *Journal of Financial Economics*, 102(3), 579–601.

Loughran, Tim and Jay R. Ritter. 1995. "The New Issues Puzzle." *Journal of Finance* 50, 23–51.

Loughran, Tim and Jay R. Ritter. 2002. "Why Don't Issuers Get Upset About Leaving Money on the Table in IPOs?" *Review of Financial Studies* 15, 413–443.

Loughran, Tim and Jay R. Ritter. 2004. "Why Has IPO Underpricing Changed Over Time?" *Financial Management* 33(3), 5–37.

Loughran, Tim, Jay R. Ritter, and Kristian Rydqvist. 1994. "Initial Public Offerings: International Insights." *Pacific-Basin Finance Journal* 2, 165–199.

Mankiw, N. G. 2006. "The Macroeconomist as a Scientist and Engineer." *Journal of Economic Perspectives* 20(4), 29–46.

Meoli, Michele, Stefano Paleari, and Silvio Vismara. 2013. "Completing the Technology Transfer Process: M&As of Science-Based IPOs." *Small Business Economics* 40(2), 227–248.

Migliorati, Katrin and Silvio Vismara. 2014. "Ranking Underwriters of European IPOs." *European Financial Management* 20(5), 891–925.

Nimalendran, M., Jay R. Ritter, and Donghang Zhang. 2007. "Do Today's Trades Affect Tomorrow's IPO Allocation?" *Journal of Financial Economics* 84, 87–109.

Paleari, Stefano, Andrea Signori, and Silvio Vismara. 2014. "How Do Underwriters Select Peers When Valuing IPOs?" *Financial Management* 43(4), 731–755.

Paleari, Stefano, Daniele Piazzalunga, Andrea Signori, Fabio Trabucchi, and Silvio Vismara. 2014. *Academic EurIPO FactBook 2014*, North Charleston: CreateSpace Independent Publishing.

Paleari, Stefano, Enrico Pellizzoni, and Silvio Vismara. 2008. "The Going Public Decision: Evidence from the IPOs in Italy and in the UK." *International Journal of Applied Decision Sciences* 1(2), 131–152.

Purnanandam, A. K. and B. Swaminathan. 2004. "Are IPOs Really Underpriced?" *Review of Financial Studies* 17, 811–848.

Ritter, J. R. 1984. "The 'Hot Issue' Market of 1980." *The Journal of Business* 57(2), 215–240.

Ritter, J. R. 1987. "The Costs of Going Public." *Journal of Financial Economics* 19(2), 269–281.

Ritter, J. R. 1991. "The Long-Run Performance of Initial Public Offerings." *Journal of Finance* 46, 3–27.

Ritter, J. R. 2003. "Differences between European and American IPO Markets." *European Financial Management* 9(4), 421–434.

Ritter, J. R. 2011. "Equilibrium in the Initial Public Offerings Market." *Annual Review of Financial Economics* 3, 347–374.

Ritter, J. R. 2013. "Re-energizing the IPO Market." In *Restructuring to Speed Economic Recovery*, edited by Martin Neil Bailey, Richard J. Herring, and Yuta Seki, Chapter 4, 123–145. Washington, DC: Brookings Press.

Ritter, J. R. 2015. "Growth Capital-backed IPOs." *The Financial Review* 50, 481–515.

Ritter, J., A. Signori, and S. Vismara. 2013. "Economies of Scope and IPO Volume in Europe." In *Handbook of Research on IPOs*, edited by Mario Levis and Silvio Vismara, 11–34. Cheltenham, UK: Edward Elgar.

Ritter, Jay R. and Donghang Zhang. 2007. "Affiliated Mutual Funds and the Allocation of Initial Public Offerings." *Journal of Financial Economics* 86, 337–368.

Ritter, Jay R. and Ivo Welch. 2002. "A Review of IPO Activity, Pricing, and Allocations." *Journal of Finance* 57, 1795–1828.

Vismara, S. 2016a. "Equity Retention and Social Network Theory in Equity Crowdfunding." *Small Business Economics*, 46 (4), 579–590.

Vismara, S. 2016b. "Information Cascades among Investors in Equity Crowdfunding." SSRN Working Paper.

Vismara, Silvio, Andrea Signori, and Stefano Paleari. 2015. "Changes in Underwriters' Selection of Comparable Firms Pre- and Post-IPO: Same Bank, Same Company, Different Peers." *Journal of Corporate Finance* 34, 235–250.

Vismara, Silvio, Stefano Paleari, and Jay R. Ritter. 2012. "Europe's Second Markets for Small Companies." *European Financial Management* 18(3), 352–388.

8

What an opportunity!

Per Davidsson

Background

As a contributor to this volume, I was asked to clearly articulate "my most important ideas about entrepreneurship"; their origin, and their impact. What a delightful invitation to get – and what a pretentious project to engage in, giving voice to one's own importance! I have been blessed with a reasonably favorable reception of my scholarship as reflected in citations. More importantly, I have enjoyed receiving occasional communications from young scholars expressing how my work has affected their journey. That's extremely rewarding. I also think it is fair to say that I have been a not totally negligible part of some important developments within the field of entrepreneurship research. Having said all that, I find it hard to point to any particular ideas of mine and discuss them as "important" in the bigger and longer-term scheme of things. But at least I have been given this chance, and I let others judge the importance.

As background, I am grateful for having received excellent training at the Stockholm School of Economics (SSE)[1] and its Section for Economic Psychology under Professor Karl-Erik Wärneryd in particular. The three-year undergraduate degree was jam packed and very demanding compared to any business school program I have seen elsewhere. Full-time study meant full-time study – and with the expectation of what you can achieve in full time if you qualify for elite school enrolment based on strict meritocracy. We were pushed, and for most of us it was to our advantage. Apart from a range of business subjects, the undergraduate program provided me with a good grounding in micro- and macroeconomics, economic history, economic geography, law, informatics, and a sound dose of statistics, including application of several "first generation" multivariate techniques (e.g., regression, cluster, and discriminant analysis in the Marketing Research elective, as well as the then-novel conjoint analysis approach). The PhD degree required another two years of coursework, including a half-semester (FTE) course in different theoretical schools of thought (e.g. Barney & Ouchi, 1986), reading classes demanding perusal and analysis of thick piles of published journal articles, philosophy of science, models and metaphors (from mathematical formulae to boxes and arrow graphs to verbal allegories), calculus and matrix algebra (good for not being intimidated by matrix notation in articles; it's often shorthand for something rather simple!), a deeper and more philosophical look at statistical tools (Ruist, 1990), and courses in then-state-of-the-art "second generation" multivariate techniques like LISREL and PLS delivered from or close to the horse's mouth (KG Jöreskog; Claes Fornell [as in Fornell & Larcker, 1981]). What I did not get was a single credit point of entrepreneurship studies; the closest I came were electives in product development and small business management as an undergraduate. Entrepreneurship simply did not exist as a teaching subject on any level.

There weren't any ready-to-use data sets around. This said, having to do most of the empirical work myself provided invaluable experiences. These entailed finding the (manageably small but) scattered literature in brick-and-mortar libraries around the globe, designing and conducting a pilot study based on personal interviews supplemented by secondary data and a conjoint task (Davidsson, 1986), raising money for the main study, designing its phone and mail questionnaires, and doing some 20% of the interviewing and, of course, all the analysis and writing. It was really good training. I had reasonable writing skills and command of English before my university studies, and I had the good sense not to write my thesis in Swedish, which was common practice at SSE at the time. I got no specific preparation for the journal publication game. The overt and covert indoctrination was emphatically focused on the mission of doing *good* research on *important issues* while observing *impeccable integrity*; not on *getting published* based on whatever you had and whatever level of faith in the conclusions you might have yourself in order to foster your career chances. It was very liberating. Consequently, during the first ten years after my PhD there was a great deal I did not care to send to journals because *I* didn't find it important enough. The requirements on good research training for a successful career in entrepreneurship research may look very different today, but I'm not sure they are.

Dissertation: small firm growth

In short summary the idea for my thesis was: *why is it that some firms continue to grow and develop, while most level off and become rather static?* In particular, I found it paradoxical that almost all theories and policy debates took the willingness to grow for granted. My conviction that willingness was important came in part from George Katona,[2] one of the "house gods" in my department at SSE. Katona insisted that economic behavior required both ability and willingness, and that both could be measured (Katona, 1975). Another origin of my interest was my own observation that the theories did not match what you quickly learn by talking to a few small business owner-managers. They are typically not growth or profit maximizers, and it was not a farfetched idea that the prospect of growth would trigger both positive and negative expectations for many of them.

The most important publications from this survey-based project are two articles in *Journal of Business Venturing* (Davidsson, 1989b, 1991), which reflect some of the core contents of my master's ("licentiate") and doctoral dissertations. Published as a book according to the Swedish custom, the PhD thesis (Davidsson, 1989a) was an important output in its own right, as was Wiklund, Davidsson, and Delmar (2003), where we follow up my 1989 article with more data and a stronger theoretical framing. Collectively these works currently count some 2,000 citations according to Google Scholar, so I guess some impact can be claimed. What might that impact have been? First, the research seemed to confirm that the perceived need – or willingness – to grow was at least as important as ability and opportunities to do so. Hence, with some others (e.g., Sapienza, Korsgaard, & Forbes, 2003) I might have helped establish the importance of entrepreneurs' nonfinancial goals and perceptions. Subsequent research has confirmed that growth willingness predicts actual, subsequent growth (Delmar & Wiklund, 2008; Wiklund & Shepherd, 2003). Second, the high-quality training I had been given allowed me to produce research (especially my 1991 article), which was conceptually and methodologically advanced for its time, thereby possibly having a gently nudging positive influence on the field, similar to what signified much of Arnold Cooper's long career in entrepreneurship research (e.g., Cooper, Gimeno-Gascon, & Woo, 1994; Gimeno, Folta, Cooper, & Woo, 1997).[3] Third, the work may have had some influence by casting small firm growth as and entrepreneurship issue – a view to which I have subsequently put some nuance (Davidsson, Delmar, & Wiklund, 2002). Overall, I would only claim modest influence. For starters, there was not much of a field of entrepreneurship research to influence back in those days. Further, when the explosive quantitative and qualitative growth took off after 2000 (Meyer et al., 2012), these works were already getting old, although citation stats indicate some lingering appreciation.

SMEs, job creation, and regional development

One year after finishing my PhD I left SSE, which was a countercultural move at the time. According to the self-perception of this elite institution there simply was nowhere else interesting to go (within the country). Although there was no expectation to "get out and get clean" from your alma mater I had the intuition that I should move on in order to continue to grow as a scholar. So in 1990 I joined the young and much less renowned Umeå University up north, which had a track record in small business studies.

It was fortuitous, because in Umeå I was soon pulled into a very interesting, large-scale, international-collaborative project on small and medium-sized firms (SMEs), job creation, and regional development. In general terms, my interest in this project had the same origin as my dissertation: the academic and policy neglect of small and new firms that prevailed at the time. My interest in their role may also have been a psychological reaction to growing up in a small steel town dominated by one, large (and old) company. The project's more immediate roots can be found in David Birch's seminal studies (Birch, 1979, 1987) and subsequent work in the United Kingdom and United States by upcoming entrepreneurship and small business research giants David Storey and Paul Reynolds. Acs and Audretsch's (1990) work on small firms and innovation was another trigger in the same domain. Reynolds and Storey coordinated the international project, and it is no exaggeration to say that getting the chance to work closely with them was what sparked my international career.

The project relied on archival data. In Sweden we were blessed with comparatively good business statistics collected by Statistics Sweden, a government agency. However, far from accepting data "as is" we engaged in close collaboration with register experts in order to develop the best possible data set (see Davidsson, 2004, chs. 7–8). Funding came from another government agency, so there was a strong policy interest in the project. Hence, two major reports in Swedish are among the more important outputs (Davidsson, Lindmark, & Olofsson, 1994a, 1996). As government agency reports go, they were best sellers. Out of the myriad of empirical facts they reported there was one that made it to the very top of political debate and mainstream media, namely the stylized fact that "7 out of 10 new jobs are created by SMEs". Hence, with a ten- to fifteen-year delay we triggered the Swedish version of the debate originally stirred up by David Birch. For those who frown upon empirical fact-finding and practice-oriented work I should perhaps mention that despite being mere research reports written in Swedish, each of these works count over 100 citations on Google Scholar. It is not hard to find articles published in the *Academy of Management Journal* (for example) from the same time that did worse.

This said, of greater interest to us and to academic outlets were the regional drivers and consequences of firm births, deaths, expansion, and contraction. The most important journal output was no doubt the special issue of *Regional Studies* where the seven country studies were reported, including our Swedish contribution (Davidsson, Lindmark, & Olofsson, 1994b). Although the country studies seemed to point in several directions, the harmonized analysis across all participating countries provided solid evidence of three major drivers of high regional start-up rates: agglomeration advantages (resources, markets), economic growth (demand), and a structure dominated by smaller firms (Reynolds, Storey, & Westhead, 1994). The experience of this project and special issue underscored that knowledge development is a collective endeavor and convinced me of the importance of replication across several contexts. Single studies do not provide much in the way of reliably transferable knowledge (cf. Davidsson, 2004, 2016, ch. 9).

In this research we were part of an influential movement that provided empirical evidence on the importance of the "undergrowth" in the economy. Increasingly, we also came to realize that *newness* rather than *smallness* was the name of the game; established SMEs are not great innovators or job creators (Davidsson, Lindmark, & Olofsson, 1998b; Reynolds, 1999). Empirics-heavy as these projects were, the battle was fundamentally a conceptual one: Should the economy and its development be viewed essentially as a matter of large, rather stable organizations, start-ups, and small firms being rather unimportant phenomena at the fringes? Or are dynamism and renewal of the business population the most important characteristics of the economy (cf. the chapter conclusions in Reynolds & White, 1997)?

Among those who dismissed the importance of small and new firms were labor economists Davis, Haltiwanger, and Schuh (DHS) in their widely circulated National Bureau of Economic Research (NBER) working paper (Davis, Haltiwanger, & Schuh, 1993). I was genuinely upset by this paper, because without references explaining how particular studies got it wrong, it portrayed us as simpletons who were deluded by three methods' artifacts. It would not have been totally wrong to criticize small business researchers at the time for being too much a fan club and too little neutral observers, although David Storey's rise did much to temper such tendencies (Storey, 1994). Yet, DHS' arrogance was unfathomable to me, especially as not an ounce of the counterargumentation was considered in the final publication of their work (Davis, Haltiwanger, & Schuh, 1996a, 1996b). Reading their work it was obvious to me that they were intelligent, knowledgeable, and technically skilled researchers. Surely, these men would understand that two of the three "method fallacies" they accused others of (the size distribution fallacy and confounding gross and net figures) do not systematically bias results in favor of small firms? Surely they would understand they were on thin ice when accusing others of using unsuitable data when DHS used data from the shrinking manufacturing sector in the context of discussing job creation during a period when tens of millions of new jobs were created in the United States? Of course they must have understood that the ideas that job changes over time predominantly reflect random oscillation and that firms have a long-term "natural size" were ill founded and that therefore the "corrections" they suggested would be proven unsound (Picot & Dupuy, 1998)? I could not help asking "Whose errands were these guys running?"

It was not until I had a face-to-face conversation with John Haltiwanger that I understood that conspiracy theories were not called for and that instead strongly held preconceptions within a paradigm or line of research were to blame. To his credit, Haltiwanger eventually came around and has become one of the greatest contributors of empirical evidence on the importance of new firms for job creation (Decker, Haltiwanger, Jarmin, & Miranda, 2014; Haltiwanger, Jarmin, & Miranda, 2013), thus confirming the importance of the new versus small distinction that we were starting to make in the mid-1990s.

At any rate, DHS triggered a couple of contributions on our part. In response to their "correction" suggestions I invented the principle now called *dynamic sizing,* which has been adopted by the US Bureau of Labor Statistics as one of their reporting standards (Butani et al., 2005; Davidsson, 1996; de Wit & de Kok, 2013). The principle is very simple: each job n is attributed to the size class the firm is in at the moment the nth job is created. In fact, the idea is so simple that de Wit and de Kok independently reinvented it (personal communication), but they were gracious enough to make the attribution when they realized I had suggested it long ago and that it was already in use. Simple does not equal unimportant, and I take comfort in the thought that if the reporting practice has had any influence in the right direction on any policy decision in the United States, I can probably justify my lifetime salary solely on the basis of this contribution.

Dynamic sizing addresses both the "size distribution fallacy" and the "regression fallacy". On the latter, DHS were correct in principle; it systematically biases job creation data in favor of small firms when a firm moves up and down across a size class divider over time. However, they were wrong about the practical significance of the issue. We demonstrated this empirically in Davidsson, Lindmark, and Olofsson (1998a). Our conclusion was that adjusting for the "regression fallacy" in our data amounted to correcting for fractions of a percentage point. This is because most size changes do not involve size class transitions, and when they do, they often reflect trendwise real change rather than random fluctuations. Hence, we argued that across most conceivable empirical situations, the regression fallacy is not a method problem of the magnitude DHS seem to have believed.

Apart from the substantive contributions, our close collaboration with Statistics Sweden paved the way for similar projects in years to come, where generations of researchers have enjoyed working with high-quality, customized data sets, often developed in close collaboration between the researchers and the register experts (Delmar, Davidsson, & Gartner, 2003; Hellerstedt, 2009; Wennberg, Wiklund, DeTienne, & Cardon, 2010; Witte, 2014) .

In addition to our studies based on archival data, I undertook two projects based on primary survey data to supplement the picture of regional dynamics with cultural determinants, that is, regional differences in prevailing beliefs and attitudes that may be relevant to entrepreneurship (Davidsson, 1995; Davidsson & Wiklund, 1997). One inspiration for this was surely David McClelland's macro-psychological work on achievement motivation (McClelland, 1961). My works on culture had almost no impact at the time, simply because there was not much of a scholarly conversation to which to connect. Interest seems to be growing, though – the 1995 and 1997 articles count seven to sixteen times as many citations in the last five years as they did in the five years following their publication, and neither seems yet to have peaked. A new generation of studies is emerging where the same issues are revisited with more comprehensive data and more sophisticated analyses (Obschonka et al., 2015a; Obschonka et al., 2015b).

Nascent entrepreneurship

In 1994 I joined the academic upstart that was to become the Jönköping International Business School (JIBS). I have described elsewhere (Davidsson, 2013) some of the joys of being part of this institution's journey from nothing to something in the world of entrepreneurship research (Aldrich, 2012; Crump et al., 2009; Teixeira, 2011). Shortly after I joined JIBS, Paul Reynolds reappeared as a significant figure in our story, now to make me join his quest for realizing what was to become the Panel Study of Entrepreneurial Dynamics (PSED) (Gartner, Shaver, Carter, & Reynolds, 2004; Reynolds, 2007).

The idea behind joining the high-risk, nascent entrepreneur(ship) project was that the most important contribution entrepreneurship research can make to the broader fields of economic and organizational studies is to focus on *emergence:* How do economic activities and organizations come into being in the first place? Putting this question in the foreground was part of our field's general drift away from an exaggerated focus on the enterprising individual and independently operated small firms. Major inspirations were Bill Gartner's emphasis on emergence (Gartner, 1989; Gartner, 1993; Katz & Gartner, 1988) and Paul Reynolds' persuasion, including his earlier efforts to make possible the empirical study of representative samples of ongoing start-up attempts (Reynolds & Miller, 1992; Reynolds & White, 1992).

Two things are undeniable. First, Paul D. Reynolds is the giant of nascent entrepreneurship research. Without him, we would not have had the Global Entrepreneurship Monitor and the collection of PSED-type projects in anything like their current form. As a consequence there are some 200+ journal articles on early-stage business development that would not have existed without him (Bergmann, Mueller, & Schrettle, 2014; Davidsson, 2005b; Davidsson & Gordon, 2012; Frid et al., 2016). Second, for better or for worse, I have been one of the major players in this research stream. I was on the design team for the original PSED, the driving principal investigator (with F. Delmar) on the Swedish counterpart study, had some involvement in the design of PSED II (Reynolds & Curtin, 2008), and led the work behind an Australian counterpart study, CAUSEE (Davidsson & Steffens, 2011). I think my (still ongoing) contributions within this research stream can be described as falling neatly into four categories: mapping out the phenomenon, substantive contributions to theory and empirical generalizations, taking stock and giving direction to future research, and providing data that allow others to make further contributions.

I have been part of empirically mapping out the phenomenon of business start-up activity (e.g. Crawford et al., 2015; Davidsson, Steffens, Gordon, & Reynolds, 2008; Delmar & Davidsson, 2000; cf. Reynolds, Carter, Gartner, & Greene, 2004). As Paul Reynolds has pointed out many times, when we started this journey we did not have much of a clue. Not of the prevalence of nascent entrepreneurs, nor of what proportion were successful, how long they took, what resources they used, etc. Some would scorn this type of fact finding as not being very interesting, sophisticated, or important in scholarly terms. Others would be concerned about the "modest majority" nature of representative samples of start-ups (Davidsson & Gordon, 2012). To these I say, first, that given the 750+ Google Scholar citations attributed to the admittedly very simple, fact-finding Delmar & Davidsson (2000) article, I think we will be "crying all the way to the bank". Second, we had to do the mapping of the territory to find out about the composition of the population, didn't we? Third, bigger minds than yours have pointed out that mapping out the phenomenon is a necessary step in developing theory that has some solid legs to stand on – it isn't properly done in the context of writing the front part of a single article (Hambrick, 2007; Locke, 2007; Locke & Latham, 2002). Finally, if the PSED data do not fit your theory or your understanding of the phenomenon, why don't you devote years of your scholarly life to creating a massive data set that can do the job? Better still, why don't you also share that data set with colleagues around the world so that they also get a chance to contribute to our collective understanding of the phenomenon you find so important? Enough said.

It is no doubt the case that the important but less ubiquitous "high end" of entrepreneurship drowns in representative samples and that such samples are not ideal for developing or testing prescriptive theory on entrepreneurial decision making and action. Hence my suggestion that now that we have the broader phenomenon mapped out in representative samples, the "early catch and follow over time" approach should be applied to more homogenous and "higher potential" samples. However, for policy making it is crucially important to understand what the totality of business start-up activity looks like. Further, PSED-type studies allow the development and testing of theory that has a more realistic view of the phenomenon as its vantage point. This is happening – thanks to the empirical fact finding (e.g., Kim, Longest, & Lippmann, 2014).

In terms of substantive contributions, Davidsson and Honig (2003) has become not only my best-cited article but the best-cited article (so far) ever published in the *Journal of Business Venturing*.[4] This is an unexpected feat for a regular, empirical article. I think its apparent influence has a lot to do with timing. It was one of the first in the entrepreneurship literature to address issues pertaining to education, experience, and networks in the theoretical language of human and social capital (entirely Benson Honig's achievement). Moreover, it was one of the first to reach publication based on longitudinal data from a random sample of nascent entrepreneurs. This makes it an early example of taking the notion of entrepreneurship *as process* seriously – a theme which more than a decade later is still just about to take off seriously in the empirically based mainstream (McMullen & Dimov, 2013). Although I appreciate every one of the citations, I do not necessarily see that article as more important than Samuelsson and Davidsson (2009), which remains one of the all too few articles to investigate variance in the "opportunity" side of Shane and Venkataraman's (2000) "individual-opportunity nexus" (Davidsson, 2015).[5] I also hope some of my recent papers will have impact, for example, our providing one of the first quantitative tests of the effects of using a bricolage approach to starting a new business (Senyard, Baker, Steffens, & Davidsson, 2014) or our opportunistic use of the global financial crisis as a natural experiment (Davidsson & Gordon, 2015). The latter study indicates a surprising absence of response to a major macroeconomic crisis on the part of nascent ventures.

Taking stock of a research stream is hard work, and giving direction is a delicate matter. Howard Aldrich's wise words are always at the back of my mind:

> What lesson can be learned from history? Influence comes from exemplary research, not from propagation of rules or admonition. The field will be shaped by those who produce research that interests and attracts others to build on their work (. . .). Those who believe they know the path forward need to do such work themselves and (. . .) provide exemplars that attract others to follow.
>
> *Aldrich & Baker (1997, p. 398)*

And then I forget and do it all the same: tell others how they ought to conduct their research. Often this is appreciated, and people tell me so, because it prevents them from unnecessarily repeating my mistakes. I am sure on other occasions it is less appreciated, but then you are more likely to hear about it than I am! At any rate, with regard to stock taking and agenda setting my most important contributions to the nascent entrepreneurship stream are arguably Davidsson (2006), Davidsson and Gordon (2012), and Davidsson and Wiklund (2001). I hope these works have helped others refine their research questions and their approach to addressing them.

Creation of data sets and making them available to others are sorely underrated activities in all formal appraisal systems I have ever come across. What should we value more highly: an article in a top journal or creating a data set allowing others to make dozens of contributions, including one or more such articles? I have done nothing near what Paul Reynolds has done in terms of providing others with data, but the Swedish PSED certainly allowed others on our extended team to contribute somewhat influential papers (Chandler, Honig, & Wiklund, 2005; Delmar & Shane, 2003, 2004, 2006; Eckhardt, Shane, & Delmar, 2006; Honig & Karlsson, 2004; Shane & Delmar, 2004). Other data sets we created at JIBS similarly benefitted a broader team than those involved in fundraising, design, and data collection, and the same is true for the Australian CAUSEE study, which has now also been put in the public domain (see http://eprints.qut.edu.au/49327/).

Further studies of small firm growth

Throughout my career I have repeatedly come back to my dissertation topic of small firm growth. The main driver of this research has been to nuance simplistic views – prevalent in both policy debates and academic contexts – of firm growth as 1) a homogenous phenomenon and 2) inherently good. Insights into these issues came from working with growth as a research topic and from policy and media hypes about "gazelles" as heroes and saviors.

In fact, growth was a subtopic in our research on SMEs, job creation, and regional development. In the next major collaboration with Statistics Sweden it was the main topic. Thanks to the close collaboration, in the "high growth firms" study we could come up with a solution to something I found intuitively must be very important but which had never been done, namely to distinguish between organic and acquisition-based growth in a broadly based, longitudinal data set built from official business statistics. I had little sense of how unique and innovative this made our data set; it is not until very recently that I have seen the same feat achieved in other broadly based data sets (Criscuolo et al., 2014). Making this distinction is particularly important from a job creation perspective: firm-level growth achieved by transferring activities from one organization to another does *not* reflect job creation.

It paid off. As a social scientist, you typically do not make what you could call "scientific discoveries". Our experience with the high-growth firms' (HGFs) data broken down by organic vs. acquisition-based growth by firm age and firm size is probably as close as I will ever get. The "effect sizes" were larger than almost anything I have seen: young HGFs in our data grew almost exclusively through the organic mode, whereas among HGFs older than ten years, 84% of the growth was acquisition based. It was the same with size class breakdowns; in fact, HGFs in the largest size class decreased their employment by a non-negligible amount in organic terms. The implication is that the contribution to job creation by young (and small) firms is much larger still than what is suggested by data that cannot make the organic-acquired distinction. Unfortunately, we did not make our findings widely available in English[6] until mentioned in passing in Davidsson (2004) and in a (re-)publication of a 1998 working paper as a book chapter (Davidsson & Delmar, 2006).

Instead Delmar et al. (2003) became the internationally most influential paper from the study. In this article, we demonstrate that what is portrayed as a "high-growth firm" depends a whole lot on how and when you measure growth, for example, in sales or employment, in absolute or percentage terms, and including or excluding acquisition-based growth (cf. Shepherd & Wiklund, 2009). Rather than a homogenous and stable group of HGFs we found no fewer than seven different types, several of which had highly irregular growth patterns over time. Extremely few firms have a stable, enduring existence as HGFs. Through this work, we became part of a movement away from viewing growth as homogenous and HGFs as a distinct "species" of firm. In its place has come a view of growth as a set of related but different phenomena and of "high growth" as a (risky) stage some, but not all, firms go through (Davidsson, Achtenhagen, & Naldi, 2010; McKelvie & Wiklund, 2010). A conceptual forerunner to this more fine-tuned understanding of firm growth was Davidsson and Wiklund (2000). Several of my more recent empirical works take the idea of different growth modes seriously by focusing narrowly on international and entrepreneurial growth (Naldi & Davidsson, 2014) and sales growth vs. employment growth (Chandler, McKelvie, & Davidsson, 2009) or organic- vs. acquisition-based growth (Lockett, Wiklund, Davidsson, & Girma, 2011) as theoretically distinct forms rather than as operationalization alternatives. The latter uses our original HGF data set so 14 years after we cracked how to partial out organic growth in the data, some results actually found their way into a high-tier journal.

Of these, the articles lead-authored by Lockett and Naldi, respectively, pertain to refined ideas about the conceptual relationship between growth and entrepreneurship (Davidsson, 2005a; Davidsson, Delmar, & Wiklund, 2002). Over time, I have come to embrace the notion that entrepreneurship is about the creation of new economic activities, not about anything and everything that concerns owner-managers of independent businesses.[7] In line with this, I argue that there are two ways in which growth can be seen as manifestations of entrepreneurship. First, under Gartner's (1990) "emergence" view, the question is when emergence ends and business as usual starts. Gartner emphasizes "the creation of new organizations", thus affording to entrepreneurship research the task of filling the gap between nonexistence, on the one hand, and existence as an organization as understood in organization theory on the other. Under this view, new cases of individual self-employment may not suffice even if the entities are trading regularly in the market. Hence, what others would call "early growth" may have to be included in the notion of "entrepreneurship", at least up to a point where division of labor and other markers of an independent organizational identity exist. Under a more market-oriented view, any growth that stirs up the market, thereby "driving the market process" (Kirzner, 1973), would qualify. Hence, growth achieved through introduction of new products and entry into new markets is entrepreneurial; acquisitions and mere volume growth to meet growing demand are not (Davidsson, 2016, ch. 1).

In Davidsson, Steffens, and Fitzsimmons (2009) – a work on my personal favorites list, although I may now have disqualified it as entrepreneurship research – we take on the notion that growth equals high performance. Using longitudinal data sets from two countries we argue and show that reaching the enviable position of combining high growth with high profitability more likely starts with reaching high profitability. On this basis firms can subsequently engage in sound, sustainable growth. Conversely, you don't typically become profitable as a result of your growth. Those firms embarking on a growth trajectory starting from a low-profitability position more likely become low performers on both dimensions in subsequent periods. Other researchers have subsequently nuanced this picture by reporting positive associations between growth and profit-ability (e.g., Delmar, McKelvie, & Wennberg, 2013; Lee, 2014). However, they have not asked quite the same question. We expected disjunctive effects of growth depending on the initial profitability position, and this has not been directly addressed in other studies. We rationalized our findings as follows. If you embark on a growth trajectory starting from low profitability, it probably means your product-market offering is not unique enough to allow high margins. Consequently, you will have to "buy" your growth through lower prices or increased marketing efforts, neither of which improves your profitability unless there are significant economies of scale. Hence, growth may neither be sustainable nor contribute to increased profitability. If, on the other hand, you show high profitability at small scale it probably means you have come up with something that impresses the market and that can be a sound basis for sustainable, profitable growth. We could not test directly that these were the mechanisms that led to our supportive results, so further research capturing the mechanisms as well as the resulting growth–profit con-figurations would be very interesting.

Conceptualization of entrepreneurship and "entrepreneurial opportunities"

If you really pressure me to discuss ideas of mine that I find somewhat important, it would have to be my ideas about what entrepreneurship and entrepreneurship research fundamentally are and on how to deal with the increasingly central notion of "entrepreneurial opportunities". I have developed these thoughts in Davidsson (2003, 2004 [ch. 1–2], 2015, 2016 [chs. 1–2; 8]) and whatever merit these works have or lack, I can at least honestly say they have been among the intellectually most demanding in my scholarly production. The space here naturally does not allow a full account, but it suffices to outline some core ideas.

The concepts "entrepreneur" and "entrepreneurship" are still debated, but they were even more so back in the 1990s. There were partial disagreements on many dimensions, for example, the extent to which novelty, intention, profit orientation, and independent ownership are neces-sary requirements. One implicit or explicit view equates entrepreneurship with anything that concerns founder-owners of independent businesses. This is how succession problems in mature family firms end up under the entrepreneurship label. It is a view our field and I have been drifting away from over time, and I am now squarely with the majority that subscribes to a view focusing on "creation of new economic activity" as representing entrepreneurship. Note that with this view we can more comfortably talk about "entrepreneurship" than about "entrepreneurs". Comparing flesh-and-blood individuals as "entrepreneurs" vs. "non-entrepreneurs" is sometimes akin to comparing people who are currently on vacation with those who currently are not; that is, it leads to confounding of person-based and situational factors (Ross, 1977). Although he slipped towards the end of his famous second chapter of *The Theory of Economic Development*, Schumpeter (1934) in his sharpest moments discussed the entrepreneur as an economic function, not as a flesh-and-blood individual. Over their life course, many individuals occasionally perform the entrepreneurial function. Although some do it more consistently than others, the entrepreneur vs. non-entrepreneur dichotomy is not very helpful for scholarly purposes.

A particularly important point of diverging views is whether "success" or "impact" is required or if entrepreneurship only requires an attempt to create new economic activity. On the one hand, it might lead wrong in many ways to have a success or favorability bias in the very definition of the concept; on the other hand, it is hard to accept the inclusion of any delusional attempt that has absolutely no impact on the economic system.

At least in business school research on entrepreneurship, Shane and Venkataraman's (2000) "Promise" article became a very important milestone. One important step they took was to try to delineate the scholarly domain of entrepreneurship rather than yet again trying the hopeless task of coming up a definition of the economic/societal phenomenon that we could all agree on. However, they did not quite complete this stride, but got stuck halfway towards fully distinguishing between the phenomenon and the scholarly domain. This has created some problems, not least with regard to the "opportunity" construct, which is a centerpiece in their argument.

They define the domain as

> [T]he scholarly examination of how, by whom, and with what effects opportunities to create future goods and services are discovered, evaluated, and exploited (Venkataraman, 1997). Consequently the field involves the study of sources of opportunities; the processes of discovery, evaluation, and exploitation of opportunities; and the set of individuals who discover, evaluate, and exploit them.
>
> *(Shane & Venkataraman, 2000: 218)*

A few lines earlier they explain a thought underlying this definition: "entrepreneurship involves the nexus of two phenomena: the presence of lucrative opportunities and the presence of enterprising individuals". When they say this, they are implicitly placing themselves at the end of one or more successful processes, looking back. Under the influence of Austrian economists they are really discussing the phenomenon of entrepreneurship in the economic system, emphasizing the point that prior micro-level research had been too myopically occupied solely with the individual side of the nexus. I hold that entrepreneurship researchers should surely try to contribute understanding to this phenomenon, but they would not do that very effectively if they restricted themselves to retrospective studies of success stories, that is, those where a lucrative opportunity and an enterprising individual were undeniably present. In other discussions we would scorn such an approach as "sampling on the dependent variable". Hence, the *domain* of entrepreneurship research should include the scholarly examination of entrepreneurial action and inaction in response to situations that are favorable and less so: the completion, termination, and reorientation of entrepreneurial processes, and the failure as well as the success as the final outcome of it.

In Davidsson (2004, 2016) I devote the first two chapters to complete what Shane and Venkataraman started by developing detailed, separate accounts of entrepreneurship as societal phenomenon (as a function in the economic system) and entrepreneurship as scholarly domain. For the former purpose I lean on Kirzner's notion of "driving the market process". Entrepreneurship is new-to-the-market economic activities, ranging from a new competitor to a new-to-the world innovation. Such activity has the effects of 1) providing customers new alternatives that suit some of them better, 2) giving incumbents reason to shape up in response, and 3) attracting followers that perceive the original actor as potentially successful – followers who further enhance the effects of (1) and (2). Hence, when discussing the societal phenomenon, I do not hesitate to include the outcome in the definition. In fact, I go so far as to suggest that only activities that have a long-term positive effect on effective resource utilization qualify; actions that enrich particular agents at the cost of the functioning of the system do not qualify.[8] However, success on the micro-level is not required – first movers do not always reap the benefits – but overall there is a developmental effect on the economics system, however small (like some customers benefitting from a more conveniently located new hairdresser).

With regard to the scholarly domain I offer this somewhat verbose delineation:

> Starting from assumptions of uncertainty, heterogeneity, and disequilibrium, the domain of entrepreneurship research encompasses the study of processes of (real or induced, and completed as well as terminated) emergence of new economic ventures, across organizational contexts. This entails the study of new venture ideas and their contextual fit; of actors and their behaviors in the interrelated processes of discovery and exploitation of such ideas, and of how the characteristics of ideas, actors and behaviors link to antecedents and outcomes on different levels of analysis.

Yes, there is quite a bit of thought packed into those few lines, and I will not even try to elaborate here, as I have already elaborated on every element of the delineation elsewhere. The most recent version of the full account can be found in Davidsson (2016, ch.2). Earlier versions appear in Davidsson (2003, 2004). Suffice it here to say that the delineation allows for both individual and corporate entrepreneurship, social and commercial entrepreneurship ("economic" is broader than "commercial"), and success as well as failure. Further, it is agnostic about outcomes; explaining favorable and unfavorable outcomes at different levels of analysis is what much of the research in the domain focuses on.

In my domain delineation, the term "opportunity" is conspicuously absent. Shane and Venkataraman's (2000) strong emphasis on "opportunities" triggered a veritable explosion of articles using this concept in a central role. A review published in 2010 identified sixty-eight articles in leading journals using opportunity (in the entrepreneurial sense) in the title, keywords, or abstract (Short, Ketchen Jr, Shook, & Ireland, 2010). Only eight of them were published prior to 2000. When I revisited the same journals in 2014 the number of qualifying, post-2000 items had grown to a whopping 210 articles. Yet, Shane himself found reason to lament the limited progress that has been achieved in our understanding of "opportunities" (Shane, 2012). Notwithstanding some excellent contributions, we have mostly seen conceptual confusion and endless philosophical debates (Davidsson, 2015).

I trace this back to Shane and Venkataraman's incomplete step from defining the phenomenon to delineating the domain. I am not one to deny the existence of objective, agent-independent opportunity. In fact, such existence can be said to follow directly from the theoretical assumption of disequilibrium. It also accords with historical experience: in each time period entrepreneurial agents try new things, and some of them are successful. Ergo, there was opportunity for successful entrepreneurial action. Shane and Venkataraman had reason to point out that "enterprising individuals" cannot capture the full story; what "they act upon" also matters. However, as soon as we try to identify and label particular entities as pre-existing, agent-independent "objective opportunities" we run into trouble. More often than not, it is the favorability connotation that necessarily comes with any definition of "opportunity" that creates the problems. It is usually much easier to agree on the objective existence of something than on its (pre-agency; agency-independent) favorability.

More importantly, in forward-looking, micro-level theory and empirical research, we should not start solely from agents known to be "entrepreneurial" or situations known to represent "opportunities" defined as "an economic circumstance where if the correct good or service were to be properly organized and offered for sale that the result would be profitable" (Eckhardt & Shane, 2010, p. 48). Potential entrepreneurial agents do not act on "opportunities"; they are not able to identify the full confluence of circumstances that will affect their chances of success. Neither are researchers who would want to study such entities (cf. the Metro example in Davidsson, 2016, ch. 8 and ponder the impossibility). Potential entrepreneurial agents do not evaluate "opportunities"; they evaluate ideas and (interpretations of) situations in order to determine if *they* think that it *might* be an *opportunity for them* (McMullen & Shepherd, 2006). The notion of "opportunity evaluation" is an oxymoron, because when afforded "opportunity" status, the entity has already been given an evaluative label. When someone choses one among several "opportunities", what justifies that label for the selected and deselected entities? A positive evaluation by one potential agent is hardly a reason for the researcher to use the o-word, and for the deselected entities we have neither the agent's subjective evaluation nor proof of a favorable outcome as justification. Equally awkward is the "opportunity" label for entities that potential entrepreneurial agents abandon after some further exploration, or cling to in a process that ends in spectacular failure. The list goes on.

Ironically, "opportunity" was always the wrong notion for the entity Shane and Venkataraman really wanted us to study when they launched the "nexus" idea. If we want to understand how entrepreneurial action and outcomes are shaped by characteristics of the agent *and* the entity they are "working on" *and* the fit between these two, then we cannot start by restricting one part of the nexus to defined-as-favorable entities. If we do, only characteristics of the agent can explain nonaction and failure, so we would end up with the person-centered view of which they meant to stay clear.

The focus on opportunities has led to conceptual overlap between independent and dependent variables, between actor and the entity acted upon, between external conditions and subjective perceptions, and between the contents and the favorability of the entity acted upon. In Davidsson (2016) I develop in great detail a set of constructs that can jointly capture the many ideas that have previously been packed into the "opportunity" concept while avoiding tautologies and conceptual confusion. These theoretical constructs are *New Venture Ideas* for imagined future ventures of any subjective or objective quality, *External Enablers* for objective, aggregate-level circumstances which may affect a variety of new venture creation attempts, and *Opportunity Confidence* strictly for a particular actor's subjective evaluation of the attractiveness – or lack thereof – of an External Enabler or a New Venture Idea as the basis for entrepreneurial activity. The article develops the nature of these constructs in great detail in order to achieve – for once – a satisfactory level of clarity regarding the meaning of our most central concepts (Suddaby, 2010).

My use of "Opportunity" in the title of this chapter is unlikely to have a detrimental effect on communication effectiveness, and "Entrepreneurial Opportunity" is such an intuitive notion that it is almost impossible to avoid in any casual conversation about entrepreneurship. Hence, it can be hard to see or accept that it is not very suitable for the more demanding role of serving as a core theoretical construct in a field of research. But this is what I have concluded by delving deep into and thinking hard about this issue. I therefore hope I can get some colleagues and research students to accept as one of the most important ideas I have contributed to this field is that for many of our scholarly purposes "entrepreneurial opportunity" is an idea we should put on the back burner. If the acceptance also included replacing that term with my triplet of alternatives, I would be most delighted.

Notes

1 The translated name is actually a misnomer; notwithstanding some famous economists it is a business school, as its Swedish name *Handelshögskolan i Stockholm* conveys.
2 Katona, who features also in Howard Aldrich's chapter in this volume, is generally regarded the father, or at least one of the originators, of economic psychology/behavioral economics.
3 Remember this was a time when there weren't scores of brilliant young people from the best universities around doing entrepreneurship research. If you are one of those, think twice, however, before you look down on those who went before you, because without them there would not have been a field of entrepreneurship research for you to enter. Your supervisor would not have allowed it because the field wouldn't have had enough legitimacy, and you would not have dared what these forerunners did: address a phenomenon because it was important and underresearched, not because it looked like a good career option.
4 William Baumol's much more important article on entrepreneurship as productive, unproductive, and destructive was originally published elsewhere (Baumol, 1990), and many of the Google Scholar citations are misattributed.
5 As explained further later I strongly prefer other labels than "opportunity" for the nonagent side of the nexus.
6 They appeared in Swedish reports, conference papers, and policy documents in English – and in a French-Canadian (!) journal article (Davidsson & Delmar, 2001). This reflects that as late as 2000 we were still not under strong pressure to publish in top journals, nor did we realize that such publication would be the way to maximize impact. Similarly, Delmar et al. (2003) achieved journal publication (five years after conference presentation) only thanks to Bill Gartner joining the team and driving the publication process.
7 See also the next main section of this chapter. In order not to alienate a large share of the 3,000-strong membership the Entrepreneurship Division of the Academy of Management acknowledges both views (Mitchell, 2011).
8 In this my use of the "e-words" differs from Baumol's (1990). Under my definition, activities that are unproductive or destructive from the perspective of the economic system are not examples of entrepreneurship. This said, when we discuss the societal phenomenon (the function in the economic system), the interest is directed at the overall effects on the economic system and not in teasing out exactly which micro-level cases qualify or not for the entrepreneurship label.

References

Acs, Z. J., & Audretsch, D. B. 1990. *Innovation and Small Firms*. Cambridge, MA: MIT Press.
Aldrich, H. E. 2012. The emergence of entrepreneurship as an academic field: A personal essay on institutional entrepreneurship. *Research Policy*, 41(7): 1240–1248.
Aldrich, H. E., & Baker, T. 1997. Blinded by the cites? Has there been progress in the entrepreneurship field? In D. Sexton, & R. Smilor (Eds.), *Entrepreneurship 2000*: 377–400. Chicago, IL: Upstart Publishing Company.
Barney, J. B., & Ouchi, W. G. 1986. *Organizational Economics*. San Francisco, CA: Jossey-Bass.
Bergmann, H., Mueller, S., & Schrettle, T. 2014. The use of global entrepreneurship monitor data in academic research: A critical inventory and future potentials. *International Journal of Entrepreneurial Venturing*, 6(3): 242–276.
Birch, D. L. 1979. *The Job Generating Process, Final Report on Economic Development Administration*. Cambridge, MA: MIT Program on Neighborhood and Regional Change.
Birch, D. L. 1987. *Job Creation in America: How the Smallest Companies Put the Most People to Work*. New York: The Free Press.

Butani, J., Clayton, R. L., Kapani, V., Spletzer, J. R., Talan, D. M., & Werking, G. S. J. 2005. Business Employment Dynamics:Tabulations by Employer Size. US Bureau of Labor Statistics, Working Paper 385.

Chandler, G. N., Honig, B., & Wiklund, J. 2005. Antecedents, moderators and performance consequences of membership change in new venture teams. *Journal of Business Venturing*, 20: 705–725.

Chandler, G. N., McKelvie, A., & Davidsson, P. 2009. Asset specificity and behavioral uncertainty as moderators of the sales growth – Employment growth relationship in emerging ventures. *Journal of Business Venturing*, 24(4): 373–387.

Cooper, A. C., Gimeno-Gascon, F. J., & Woo, C. Y. 1994. Initial human and financial capital as predictors of new venture performance. *Journal of Business Venturing*, 9(5): 371–395.

Crawford, G. C., Aguinis, H., Lichtenstein, B., Davidsson, P., & McKelvey, B. 2015. Power law distributions in entrepreneurship: Implications for theory and research. *Journal of Business Venturing*, 30(5), 696–713.

Criscuolo C., Gal, P. N., & Menon, C. 2014. The dynamics of employment growth: New evidence from 18 countries, OECD Science, Technology and Industry Policy Papers No 14.

Crump, M.E.S, Abbey, A., & Zu, X. 2009. Rankings of top entrepreneurship researchers and affiliations: 1995 through 2006. Paper presented at the Academy of Management Annual Meeting, Chicago.

Davidsson, P. 1986. *Tillväxt i små företag: en pilotstudie om tillväxtvilja och tillväxtförutsättningar i små företag* (Small Firm Growth: A Pilot Study on Growth Willingness and Opportunity for Growth in Small Firms). Stockholm: Stockholm School of Economics.

Davidsson, P. 1989a. *Continued Entrepreneurship and Small Firm Growth*. Doctoral dissertation. Stockholm: Stockholm School of Economics.

Davidsson, P. 1989b. Entrepreneurship – and after? A study of growth willingness in small firms. *Journal of Business Venturing*, 4(3): 211–226.

Davidsson, P. 1991. Continued entrepreneurship: Ability, need, and opportunity as determinants of small firm growth. *Journal of Business Venturing*, 6(6): 405–429.

Davidsson, P. 1995. Culture, structure and regional levels of entrepreneurship. *Entrepreneurship & Regional Development*, 7: 41–62.

Davidsson, P. 1996. Methodological Concerns in the Estimation of Job Creation in Different Firm Size Classes. Working Paper, Jönköping International Business School. Available for the author.

Davidsson, P. 2003. The domain of entrepreneurship research: Some suggestions. In J. Katz, & D. Shepherd (Eds.), *Cognitive Approaches to Entrepreneurship Research*, Vol. 6: 315–372. Oxford, UK: Elsevier/JAI Press.

Davidsson, P. 2004. *Researching Entrepreneurship*. New York: Springer.

Davidsson, P. 2005a. Entrepreneurial growth. In M. A. Hitt, & R. D. Ireland (Eds.), *Entrepreneurship*, (2 ed.), Vol. III: 80–82. Maden, MA: Blackwell.

Davidsson, P. 2005b. Paul Davidson Reynolds: Entrepreneurship research innovator, coordinator and disseminator. *Small Business Economics*, 24(4): 351–358.

Davidsson, P. 2006. Nascent entrepreneurship: Empirical studies and developments. *Foundations and Trends in Entrepreneurship*, 2(1): 1–76.

Davidsson, P. 2013. Some reflection on research 'Schools' and geographies. *Entrepreneurship & Regional Development*, 25(1–2): 100–110.

Davidsson, P. 2015. Entrepreneurial opportunities and the entrepreneurship nexus: A re-conceptualization. *Journal of Business Venturing*, 30(5), 674–695.

Davidsson, P. 2016. *Researching Entrepreneurship: Conceptualization and Design*, (2 ed.). New York: Springer.

Davidsson, P., Achtenhagen, L., & Naldi, L. 2010. Small firm growth. *Foundations and Trends in Entrepreneurship*, 6(2): 69–166.

Davidsson, P., & Delmar, F. 2001. Les entreprises à forte croissance et leur contribution à l'emploi: le cas de la Suède 1987–1996. *Revue Internationale PME*, 14(3–4): 164–187.

Davidsson, P., & Delmar, F. 2006. High-growth firms and their contribution to employment: The case of Sweden 1987–96. In P. Davidsson, F. Delmar, & J. Wiklund (Eds.), *Entrepreneurship and the Growth of Firms*: 156–178. Cheltenham, UK: Elgar.

Davidsson, P., Delmar, F., & Wiklund, J. 2002. Entrepreneurship as growth; growth as entrepreneurship. In M. A. Hitt, R. D. Ireland, S. M. Camp, & D. L. Sexton (Eds.), *Strategic Entrepreneurship: Creating a New Mindset*: 328–342. Oxford, UK: Blackwell.

Davidsson, P., & Gordon, S. R. 2012. Panel studies of new venture creation: A methods-focused review and suggestions for future research. *Small Business Economics*, 39(4): 853–876.

Davidsson, P., & Gordon, S. R. 2015. Much ado about nothing? The surprising persistence of nascent entrepreneurs through macroeconomic crisis. *Entrepreneurship Theory and Practice*. DOI: 10.1111/etap.12152.

Davidsson, P., & Honig, B. 2003. The role of social and human capital among nascent entrepreneurs. *Journal of Business Venturing*, 18(3): 301–331.

Davidsson, P., Lindmark, L., & Olofsson, C. 1994a. *Dynamiken i svenskt näringsliv (Business Dynamics in Sweden)*. Lund, Sweden: Studentlitteratur.

Davidsson, P., Lindmark, L., & Olofsson, C. 1994b. New firm formation and regional development in Sweden. *Regional Studies*, 28: 395–410.

Davidsson, P., Lindmark, L., & Olofsson, C. 1996. *Näringslivsdynamik under 90-talet (Business Dynamics in the 90s)*. Stockholm: NUTEK.

Davidsson, P., Lindmark, L., & Olofsson, C. 1998a. The extent of overestimation of small firm job creation: An empirical examination of the 'regression bias'. *Small Business Economics*, 10: 87–100.

Davidsson, P., Lindmark, L., & Olofsson, C. 1998b. Smallness, newness and regional development. *Swedish Journal of Agricultural Research*, 28(1): 57–71.

Davidsson, P., & Steffens, P. 2011. Comprehensive Australian Study of Entrepreneurial Emergence (CAUSEE): Project presentation and early results. In P. D. Reynolds, & R. T. Curtin (Eds.), *New Business Creation*: 27–51. New York: Springer.

Davidsson, P., Steffens, P., & Fitzsimmons, J. 2009. Growing profitable or growing from profits: Putting the horse in front of the cart? *Journal of Business Venturing*, 24(4): 388–406.

Davidsson, P., Steffens, P., Gordon, S., & Reynolds, P. D. 2008. Anatomy of New Business Activity in Australia: Some Early Observations from the CAUSEE Project. Brisbane: QUT Business School. Available at: eprints.qut.edu.au/archive/00013613.

Davidsson, P., & Wiklund, J. 1997. Values, beliefs and regional variations in new firm formation rates. *Journal of Economic Psychology*, 18: 179–199.

Davidsson, P., & Wiklund, J. 2000. Conceptual and empirical challenges in the study of firm growth. In D. Sexton, & H. Landström (Eds.), *The Blackwell Handbook of Entrepreneurship*: 26–44. Oxford, MA: Blackwell Business.

Davidsson, P., & Wiklund, J. 2001. Levels of analysis in entrepreneurship research: Current practice and suggestions for the future. *Entrepreneurship Theory & Practice*, 25(4, Summer): 81–99.

Davis, S. J., Haltiwanger, J., & Schuh, S. 1993. Small Business and Job Creation: Dissecting the Myth and Reassessing the Facts: National Bureau of Economic Research. National Bureau of Economic Research Discussion Paper no. 4492, October 1993.

Davis, S. J., Haltiwanger, J., & Schuh, S. 1996a. *Job Creation and Destruction*. Boston, MA: MIT Press.

Davis, S. J., Haltiwanger, J., & Schuh, S. 1996b. Small business and job creation: Dissecting the myth and reassessing the facts. *Small Business Economics*, 8(4): 297–315.

Decker, R., Haltiwanger, J., Jarmin, R., & Miranda, J. 2014. The role of entrepreneurship in US job creation and economic dynamism. *The Journal of Economic Perspectives*, 28(3), 3–24.

Delmar, F., & Davidsson, P. 2000. Where do they come from? Prevalence and characteristics of nascent entrepreneurs. *Entrepreneurship & Regional Development*, 12: 1–23.

Delmar, F., Davidsson, P., & Gartner, W. 2003. Arriving at the high-growth firm. *Journal of Business Venturing*, 18(2): 189–216.

Delmar, F., McKelvie, A., & Wennberg, K. 2013. Untangling the relationships among growth, profitability and survival in new firms. *Technovation*, 33(8): 276–291.

Delmar, F., & Shane, S. 2003. Does business planning facilitate the development of new ventures? *Strategic Management Journal*, 24: 1165–1185.

Delmar, F., & Shane, S. 2004. Legitimating first: Organizing activities and the survival of new ventures. *Journal of Business Venturing*, 19(3): 385–410.

Delmar, F., & Shane, S. 2006. Does experience matter? The effect of founding team experience on the survival and sales of newly founded ventures. *Strategic Organization*, 4(3): 215–247.

Delmar, F., & Wiklund, J. 2008. The effect of small business managers' growth motivation on firm growth: A longitudinal study. *Entrepreneurship Theory and Practice*, 32(3): 437–457.

de Wit, G., & de Kok, J. 2013. Do small businesses create more jobs? New evidence for Europe. *Small Business Economics*, 42(2), 1–13.

Eckhardt, J. T., & Shane, S. 2010. An update to the individual-opportunity nexus. in Acs, Z., & Audretsch, D. B. (eds), *Handbook of Entrepreneurial Research*, New York/Heidelberg: Springer, chapter 3, 47–76.

Eckhardt, J., Shane, S., & Delmar, F. 2006. Multistage selection and the financing of new ventures. *Management Science*, 52(2): 220–232.

Fornell, C., & Larcker, D. F. 1981. Evaluating structural equation models with unobservable variables and measurement error. *Journal of Marketing Research*, 18: 39–50.

Frid, C. et al. 2016. Publications based on the Panel Study of Entrepreneurial Dynamics. Available at: www.psed.isr.umich.edu/psed/documentation.

Gartner, W. B. 1989. Who is an entrepreneur? is the wrong question. *Entrepreneurship Theory and Practice*, 12: 47–64.

Gartner, W. B. 1990. What are we talking about when we talk about entrepreneurship? *Journal of Business Venturing*, 5(1): 15–28.

Gartner, W. B. 1993. Words lead to deeds: Towards an organizational emergence vocabulary. *Journal of Business Venturing*, 8: 231–239.

Gartner, W. B., Shaver, K. G., Carter, N. M., & Reynolds, P. D. 2004. *Handbook of Entrepreneurial Dynamics: The Process of Business Creation*. Thousand Oaks, CA: Sage.

Gimeno, J., Folta, T. B., Cooper, A. C., & Woo, C. Y. 1997. Survival of the fittest? Entrepreneurial human capital and the persistence of underperforming firms. *Administrative Science Quarterly*, 42: 750–783.

Haltiwanger, J., Jarmin, R. S., & Miranda, J. 2013. Who creates jobs? Small versus large versus young. *Review of Economics and Statistics*, 95(2): 347–361.

Hambrick, D. C. 2007. The field of management's devotion to theory: Too much of a good thing? *Academy of Management Journal*, 50(6): 1346–1352.

Hellerstedt, K. 2009. *The Composition of New Venture Teams: Its Dynamics and Consequences*. Doctoral dissertation. Jönköping, Sweden: Jönköping, International Business School.

Honig, B., & Karlsson, T. 2004. Institutional forces and the written business plan. *Journal of Management*, 30(1): 29–48.

Katona, G. 1975. *Psychological Economics*. New York: Elsevier.

Katz, J., & Gartner, W. B. 1988. Properties of emerging organizations. *Academy of Management Review*, 13(3): 429–441.

Kim, P. H., Longest, K. C., & Lippmann, S. 2014. The tortoise versus the hare: Progress and business viability differences between conventional and leisure-based founders. *Journal of Business Venturing*, http://dx.doi.org/10.1016/j.jbusvent.2014.02.005.

Kirzner, I. M. 1973. *Competition and Entrepreneurship*. Chicago, IL: University of Chicago Press.

Lee, S. 2014. The relationship between growth and profit: Evidence from firm-level panel data. *Structural Change and Economic Dynamics*, 28: 1–11.

Locke, E. A. 2007. The case for inductive theory building. *Journal of Management*, 33(6): 867–890.

Locke, E. A., & Latham, G. P. 2002. Building a practically useful theory of goal setting and task motivation: A 35-year odyssey. *American Psychologist*, 57(9): 705.

Lockett, A., Wiklund, J., Davidsson, P., & Girma, S. 2011. Organic and acquisitive growth: Re-examining, testing and extending penrose's growth theory. *Journal of Management Studies*, 48(1): 48–74.

McClelland, D. C. 1961. *The Achieving Society*. Princeton, NJ: Van Nostrand.

McKelvie, A., & Wiklund, J. 2010. Advancing firm growth research: A focus on growth mode instead of growth rate. *Entrepreneurship Theory and Practice*, 34(2): 261–288.

McMullen, J. S., & Dimov, D. 2013. Time and the entrepreneurial journey: The problems and promise of studying entrepreneurship as a process. *Journal of Management Studies*, 50(8): 1481–1512.

McMullen, J. S., & Shepherd, D. 2006. Entrepreneurial action and the role of uncertainty in the theory of the entrepreneur. *Academy of Management Review*, 31(1): 132–152.

Meyer, M., Libaers, D., Thijs, B., Grant, K., Glänzel, W., & Debackere, K. 2012. Origin and emergence of entrepreneurship as a research field. *Scientometrics*, 98(1)1–13.

Mitchell, R. K. 2011. Increasing returns and the domain of entrepreneurship research. *Entrepreneurship Theory and Practice*, 35(4): 615–629.

Naldi, L., & Davidsson, P. 2014. Entrepreneurial growth: The role of international knowledge acquisition as moderated by firm age. *Journal of Business Venturing*, 29(5): 687–703.

Obschonka, M., Stuetzer, M., Audretsch, D. B., Rentfrow, P. J., Potter, J., & Gosling, S. D. 2015a. Macro-psychological Factors Predict Regional Economic Resilience during a Major Economic Crisis. *Social Psychological and Personality Science*, DOI:10.1177/1948550615608402.

Obschonka, M., Stuetzer, M., Gosling, S. D., Rentfrow, P. J., Lamb, M. E., Potter, J., & Audretsch, D. B. 2015b. Entrepreneurial regions: Do macro-psychological cultural characteristics of regions help solve the "Knowledge Paradox" of economics? *PLoS One*, 10(6): e0129332.

Picot, G., & Dupuy, R. 1998. Job creation by company size class: The magnitude, concentration and persistence of job gains and losses in Canada. *Small Business Economics*, 10(2): 117–139.

Reynolds, P. D. 1999. Creative destruction: Source or symptom of economic growth. In Z. J. Acs, B. Carlsson, & K. Karlsson (Eds.), *Entrepreneurship, Small and Medium-sized Firms and the Macroeconomy*: 97–136. Cambridge: Cambridge University Press.

Reynolds, P. D. 2007. New firm creation in the US: A PSED overview. *Foundations and Trends in Entrepreneurship*, 3(1): 1–151.

Reynolds, P. D., Carter, N. M., Gartner, W. B., & Greene, P. G. 2004. The prevalence of nascent entrepreneurs in the United States: Evidence from the Panel Study of Entrepreneurial Dynamics. *Small Business Economics*, 23(4): 263–284.

Reynolds, P. D., & Curtin, R. T. 2008. Business creation in the United States: Panel study of Entrepreneurial Dynamics II initial assessment. *Foundations and Trends in Entrepreneurship*, 4(3), 155–307.

Reynolds, P. D., & Miller, B. 1992. New firm gestation: Conception, birth and implications for research. *Journal of Business Venturing*, 7: 405–417.

Reynolds, P. D., Storey, D. J., & Westhead, P. 1994. Cross-national comparisons of the variation in new firm formation rates. *Regional Studies*, 28(4): 443–456.

Reynolds, P. D., & White, S. B. 1992. Finding the nascent entrepreneur: Network sampling and entrepreneurship gestation. In N. C. Churchill, S. Birley, W. D. Bygrave, C. Wahlbin, & W. E. J. Wetzel (Eds.), *Frontiers of Entrepreneurship Research 1992*: 199–208. Wellesley, MA: Babson College.

Reynolds, P. D., & White, S. B. 1997. *The Entrepreneurial Process: Economic Growth, Men, Women, and Minorities.* Westport: CT: Quorum Books.

Ross, L. 1977. The intuitive psychologist and his shortcomings: Distortions in the attribution process. In L. Berkowitz (Ed.), *Advances in Experimental Social Psychology*, Vol. 10: 173–240. Orlando, FL: Academic Press.

Ruist, E. 1990. *Modellbygge för empirisk analys: att se vad som sker i det som synes ske (Model building for Empirical Analysis: To See What Is Happening in What Appears to Be Happening).* Lund: Studentlitteratur.

Samuelsson, M., & Davidsson, P. 2009. Does venture opportunity variation matter? Investigating systematic process differences between innovative and imitative new ventures. *Small Business Economics*, 33(2): 229–255.

Sapienza, H. J., Korsgaard, M. A., & Forbes, D. P. 2003. The self-determination motive and entrepreneurs' choice of financing. In J. Katz, & D. Shepherd (Eds.), *Cognitive Approaches to Entrepreneurship Research: Advances in Entrepreneurship, Firm Emergence, and Growth*, Vol. 6: 107–140. Oxford, UK: Elsevier/JAI Press.

Senyard, J., Baker, T., Steffens, P., & Davidsson, P. 2014. Bricolage as a path to innovativeness for resource-constrained new firms. *Journal of Product Innovation Management*, 31(2): 211–230.

Shane, S. 2012. Reflections on the 2010 AMR Decade Award: Delivering on the promise of entrepreneurship as a field of research. *The Academy of Management Review*, 37(1): 10–20.

Shane, S., & Delmar, F. 2004. Planning for the market: Business planning before marketing and the continuation of organizing efforts. *Journal of Business Venturing*, 19: 767–785.

Shane, S., & Venkataraman, S. 2000. The promise of entrepreneurship as a field of research. *Academy of Management Review*, 25(1): 217–226.

Shepherd, D., & Wiklund, J. 2009. Are we comparing apples with apples or apples with oranges? Appropriateness of knowledge accumulation across growth studies. *Entrepreneurship Theory and Practice*, 33(1): 105–123.

Short, J. C., Ketchen Jr, D. J., Shook, C. L., & Ireland, R. D. 2010. The concept of "Opportunity" in entrepreneurship research: Past accomplishments and future challenges. *Journal of Management*, 36(1): 40–65.

Storey, D. J. 1994. *Understanding the Small Business Sector.* London: Routledge.

Suddaby, R. 2010. Editor's comments: Construct clarity in theories of management and organization. *The Academy of Management Review*, 35(3): 346–357.

Teixeira, A. A. C. 2011. Mapping the (in) visible college (s) in the field of entrepreneurship. *Scientometrics*, 89(1): 1–36.

Venkataraman, S. (1997). The distinctive domain of entrepreneurship research. *Advances in Entrepreneurship, Firm Emergence and Growth*, 3(1): 119–138.

Wennberg, K., Wiklund, J., DeTienne, D. R., & Cardon, M. S. 2010. Reconceptualizing entrepreneurial exit: Divergent exit routes and their drivers. *Journal of Business Venturing*, 25(4): 361–375.

Wiklund, J., Davidsson, P., & Delmar, F. 2003. What do they think and feel about growth? An expectancy-value approach to small business managers' attitudes towards growth. *Entrepreneurship Theory & Practice*, 27(3): 247–269.

Wiklund, J., & Shepherd, D. 2003. Aspiring for, and achieving growth: The moderating role of resources and opportunities. *Journal of Management Studies*, 40(8): 1911–1941.

Witte, F. C. 2014. *When Employees Leap to Self-Employment: Do Business Ideas, Occupations and Policy Matter?* Doctoral dissertation. Lund: Lund University.

9

Finding myself staring at the future

Dimo Dimov

Introduction

Imagine thinking about a theory of something, whereby your thinking process about the some-thing is a very example of the theory you are trying to develop. The image that comes to mind is of Baron Munchausen trying to pull himself out of the water. In a way, it seems that what I have been trying to capture in my mind is myself trying to capture myself in my mind . . .

A theory is a sort of intellectual taming, of containing an object or situation in your mind. As such, an intellectual journey represents an attempt to rise to and stay on top of the subject of inquiry. The goal is to find a firm ground on which to stand and grasp the subject in full view – akin to watching a tiger at the zoo from behind a glass wall. The observer has the power, the subject having fully revealed itself, to distill the essence of the subject in his or her mind. But again, what if your own thinking process is part of the subject of inquiry?

Now imagine this intellectual effort against the constant flow of time. The firm ground is a position somewhere ahead from which you can take in what has happened so far. But you are soon overtaken by the flow of time and find yourself part of the past. Think of trying to take a close-up picture of people running towards you: you run ahead, turn back, shoot; then run ahead again, turn back, and shoot. You have to keep running. And your picture turns 'old' the very moment it is taken.

The process of intellectual distillation is well represented by Piaget's (1950) theory of cogni-tive development, based on an interplay between assimilation and accommodation. The former entails perceiving new objects through existing mental schemas, whereas the latter entails adapt-ing the schema to incorporate ill-fitting objects or situations. This idea forms the basis of experi-ential leaning theory (Kolb, 1984), which also specifies – as part of an overall learning cycle – the way new schemas arise through reflective observation and abstract conceptualization and the way they are put to the test through active experimentation and concrete experience.

The interplay of assimilation and accommodation captures well the engine of my intellectual journey. But its subject of inquiry – entrepreneurial opportunity – has been tricky on two fronts. First, it inevitably involves a person, and there is no a priori reason why that person could not be me. Second, it pertains to the future and, to the extent that the future has not yet happened, the best viewpoint for it is now. And the most accessible *now* is the one in which I am in. As a result, much of the churn of assimilation and accommodation has been contained within myself, steered and intensified through the various experiences of my academic career and visible only through the papers I have written.

Hooked on opportunity

I enrolled in the PhD program at London Business School (LBS) in October 2000. The decision to pursue a PhD degree was sudden, stressful, and exciting all at the same time. I had given no previous thought to becoming an academic, even if the career profile from my MBA study suggested 'college professor' to be one of the suitable realizations. And I was poised on a steep career trajectory in the industry I loved: hospitality. Just eighteen months earlier, at the age of twenty-four, I had become CFO of two Marriott hotels in Budapest, Hungary, and oversaw a business with $25 million turnover, over 400 employees, and over $100 million of serviced debt. Oh, and I had recently met the person who would become my life partner and we were on course to getting married.

I received an email in late January 2000 announcing that LBS was starting a new PhD program in entrepreneurship and looking to recruit the first cohort of students. The context of this was the dot.com boom of the late 1990s where entrepreneurship had become hot and all the talk was about the next economy where none of the old rules applied (e.g., Dow 36,000). The premise of the LBS initiative was an expected surge in demand for entrepreneurship faculty over the following decade. The application deadline was in a week's time.

I was sold on the opportunity, not because of what it would bring, but because of what it would not if I had stayed on the career path that looked familiar and well trodden. When I received the offer letter, my wife and I shared a sense of not wanting to wonder for the rest of our lives what would have happened if I had gone down the PhD route. I faxed in my acceptance from our honeymoon hotel. My farewell present from Marriott – a picture of the Budapest Marriott Hotel signed by my colleagues – is a constant reminder of the uncertainty that lay ahead, despite the retrospective clarity with which I can look back now.

Coming from a finance background, I wanted to do something related to finance, and venture capital (VC) seemed to be the closest fit. My start of PhD training coincided with the publication of Shane and Venkataraman's *Academy of Management Review* paper "The Promise of Entrepreneurship as a Field of Research", which placed the research focus on the study of opportunities. The paper took center stage in my first PhD seminar in entrepreneurship, taught by Professor Paul Reynolds. Just as the seed of 'opportunity' was being planted in my head, another intellectual imprinting from those early days was Paul Reynolds's consisted retort "Yes, but how are you going to measure it?" to any attempts to go off on a theoretical tangent when discussing the phenomenon of entrepreneurship. Thus, the assimilation–accommodation cycle was set in motion, whereby any emerging conception of opportunity was followed by a search for empirical manifestation.

At the intersection of venture capital and opportunity lay the investment selection decision, which formed my initial focus of inquiry. Against the theoretical background of normative decision theory, early work on venture capital decision making was highlighting the role of intuition and the inability to make decision-making criteria explicit. Taking an opportunity as given, there was a sense that certain characteristics would place some individuals in a superior position to recognize it.

The glasses of experience

Reading Ana Lee Saxenian's *Regional Advantage* (1994) was a key early influence. It was the early story of Silicon Valley that left an imprint, and particularly the origins of Kleiner Perkins, the pre-eminent venture capital firm. I found out that Eugene Kleiner had come from Fairchild

Semiconductor (as his teammates Andy Grove and Gordon Moore had gone off to found Intel) and that Tom Perkins came from Hewlett Packard. This did not square with preconceived notions about the backgrounds of venture capitalists and certainly not with my observations of the decision-making processes inside a venture capital firm. I had attended the investment committee meetings of a London VC firm. The idea that experience shapes what we see was born and was to take shape as part of my PhD dissertation.

The quest for the intellectual underpinning of this idea led me to experiential learning theory (Kolb, 1984) and its central idea of learning as the transformation of experience. I read everything I could about experiential learning theory and kept coming to Kolb's seminal book for missed insights. Learning style emerged as a construct that could differentiate among individuals on the basis of their different patterns of experience and thus different ways of grasping and transforming new experience.

In search for some sort of empirical validation, I started looked at the background profiles of venture capital partners. As I captured this information in a data set, I tallied this with the firms' investment activity and performance extracted from the VentureXpert database. The result was a simple data set that enabled me to explore the relationship between background experience and investment performance. I presented the paper at my first conference, the 2002 Babson conference at the University of Colorado, where I also participated in the doctoral consortium.

Dean Shepherd was one of the consortium facilitators, and I was familiar with his work on venture capital decision making at the time. After some productive discussion at the consortium, I sent Dean the draft paper for feedback, and we started working on it together to develop it for publication. This eventually became the 2005 *Journal of Business Venturing* piece "Human Capital Theory and Venture Capital Firms" (Dimov and Shepherd, 2005) from which two main insights came out. The first was that there was more to human capital than simple proxies (as used in economics); its qualitative composition mattered. The second was that maximizing success and minimizing failure were distinct forms of success, each linked to distinct backgrounds and experiences. One set of factors was associated with more successful exits (IPOs or "Home Runs") and another with fewer failures (bankruptcies or "Strike Outs"). These threads would be picked up and developed in later work.

I viewed the investment selection by venture capitalists as a form of opportunity recognition. Such recognition was second-order in nature, that is, it pertained to opportunities already recognized by entrepreneurs presenting them. Thus, it was logical to extend the PhD inquiry and its emerging theoretical framework to the first-order recognition, that is, by the entrepreneurs themselves. In including the entrepreneur's side of opportunity, the idea was that entrepreneurs and investors look at different sides of the same thing: entrepreneurs recognize them, whereas investors select them. The next step was to develop experiments that would capture how differences in experience and learning styles would translate into differences in opportunity recognition. But how was opportunity recognition to be measured?

From insight to intention

This question was a crucial aspect of the research design. But it was also more than an empirical issue since any measure reflected implicit assumptions about the nature of opportunities and the nature of recognition. Without facing these assumptions head on, there was no firm ground to stand on. It was at that time that John Butler invited me to contribute a chapter on opportunities to a book, *Research in Entrepreneurship in Management* (Dimov, 2004). This offered a disciplining chance to conduct a critical review of prior literature on entrepreneurial opportunities and flesh out the formal premises for development of the topic. These emerged from the need to explain the intuition that what individuals see as opportunities is rather idiosyncratic, that the same individual would see different things in a different context, and that different individuals would see different things in the same context.

The first premise pertained to clarifying the nature of opportunities at the same level of analysis as the factors seeking to explain opportunity recognition, that is, the individual prospective entrepreneur. At that level, it is impossible to separate an opportunity and its recognition. Equally, some sort of enactment is necessary to maintain a distinction from pure ideas or imagined possibilities. The second premise related to making the nature of the context more explicit, particularly in terms of the information it conveys to prospective entrepreneurs. The third premise related to specifying the nature of individual differences that can not only account for making different sense of the same information, but also evolve with experience.

These ideas were put together in the first study as part of my dissertation, an early version of which was presented at the Babson Conference in 2003 (Dimov, 2003). The paper introduced the ideas of opportunity recognition as an outcome of an experiential learning process and of representing the contexts in which it occurs in terms of different epistemological structures or logical leaps from informational premises to insights/hypotheses. The early results were very encouraging in that they highlighted a person–situation interaction. This idea was developed further in the paper "From Opportunity Insight to Opportunity Intention" published in *Entrepreneurship Theory and Practice* (Dimov, 2007a). The concept of "person–situation learning match" captured the person-situation and emerged as a regulator of the relationship between prior knowledge and opportunity intention. This paper also helped draw a distinction between opportunity insight and opportunity intention (i.e., pure vs. enacted idea), as well as between entrepreneurial intention and opportunity intention (i.e., the general intention to pursue opportunities vs. the intention to pursue a specific opportunity).

Beyond single person, single insight

My PhD dissertation had zoomed in on the momentary nature of opportunity recognition, whereby one's prior experience blends with situational circumstances to produce a sense of perceived possibility and to propel some action towards it. Having completed the PhD, I started looking to unclasp the boundary conditions that had been necessary for isolating and taking a close look at that momentary transformation. At the same time, I took my first faculty job at the Instituto de Empresa (now the IE Business School) in Madrid and started preparing to teach entrepreneurship in its top-ranked MBA program. As entrepreneurship emerged as one of the distinguishing features of the program, there was an opportunity – upon joining the IE Business School – to redesign its entrepreneurship curriculum. Thus, the first of three courses in this area focused on the generation and development of entrepreneurial opportunities.

The most important boundary condition to open up was the gateway to thereafter, that is, what happens after opportunity recognition and early action. Although the typical account of a great entrepreneurial story would suggest that 'the rest is history', there is not such sense of history making when the gate of time is open. This point was vividly made in the entrepreneurship classes, where students burst with excitement and confidence when pitching their initial ideas, only to become dejected and frustrated a few weeks later. The initial excitement was undeniable, but so was the eventual dejection. What happened in between was a search for validation of their initial hunches as well as attempts to work around the various setbacks or retreat from dead ends. By the time of the final pitches the ideas inevitably looked different. Not only did they have new or modified elements, but also these elements came from various inputs from third parties as part of the research process.

This empirical reality did not square with the existing conception of opportunity as a single entity, attributed to a particular person and represented as one particular insight. An evolving idea represented a particular challenge for being contained within what had essentially been a static conception. On the one hand, when first articulated, and as long as it compels someone to take some action in its pursuit, an idea cannot be ruled out as being a nonopportunity. But, on the other hand, does this mean it should be considered an opportunity? As soon as action is taken, everything needs to be reassessed in the light of the new information that had been revealed only because of the action. And so on. In other words, as long as action continues to take place, the possibility of opportunity remains alive.

Indulging these thought experiments formed the backbone of another paper published in *Entrepreneurship Theory and Practice* (Dimov, 2007b). The paper was framed around an analogy with the fundament attribution error in psychology, whereby individual factors are overplayed and situational factors downplayed. In this case the situational factors were compressed in 'the rest is history', whereby the only meaningful marker of the entrepreneurial process is often seen as the initial idea and the person behind it. Separating idea from opportunity and placing them at opposite ends of a time continuum shines the light on the process that connects the two. The process is essentially one of development, of keeping the possibility of opportunity alive by working around various situational and social contingencies. Thus, this paper signified a move in thinking about opportunities from instantaneous recognition to gradual, iterative development.

Opportunity confidence and two types of success

The idea of opportunity development as a gradual, iterative process called for revisiting the fate of the original opportunity insight and opportunity intention, that is, they get the process going, but for how long? Keeping the possibility of opportunity alive in the face of various contingencies implies a repeated judgment of whether to go on or abandon the entrepreneurial effort. The interesting question that arose was whether abandoning the effort could be seen as the best decision in certain circumstances. Again, the thought experiments that followed, blended with the personal experience of teaching entrepreneurship, revealed a host of implicit assumptions.

Teaching the case "3M Optical Systems: Managing Corporate Entrepreneurship" brought to the fore the idea of well-intentioned failure. It was the kind of failure that deserves praise and not punishment and that is seen as an essential component of an innovation process, as captured in A. G. Lafley's insightful quote "the key is to fail early, fail cheaply, and don't make the same mistake twice" or in IDEO's slogan "fail fast in order to succeed early" from *The Deep Dive* documentary. These ideas spurred a lot of class debates about how to draw the line between persistence as a virtue and persistence as a folly or between giving up as a weakness and giving up as a wisdom.

The arguments arising from the practicalities of persistence did not square with the academic literature on nascent entrepreneurship, which drew a dichotomous distinction between reaching operating status and abandoning the effort, implicitly treating abandonment as a 'bad' outcome. To the extent that the decision to abandon was based on a reasonable judgment, given how the promise of the original business idea had unfolded, it should be treated more appropriately as optimal rather than 'bad'. But how to distinguish shades of abandonment?

This question drove further reflection and analysis that became the basis of the paper "Nascent Entrepreneurs and Venture Emergence" published in the *Journal of Management Studies* (Dimov, 2010). I had worked with the Panel Study of Entrepreneurial Dynamics (PSED) data set as part of my dissertation. In fact, the very first version of the paper – which bore little resemblance to the one published eventually – came out of the dissertation and aimed to find patterns in the human capital of nascent entrepreneurs that corroborated the person–context interactions established in the earlier study on opportunity intention. The review process quickly steered the paper towards the more meaningful outcome of venture emergence and ruled out that the concept of learning match could be validly operationalized with the PSED data.

With the focus on venture emergence, the aim was to take advantage of the longitudinal nature of the data. This meant recognizing that judgments about the merits of the pursued opportunity could vary across the waves of data collection and that these judgments could be the most proximate explanation for the venturing outcome at each stage. I termed this intermediate judgment 'opportunity confidence' as a way of reflecting its target and of keeping up with the 'opportunity' series of constructs: insight, intention, development, confidence.

The theoretical breakthrough for the paper was to recognize that in the context of uncertainty, things could really go either way in between actions and that at least some of the consequence of actions cannot be known before the actions are undertaken. This suggests that there are two distinct considerations behind a persistence decision: (1) discontinuing the pursuit of opportunities that show no promise and (2) continuing to convert the opportunities that show promise into viable businesses. Empirically, the crucial bit for validating this logic came through demonstrating that the different status descriptions for the venturing efforts (gave up, inactive, active, operating) were indeed ordered in nature, that is, the baseline probabilities of transitioning across categories were different.

The key finding of the paper was that opportunity confidence mediates the effects of entrepreneurial experience and early planning on venture emergence. It demonstrates the endogenous nature of opportunity development – one of gradual resolution of uncertainty – whereby initial assumptions are converted into positive or negative signals. In this regard, the skills and actions that are instrumental for teasing out the initial assumptions enable the entrepreneur to make a more informed judgment down the line, but cannot guarantee that this judgment would be positive. Thus, simply connecting inputs such as human capital and planning to eventual outputs while ignoring the endogenous considerations in between is a weakness in research design. The final reflection of the paper suggests a need to distinguish and more explicitly consider two types of success in entrepreneurship: type I (sticking with the good ideas) and type II (abandoning the bad ones).

Grappling with the unbearable elusiveness

Eight years into studying opportunities I still had not observed one. The closest I had gotten to them were the reactions of the entrepreneurs engaged with them – insight, intention, confidence, as represented in the constructs proposed so far – as well as the overarching sense of the process (i.e., development) in which these reactions are embedded. It was intuitively clear that opportunities were obvious in retrospect but quite opaque and nebulous in prospect. Hence the persistent question of how to study something that cannot be observed, something that had become "unbearably elusive". Two different strands of experience converged into what eventually became the namesake paper in *Entrepreneurship Theory and Practice* that aimed to outline an empirical research program around entrepreneurial opportunities (Dimov, 2011).

The first was the ever-vibrant and stimulating classroom experience. I had moved to the University of Connecticut and started teaching undergraduate classes on opportunity generation and assessment, in which the gist was to work with students to develop opportunities. I was constantly looking for examples to share in class. I identified a company, Chegg, that had recently received first-round venture capital funding. I was portraying it in class as an example of analogical reasoning (Netflix-type rentals for textbooks) and I picked up a CNBC video to demonstrate that transferring insights across domains can be a great starting point. The video was perfect in the sense that it said exactly what I wanted to hear: when asked "Where did you get this idea, text-book rentals?" the Chegg CEO replied, "Well, it is a lot like Netflix, but for college textbooks".

Little did I know that I had fallen into the trap of retrospective clarity. Looking further back into the history of the company proved to be a slippery slope. Various contemporaneous news-paper accounts suggested that the company had gone through different identities in the textbook space: first Craigslist (classified ads), then eBay (online marketplace), then Netflix (rentals). All of a sudden, my classroom story rang very hollow: its retrospective telling of the story had little to do with its prospective construction. This eventually became the opening premise of the paper, but the problem was that it was not clear for a while how the paper was to unfold from there. I had a promising beginning but no real end in sight.

As an aside, the rummaging into the history of Chegg uncovered over 350 Chegg-alike ven-tures in the United States, all student led and all looking to solve the problem of high textbook prices. This reinforced the idea that Chegg was not really very special at its outset, even if it is a very special, billion-dollar unicorn today. The scale and dynamics of the entrepreneurial effort to solve the same overarching problem became the basis of a great (we thought) paper written with David Gras, who was a PhD student at the University of Connecticut at the time, and presented at the Babson conference (Dimov and Gras, 2010). To this day, the paper is still looking for a home and has fallen into obscurity, just like most of the ventures it studied.

The second strand of experience was taking part in the workshop "The Future of Entrepre-neurship Research", organized by Johan Wiklund and Per Davidsson in Sweden in the summer of 2008 and aimed at laying the groundwork for a special issue at *Entrepreneurship Theory and Practice*. My presentation had the mundane title "From Opportunity Formation to Business Creation" and invited a discussion of what to study (empirically). Even today, the transcript of the discussion easily brings back the sense of confusion, lack of consensus, and complexity when trying to explain a realized end from some beginning. There was no clear direction from the workshop, except for sense of a need to look for ideas elsewhere and to revisit the deterministic frame that was implicit as a logic of explanation.

Thus started an intellectual excursion that continues to this day, uncovering thread after thread of new ideas, each putting the notion of opportunity in a new light and taking me away from the comfort zone of my training. Its early markers were evident in the fact that the eventual paper went through three different versions as part of the review process, each with a different title, suggesting different resolution to the problem of "unbearable elusiveness":

1   The unbearable elusiveness of entrepreneurial opportunities: Time to let go?
2   Away from the unbearable elusiveness of entrepreneurial opportunities: A new conversation about emergence and the sociology of markets.
3   Grappling with the unbearable elusiveness of entrepreneurial opportunities.

The Chegg story, as well as other stories, suggested that chance had played a role in how its opportunity had developed. Thinking about the relationship between chance and determinis-tic explanation raised interesting philosophical questions to which, to my surprise, there were already some answers elsewhere. In fact, there was quite a lot of frustration in realizing that what I thought might be an original insight had already been uncovered in the broader academic field. The prospective-retrospective asymmetry was nothing more than a reflection of the one-directional nature of time's arrow. One of the key influences at the time was Anderson's (1972) idea of the "broken symmetry" between levels of analysis and the insight that the ability to reduce something to a simple explanation does not imply an ability to reconstruct it from that explanation. This thread about emergent phenomena would resurface later on. It was not long before I ran into Abbott's paper (1988) "Transcending General Linear Reality" that opened the door to the world of process.

The new ideas were overwhelming and ever expanding but there was also the time pressure of producing a coherent paper. In the end I had to stop reading (albeit for a little while), make sense of what I had read, and synthesize it into the paper. Two main ideas came out. The first was the distinction between formal and substantive conceptions of entrepreneurial behavior. A formal conception, through its basic requirement for an opportunity to be defined exogenously, effectively steps out of the realm of uncertainty and limits the study of opportunity to pure theorizing. In contrast, a substantive conception aims to make sense of how entrepreneurs act in the face of uncertainty and an opportunity represents the lens for doing so.

The second idea was to elaborate on the substantive premises for studying opportunities, namely as happening through ideas, expressed in actions, and instituted in market relationships. For each of these, there is an asymmetry between the ex ante possible and the ex post particular. Accordingly, the research implications outlined the need to apply (1) process explanation to the specific instances of ideas, actions, and relationships observed in a given entrepreneurial journey; and (2) variance explanation for the possibilities in general representations.

The punchline of the paper was perhaps personally the most insightful. It suggested that the process of developing the paper was the epitome of the very process of opportunity development that the paper was trying to capture. Thus, what had seemed "unbearably elusive" for quite a while turned out to be like my shadow – always there but not always noticed.

No time for time

This was the initial title of the paper with Jeff McMullen "Time and the Entrepreneurial Journey" published in the *Journal of Management Studies* (McMullen and Dimov, 2013). At the Academy of Management meeting in Boston in 2012, Jeff and I brainstormed ideas for a paper that could offer a forward-looking perspective for entrepreneurship in the context of the fiftieth anniversary issue of JMS. We settled on reclaiming entrepreneurship as a journey through facilitating process-oriented research, always called for but rarely done. Our both attending the Darden-Lally-Leeds retreat in Boulder, Colorado, in October 2012 enabled us to hash out an outline. The development of the paper presented an opportunity to integrate some of our long-brewing ideas under the constructive editorial guidance of Andrew Corbett.

The paper offers a distillation of the main premises of process explanation, highlighting in particular the distinction between vertical and horizontal partitioning of the observation space. The former "chops" a journey into discrete variables, treating them as replications of an underlying factor and aiming to analyze their patterns of variation and co-variation. This effectively squeezes time out. In contrast, the latter retains the creative force of time by keeping the journey intact as a unit of explanation and acknowledging that everything that transpires in it is part of the same. Having established the need for such holistic grasp of the journey, the paper discusses five key questions related to its nature, boundaries, constituent elements, and permanent essence. It recognizes that although the journey may be driven by the energy and momentum of evolving individual intent, its ultimate realization is part of a broader system with complex behavior. The methodological implications call for understanding that complexity through interdisciplinary collaboration.

The paper also represented a shift in my personal intellectual journey. Grappling with the unbearable elusiveness of opportunities had opened up the gateway to understanding process and its logic. It had been a push away from my comfort zone towards an interdisciplinary space, an effort that continues to the present day in pursuit of various threads uncovered along the way.

In the meantime, I moved from the United States to the United Kingdom, first to Newcastle University and then to the University of Bath.

Where next?

The Innovation Journey by Van de Ven and colleagues (Van de Ven et al., 1999) had been a watershed influence along the way, triggering a cascade of new pursuits. In its conceptual representation of the trajectory of a new venture, it made reference to chaos – as distinct from randomness – as a deterministic yet nonpredictable process. This concept resonated with the inherent open-endedness of the entrepreneurial journey and invited further exploration. It opened up the world of complexity science, which in turn resonated with the idea of moving away from a general linear model of reality. In turn, attending a Professional Development Workshop on using simulation in entrepreneurship research at the 2011 Academy of Management Meeting in San Antonio, organized by Christopher Crawford, revealed the power and distinct, bottom-up logic of computational modelling. Alongside a constant stream of books and papers in this space, I completed a series of online courses: Modelling, Network Analysis, Introduction to Complexity, Nonlinear Dynamics and Chaos and, just recently, Fractals and Scaling. These were driven by a sense of relevance that is gradually beginning to crystallize.

A couple of new ideas have emerged from this so far, set to be developed further. The first is of opportunity as social structure, as outlined in Crawford, Dimov, and McKelvey (2015) in response to continued attempts to perpetuate debates about the ontology of opportunities. An opportunity is perhaps best seen as an emergent phenomenon, consisting of ontologically real components (products, customers, suppliers, etc.) and epistemologically real functional relationships between them. In this sense, the role of the entrepreneur is to weave together the relationships through a multitude of actions and interactions. The logic of explanation falls within the broader realm of generative process theory in sociology, whereby interactions give rise to social forms (Cederman, 2005).

The second idea is that the focal engine of the process that generates the social structure of opportunity is recursive action, that is, repeated action in which the outcome of one step becomes the input to the next. The underlying rules link positional information to action (Drazin and Sandelands, 1992). The central idea of chaos theory is that simple, deterministic rules, when applied recursively, can lead to nonpredictable outcomes that are highly sensitive to initial conditions (May, 1976). In this regard, recursivity is a powerful yet simple mechanism that can open nonlinear paths and generate complex structures. This can be seen as a blindspot in current conceptions of the entrepreneurial process and offers an opportunity to elaborate on the cognitive and affective underpinnings of recursive action (Gregoire et al., 2015).

With all the thinking about opportunity, one simple question has remained unanswered: how to study the future? This entails looking forward, together with the entrepreneur, rather than backward, to make sense of what she or he has done. To the extent that our goal is to describe and explain, we have to wait for something to happen before deploying analysis. But whether this is the only goal has underpinned the latest strand of thought, emerging from the idea of entrepreneurship as science of the artificial. It was triggered by Selden and Fletcher's (2015) discussion of the creation of artifacts as the essence of an entrepreneurial journey; I was the handling editor of the paper at the *Journal of Business Venturing*. It connected to the earlier writings by Sarasvathy (2003) on the topic and led to being energized by Simon's (1969) distinction of natural and artificial phenomena: the former are defined by necessity and the latter by contingency, molded by goals and purposes.

The ideas arising from this are still being shaped, but they all center on a core premise: the past is natural, the future artificial. As such, entrepreneurship is both a natural and an artificial phenomenon, depending on whether one looks back or forward. Design is about looking forward with some purpose. It represents a distinct mode of research (Romme, 2003), whereby the beacon of opportunity poses the question of what to do.

In the spirit of the intellectual quest described in this chapter, it would be inappropriate to offer any conclusion. I have just organized these thoughts into a new paper, aptly named "Towards a Design Science of Entrepreneurship" (Dimov, 2016).

References

Abbott, A. 1988. Transcending general linear reality. Sociological Theory, 6(2); 169–186.

Anderson, P.W. 1972. More is different. Science, 177(4047): 393–396.

Cederman, L.E. 2005. Computational models of social forms: Advancing generative process theory. American Journal of Sociology, 110(4): 864–893.

Crawford, G.C., Dimov, D. and McKelvey, B. 2015. Realism, empiricism, and fetishism in the study of entrepreneurship. Journal of Management Inquiry, 25: 168–170.

Dimov, D. 2004. The individuality of opportunity identification: A critical review and extension. In J. Butler (Ed.) Research in Entrepreneurship and Management, Vol. 4: Opportunity Identification and Entrepreneurial Behavior: 135–161. Greenwich, CT: Information Age Publishing.

Dimov, D. 2007a. From opportunity insight to opportunity intention: The importance of person–situation learning match. Entrepreneurship Theory & Practice, 31(4): 561–583.

Dimov, D. 2007b. Beyond the single person, single insight attribution in understanding entrepreneurial opportunities. Entrepreneurship Theory & Practice, 31(5): 713–731.

Dimov, D. 2010. Nascent entrepreneurs and venture emergence: Opportunity confidence, human capital, and early planning. Journal of Management Studies, 47(6): 1123–1153.

Dimov, D. 2011. Grappling with the unbearable elusiveness of entrepreneurial opportunities. Entrepreneurship Theory & Practice, 35(1): 57–81.

Dimov, D. 2016. Towards a design science of entrepreneurship. In A.C. Corbett and J.A. Katz (Eds.) Advances in Entrepreneurship, Firm Emergence and Growth, Vol. 18: Models of Start-up Thinking and Action: in press. Bingley, UK: Emerald Insight.

Dimov, D. and Gras, D. 2010. The emergence and evolution of an opportunity: A historical analysis. (Summary). Frontiers of Entrepreneurship Research, 30(15): Article 11.

Dimov, D. and Shepherd, D.A. 2005. Human capital theory and venture capital firms: Exploring 'home runs' and 'strike outs'. Journal of Business Venturing, 20: 1–21.

Dimov, D. P. 2003. The nexus of individual and opportunity: Opportunity recognition as a learning process. Frontiers of Entrepreneurship Research, 23(16): Article 2.

Drazin, R. and Sandelands, L. 1992. Autogenesis: A perspective on the process of organizing. Organization Science, 3(2): 231–249.

Grégoire, D.A., Cornelissen, J., Dimov, D. and Van Burg, E. 2015. The mind in the middle: Taking stock of affect and cognition research in entrepreneurship. International Journal of Management Reviews, 17: 125–142.

Kolb, D. A. 1984. Experiential Learning: Experience as The Source of Learning and Development. Englewood Cliffs, NJ: Prentice Hall.

McMullen, J.S. and Dimov, D. 2013. Time and the entrepreneurial journey: The problems and promise of studying entrepreneurship as a process. Journal of Management Studies, 50(8): 1481–1512.

May, R.M. 1976. Simple mathematical models with very complicated dynamics. Nature, 261: 459–467.

Piaget, J. 1950. The Psychology of Intelligence. London: Routledge & Kegan Paul (2nd Edition 2001 by Routlege).

Romme, A.G.L. 2003. Making a difference: Organization as design. Organization Science, 14: 558–573.

Sarasvathy, S.D. 2003. Entrepreneurship as a science of the artificial. Journal of Economic Psychology, 24: 203–220.

Selden, P.D. and Fletcher, D.E. 2015. The entrepreneurial journey as an emergent hierarchical system of artifact-creating processes. Journal of Business Venturing, 30(4): 603–615.

Simon, H. A. (1969/1996). The Sciences of the Artificial (first edition published in 1969; third edition in 1996). Cambridge, MA: MIT Press.

Van de Ven, A. H., Polley, D. E., Garud, R. and Venkataraman, S. (1999). The Innovation Journey. New York: Oxford University Press.

10

Judgement, the theory of the firm, and the economics of institutions

My contributions to the entrepreneurship field

Nicolai N. Foss

Introduction: the reluctant entrepreneurship scholar

There are obvious learning economies to an organization of science where fields are relatively narrow and self-contained and identities are strong. However, there is also the danger that important opportunities for cross-fertilization between fields are, highly apropos, not imagined and realized. I have never considered myself an entrepreneurship scholar per se. My identity has rather been lying within the field of economics and, within management research, within the strategy and organization fields. In fact, my interest in entrepreneurship has mainly involved exploring relations between entrepreneurship and neighboring and related fields, such as the theory of the firm and the economics of institutions, and has derived from a long-standing interest in Austrian economics.

And yet, after being invited by David Audretsch and Erik Lehman to contribute to the present chapter, I realized that a considerable part of my academic output can be clearly related to, and sometimes placed squarely within, entrepreneurship research. Moreover, it may even be that my work on entrepreneurship forms a reasonably coherent, distinct perspective; in any case, the following is written on the basis of the conjecture that this is in fact the case. Apparently, and to paraphrase a noted Danish philosopher, I have apparently been living my life as an entrepreneurship scholar forwards, and must now try to understand it backwards. Thus, what follows is an chapter in reconstruction.

Personal background[1]

My interest in entrepreneurship as a phenomenon and a field has been heavily shaped by my educational background and my other research interests. I studied economics at the University of Copenhagen from 1983 to 1989. Economics at the university in those days were split between macro-oriented empiricists and mathematical, general equilibrium theorists, a distinction, even schism, that is (luckily) less strongly felt in contemporary economics. Only one or two professors did applied price theory, so the use of economics as a tool to make sense of the choices people make in the real world and how these choices aggregate —my main motivation for studying economics —was not stressed. The implications of the missing linkages between these areas were very clear in the teaching that students were exposed to (although it is nothing like the disciplinary diversity that management students are exposed to): Things didn't really seem to connect – and no one believed the "neoclassical synthesis" sugar-coating anyway – so students made early choices to focus on either "micro" or "macro."

The majority of the teaching in the bachelor part of the economics program centred on macro-issues, and I confess to finding the macro-drill that we were exposed to highly demotivating. Things began to change when I realized in the second year of my economics study that there were strong alternatives to the Keynesian macroeconomics and macro-econometric modelling focus of so much of the teaching. In particular, the methodological essays of Robert Lucas (1977, 1980) and Milton Friedman's Presidential Address to the American Economic Association (Friedman, 1968) captured my interest, no doubt because they were uniformly bashed by my macro professors.

At one of my raids at the Economics Department library, I picked up an old volume with the title, *The Fallacy of the New Economics* (Hazlitt, 1959). It turned out to be an energetic (though over-the-top) smashing of the Keynesian revolution. When researching the author, I found out that he had been associated with an "Austrian School of Economics." At about the same time I was reading Axel Leijonhufvud's brilliant *On Keynesian Economics and the Economics of Keynes* (1968), a very different attempt (and one with which I felt more sympathetic) to furnish microfoundations for macroeconomics than new classical macroeconomics. That book contained references to a "Friedrich Hayek," and when checking up on that name I again encountered the enigmatic "Austrian School."

This led, of course, to the discovery of the writings of Hayek, as well as Mises, Kirzner, Lachmann, and other modern Austrians. Kirzner's (1973) book, *Competition and Entrepreneurship*, and Hayek's (1948) essay collection, *Individualism and Economic Order*, were the first two Austrian books I read, both profoundly shaping my perspective. Lachmann's thinking was a strong influence also (Lachmann, 1956, 1986), and his work led me to the kindred work of George Shackle (Shackle, 1972). These two so-called "radical subjectivists" strongly stressed that although the future is unknowable, it is not unimaginable. However, because the future is the product of creative human choice, the set of possible outcomes of any decision that reaches nontrivially into the future cannot be entirely identified, and putting probabilities on outcomes is meaningless. Shackle in particular published work after work exploring and meditating upon this theme, arguing the case that the fundamental creativity of the human mind cannot easily be aligned with mainstream economics. Although I found Shackle's work intoxicating, I also realized its potentially nihilistic implications, because social regularities do not seem to exist in Shackle's "kaleidic society" which can at any moment be upset by the results of creative (entrepreneurial) imagination. It seemed to me that Lachmann gave an answer that Shackle didn't, namely that societal institutions added stability and predictability and put bounds, as it were, on expectations and imaginations (Foss & Gazarelli, 2007). Thus, I have always disagreed with the critique from some quarters in Austrian economics that Lachmann was a "veteran nihilist" whose theorizing was destructive of economics.

I did not become a die-hard Austrian (I never have been; I have usually thought of myself as a fellow traveller), but I found, and continue to find, the basic Austrian vision congenial and inspiring. However, I fundamentally like and admire so-called mainstream economics, and although disequilibrium, process, entrepreneurship, capital heterogeneity, and the subjectivism of knowledge and expectations continue to be soft spots in the mainstream corpus, mainstream economics seems to me to make very serious and sustained attempts at coming to grips with the kinds of issues that have been central to the Austrians.[2] I decided to write my master thesis, completed in late 1988, on the business cycle theory of Hayek (e.g., Hayek, 1931; some results from the thesis were published as Foss, 1995).

Moving to the Copenhagen Business School (CBS) in 1989, I was enthused to recognize that many of the ideas that I associated with the Austrians, such as privately held knowledge, dynamics, impediments to exchange, and rational agents circumventing those impediments by developing institutions and engaging in entrepreneurial acts, were part and parcel of the business school curriculum. Although entrepreneurship was not taught at CBS at that time, much of the theorizing in strategy, particularly ideas on resources and capabilities, resonated with a basic Austrian outlook (see Jacobson (1992) for this point). Thus, I became a huge fan of the work of "post-Marshallian" economists such as Edith Penrose (1959), George Richardson (1960, 1972), and Brian Loasby (1976), as well as of evolutionary economists Nelson and Winter (1982) (Foss, 1996c).

As is well known, Penrose supplied fundamental insights in firm-specific capabilities that in her theorizing formed the basis of a disequilibrium theory of growth through related diversification.(In contrast, she did not anticipate the resource-based analysis of sustained competitive advantage although she is often cited to that effect; see Foss, 2000). However, at the foundation of her theory lay a conceptualization of the top management team as fundamentally entrepreneurial, imagining the firm's "productive opportunity set" on the basis of an intimate knowledge of which services could be extracted from the firm's resource bundle. Penrose's ideas formed a very important input into the work of George Richardson, who combined her ideas with those of Hayek to build pioneering insight into how firm-level capabilities have implications for firm organization (Foss, 1994a, 1995; Foss & Loasby, 1998). Unfortunately, the work of Richardson, unlike that of Penrose, is not much known among management scholars, including entrepreneurship scholars. Finally, the highly original and eclectic work of Brian Loasby, which creatively tied many of the previous sources together, was a huge inspiration to me.

My PhD thesis, submitted in 1992, was essentially an application of capabilities and transaction cost economics to the issue of the organization of technological innovation, an undertaking that was heavily inspired by the work of David Teece (1986) and Richard Langlois (1988, 1992). Langlois in particular was a continuing source of inspiration in my early career. He was interested in many of the same issues and writers that interested me and approached these issues with a creative mind and an excellent writing style. Langlois, like Richardson and Loasby before him, has in my opinion not received anything like the recognition and respect he deserves from management scholars, partly because he has preferred to publish in economics rather than in management journals.[3]

Early work

As is usually the case, the research I did for my PhD thesis has very much shaped my subsequent work. My thesis work drew on the industrial economics tradition of post-Marshallians such as Edith Penrose (1959), George Richardson (1972), and Brian Loasby (1976); evolutionary economics in the Nelson and Winter (1982) tradition; and Williamsonian transaction cost economics (Williamson, 1985, 1996), and was essentially six loosely connected thought pieces that, among other things, compared governance and capabilities perspectives on economic organization, discussed Frank Knight's entrepreneurial theory of economic organization (Knight, 1921), and discussed how firm boundaries in the context of technology life-cycle theory. It only contained empirics by way of illustrations. It had plenty methodology and doctrinal history context. In other words, it was a thesis of the kind that would not be allowed nowadays.

However, most of the thesis papers got published (e.g., Foss, 1991, 1993a, 1993b, 1996a, 1996b, 1996c), and a number of these have flag entrepreneurship themes. Thus, one paper argued against the critics of Williamsonian transaction cost economics (e.g., Boudreaux & Holcombe, 1989) that at the heart of transaction cost economics is an ontology that is not so different from that of, for example, Knight, as manifest in the insistence in transaction cost economics on incomplete contracts, bounded rationality, and unexpected contingencies (Foss, 1993a). And yet, Knight's specific insights in economic organization differed from those of the originator of transaction cost economics, namely Ronald Coase (Foss, 1996a; see also Langlois & Cosgel, 1993). A third paper in this stream (Foss, 1993b) argued that capabilities ideas in strategy and evolutionary economics could be extended to the boundaries of the firm by means of ideas on costly knowledge exchange (the paper anticipated arguments later made by, e.g., Alvarez & Barney, 2005, 2007). The argument is that capabilities represent firm-specific knowledge that is costly to transfer and communicate and that economizing with the costs of such transfer and communication shapes the boundaries of the firm.

A somewhat later paper reached back to Kirzner rather than to Knight, applying Kirznerian ideas to business ethics and specifically to assessing the ethical implications of the dominant frameworks in the firm strategy literature. Thus, I contrasted Michael Porter's (1980) framework with resource-based theory (Barney, 1986, 1991). In Porter the basic analytical engine is the familiar monopoly model of the basic microeconomics textbook. Given this starting point, making above-normal profits is tantamount to imposing a deadweight welfare loss on consumers/customers. Thus, profit making has problematic ethical implications. In contrast, the resource-based view does not consider strategic success a matter of curtailing product markets, but of serving customer preferences in the best possible manner and/or driving down costs of production. Moreover, the resource-based view fundamentally has an entrepreneurial mechanism at the center of its theorizing. Thus, above-normal returns can only be enjoyed by firms that purchase resources at a price below their net present value (Barney, 1986). Firms may do so because of luck or because of essentially entrepreneurial superior insight. In turn, the discovery of resources at prices below their net present value (NPV) can be linked to a finders-keepers ethics in the finder (the firm acting on the demand side of the strategic factor market) is entitled to the returns that the resource yields.

My increasing involvement with the resource-based view throughout the 1990s led me to ponder the issue: Where does new resource value come from? Resource-based theory is, in its pure form, a set of conditions that a resource must conform to give rise to sustained competitive advantage. It says little about the creation of strategic resources (those that are high in appropriable value) beyond very general statements about firm-specific knowledge being the source of factor market advantages. However, new resources do emerge and are consciously created by enterprising businessmen; hence, the resource-based view should be complemented with a theory of entrepreneurship.

Three attempts to deliver on this are Foss and Ishikawa (2007), Foss and Foss (2008), and Foss, Klein, Kor and Mahoney (2008). The first paper of the three links theories of search over rugged landscapes (Levinthal, 1997) to entrepreneurship. The idea is that resource (or capital) combinations define the landscape. Entrepreneurs then search for the peak that they think is associated with the highest level of appropriable value creation (this is also discussed in Stieglitz & Foss, 2009). The paper with Klein, Kor, and Mahoney adds Austrian subjectivism to the top-management team level. Thus, the paper unfolds the Penrosian idea of the firm's "productive opportunity set" as a cognitive construct held at the top management team (TMT) level. The final paper with Kirsten Foss also deals with firm-level entrepreneurship, but adds transaction cost and property rights to the mix of capabilities and entrepreneurship ideas. Our key idea is that property rights and transaction costs are key antecedents of the entrepreneurial discovery of opportunities. Thus, transaction costs influence the ease with which resources can be combined in the realization of opportunities. Entrepreneurs perceiving that some paths of entrepreneurial activities are too costly will shut these off, as it were, and look for less costly resource combinations. This introduces path dependency in entrepreneurial opportunity discovery and exploitation. Additionally, such path dependence is influenced by the costliness of protecting property rights to new discoveries. Although this is obvious for the case of intellectual property, we argue that the reasoning has applicability beyond such property.

Entrepreneurship, governance, and organizational design

This mix of Austrian ideas on entrepreneurship, capabilities, and transaction costs and property rights began to coalesce into a coherent vision around 2005. One key event in my evolving thinking on entrepreneurship was working with Peter G. Klein, then at the University of Missouri. I had known Peter since the mid-1990s and we shared a similar intellectual background, primarily Austrian and transaction cost economics (see Peter's chapter elsewhere in this volume). Peter and I organized a small conference in Copenhagen on Austrian economics and the firm. The conference papers were published as Foss and Klein (2002).

More importantly, however, Peter introduced me to a different perspective on entrepreneurship in the Austrian tradition. I had thought of the Austrian tradition as it pertains to entrepreneurship it as relatively homogenous. It wasn't and isn't; Kirzner's conceptualization of entrepreneurship as alertness to hitherto unnoticed opportunities is fundamentally different from, in particular, Mises' (1949) notion of the entrepreneur. Mises' entrepreneur holds ownership to assets that he deploys in the uncertain pursuit of satisfying future unknown consumer preferences (Salerno [2008] is a brilliant exposition of Mises' views). Ownership, appraisal of future possibilities of action, and uncertainty are key in Mises; Kirzner's entrepreneur may be "poor and penniless" and can perform his function even in the total absence of uncertainty (ignorance rather than uncertainty is key in his theorizing).

In fact, the entrepreneur is so "thinly" described in Kirzner that it is somewhat enigmatic why his conception of entrepreneurship has been so hugely influential in entrepreneurship research in management over the last fifteen years or so (Shane, 2000; Shane & Venkataraman, 2000). Of course, Kirzner's theory isn't a theory of the entrepreneur as much as it is a theory of market equilibration. Thus, Kirzner is addressing the fundamental challenge to economics that Hayek (1937) posed: How can a system of decentralized actors, each possessing mainly knowledge of their own local circumstances, possibly achieve a state in which their forward-looking plans become consistent (i.e., an economic equilibrium)? Kirzner's solution to the Hayekian puzzle was to bring in the entrepreneur as the "device" that by discovering and exploiting undiscovered profit opportunities drives the system towards an equilibrium.

Entrepreneurship and the classical Coasian questions[4]

Mises' and in particular Frank Knight's, portrayal of the asset-owning, uncertainty-bearing entrepreneur is closer to real entrepreneurs and a better starting point for linking entrepreneurship and the firm. In fact, key to my work since 2005, much of it in conjunction with Peter Klein, is that the theory of entrepreneurship and the theory of the firm should be treated together. Entrepreneurial behavior does not occur in a vacuum, and much of the relevant context is constituted by the firms entrepreneurs lead, own, work in, or start to realize their judgment about resource uses. Moreover, both the entrepreneurship field and the theory of the firm deal with new firm formation, new value creation, sustained performance differences, and so on. Thus, one would naturally expect the two fields to be engaged in substantial cross-fertilization.

However, the modern theory of the firm (i.e., transaction cost economics, agency theory, property rights theory) ignores entrepreneurship, and the literature on entrepreneurship in economics and management research has limited use for the economic theory of the firm. Foss and Klein (2005) explored the reasons for this state of affairs and concluded that the separation between entrepreneurship and the theory of the firm is not due to any inherent incompatibility, but is largely an idiosyncratic consequence of the way the field of economics developed, particularly after World War II, towards "closed" equilibrium models with little or nothing for entrepreneurs to accomplish (Foss & Klein, 2005). Additionally, the entrepreneurship literature typically sees entrepreneurship as a theory of firm creation; once created, however, the firm ceases to be "entrepreneurial" and is dominated by "managerial" motives – a partial legacy of Schumpeter's early and influential work on innovation (Schumpeter, 1911; Foss & Klein, 2012).

To be sure, over the last few decades, economists have increasingly tried to incorporate entrepreneurship in formal economic models and have tried to forge analytical links between the exercise of entrepreneurship and firms. For example, Lucas' (1978) general equilibrium model, the starting point for much modern economics work on entrepreneurship, examines the matching of firms and entrepreneurial talent (that includes entrepreneurial, managerial, and ownership skills), given that entrepreneurial talent is unequally distributed. In Lucas' model, firms of varying sizes are matched with entrepreneurial talent, with the most able entrepreneurs running the largest firms. However, it is unclear in Lucas' treatment why entrepreneurs would need firms at all. Why can't they perform their coordinating function simply by using contracts (i.e., they act as consultants for firms)? Why are the governance mechanisms of the firm required?

These are the kinds of questions that a transaction cost perspective prompts one to raise (Coase, 1937; Williamson, 1985, 1996). They are essentially variations of the three questions that Ronald Coase (1937) posed in 1937: Why do firms exist? What explains their boundaries? And what explains the form that their internal organizations take? Foss, Foss, Klein and Klein (2007) and Foss, Foss and Klein (2007) followed up on the argument in Foss and Klein (2005) that gains to trade could be made by bringing the modern (Coasian) theory of the firm into contact with the entrepreneurship literature. We specifically argue that both fields stand to gain from exposure to the other. Foss, Foss, Klein and Klein (2002, 2007) argued that the fundamental starting point for an entrepreneurial theory of economic organization is the relation between an entrepreneur who has formed an entrepreneurial judgment (i.e., he has envisioned how he can satisfy future customer preferences by deploying heterogeneous, complementary assets to production) and a set of heterogeneous, multiattribute assets. In a world with perfect foresight and full information, assuming ownership to such assets would not make sense, as their services could be costlessly contracted for. However, if asset attributes (characteristics, functionalities, services of resources; see Foss & Foss, 2005) are costly to discern, discover, measure, write down in contracts, coordinate, etc., asset ownership becomes an instrument in the service of minimizing transaction costs.

It may be objected that rather than acquiring ownership title to such assets, the entrepreneur could realize profits from his judgment by selling it. However, entrepreneurship represents judgment that cannot be assessed in terms of its marginal product and which cannot, accordingly, be paid a wage (Knight, 1921: 311). Additionally, noncontractibility arises because "[t]he decisive factors . . . are so largely on the inside of the person making the decision that the 'instances' are not amenable to objective description and external control" (Knight, 1921: 251). A nascent entrepreneur may be unable to communicate his "vision" in such a way that other agents can assess its economic implications.

In other words, there is no market for the judgment that entrepreneurs rely on, and therefore exercising judgment requires the person with judgment to own productive assets (Foss, 1993b); thus, in contrast to Kirznerian "alertness", judgment implies asset ownership. At the same time, these ideas form a basic theory of why firms (in their elemental forms: the entrepreneur plus the asset he owns) emerge that puts the emphasis on difficulties of trading judgment.

Foss, Foss and Klein (2007) extended these ideas to the two remaining Coasian questions: namely what explains the boundaries and the internal organization of the firm. Thus, we consider a simple set-up with two cooperating individuals who work with an asset and who can both exercise judgment. The two individuals do not know all relevant present and future attributes of the asset. Instead, attributes must be created or discovered over time as the asset is deployed in production. Using a simple semi-formal model and making specific assumptions about the ability to exercise judgment, we identify the individual who will assume the role of employer and the individual who will be the employee. We also show that efficiency implies that the employer shall own the asset because this gives him power to constrain the employee's actions. Thus, this is a simple model of the authority relation that is derived from very different premises from those of Coase (1937).[5]

The basic neoclassical theory of the firm makes the simplifying assumption that factors of production are homogenous within categories. That is, one piece of capital equipment is like another one (what Robert Solow called "Shmoo" capital). Although this assumption may be a useful simplification for some purposes, it can sometimes lead analysis astray. One example is the analysis of economic policy, where failure to take capital heterogeneity explicitly into account may lead to too optimistic assessments of the potential of stimulus policies (Agarwal, Barney, Foss, & Klein, 2009). Another example is entrepreneurship. Thus, if capital were homogenous, conceiving, coordinating, and implementing plans for producing, marketing, and selling goods and services would be simple. If capital is heterogeneous, production plans are much more difficult to conceive, coordinate, and implement. As Lachmann (1956: 16, original emphasis) suggests:

> [T]he entrepreneur's function . . . is to *specify* and make decisions on the concrete form the capital resources shall have. He specifies and modifies the layout of his plant . . . As long as we disregard the heterogeneity of capital, the true function of the entrepreneur must also remain hidden. In a homogenous world there is no scope for the activity of specifying.

Given that the optimal relationships among assets is often shrouded in uncertainty *ex ante*, some kind of experimental process is typically required (Hayek, 1948; Foss & Foss, 2002). "Experiments" should be understood in a wide sense, ranging all the way from setting up and fine-tuning an assembly line to designing and implementing organizational architectures to inventing and commercializing new product. Often firms can organize such experiments at a low cost internally (as compared to organizing them with other firms, across the boundaries of the firm) for reasons of shared knowledge and norms and the efficacy of authority in coordinating systems with highly complementary components (Foss & Foss, 2002; Foss, Foss, Klein, & Klein, 2007). This provides a basic story of firm boundaries (for more detail, see Foss & Klein, 2012: ch. 8).

Entrepreneurship and organizational design in the established firm

In a separate stream of research, most of it done with Jacob Lyngsie, I have further pursued the theme of entrepreneurship in the context of the internal organization of firms. This is a theme with particular relevance for established firms, as start-ups are often small and have a very basic organizational structure. The emphasis on established firms helps to redress an imbalance in the entrepreneurship literature, which often seems premised on the founding of new firms (e.g.,

Gartner & Carter, 2003: 196). However, once entrepreneurship is understood as the exercise of judgment over the use of heterogeneous resources in the pursuit of uncertain profits from satisfying future preferences, it is clear that there is nothing conceptually wrong with thinking of established firms as acting entrepreneurially. Of course, some of the key contributors to the economics of entrepreneurship, notably Baumol (1993), have held this view, but the field at large has had a start-up bias, perhaps following Schumpeter's (1911) notion that once firms gets established they cease being entrepreneurial. However, if entrepreneurship is the general function of deploying scarce, heterogeneous resources to production under uncertainty and in the expectation of future profits, obviously it is a general kind of behavior that extends much beyond the start-up.

However, the analysis of how entrepreneurship unfolds may differ between start-ups and established firms. Notably, established firms are likely to be larger and to have an established organizational design. Whereas all entrepreneurial behaviors in the small firm may be concentrated on the owner/founder, the larger established firm may organize an "entrepreneurial division of labor" (Foss & Lyngsie, 2014) that pertains not only to the recognition of opportunities, but also to the evaluation and exploitation of opportunities and allocates these behaviors to different organizational functions, departments, projects, etc. Thus, entrepreneurial efforts are supported by an organizational infrastructure of structure and control. As the strategic entrepreneurship literature argues, they are often initiated and managed by senior managers who believe they are capable of exercising superior judgment regarding how to direct actions, assets, and investments to servicing future preferences. However, missing from the current strategic entrepreneurship literature is a consistent focus on how the firm's administrative framework helps coordinate the entrepreneurial division of labor (Foss & Lyngsie, 2014).[6]

A research program that articulates how different kinds of organizational structure and control influence different kinds of entrepreneurial behaviors across the organization and how these behaviors aggregate to firm-level entrepreneurship is a massively ambitious undertaking. It is best approached in a piecemeal fashion. Two examples of such research are Foss, Lyngsie and Zahra (2013, 2015). Thus, Foss, Lyngsie and Zahra (2013) link the open innovation and strategic entrepreneurship literatures with organization design theory. We focus in particular on opportunity exploitation (as distinct from opportunity recognition and evaluation). We note that much recent research has highlighted the role of external knowledge sources in the recognition of strategic (usually innovation) opportunities (e.g., Laursen & Salter, 2006), but is less forthcoming with respect to the role of such sources during the process of exploiting or realizing opportunities. We build on the knowledge-based view to propose that realizing opportunities often involves significant interactions with external knowledge sources. Additionally, we argue that organizational design can facilitate a firm's interactions with these sources, while achieving coordination among organizational members engaged in opportunity exploitation. Our analysis of a double-respondent survey involving 536 Danish firms shows that the use of external knowledge sources is positively associated with opportunity exploitation, but the strength of this association is significantly influenced by organizational designs that enable the firm to access external knowledge during the process of exploiting opportunities.

Using the same data set, a follow-up paper arrives at a more provocative conclusion. Thus, Foss et al. (2015) suggest that the same organizational designs support the realization as well as the discovery of opportunities. Specifically, decentralized structures are associated with opportunity realization as well discovery, and this effect is reinforced by formalization. Decentralization gives managers the discretion and autonomy needed to recognize *and* realize opportunities, whereas formalization enables the standardization and codification of actions and processes. These ideas are empirically corroborated. This is provocative because it runs counter to prevalent ideas that firms need very different organizational set-ups to deal with different entrepreneurial processes.

Thus, research suggests that for optimal performance over time firms need to either vacillate between organizational designs or adopt ambidextrous designs, processes that are costly and difficult to successfully design. Foss et al. (2014) suggest that this is not necessary, because firms can realize different entrepreneurial processes with the same organizational set-up.

In a third paper with Jacob Lyngsie, we focus less on organization design and more on organizational members (Foss & Lyngsie, 2015). In particular, we study the association between firms' entrepreneurial outcomes and their gender composition. By matching a paired-respondent questionnaire survey (responses from HR executives as well as CEOs) with population-wide employer–employee data (the IDA database held by Statistics Denmark), we find evidence that the presence of female top managers is positively related to entrepreneurial outcomes in established firms. Yet, this relation is nonlinear in the proportional difference between male and female top managers. We also find evidence that the overall proportion of women in the firm's workforce negatively moderates the relation between female top managers and entrepreneurial outcomes. This is a striking and surprising finding that is difficult to explain, particularly as we cannot observe the relevant mechanisms. By means of a series of robustness tests, we lend credibility to an explanation that stresses identity and categorization: women who enter the top management team are recategorized as "just" top-managers, which may have negative attitudinal and motivational consequences for women at lower levels in the firm.

Entrepreneurship, institutions, and economic growth

Institutions and the consequences of entrepreneurship

My latest and so far smallest research stream in entrepreneurship is taken up with the links between entrepreneurship, institutions, and growth (Bjørnskov & Foss, 2008, 2012, 2013, 2016). Indeed, much of the reason social scientists care about entrepreneurship is because it matters to resource allocation, growth, and social change more generally. Thus, identifying the multilevel antecedents of entrepreneurship should be very high on the research agenda of social scientists, as should understanding how the entrepreneurship of firms and individuals aggregate up to economy-wide outcomes (cf. also Shepherd, 2011). However, little work seeks to links the antecedents of entrepreneurship, entrepreneurial activity itself, and the consequences thereof in a unified, multilevel framework. The reasons are that multilevel inquiry into the causes and consequences of entrepreneurial decisions and actions is highly complex, involving many different potential explanatory mechanisms, and that useful data sources have, until recently, been very few (Bjørnskov & Foss, 2016). Thus, the first data set (i.e., the Global Entrepreneurship Monitor) that allows for meaningful cross-national comparisons of entrepreneurship was not made available until 1999.

In my first paper with Christian Bjørnskov (Bjørnskov and Foss, 2008), one of the very first papers to empirically link institutions and entrepreneurship, we observe that the classical writers on entrepreneurship in economics – notably, Schumpeter (1911), Knight (1921), Mises (1949), Kirzner (1973) and Casson (1982) – have surprisingly little to say about the antecedents of entrepreneurship, concentrating on personal characteristics or simply the lure of profit. Thus, none of them systematically links institutions and entrepreneurship. The key concern of the classical writers on entrepreneurship was to define the entrepreneurship construct and clarify its role in economic theory. And yet, institutions (and economic policy) would seem to antecede entrepreneurship in fairly predictable ways (cf. also Henreksson, 2005). Thus, Bjørnskov and Foss (2008) explain cross-country differences in the level of entrepreneurship in terms of differences in economic policy and institutional design. Our data for regressors come from the Economic Freedom Index issued on a yearly basis by the Fraser Institute, and the entrepreneurship data are from the Global Entrepreneurship Monitor (hence, this implies that entrepreneurship is – narrowly – identified with start-ups). We find that the size of government is negatively correlated and sound money is positively correlated with entrepreneurial activity. Other measures of economic freedom are not significantly correlated with entrepreneurship.

It is also only rather recently that social scientists have begun to systematically model and measure the economy-level *consequences* of entrepreneurship (cf. Bjørnskov & Foss, 2013), beginning with Schmitz (1989), Baumol (1990, 1993), and Aghion and Howitt (1992). Bjørnskov and Foss (2012, 2013) focus on the total factor productivity effects of entrepreneurial activity. Both papers first estimate the institutional effects on entrepreneurial activity. We find similar results to other papers that regress entrepreneurship data against economic freedom measures. In particular, we find that a big public sector is harmful to the incidence of entrepreneurship. We subsequently estimate the productivity consequences of entrepreneurship. A surprising finding is that the *marginal* productivity effects of entrepreneurship are significantly larger in countries with large public sectors and high taxes. We interpret this evidence by arguing that the higher marginal effect is due to the smaller supply of activity – that is, a situation consistent with decreasing marginal productivity gains from entrepreneurial activity.

The literature on entrepreneurship, institutions, and aggregate economic performance, although still small and emerging, has made important progress over the last decade (see also, e.g., Nyström, 2008). What may be called "Schumpeter's conjecture" – that entrepreneurial activity has positive long-run economic consequences in terms of wealth, productivity, and growth – can now be considered fairly well established. It is similarly well established that institutions influence entrepreneurial activity and that this is a key way in which institutions affect aggregate performance. However, we are more in the dark when it comes to identifying which institutional features matter most and why they matter. Thus, the mediating mechanisms through which the influence of institutions on growth plays out in terms of influencing entrepreneurship are not particularly well understood. Part of the reason is that extant empirical work examines these mechanisms in terms of start-up activity. However, the entrepreneurial activities of established firms are very much part of the equation and need to be considered, data permitting.

The judgment view may contribute to the theoretical understanding of the "transmission mechanism" between institutions and aggregate outcomes. In the "macro" world of most of mainstream economics, as noted earlier, factors of production, or resources, are taken as homogenous within categories. In such a world it is hard to define a meaningful role for the entrepreneur (cf. Agarwal et al., 2009). Homogeneous resources are uncomplicated to search for, measure, monitor, combine, and coordinate. Essentially, the transaction costs associated with such activities are low or even zero. In actuality, resources are, of course, heterogeneous (Lachmann, 1956; Barney, 1991), and combining them in the uncertain pursuit of profits is the essence of entrepreneurship. Resource heterogeneity is also the source of many transaction costs, not just because of the well-known problems that asset specificity and complementarity may cause, but also because resource heterogeneity means that resources have different levels and kinds of valued attributes (Foss & Foss, 2005), and self-interest will motivate agents to expend resources on measuring such attributes, discover new attributes, and so on.

However, exactly because such attributes are not known ex ante to agents, learning and experimentation is called for; the optimal combination of resources results from experimental processes of resource learning based on entrepreneurial judgment – it is not something that is given to firms (Nelson & Winter, 1982). Also, processes of mergers, divestments, spin-offs, new firm formation, etc., reallocate resources across firms in response to price signals and entrepreneurial judgment and make the economy track its (moving) production possibility frontier (e.g., Foster, Haltiwanger, & Krizan, 2002).

The role of institutions[7]

Experimental processes of resource combination are influenced by institutions and policy. In general, there is much evidence that institutions have a strong impact on growth (see in particular, Rodrik, Subramanian, & Trebbi, 2004). As North (1990: 6) explains, the major role of institutions in a society is to reduce uncertainty by establishing a stable (but not necessarily efficient) structure to human interaction. The overall stability of an institutional framework makes complex exchange possible across both time and space.

Such higher certainty translates into lowered transaction costs. Specifically, higher certainty means that the costs of contracting and of protecting property are lowered. In turn, this means that more entrepreneurial projects will be undertaken as their expected value increases. More start-ups and more entrepreneurial activity on the part of established firms may be expected. As Bjørnskov and Foss (2013) argue, incentives for productive behaviors are particularly strongly influenced by the extent to which private property rights are protected, including dimensions such as generality (i.e., equals are treated equally), transparency in public decision making, accountability in public decision making, and, importantly, an expectation that property rights are effectively enforced by the courts of justice.

Many social scientists have made similar points; yet, the way in which institutions and entrepreneurial activities are related have seldom been pinned down with much precision (but see Henreksson, 2005). If one accepts the argument that economic growth is to a large extent the result of the introduction of new modes of organization, ways of better allocating resources to preferred uses, and so on, the *flexibility* (i.e., costliness) with which these changes can be made becomes a central concern (Bjørnskov & Foss, 2013). The economics of production captures such flexibility in terms of the "elasticity of factor substitution" construct (Klump & de la Grandville, 2000).[8] A high elasticity of substitution means high factor productivity, as it means that resources are more easily allocated to highly valued uses. The elasticity of substitution is not a purely technical parameter, and is in actuality endogenous to institutional variables. Thus, a high positive impact on factor productivity of high elasticity of substitution may be caused by low transaction costs in searching for contract partners, bargaining, and monitoring and enforcing contracts, which positively influence the ease, speed, and flexibility with which resources can be identified, allocated, combined, etc., by entrepreneurs. In turn, low transaction costs result from well-defined and enforced property rights. Thus, institutional and political features, such as the quality of regulations and the judicial system, that directly influence property rights influence the relation between entrepreneurship and total factor productivity, and therefore growth.

Christian Bjørnskov and I deploy the aforementioned kinds of arguments in our cross-country examination of the links between institutions and entrepreneurship (Bjørnskov & Foss, 2013). However, although we theorize on the mechanisms, they remain unobserved. The reason lies in a general lack of appropriately nested data across a sufficient number of countries (or regions) that can be used to test and otherwise further theorize in this domain. However, there are reasons to expect progress in this area, as data relevant to understanding the mechanics of the growth process become increasingly available.

Coda

I am very grateful to David Audretsch and Erik Lehmann for inviting me to contribute to this volume. Not only do I find myself in highly distinguished company, writing this chapter has also afforded me the opportunity to provide some retrospective intellectual stock taking and, in particular, sense making. I can now see a path from my early interests in Austrian economics and new institutional economics, including transaction cost economics, to my attempts to update, expand, and relaunch Frank Knight's entrepreneurial vision and to examine the links between institutions, entrepreneurship, and aggregate economic performance. Because of David and Erik I can see that I may have been an entrepreneurship scholar all along, although I have never really published in entrepreneurship journals or even been a member of the Academy of Management's entrepreneurship division.

Although there is, of course, thematic overlap with the contributions made by many of the other contributors to this book, I think the intellectual path I have traveled, alone and with others, means that what Peter Klein and I call the "judgment view" has a certain claim to intellectual uniqueness on the contemporary entrepreneurship scene. As I see it, it has certain advantages relative to other perspectives (e.g., its natural links to ownership and firm organization) and although the view is currently less influential than ideas on effectuation, opportunity discovery, and creation opportunities, I expect the judgment view to become increasingly influential over the coming years. The view is best summarized in my book with Peter, *Organizing Entrepreneurial Judgment* (Foss & Klein, 2012).

The judgment view, as well as much of my other work on entrepreneurship, has emerged from interactions with a number of co-authors. My most frequent co-authors in my entrepreneurship stream are Christian Bjørnskov, Kirsten Foss, Peter G. Klein, Jacob Lyngsie, and Shaker Zahra, and I am extremely grateful to them for fruitful collaboration over the years.

Notes

1 This section draws on the autobiographical Introduction to Foss (2009).
2 Thus, the theme of my 1994 book, *The Austrian School and Modern Economics: Essays in Reassessment* (Foss, 1994a), written as a hobby project while I was working on my PhD thesis, is that although the Austrians, particularly Mises and Hayek, anticipated numerous themes that later became prominent in mainstream economics (e.g., asymmetric information, the agency problem, property rights), they failed to develop these ideas sufficiently and they failed to do concrete theorizing with them. As an example, although the Austrians had many of the necessary ingredients of an economic approach to organization before anyone else, they never thought of piecing them together (Foss, 1994b). See also Foss (1999) on Austrian economics and game theory.
3 For example, much of the recent work in management research on the relations between capabilities and transaction costs in driving firm boundaries was anticipated by Langlois (e.g., Langlois, 1992).
4 This subsection draws on Foss and Klein (2005, 2012).
5 Rajan (2012) develops similar ideas.
6 An exception is Ireland, Covin and Kuratko's (2009) view that "pro-entrepreneurship organizational instruments," namely organization structures, cultural norms, reward systems, internal procedures for resource allocation, and firm strategy, aim at fostering entrepreneurship.
7 This section draws on Bjørnskov and Foss (2016).
8 This elasticity measures the percentage change in factor proportions due to a change in the marginal rate of technical substitution.

References

Agarwal, R., Barney, J.B., Foss, N.J. & Klein, P.G. 2009. Heterogeneous Resources and the Current Crisis: Implications of Strategic Management Theory. *Strategic Organization* 7: 467–484.

Aghion, P. & Howitt, P. 1992. A Model of Growth Through Creative Destruction. *Econometrica* 60(2): 323–351.

Alvarez, Sharon A. & Barney, Jay B. 2005. How do Entrepreneurs Organize Firms under Conditions of Uncertainty. *Journal of Management* 31(5): 776–793.

Alvarez, Sharon A. & Barney, Jay B. 2007. Discovery and Creation: Alternative Theories of Entrepreneurial Action. *Strategic Entrepreneurship Journal* 1(1–2): 11–26.

Barney, Jay B. 1986. Strategic Factor Markets. *Management Science*, 32: 1231–1241.

Barney, Jay B. 1991. Firm Resources and Sustained Competitive Advantage. *Journal of Management* 17: 99–120.

Baumol, W.J. 1990. Entrepreneurship: Productive, Unproductive, and Destructive. *Journal of Political Economy* 98(5): 893–921.

Baumol, William J. 1993. *Entrepreneurship, Management and the Structure of Pay-Offs*. Cambridge, MA: MIT Press.

Bjørnskov, C. & Foss, N.J. 2008. Economic Freedom and Entrepreneurial Activity: Some Cross-country Evidence. *Public Choice* 134: 307–328.

Bjørnskov, C. & Foss, N.J. 2012. How institutions of liberty promote entrepreneurship and growth, in F. McMahon, ed. *Economic Freedom of the World: 2012 Annual Report*. Vancouver, Canada: Fraser Institute.

Bjørnskov, C. & Foss, N.J. 2013. How Strategic Entrepreneurship and the Institutional Context Drive Economic Growth. *Strategic Entrepreneurship Journal* 7: 50–69.

Bjørnskov, C. & Foss, N.J. 2016. Entrepreneurship, Institutions and Economic Growth. *Academy of Management Perspectives* (forthcoming).

Boudreaux, D. & Holcombe, R. 1989. The Coasian and Knightian Theories of the Firm. *Managerial and Decision Economics* 10: 147–154.

Casson, M. 1982. *The Entrepreneur: An Economic Theory*. Maryland: Rowman & Littlefield.

Coase, R.H. 1937. The Nature of the Firm. *Economica* 4: 386–405.

Foss, K. & Foss, N.J. 2002. Organizing Economic Experiments: The Role of Firms. *Review of Austrian Economics* 15: 297–312.

Foss, K. & Foss, N.J. 2005. Value and Transaction Costs: How the Economics of Property Rights Furthers the RBV. *Strategic Management Journal* 26: 541–553.

Foss, K. & Foss, N.J. 2008. Understanding Opportunity Discovery and Sustainable Advantage: the Role of Transaction Costs and Property Rights. *Strategic Entrepreneurship Journal* 2: 191–207.

Foss, K., Foss, N. & Klein, P.G. 2007. Original and Derived Judgment: An Entrepreneurial Theory of Economic Organization. *Organization Studies* 28: 1893–1912.

Foss, K., Foss, N., Klein, P.G. & Klein, S. 2002. Heterogeneous Capital, Entrepreneurship, and Economic Organization. *Journal des Economistes et des Etudes Humaine* 12: 79–96.

Foss, K., Foss, N., Klein P.G. & Klein, S. 2007. Heterogenous Capital and the Organization of Entrepreneurship. *Journal of Management Studies* 44: 1165–1186.

Foss, N.J. 1991. The Suppression of Evolutionary Approaches in Economics: The Case of Marshall and Monopolistic Competition. *Methodus* 3: 65–72.

Foss, N.J. 1993a. More on Knight and the Theory of the Firm. *Managerial and Decision Economics* 14: 269–276.

Foss, N.J. 1993b. Theories of the Firm: Contractual and Competence Perspectives. *Journal of Evolutionary Economics* 3(2): 127–144.

Foss, N.J. 1994a. *The Austrian School and Modern Economics: Essays in Reassessment*. Copenhagen: Copenhagen Business School Press/Munksgaard.

Foss, N.J. 1994b. The Theory of the Firm: The Austrians as Precursors and Critics of Contemporary Theory. *Review of Austrian Economics* 7(1): 31–65.

Foss, N.J. 1995. The Economic Thought of an Austrian Marshallian: George Barclay Richardson. *Journal of Economic Studies* 22: 23–44.

Foss, N.J. 1996a. The "Alternative" Theories of Knight and Coase, and the Modern Theory of the Firm. *Journal of the History of Economic Thought* 18: 76–95.

Foss, N.J. 1996b. Firms, Incomplete Contracts, and Organizational Learning. *Human Systems Management* 15: 17–26.

Foss, N.J. 1996c. Post-Marshallian and Austrian Economics: Towards a Fruitful Liaison? *Advances in Austrian Economics* 3: 213–221.

Foss, N.J. 1997. Ethics, Discovery, and Strategy. *Journal of Business Ethics* 16: 1131–1142.

Foss, N.J. 1999. The Use of Knowledge in Firms. *Journal of Institutional and Theoretical Economics* 155(3): 458–486.

Foss, N.J. 2000. Equilibrium and Evolution: The Conflicting Legacies of Demsetz and Penrose, in Nicolai J. Foss and Paul L. Robertson, eds. *Resources, Technology, and Strategy*. London: Routledge.

Foss, N.J. 2009. *Knowledge, Economics Organization, and Property Rights: Selected Essays of Nicolai J. Foss*. Cheltenham: Edward Elgar.

Foss, N.J. & Garzarelli, G. 2007. Institutions as Knowledge: Ludwig Lachmann's Institutional Economics. *Cambridge Journal of Economics* 31: 789–804.

Foss, N.J. & Ishikawa, I. 2007. Toward a Dynamic Resource-based View. *Organization Studies* 28: 749–772.

Foss, N.J. & Klein, P.G. 2002. *Entrepreneurship and the Firm: Austrian Perspectives on Economic Organization.* Aldershot: Edward Elgar.

Foss, N.J. & Klein, P.G. 2005. Entrepreneurship and the Theory of the Firm: Any Gains from Trade? in Rajshree Agarwal, Sharon A. Alvarez, and Olav Sorenson, eds. *Handbook of Entrepreneurship: Disciplinary Perspectives.* Berlin: Springer.

Foss, N.J. & Klein, P.G. 2012. *Entrepreneurial Judgment and the Theory of the Firm.* Cheltenham: Cambridge University Press.

Foss, N.J., Klein, P.G., Kor, Y. & Mahoney, J. 2008. Entrepreneurship, Subjectivism, and the Resource-Based View: Towards a New Synthesis. *Strategic Entrepreneurship Journal* 2: 73–94.

Foss, N.J. & Loasby, B.J. 1998. *Economic Organization, Capabilities and Coordination.* New York: Routledge.

Foss, N.J. & Lyngsie, J. 2014. The Strategic Organization of the Entrepreneurial Established Firm. *Strategic Organization* 12: 208–215.

Foss, N.J. & Lyngsie, J. 2015. The More, the Merrier? The Role of Gender in Explaining Firms' Entrepreneurialism. *Strategic Management Journal* (forthcoming).

Foss, N.J., Lyngsie, J. & Zahra, S. 2013. The Role of External Knowledge Sources and Organizational Design in the Process of Opportunity Exploitation. *Strategic Management Journal* 34(12): 1453–1471.

Foss, N.J., Lyngsie, J. & Zahra, S. 2015. Organizational Design Correlates of Opportunity Realization. *Strategic Organization* 13: 32–60.

Foster, L., Haltiwanger, J. & Krizan, C.J. 2002. The Link between Aggregate and Micro Productivity Growth: Evidence from Retail Trade. *NBER Working Paper No. 9120.*

Friedman, M. 1968. The Role of Monetary Policy. *American Economic Review* 68: 1–17.

Gartner, W.B. & Carter, N.M. 2003. Entrepreneurial Behavior and Firm Organizing Processes, in Z.J. Acs and D.B. Audretch, eds. *Handbook of Entrepreneurship Research.* Boston: Kluwer: 195–221.

Hayek, F.A. von. 1931. *Prices and Production.* New York: Augustus M. Kelly Publishers.

Hayek, F.A. von. 1937. Economics and Knowledge. In Hayek, F.A. von. 1948. *Individualism and Economic Order.* Chicago: University of Chicago Press.

Hayek, F.A. von. 1948. *Individualism and Economic Order.* Chicago: University of Chicago Press.

Hazlitt, H. 1959. *Failure of the 'New Economics'.* Alabama: Ludwig von Mises Institute.

Henreksson, M. 2005. Entrepreneurship: A Weak Link in the Welfare State? *Industrial and Corporate Change* 14(3): 437–467.

Ireland, R.D., Covin, J.G. & Kuratko, D.F. 2009. Conceptualizing Corporate Entrepreneurship Strategy. *Entrepreneurship Theory and Practice* 33(1): 19–46.

Jacobson, R. 1992. The "Austrian" School of Strategy. *Academy of Management Review* 17: 782–807.

Kirzner, I.M. 1973. *Competition and Entrepreneurship.* Chicago: University of Chicago Press.

Klump, R. & de La Grandville, O. 2000. Economic Growth and the Elasticity of Substitution: Two Theorems and Some Suggestions. *American Economic Review* 90: 282–291.

Knight, F.H. 1921. *Risk, Uncertainty, and Profit.* New York: Augustus M. Lelley.

Lachmann, L.M. 1956. *Capital and Its Structure.* Kansas City, MO: Sheed Andrews and McMeel.

Lachmann, L.M. 1986. *The Market as an Economic Process.* Oxford: Basil Blackwell.

Langlois, R.N. 1988. Economic Change and the Boundaries of the Firm. *Journal of Institutional and Theoretical Economics* 144: 635–657.

Langlois, R.N. 1992. Transaction Cost Economics in Real Time. *Industrial and Corporate Change* 1(1): 99–127.

Langlois, R.N. & Cosgel, M. 1993. Frank Knight on Risk, Uncertainty, and the Firm: A New Interpretation. *Economic Inquiry* 31: 456–465.

Laursen, K. & Salter, A. 2006. Open for Innovation: The Role of Openness in Explaining Innovation Performance among U.K. Manufacturing Firms. *Strategic Management Journal* 27(2): 131–150.

Levinthal, D.A. 1997. Adaption on Rugged Landscapes. *Management Science* 43(7): 934–950.

Loasby, B.J. 1976. *Choice, Complexity, and Ignorance.* Cambridge: Cambridge University Press.

Lucas. R.E. 1977. Understanding Business Cycles, in K. Brunner and A. Meltzer, eds., *Stabilization of the Domestic and International Economy*, North-Holland. Carnegie-Rochester Conference Series on Public Policy, Vol 5, a supplementary series to the *Journal of Monetary Economics.*

Lucas, R.E. 1978. On the Size Distribution of Business Firms. *Bell Journal of Economics* 9: 508–523.

Lucas, R.E. 1980. Methods and Problems in Business Cycle Theory. *Journal of Money, Credit and Banking* 12: 696–717.

Mises, L. von. 1949. *Human Action*. New Haven: Yale University Press.

Nelson, R.R. & Winter, S.G. 1982. *An Evolutionary Theory of Economic Change*. Cambridge, MA: The Belknap Press.

North, D.N. 1990. *Institutions, Institutional Change, and Economic Performance*. Cambridge, UK: Cambridge University Press.

Nyström, K. 2008. The Institutions of Economic Freedom and Entrepreneurship: Evidence from Panel Data. *Public Choice* 136: 269–282.

Penrose, E.T. 1959. *The Theory of the Growth of the Firm*. Oxford: Oxford University Press.

Porter, M.E. 1980. *Competitive Strategy: Techniques for Analyzing Industries and Competitors*. New York: Free Press.

Rajan, R. 2012. Presidential Address: The Corporation in Finance. *Journal of Finance* 67: 1173–1217.

Richardson, G.B. 1960. *Information and Investment*. Oxford: Oxford University Press.

Richardson, G.B. 1972. The Organisation of Industry. *Economic Journal* 82: 883–896.

Rodrik, D., Subramanian, A. & Trebbi, F. 2004. Institutions Rule: The Primacy of Institutions Over Geography and Integration in Economic Development. *Journal of Economic Growth* 9(2): 131–165.

Salerno, J. 2008. The Entrepreneur: Real and Imagined. *Quarterly Journal of Austrian Economics* 11(3): 188–207.

Schmitz, J. 1989. Imitation, Entrepreneurship and Long-run Growth. *Journal of Political Economy* 97(3): 721–739.

Schumpeter, J.A. 1911/1934. *The Theory of Economic Development*. Cambridge, MA: Harvard University Press.

Shackle, G.L.S. 1972. *Economics and Epistemics*. Cambridge: Cambridge University Press.

Shane, S. 2000. *A General Theory of Entrepreneurship: The Individual-opportunity Nexus*. Cheltenham: Edward Elgar.

Shane, S. & Venkataraman, S. 2000. The Promise of Entrepreneurship as a Field of Research. *Academy of Management Review* 25: 217–226.

Shepherd, D. 2011. Multilevel Entrepreneurship Research: Opportunities for Studying Entrepreneurial Decision Making. *Journal of Management* 37: 412–420.

Stieglitz, N. & Foss, N.J. 2009. Entrepreneurship and Transaction Costs. *Advances in Strategic Management* 26: 67–96.

Teece, D.J. 1986. Profiting from Technological Innovation: Implications for Integration, Collaboration, Licensing and Public Policy. *Research Policy* 15(6): 285–305.

Williamson, O.E. 1985. *The Economic Institutions of Capitalism*. New York: The Free Press.

Williamson, O.E. 1996. *The Institutions of Governance*. Oxford: Oxford University Press.

11

Entrepreneurship and growth

A personal story[1]

Michael Fritsch

Introduction

During the last two decades, one of the main topics of my research has been the effect of new business formation on regional development. Thus, in accordance with the theme of this book, I will describe the process of my personal discovery in this field: how I became attracted to the topic, the colleagues and collaborators who made significant contributions, the dominant research questions over time, what did I find, and what followed from all of this. It is my hope that this description of my research process will make understandable why and how I did things. I believe it will provide some insight into the different stages of my research on entrepreneurship and growth that would not be possible to discover from simply reading individual papers. It is a personal story of an ongoing research process that provided explanations for important phenomena and, of course, gave rise to new questions.[2]

Finding the topic

I was born in the western part of Berlin (Germany) and spent the first forty years of my life in this exciting city. There were two entrepreneurs in my family. After the heavy destruction of World War II, my uncle Willy started a quite successful business as a scrap dealer. My father ran a business in the same industry but went bankrupt in the early 1960s when the economic environment deteriorated due to the erection of the Berlin Wall, which isolated West Berlin from its surroundings. He was dependently employed for the rest of his life – but always dreamed of running his own business again. The ruin of my father's business significantly lowered our family's standard of living, and we had to move into a much smaller apartment in a poorer quarter of the city where the quality of schooling was considerably lower. This experience, however, did not prevent two of my four brothers from becoming self-employed, thereby confirming empirical evidence on the intergenerational transmission of entrepreneurship. Perhaps my own interest in entrepreneurship as a research topic was in at least some way inspired by my family's tendency toward self-employment, although the direction of my academic path was much more strongly influenced by peer effects generated by colleagues I met later in my life.

I became interested in regional development processes while studying economics at the Technical University of Berlin. In my final year of study I participated in a teaching project on regional development and planning. This interest in regional topics led me to choose "agglomeration taxes" as the topic of my diploma thesis. The thesis dealt with the idea of imposing higher taxes in prosperous high-density areas to correct for externalities and limit the growth of larger cities. My thesis supervisor was Dieter Biehl, at that time chair of Public Finance at the Technical University of Berlin, who had done some interesting research on regional development and fiscal policy in the federal system of the European Union. Directly after taking my exam in the summer of 1977, I worked for some months in the European Regional Policy Group at the Science Center Berlin on a project on "deglomeration" policies, that is, measures aimed at restricting the growth of large agglomerations, a concept closely related to my diploma thesis. Already at this early phase of my career I had a significant interest in questions of regional development.

It was during my few months at the Science Center in late 1977 that I met Hans-Juergen Ewers, who had just finished his habilitation at the University of Muenster (Germany) and at that time prepared a research program on innovation-oriented regional policy (Ewers and Wettmann 1980), which was a novel idea at that time.[3] Juergen became chair of Economic Policy at the Technical University of Berlin in 1979, after which he engaged me as a junior researcher, and we worked closely and very productively together for more than ten years. However, before I became a junior researcher under Juergen Ewers, I worked for a year and a half at the Chair of Macroeconomics of the Technical University, teaching theories of the business cycle and economic growth.

In addition to issues of regional development, another main field of interest for me was the justification of public intervention. This was another interest shared by Juergen Ewers, who was a proponent of the ideas of Joseph Schumpeter and had also studied the writings of liberal philosophers such as Karl Popper and Friedrich August von Hayek. Juergen supported my idea to write my PhD thesis on the economic theory of constitutions and acted as my supervisor in this endeavor. While working on my thesis, I read a great deal of literature in the field of economic and social philosophy, particularly the works of James Buchanan and John Rawls. However, after finishing my thesis (Fritsch 1983), I did not find this topic interesting or promising enough for an academic career. Hence, I switched to the empirical analyses of growth and, specifically, the role of innovation in a regional context, which was also the chief focus of Juergen Ewers's research at that time.

Soon after finishing my PhD thesis, I became involved in a study of the role played by smaller firms in job creation. This work was largely inspired by the famous study of David Birch (1979, 1981), who claimed that it is small firms and, especially, young firms that make a relatively large contribution to employment growth. However, due to poor availability of data, the results of these research attempts remained speculative. In particular, the research suffered from the nonavailability of data on new business formation. Together with others, Juergen Ewers and I organized a workshop at the Science Center in Berlin about job creation in small and large firms which is where I met David Storey for the first time.[4] David was one of the pioneers in the fields of regional new business formation and the employment effects of small and new firms. In the following years, the main focus of my research was on the spatial diffusion of new technologies, the growth and decline of manufacturing establishments, and the effect of computerized technologies on firm performance, most of it based on micro data at the establishment level. It was during this time, the late 1980s, that I got into contact with Zoltan Acs and David Audretsch, both of whom worked at the Science Center Berlin. The two organized several conferences and workshops at the Science Center at which I met a number of scholars in the emerging field of entrepreneurship research.

In early 1989, I submitted my habilitation thesis about the growth of manufacturing establishments (Fritsch 1990) to the economics department of the Technical University of Berlin and took the exam in the summer of that same year. My thesis revealed strong effects of product innovation and firm age on firm growth, but a detailed empirical analysis of the role of new business formation was still impossible due to lacking data. At the end of 1989, just around the time the Berlin Wall came down, Juergen Ewers accepted a position at his old university in Muenster. I took over his teaching obligations in the spring of 1990, becoming the interim chair of Economic Policy. It was at this time that I also felt the need to decide on the future direction of my research. The two main research projects that I had been involved in during the previous years – my habilitation project and a huge empirical study on the effect of computerized technologies in manufacturing establishments (Ewers, Becker, and Fritsch 1990a, 1990b) – were finished. Moreover, my collaboration with Juergen Ewers came to an end when he left for Muenster and began to work on rather different topics.

The effect of new businesses on regional development

Early analyses

Soon after finishing my habilitation, I began to more closely collaborate with two other scholars at the Technical University of Berlin, Gernot Weisshuhn and Andreas Koenig, who had obtained data from the German Social Insurance Statistics. We developed a simple way of identifying new businesses in these data, and I started research into the determinants of regional new business formation (Fritsch 1992) and its impact on growth.[5] Some of this work was done in cooperation with David Audretsch, who connected me with an international research project on the determinants of regional new business formation led by Paul Reynolds and David Storey. This project resulted in a 1994 special issue of *Regional Studies* on the topic (see Reynolds, Storey, and Westhead 1994; Audretsch and Fritsch 1994a, 1994b).

With only a few successive years of data on start-ups and regional employment, David Audretsch and I could not find any significant positive effect of new business formation on growth (Audretsch and Fritsch 1996; Fritsch 1996, 1997). Our colleagues' reaction to these results was benevolent, but somewhat skeptical, along the lines of "nice guys, but something in their analysis must be completely wrong." Almost everybody seemed to believe that new businesses *must* be a source of growth, but hardly anyone had solid empirical evidence to back up this belief. Of course, there were stories about the extraordinary Silicon Valley and Route 128 near Boston, where innovative new businesses obviously played an important role, but more general evidence was largely missing. Paul Reynolds was the single exception in that he had detected a positive relationship between new business formation and regional growth for regions of the United States (Reynolds and Maki 1990; Reynolds 1994, 1999). Reynolds's analyses clearly showed that the strength of the effect of start-ups on growth was not uniform, but varied considerably across regions and over time.

In October 1992, I obtained my first tenure position as a full professor and chair of Economic Policy at the Technical University Bergakademie Freiberg. This is a rather small university with a long tradition in engineering and, particularly, in mining that is located in the southern part of East Germany, quite close to the city of Dresden and not far from the Czech border. During the transformation of the former socialist East German system of research and higher education, the old Department of Management at this university had been closed down and a new department founded and staffed almost in its entirety with professors from the West. Building a new department in this turbulent environment was an exciting experience. Due to my direct involvement in the transformation process, as well as my personal history of having lived so long in Berlin at a time when the city was surrounded by a socialist regime, development of the East German economy became an important topic of my research.

Together with Horst Brezinski, a new colleague at Freiberg University, I organized a conference on "Bottom-up Transformation in Eastern Europe" in Freiberg in September 1993, at which scholars from different countries presented early research on new business formation in the former socialist economies.[6] The contributions dealt with problems of and perspectives on entrepreneurship in these countries but, due to the very early stage of the transformation process, very little evidence on the effects of entrepreneurship was presented. What little empirical evidence there was, however, made it very clear that entrepreneurship in the transformation process was different from that occurring in developed Western-type market economies. Most of my research at that time was devoted to investigating the reasons for the low productivity of the East German economy (see, e.g., Fritsch and Mallok 1998) and on innovation systems in several European regions, including parts of East Germany (Fritsch 2000, 2003, 2004b).

During this period, Frieder Meyer-Krahmer, who I knew from earlier research collaboration, was director of the Fraunhofer Institute for Systems and Innovation Research (ISI) in Karlsruhe. This institute had hired a former East German professor of mechanical engineering, Franz Pleschak, and wanted to affiliate him and his team with a university. We managed to set up the "Research Unit for Economics of Innovation" (*Forschungsstelle Innovationsökonomik*) in Freiberg as a joint institution of Freiberg University and the Fraunhofer Institute that hosted Franz Pleschak and his group, with Frieder Meyer-Krahmer and me as the managing directors. Franz Pleschak was a very creative and extremely productive researcher who mainly worked on innovation processes in the transforming East German economy. His particular interest was in innovative start-ups, and during our cooperation (which ended with his sudden death in 2003) he stimulated my interest in this particular type of entrepreneurship. I also learned a great deal from him about research organization and policy consulting.

Analyzing longer time series of data

In 1997, I began to more closely cooperate with the Institute of Employment Research (IAB) at the Federal Employment Agency (Nuremberg), which is responsible for compiling the German Social Insurance Statistics.[7] The project partner at the IAB was Udo Brixy, who had just completed his PhD thesis on the role of new businesses in the development of East German regions (Brixy 1999). This cooperation gave me better access to data so that my time series on new business formation and employment in German regions became considerably longer. David Audretsch, with whom several years past I had done some research on the determinants and the effects of new business formation, had moved from Berlin back to the United States around the mid-1990s and become a professor at Indiana University at Bloomington. When I visited him there in February 2000 we had another look at the now longer time series of data.

One main result of our analyses based on the new data was that new business formation in West German regions in the early 1980s could not explain growth in this decade – however, our regressions showed that it could explain, at least partially, growth in the following decade, the 1990s. This result implied that the effects of new business formation take a relatively long time to manifest. Moreover, the relationship between new business formation and growth varied considerably across regions. We made a simple classification of regions into four types of different growth regimes understood as constellations in which new businesses played different roles. We argued, however, that new business formation plays an important role in all these constellations in the long run. We summarized our new analyses in the paper "Growth Regimes over Time and

Space" (Audretsch and Fritsch 2002). An early version of this paper had been sent to a number of colleagues, and we received helpful comments from David Storey, among others.

In the following years, David Audretsch did some interesting work with Max Keilbach and Erik Lehmann on the effect of new business formation on growth, mainly based on regional production functions that included start-up rates as indicators for entrepreneurship (Audretsch and Keilbach 2004; Audretsch, Keilbach, and Lehmann 2006). My next research topics in this area were the development of start-up cohorts and the time lags of the effects of start-ups. The analysis of rather long time series for the development of start-up cohorts clearly showed that after some few years, employment in these cohorts declined below the initial level (Fritsch and Weyh 2006). This was obviously caused by the high exit rates among the new businesses and the low growth rates of the survivors. In particular, most of the surviving businesses remained small, and only a very small fraction of them created a significant number of jobs.[8] Performing the analysis separately for East and West Germany revealed drastic differences clearly demonstrating that the two parts of the country were characterized by different types of growth regime (Fritsch 2004c).

The structure of the time lags

Inspired by my paper with David Audretsch on regional growth regimes (Audretsch and Fritsch 2002), André van Stel and David Storey analyzed the lag structure of the effects of regional new business formation on growth for regions of the United Kingdom. A major problem in such an analysis of the lag structure is that there is a very high correlation between the start-up rates of successive years, which causes high levels of multicollinearity in empirical models. To deal with this problem, André van Stel and David Storey applied the Almon lag procedure, an econometric technique that attempts to identify the "true" lag structure based on a polynomial that may be of second, third, fourth, or higher order (Greene 2012). Assuming a second-order polynomial, van Stel and Storey (2004) found that the effect of new business formation on regional growth over time is positive and follows an inverted U-shaped pattern: it increases in strength over the first four years, and then, after having reached a maximum in the fourth year, decreases and finally becomes statistically insignificant after about eight years. Over this eight-year period, the effect of new business formation on regional employment was clearly positive.

In late 2003, my PhD student Pamela Mueller and I tried to replicate this result with German data. In contrast to van Stel and Storey (2004), we found the relationship between regional new business formation and employment growth to be U-shaped when we assumed a second-order polynomial. The effect was slightly positive in the first year, then turned negative, becoming positive again after about eight years. For new business formation that lagged by more than ten years, the relationship was statistically insignificant. A crucial limitation of a second-order polynomial is that it allows for only one inflection point, whereas higher-order polynomials can have more than one inflection point. When we assumed a polynomial of a higher than second order, we found that the lag structure was S-shaped with two inflection points. Accordingly, the effect of new business formation on growth is positive in the first year, then turns negative, becoming positive again after five years, with this positive effect peaking after about eight years. Beyond this maximum, the effect decreases and becomes insignificant after about ten years. Figure 11.1 shows the result for the lag structure with and without application of the Almon lag procedure.

This S-shaped pattern matched the expectations I had developed previously in two papers (Fritsch 2004d, 2005). According to my interpretation, the positive effect of new business formation in the first year (Section I in Figure 11.1) was due to the additional employment in the new businesses and possibly also due to their demand for equipment. The competition that emerges between the newcomers and the incumbents may then lead to decreased employment

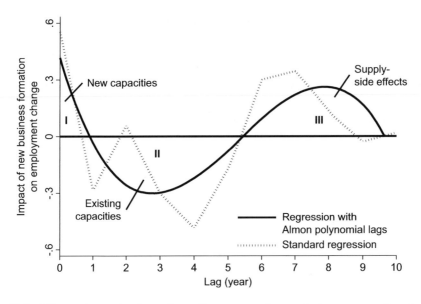

Figure 11.1 Effects of new business formation on employment change over time in West Germany – regression coefficients for start-up rates and the results of the Almon lag procedure assuming a third-order polynomial

Source: Fritsch 2008.

in the established firms (displacement effect), or the newly founded firms may turn out to be not sufficiently competitive and are forced to exit the market. In any case, a competitive process along the lines of "survival of the fittest" should result in increased productivity that leads to a reduction of labor inputs at a given output level. This can explain the negative effect of new business formation on employment that we observe between the first and the fifth year (Section II in Figure 11.1). The positive effect after the fifth year (Section III in Figure 11.1) cannot be explained by later growth of the newly founded businesses because available empirical analyses (for Germany, see Fritsch and Weyh 2006; Schindele and Weyh 2011) of the development of start-up cohorts find a constant employment decrease after the first years. I concluded that the reason for the increase in employment that we found after the fifth year must be improved competitiveness in the region that is attracting in additional demand.

This new evidence on the lag structure could explain why David Audretsch and I, more than ten years previously, did not find any significant positive effect when we related regional start-up rates to employment growth in the successive three-year period (Audretsch and Fritsch 1996; Fritsch 1997). The time period that we had available at that time was simply too short to allow discovery of the positive supply-side effects that begin to dominate the development after the fifth year! Our evidence was also in accord with empirical research into the impact of entry (and exit) on average productivity at the industry level.[9] That this productivity increase often becomes visible only after several years suggests that the market process requires some time to achieve the positive effects of competition on market performance.

Our findings and their interpretation had a number of important implications. First, for a positive effect of new business formation on growth, it is essential that the market process is one of survival of the fittest. Exit of noncompetitive firms is a key element of this process, and policy should avoid anything that may distort market selection. Second, the employment effect of new business formation on economic development is not due only to new jobs created by the new entities, the "direct" effect, but also to an important "indirect" effect, namely, increased productivity and employment in the incumbents. Third, the intensity of the competitive pressure that newcomers exert on incumbents, as well as the incumbents' reaction, should be important determinants of the magnitude of the effects. This suggests that it is especially the challenging type of start-up that is responsible for a positive effect on regional development. Hence, the "quality" of the new businesses in terms innovativeness, as well as the competitive response of the incumbent firms, should play a role here. These reasons make it clear that the effect of new business formation on employment will vary across regions.

Pamela Mueller and I finished a first version of a paper containing these results and interpretations during the 2003 Christmas holidays, exchanging drafts by e-mail. On New Year's Day of 2004 I sent this paper to several colleagues. Some weeks later, Zoltan Acs sent me an e-mail asking if we would agree to have the paper considered for a special issue of *Regional Studies* that he was editing with David Storey. After a speedy review process and some revisions, the final version of the paper (Fritsch and Mueller 2004) appeared in this special issue in the summer of that same year.

However, it was still unclear whether our results would hold for countries other than West Germany. As luck would have it, my old friend David Audretsch provided a great opportunity to explore this question. In the fall of 2003, David became director of the department of "Entrepreneurship and Public Policy" at the Max Planck Institute for Economics in Jena, located about 140 km from my university in Freiberg. The institute provided a fantastic environment for economic research and was a leading center of entrepreneurship research until David stepped down from directorship in 2009. Our proximity allowed us intensified contact with each other. David offered me the opportunity to organize a workshop at the Max Planck Institute, at which I could invite scholars to present results for other countries applying the same methodology. My requests for such empirical analyses were quite successful,[10] and in July 2005, empirical evidence was presented for a number of countries, all of which confirmed the basic pattern we had found for Germany. Right after the workshop, I asked Zoltan Acs and David Audretsch, the founders and editors of *Small Business Economics*, to publish a special issue of that journal in which the Jena workshop contributions could be published. They agreed and the special issue was published in 2008 (see Fritsch 2008).

Differences across regions, types of entry, and indirect effects

The papers presented at the Max Planck workshop in 2005 confirmed the basic pattern of the effects of new business formation for a number of countries,[11] but also revealed considerable differences across countries and regions. For example, Pamela Mueller, André van Stel, and David Storey (2008) conducted their analysis for Great Britain as a whole and then separately for Scotland, Wales, and the southeast of England, finding significant differences between these three regions. Most remarkably, whereas the overall effect of new business formation was quite positive for southeast England, it was negative for Scotland. In our analysis of West Germany, Pamela Mueller and I found that the positive as well as the negative effects of new business formation on employment were most pronounced in agglomerations and weakest in rural regions (Fritsch and Mueller 2004, 2008). André van Stel and Kashifa Suddle (2008) showed a positive effect of new business formation in the urban areas of the Netherlands but a clearly negative result in that country's rural regions. The evidence on the effect of entries with different characteristics (Acs and Mueller 2008; Baptista and Preto 2010) suggested that not all start-ups are equally important for economic development but that the quality of the newcomers does play a decisive role. However, the results were by no means uniform.

In the fall of 2006, I left Freiberg University for the Friedrich Schiller University Jena where I became chair of Business Dynamics, Innovation, and Economic Change. One of my functions in this position was to act as an interface between the university and David Audretsch's department at the Max Planck Institute. In Jena, I began to investigate in more detail the differences in the effects of new business formation across regions, as well as the indirect effects. Alexandra Schroeter and I identified population density as the key variable for differing regional effects (Fritsch and Schroeter 2011). However, we still could not say anything about the forces behind this variable, which may include a variety of factors, such as knowledge spillover, thick markets, intensity of competition, qualification of the workforce, the challenging quality of start-ups, and the like.

Florian Noseleit and I distinguished between the jobs created in the new businesses and the effect of start-ups on employment in incumbent businesses (Fritsch and Noseleit 2013a). This analysis showed that the effect of new business formation on incumbents over a period of ten years was clearly positive in most German regions. Moreover, we found that the S-shape of the lag structure (see Figure 11.1) is entirely due to the effects new business formation has on incumbents. Comparing the employment generation by the newcomers[12] and the positive employment effect on the incumbents over a period of ten years after entry, we found that the effect on the incumbents was considerably larger and constituted about two-thirds of the overall effect. Performing the analysis separately for agglomerations, moderately congested regions, and rural areas, we showed that regional differences were almost entirely due to indirect effects on incumbents. Still, the forces behind this effect of population density remained unclear.

A plausible explanation for the stronger effect of new business formation in high-density areas is that these regions are characterized by a higher level of competition. Such competition may occur on the output market as well as on the input markets, for example, the labor market or the market for floor space. Competition on the input market may be relevant because increased demand for inputs should lead to higher input prices, which may pressure incumbents to increase their productivity. I investigated these two types of competition in studies with Florian Noseleit and Javier Changoluisa. Fritsch and Noseleit (2013b) found that the effect of new business formation on employment in incumbents was higher in regions where the industry structure of the newcomers is similar to the industry structure of the incumbents. This might indicate that the effects depend to some degree on competition on the output markets. Fritsch and Changoluisa (2014) revealed that the positive effect of new business formation on the labor productivity of incumbent firms only occurs when the new firms are in the same two-digit industry as the incumbents. In contrast, the level of new business formation in other industries, which may signal the intensity of competition on input markets, had no significant effect. Hence, both studies find that competition on the output side is more important than competition on the markets for inputs in regard to the growth effects of new businesses.[13]

My study with Javier Changoluisa (Fritsch and Changoluisa 2014) confirmed the claim by Aghion et al. (2009) that firms that operate close to the technological frontier are likely to respond to the challenge of entry with improvements, whereas those who are far from the frontier tend to be discouraged and exit the market. This provides support for the hypothesis that the quality of the incumbent firms is an important factor in the effect that new businesses have on economic development.

The available data are insufficient for assessing the quality of new businesses and the role such quality (or lack thereof) plays in regional development. Based on an idea of my former PhD student Oliver Falck (Falck 2007), Florian Noseleit and I classified new businesses based on the length of time they survive in the market. New businesses that exit the market rather soon after entry, the "mayflies," can be regarded as of relatively low quality; those that are able to survive for several years can be assumed to be more of a challenge to incumbents. When analyzing the effect of short- and long-term survivors on employment growth, we found that the effect was statistically significant for the long-term survivors and not at all significant for the mayflies (Fritsch and Noseleit 2013c). A similar result was found by Udo Brixy (2014), who used productivity growth as the dependent variable.

A surprising result of all these studies was that the effect of new business formation on regional productivity and employment is concentrated in the same planning region in which the new businesses are started. Quite frequently, tests that also included measures for entry in adjacent regions showed no significant effect. These findings mean that it is not only the formation of new businesses that has to be regarded as a "regional event" (Feldman 2001), but that the processes through which newcomers lead to economic growth are also largely region specific.

Regional entrepreneurship culture

When I moved to Jena University in the fall of 2006, I became aware of a group of political science, sociology, and psychology scholars who were engaged in research about the transformation of East German society after German reunification. The group was funded by the German Research Foundation (DFG) as a Collaborative Research Center (*Sonderforschungsbereich*). I became a member of this group during the final funding phase of the program from 2008 to 2012. The topic of my project was the development of entrepreneurship and its role in the transformation process. One of the three PhD students I engaged for this project was Michael Wyrwich, who had just finished his master thesis under my supervision. By chance, I discovered data about self-employment in East Germany as of September 1989, directly before the socialist GDR regime collapsed. Michael Wyrwich prepared these data for empirical analysis and found that regions with relatively high levels of self-employment in 1989 had high levels of new business formation in the following years.[14]

Generous funding by the German Research Foundation permitted the labor-intensive preparation of historical data on firms and employment status of the German labor force in 1925. Based on these data, we discovered that the spatial pattern of self-employment in East Germany in 1925 was remarkably similar to the pattern of remaining self-employment in 1989, as well to the level of new business formation in subsequent years. This was surprising given the drastic economic and social disruption of World War II, the more than forty years of socialist rule in East Germany during which attempts were made to extinguish all private businesses, and the region's shock transformation to a market economy. When performing the analysis for West Germany, we again found a significant persistence of entrepreneurship over a period of eighty years. We interpreted the long-term persistence of regional entrepreneurship as the result of a regional culture, that is, an informal institution (see Fritsch and Wyrwich 2014). Such long-term persistence of cultural values and beliefs was discovered in a number of respects in previous research (see, for example, Nunn 2009, 2012). I myself was involved in another research project in which we found a long-term artistic culture (Falck, Fritsch, and Heblich 2011), but we were the first to find such long-term persistence with regard to entrepreneurship.

Our research on entrepreneurship in East Germany after the transformation process led us to conclude that regions with a relatively high level of new business formation were the most successful in coping with the transformation to a market economy and that many of these regions already had relatively high levels of entrepreneurial activity in 1925 and in 1989 (Fritsch et al. 2014).[15] This suggested that a regional culture of entrepreneurship could be an important source of economic growth. At around the same time that we conducted this analysis for East Germany,

Glaeser, Kerr, and Kerr (2015) published a paper containing similar results for the United States. Assuming that a regional concentration of the mining sector implies the presence of large firms and low levels of entrepreneurship, they used the geographic distance of a region to the nearest coal mine around the year 1900 as an indicator for historic levels of entrepreneurship and found a significantly positive link with entrepreneurship and regional growth today. Because East Germany does not have a sufficiently large number of regions of the size that would allow investigating the role played by a regional culture of entrepreneurship in economic growth with refined econometric methods, Michael Wyrwich and I had to limit our analysis to West Germany. We found that a pronounced regional culture of entrepreneurship as measured by high levels of self-employment in 1925 not only leads to relatively high levels of new business formation, but also to higher growth due to its effect on start-up activity (Fritsch and Wyrwich 2016).

Conclusions and further questions

Entrepreneurship not only makes an important contribution to growth – it may be its key driver. The results of the empirical analyses that I have described here clearly show that the effect of new business formation on growth emerges through the competition between newcomers and incumbents. Hence, the growth effects depend on the intensity of this competition, particularly the significance of the challenge that the newcomers exert on the incumbents and the incumbents' response to this challenge that determine the magnitude of the effect. Both start-ups and incumbents are key players in the manifestation of growth effects, and thus it is plausible that the quality of both types of actors contributes to explaining observed regional variations in start-up–induced growth. The results of the empirical research further suggest that the employment effects of the competitive process between start-ups and incumbents are to some degree limited to the region where the new businesses emerge. This clearly indicates that region-specific factors play an important role and that the region can be an important arena of entrepreneurship policy. The region's role, however, is as yet not well understood.

The relationship between entrepreneurship and growth is complex, and it may be appropriate to speak of regional systems of entrepreneurship (Qian, Acs, and Stough 2013) or regional growth regimes (Audretsch and Fritsch 2002). A number of factors may shape the quantity as well as the quality of new businesses and the way incumbents respond to these challenges. Hence, it is not just new business formation that creates growth, but the interaction of the newcomers with other businesses in their regional (and national) environment.

The long-term persistence of regional entrepreneurship and its positive effect on growth that has been found in empirical analyses raise a number of important questions. First, the main elements of a regional culture of entrepreneurship need to be identified with more specificity. How does a culture of entrepreneurship emerge, and how can it be stimulated? How is a culture of entrepreneurship transferred over time, and how can it persist despite disruptive changes in the environment? Do regions with a pronounced culture of entrepreneurship have a higher share of people with an entrepreneurial mind-set (see Obschonka et al. 2013)?[16] Do such regions attract entrepreneurial people from other regions? Second, and even more important, we should find out what all this means for policy aimed at stimulating regional growth. How can a culture of entrepreneurship be promoted? What steps could be taken to foster such a culture in regions where entrepreneurship does not play a significant role? If regional culture and levels of entrepreneurship are fairly stable over time, what is the time horizon for respective policy measures to become effective? These are important questions on my current research agenda, and I hope that I will be able to help answer them.

Notes

1 I am indebted to Javier Changoluisa and Michael Wyrwich for helpful comments on an earlier version.
2 I will not deal with my work on other topics in the field of entrepreneurship such as the determinants of new business formation (see, e.g., Fritsch and Falck 2007; Fritsch and Aamoucke 2013), survival of new businesses (Fritsch, Brixy, and Falck 2006), regional availability of venture capital (Fritsch and Schilder 2012), or the income of the self-employed (Sorgner, Fritsch, and Kritikos 2014).
3 I have reviewed the development of the concept in Fritsch (2004a).
4 Most of the papers presented at that workshop can be found in Fritsch and Hull (1987).
5 Parallel work at that time was being conducted by Tito Boeri and Ulrich Cramer; see Boeri and Cramer (1992).
6 Revised versions of these papers can be found in Brezinski and Fritsch (1996).
7 This work was funded in the framework of a priority program (*Schwerpunktprogramm*) of the German Research Association (DFG) that I organized with Juergen Schmude. The program lasted until 2004. Parts of the work conducted in this priority program are summarized in Fritsch and Schmude (2006).
8 These results were in line with earlier research of Storey and Johnson (1987), Boeri and Cramer (1992), Wagner (1994), Baldwin (1995), and Davis, Haltiwanger, and Schuh (1996).
9 E.g., Baldwin (1995), Caves (1998), Foster, Haltiwanger, and Syverson (2001), Disney, Haskel, and Heden (2003), OECD (2003), and Foster, Haltiwanger, and Krizian (2006).
10 In preparing the analysis for other the countries, it was helpful that my co-author Pamela Mueller joined the team for the case of Great Britain, and she also conducted the empirical analysis for the United States together with Zoltan Acs.
11 These countries were the Netherlands, Portugal, Spain, the United Kingdom, the United States, and several OECD countries. Another special issue of *Small Business Economics* on "Entrepreneurial Dynamics and Regional Growth" that I edited with Marcus Dejardin some years later provided empirical evidence for Belgium and Sweden also.
12 On average, an entry cohort of a particular year adds 1.8% to overall employment after two years and 1.56% after 10 years. The difference between the long-term and the short-term contribution reflects the declining employment in start-up cohorts between the second year and the tenth year after entry. See Fritsch and Schindele (2011) and Fritsch and Noseleit (2013a) for details.
13 In an analysis based on Swedish data, Martin Andersson and Florian Noseleit (2011) show that new business formation in a certain sector can have significant effects on employment in other sectors of the economy. This clearly indicates that the indirect effects of start-ups are not limited to the industry or sector in which the start-ups occur.
14 Some years earlier, Pamela Mueller and I had already found and analyzed persistence of new business formation in the regions of West Germany over a period of 20 years; see Fritsch and Mueller (2007).
15 Michael Wyrwich has conducted rather detailed analyses of the impact of forty years of socialist regime in East Germany on new business formation; see Wyrwich (2013).
16 A recent analysis by Stuetzer et al. (2016) for the United Kingdom confirms that regions with higher employment shares of large-scale industries in the nineteenth century have lower start-up and self-employment rates today, as well as a lower share of population with an entrepreneurial personality profile.

References

Acs, Zoltan J. and Pamela Mueller (2008): Employment Effects of Business Dynamics: Mice, Gazelles and Elephants. *Small Business Economics*, 30, 85–100.
Aghion, Phillippe, Richard W. Blundell, Rachel Griffith, Peter Howitt, and Susanne Prantl (2009): The Effects of Entry on Incumbent Innovation and Productivity. *Review of Economics and Statistics*, 91, 20–32.
Andersson, Martin and Florian Noseleit (2011): Start-Ups and Employment Dynamics within and Across Sectors. *Small Business Economics*, 36, 461–483.
Audretsch, David B. and Michael Fritsch (1994a): The Geography of Firm Births in Germany. *Regional Studies*, 28, 359–365.
—— and Michael Fritsch (1994b): On the Measurement of Entry Rates. *Empirica*, 21, 105–113.
—— and Michael Fritsch (1996): Creative Destruction: Turbulence and Economic Growth. In Ernst Helmstädter and Mark Perlman (eds.), *Behavioral Norms, Technological Progress, and Economic Dynamics: Studies in Schumpeterian Economics*. Ann Arbor: University of Michigan Press, 137–150.

—— and Michael Fritsch (2002): Growth Regimes over Time and Space. *Regional Studies*, 36, 113–124.

—— and Max Keilbach (2004): Entrepreneurship Capital and Economic Performance. *Regional Studies*, 38, 949–959.

——, Max Keilbach, and Erik Lehmann (2006): *Entrepreneurship and Economic Growth*. Oxford: Oxford University Press.

Baldwin, John R. (1995): *The Dynamics of Industrial Competition – A North American Perspective*. Cambridge: Cambridge University Press.

Baptista, Rui and Miguel Torres Preto (2010): Long-Term Effects of New Firm Formation by Type of Start-Up. *International Journal of Entrepreneurship and Small Business*, 11, 382–402.

Birch, David L. (1979): *The Job Generation Process*. Cambridge, MA: MIT Program on Neighborhood and Regional Change (mimeo).

Birch, David L. (1981): Who Creates Jobs? *Public Interest*, 65(Fall), 3–14.

Boeri, Tito and Ulrich Cramer (1992): Employment Growth, Incumbents and Entrants – Evidence from Germany. *International Journal of Industrial Organization*, 10, 545–565.

Brezinski, Horst and Michael Fritsch (eds.) (1996): *The Economic Impact of New Firms in Post-Socialist Countries – Bottom Up Transformation in Eastern Europe*. Cheltenham: Edward Elgar Publishers.

Brixy, Udo (1999): *Die Rolle von Betriebsgründungen für die Arbeitsplatzentwicklung*. Nuremberg: Institut für Arbeitsmarkt- und Berufsforschung.

Brixy, Udo (2014): The Significance of Entry and Exit for Regional Productivity Growth. *Regional Studies*, 48, 1051–1070.

Caves, Richard E. (1998): Industrial Organization and New Findings on the Turnover and Mobility of Firms. *Journal of Economic Literature*, 36, 1947–1982.

Davis, Steven J., John C. Haltiwanger, and Scott Schuh (1996): *Job Creation and Destruction*. Cambridge, MA: MIT Press.

Disney, Richard, Jonathan Haskel, and Ylva Heden (2003): Restructuring and Productivity Growth in UK Manufacturing. *Economic Journal*, 113, 666–694.

Ewers, Hans-Jürgen, Carsten Becker, and Michael Fritsch (1990a): *Wirkungen des Einsatzes computergestützter Techniken in Industriebetrieben*. Berlin/New York: de Gruyter.

Ewers, Hans-Jürgen, Carsten Becker, and Michael Fritsch (1990b): The Nature of Employment Effects of New Technology. In Egon Matzner and Michael Wagner (eds.), *The Employment Impact of New Technology – The Case of West Germany*. Aldershot: Avebury/Gower, 23–41.

Ewers, Hans-Jürgen and Reinhart Wettmann (1980): Innovation Oriented Regional Policy. *Regional Studies*, 14, 161–179.

Falck, Oliver (2007): Mayflies and Long-Distance Runners: The Effects of New Business Formation on Industry Growth. *Applied Economic Letters*, 14, 1919–1922.

Falck, Oliver, Michael Fritsch, and Stephan Heblich (2011): The Phantom of the Opera: Cultural Amenities, Human Capital, and Regional Economic Growth. *Labour Economics*, 18, 755–766.

Feldman, Maryann P. (2001): The Entrepreneurial Event Revisited: Firm Formation in a Regional Context. *Industrial and Corporate Change*, 10, 861–891.

Foster, Lucia, John C. Haltiwanger, and Cornell J. Krizian (2006): Market Selection, Reallocation, and Restructuring in the U.S. Retail Trade Sector in the 1990s. *Review of Economics and Statistics*, 88, 748–758.

Foster, Lucia, John Haltiwanger, and Chad Syverson (2001): Aggregate Productivity Growth: Lessons from Microeconomic Evidence. In Charles R. Hulton, Edwin R. Dean, and Michael J. Harper (eds.), *New Developments in Productivity Analysis*. Chicago: University of Chicago Press, 303–363.

Fritsch, Michael (1983): *Ökonomische Ansätze zur Legitimation kollektiven Handelns*. Berlin: Duncker & Humblot.

—— (1990): *Arbeitsplatzentwicklung in Industriebetrieben – Entwurf einer Theorie der Arbeitsplatzdynamik und empirische Analysen auf einzelwirtschaftlicher Ebene*. Berlin/New York: de Gruyter.

—— (1992): Regional Differences in New Firm Formation: Evidence from West Germany. *Regional Studies*, 25, 233–241.

—— (1996): Turbulence and Growth in West-Germany: A Comparison of Evidence by Regions and Industries. *Review of Industrial Organization*, 11, 231–251.

—— (1997): New Firms and Regional Employment Change. *Small Business Economics*, 9, 437–448.

—— (2000): Interregional Differences in R&D Activities – An Empirical Investigation. *European Planning Studies*, 8, 409–427.

—— (2003): Does Cooperation Behavior Differ between Regions? *Industry and Innovation*, 10, 25–39.

—— (2004a): Von der innovationsorientierten Regionalförderung zur regionalisierten Innovationspolitik. In Michael Fritsch (ed.), *Marktdynamik und Innovation – Gedächtnisschrift für Hans-Jürgen Ewers*. Berlin: Duncker & Humblot, 105–127.

—— (2004b): R&D-Cooperation and the Efficiency of Regional Innovation Activities. *Cambridge Journal of Economics*, 28, 829–846.

—— (2004c): Entrepreneurship, Entry and Performance of New Businesses Compared in Two Growth Regimes: East and West Germany. *Journal of Evolutionary Economics*, 14, 525–542.

—— (2004d): Zum Zusammenhang zwischen Gründungen und Wirtschaftsentwicklung. In Michael Fritsch and Reinhold Grotz (eds.), *Empirische Analysen des Gründungsgeschehens in Deutschland*. Heidelberg: Physica, 199–211.

—— (2005): Gründungen und regionale Beschäftigungsentwicklung – Empirische Evidenz und offene Fragen. In Friederike Welter (ed.), *Dynamik im Unternehmenssektor: Theorie, Empirie und Politik*. Berlin: Duncker & Humblot, 45–58.

—— (2008): How Does New Business Formation Affect Regional Development? Introduction to the Special Issue. *Small Business Economics*, 30, 1–14.

—— and Alexandra Schroeter (2011): Why Does the Effect of New Business Formation Differ Across Regions? *Small Business Economics*, 36, 383–400.

—— and Antje Weyh (2006): How Large are the Direct Employment Effects of New Businesses? – An Empirical Investigation. *Small Business Economics*, 27, 245–260.

—— and Christopher Hull (eds.) (1987): *Arbeitsplatzdynamik und Regionalentwicklung – Beiträge zur beschäftigungspolitischen Bedeutung von Groß- und Kleinunternehmen*. Berlin: Edition Sigma.

—— and Dirk Schilder (2012): The Regional Supply of Venture Capital – Can Syndication Overcome Bottlenecks? *Economic Geography*, 88, 59–76.

——, Elisabeth Bublitz, Alina Sorgner, and Michael Wyrwich (2014): How Much of a Socialist Legacy? The Re-Emergence of Entrepreneurship in the East German Transformation to a Market Economy. *Small Business Economics*, 43, 427–446.

—— and Florian Noseleit (2013a): Investigating the Anatomy of the Employment Effect of New Business Formation. *Cambridge Journal of Economics*, 37, 349–377.

—— and Florian Noseleit (2013b): Indirect Employment Effects of New Business Formation across Regions: The Role of Local Market Conditions. *Papers in Regional Science*, 92, 361–382.

—— and Florian Noseleit (2013c): Start-Ups, Long- and Short-Term Survivors, and Their Contribution to Employment Growth. *Journal of Evolutionary Economics*, 23, 719–733.

—— and Javier Changoluisa (2014): New Business Formation and the Productivity of Manufacturing Incumbents: Effects and Mechanisms, Jena Economic Research Papers # 2014–025, Friedrich Schiller University and Max Planck Institute of Economics Jena.

—— and Joern Mallok (1998): Surviving the Transition: The Process of Adaptation of Small and Medium-Sized Firms in East Germany. In Horst Brezinski, Egon Franck, and Michael Fritsch (eds.), *The Microeconomics of Transformation and Growth*. Cheltenham: Edward Elgar Publishers, 163–184.

—— and Juergen Schmude (eds.) (2006): *Entrepreneurship in the Region*. New York: Springer.

—— and Michael Wyrwich (2014): The Long Persistence of Regional Levels of Entrepreneurship: Germany 1925 to 2005. *Regional Studies*, 48, 955–973.

—— and Michael Wyrwich (2016): The Effect of Entrepreneurship for Economic Development – An Empirical Analysis using Regional Entrepreneurship Culture. *Journal of Economic Geography*, forthcoming. DOI:10.1093/jeg/lbv049.

—— and Oliver Falck (2007): New Business Formation by Industry over Space and Time: A Multi-Dimensional Analysis. *Regional Studies*, 41, 157–172.

—— and Pamela Mueller (2004): The Effects of New Firm Formation on Regional Development over Time. *Regional Studies*, 38, 961–975.

—— and Pamela Mueller (2007): The Persistence of Regional New Business Formation-Activity over Time – Assessing the Potential of Policy Promotion Programs. *Journal of Evolutionary Economics*, 17, 299–315.

—— and Pamela Mueller (2008): The Effect of New Business Formation on Regional Development over Time: The Case of Germany. *Small Business Economics*, 30, 15–29.

—— and Ronney Aamoucke (2013): Regional Public Research, Higher Education, and Innovative Start-Ups – An Empirical Investigation. *Small Business Economics*, 41, 865–885.

——, Udo Brixy, and Oliver Falck (2006): The Effect of Industry, Region and Time on New Business Survival – A Multi-Dimensional Analysis. *Review of Industrial Organization*, 28, 285–306.

—— and Yvonne Schindele (2011): The Contribution of New Businesses to Regional Employment – An Empirical Analysis. *Economic Geography*, 87, 153–170.

Glaeser, Edward L., Sari Pekkala Kerr, and William R. Kerr (2015): Entrepreneurship and Urban Growth: An Empirical Assessment with Historical Mines. *Review of Economics and Statistics*, 97, 498–520.

Greene, William H. (2012): *Econometric Analysis*, 7th ed. Harlow: Pearson.

Mueller, Pamela, André van Stel, and David J. Storey (2008): The Effect of New Firm Formation on Regional Development over Time: The Case of Great Britain. *Small Business Economics*, 30, 59–71.

Nunn, Nathan (2009): The Importance of History for Economic Development. *Annual Review of Economics*, 1, 65–92.

—— (2012): Culture and the Historical Process. *Economic History of Developing Regions*, 27, S108–S126.

Obschonka, Martin, Eva Schmitt-Rodermund, Samuel D. Gosling, and Rainer K. Silbereisen (2013): The Regional Distribution and Correlates of an Entrepreneurship-Prone Personality Profile in the United States, Germany, and the United Kingdom: A Socioecological Perspective. *Journal of Personality and Social Psychology*, 105, 104–122.

Organisation for Economic Co-operation and Development (OECD) (2003): *The Sources of Economic Growth in OECD Countries*. Paris: OECD.

Qian, Haifeng, Zoltan J. Acs, and Roger R. Stough (2013): Regional Systems of Entrepreneurship: The Nexus of Human Capital, Knowledge and New Firm Formation. *Journal of Economic Geography*, 13, 559–587.

Reynolds, Paul D. (1994): Autonomous Firm Dynamics and Economic Growth in the United States, 1986–90. *Regional Studies*, 27, 429–442.

Reynolds, Paul D. (1999): Creative Destruction: Source or Symptom of Economic Growth? In Zoltan J. Acs, Bo Carlsson, and Charlie Karlsson (eds.), *Entrepreneurship, Small and Medium-Sized Enterprises and the Macroeconomy*. Cambridge, UK: Cambridge University Press, 97–136.

Reynolds, Paul D., David J. Storey, and Paul Westhead (1994): Cross National Comparison of the Variation on the New Firm Formation Rates. *Regional Studies*, 27, 443–456.

Reynolds, Paul D. and Wilbur R. Maki (1990): Business Volatility and Economic Growth (Final Project Report). Minneapolis (mimeo).

Schindele, Yvonne and Antje Weyh (2011): The Direct Employment Effects of New Businesses in Germany Revisited – An Empirical Investigation for 1976–2004. *Small Business Economics*, 36, 353–363.

Sorgner, Alina, Michael Fritsch, and Alexander Kritikos (2014): Do Entrepreneurs Really Earn Less? Jena Economic Research Papers # 2014–029, Friedrich Schiller University and Max Planck Institute of Economics Jena.

Storey, David J. and Steven Johnson (1987): *Job Generation and Labour Market Change*. Basingstoke: MacMillan.

Stuetzer, Michael, Martin Obschonka, David B. Audretsch, Michael Wyrwich, Peter J. Rentfrow, Mike Coombes, Leigh Shaw-Taylor, and Max Satchell. (2016): Industry Structure, Entrepreneurship, and Culture: An Empirical Analysis Using Historical Coalfields. *European Economic Review*, 86, 52–72.

van Stel, André and David J. Storey (2004): The Link between Firm Births and Job Creation: Is There a Upas Tree Effect? *Regional Studies*, 38, 893–909.

van Stel, André and Kashifa Suddle (2008): The Impact of New Firm Formation on Regional Development in the Netherlands. *Small Business Economics*, 30, 31–47.

Wagner, Joachim (1994): The Post-Entry Performance of New Small Firms in German Manufacturing Industries. *Journal of Industrial Economics*, 42, 141–154.

Wyrwich, Michael (2012): Regional Entrepreneurial Heritage in a Socialist and a Post-Socialist Economy. *Economic Geography*, 88, 423–445.

Wyrwich, Michael (2013): Can Socioeconomic Heritage Produce a Lost Generation with Regard to Entrepreneurship? *Journal of Business Venturing*, 28, 667–682.

12
Anecdotes of destiny[1]

William B. Gartner

Introduction

> Autobiographies do not form indisputable authorities. They are always incomplete, and often unreliable. Eager as I am to put down the truth, there are difficulties; memory fails especially in small details, so that it becomes finally but a theory of my life.
>
> (Du Bois, 1968: 12)

The editors of this book have tasked authors to address three issues: "clearly articulate what were your most important ideas about entrepreneurship, what led you to develop those ideas into the literature, and what has been the impact of those ideas." There is a conundrum in this request. My research is about origins: the puzzle of why and how organizations come into existence. And my immersion into the nature of organization origins has humbled me with regard to considerations about the moment of conception. Where to begin? Beginnings have the possibility of an infinite regress backwards. Isn't there always something before "begin?" – a cause that precedes the cause? X leads to Y, but what led to X? The choice of a beginning seems so arbitrary. So, in considering this request to identify specific ideas about entrepreneurship that I would attach myself to and then to offer speculations about the causes that led me towards these ideas, well . . . this is not so simple.

Family and background

Should I begin with the history of my family? Is it important to know that I can trace my ancestors to the Alsace region around Strasbourg, France? At some point during the reign of Catherine the Great (Empress of Russia – 1762 to 1796), my ancestors were invited to emigrate to the Ukraine, where for some 100 years they were part of a German-speaking culture (the "Black Sea Germans") of farmers and tradespersons. In the late 1800s, as political and social conditions in the Ukraine deteriorated for individuals of German heritage, many of my relatives emigrated, again, either to the United States (to settle around a city in North Dakota they named Strasbourg) or to Argentina. Those who stayed in the Ukraine were killed in various purges or were deported to Siberia.

By the 1930s, given climate changes and economic conditions in North Dakota, a life in farming (at least for my grandparents) proved unsustainable. My father's family moved to Washington State when my father was in the fifth grade. My mother's family continued to eke out a subsistence living through construction work and other assorted occupations in North Dakota. Through the serendipity that entails love and adventure, my parents met again in their late teens – they had known each other in grade school, and through the forms of romance common in those days, eventually married (soon after they both turned twenty-one) and settled in Washington State. My father began his career as a chemist at Hanford, Washington, after graduating from Seattle University, and my mother worked at a bank until she became pregnant with me. (And I should mention that my mother was valedictorian of her high school and was not given a scholarship because the scholarship committee believed that only men should go to college). I was born in Richland, Washington, in 1953.

I suggest this story could be interpreted in two ways. One is that I come from a long line of failed farmers: individuals who left their homes and moved because they couldn't make farming work in France, the Ukraine, or North Dakota. Or, I could say that this story depicts pioneering entrepreneurs who sought new opportunities through emigration and location mobility. Does my heritage influence my intellectual predispositions towards an interest in entrepreneurship? Or is the past merely a series of events with no influence or meaning?

Are childhood, grade school, and high school experiences of importance? What would be salient and offer any insight? One story that I find of some curiousness: At my parents' fiftieth wedding anniversary, one of my grade school teachers approached me and asked about my life since leaving Richland. I told her, with some bashfulness, that I had become a university professor and that I (at that time) held the Henry W. Simonsen Chair in Entrepreneurship at the University of Southern California (impressive sounding, yes?), and she came up very close to me and said: "I am so surprised to hear this. I thought you would be in prison." Really? I have always thought of myself as a well-behaved child and the type of student who was innocuous and rarely noticed. Later I asked my mother about what might have prompted this comment, and my mother's response was: "Did you think that I spent so much time at your school as a school aide? I was constantly in the principal's office begging them to not expel you!" No, really, I think of myself as very mild mannered. In grade school I can think of only a few instances where I appeared to be the center of some misunderstanding, but then, those situations seemed to be matters of interpretation of what "trouble" meant and whether my actions might be seen as just differing points of view as to how learning might occur in the classroom. None of my experiences, as I interpreted them, would have indicated that my future path would lead to incarceration. Yet, others thought differently.

On the Myers-Briggs I score as an INTJ (Quenk & Hammer, 1998). I was a slightly better-than-average student in high school and in college (B+ or a 3.2 on a 4-point scale). I took advanced math classes in high school and college, and I had hoped to major in math, but in my sophomore year of college, when studying differential equations, I realized my mind had reached some upper limit of mathematical perspicacity. I then majored in accounting in college (the math degree for business students). At some point during the many art classes I took in high school, my art teacher ended up leaving me alone, allowing me to set up a studio in a corner of the art room to let me do what I wanted: pencil drawings of my right hand, painting the number "4" and making slab pottery. I also learned to silk-screen and I teamed up with a friend to make silk-screened t-shirts to sell at school. We decided that the best way to sell t-shirts was to form a club where the t-shirts were a requirement for membership (we could charge more per t-shirt because the t-shirt was part of the dues for club membership). Soon the school administration looked at this club as a "gang" and the club (and the t-shirt sales that were generated from this) was banned. (Does this make me a "trouble maker," an "entrepreneur," "an organizer," or someone who just wanted to make a few dollars from a newly learned skill in silk-screening?) I learned French from a Spanish teacher, and I discovered I had no facility for languages. I did poorly in any writing courses or in literature courses that required writing. My handwriting has the arrested look of letters formed by a second-grade student. In high school I purchased an IBM "correcting" Selectric typewriter to submit papers. This worked for take-home assignments, but I was not so lucky with in-class exams. I write slowly in large letters (now, using a Pentel Color Pen Fine Point #S360–101 BLACK). During the year when children switch from block printing letters to cursive (I remember this as the fourth grade), my teacher felt that left-handed writers were children of the devil, and for that year I wrote cursive with my right hand. I play golf and bat in baseball right-handed. I throw and play tennis (and other racquet sports) left-handed. If you want me to quickly respond to "turn left" or "turn right" when driving, I will have no immediate insight into which direction you are asking me to go. I will likely turn the wrong way.

I do not recognize faces very well. I would not be able to pick you out of a crowd. I would hope to know you by observing what you are wearing as the way to recognize you. So, if you change your clothes, change your hair color, wear glasses when you did not before, or wear black like everyone in Europe, then, it will take me some time to figure out who you are. It would be better for me if everyone wore a nametag.

Everything is difficult for me. I cannot think of one activity (i.e., writing, research, playing the piano, playing tennis, friendship, marriage, fatherhood, etc.) I have ever demonstrated some natural ability at. I believe I have some insights into the process of learning because everything I do has required some conscious insights and practice to master. Those transcendent moments in my life are when the body takes over and the mind can just enjoy the flow of the present. I can type these words realizing that the fingers know where to go and what to say. That makes me happy. Most of my life is about thinking, yet the pleasures I find in this world are when I am not.

Do these stories and anecdotes offer any insights into subsequent academic efforts?

Ideas and their origins

> Wisdom is never
> Mine to give. It comes from an
> Anguish of the heart.

This section of the chapter is, essentially, a retelling of stories concerning a biography of ideas and research about entrepreneurship that I have associated myself with. I have already told stories about the development of my dissertation and the ideas that emanated from that experience in Gartner (2008, 2016). I have already offered (Gartner, 2004) a rather sanitized account of the publication process involved with the article "Who Is an Entrepreneur? Is the Wrong Question" (Gartner, 1988). And I have already provided an overview of the origins and logic for twenty-one articles published from 1985 to 2010 (Gartner, 2016). Given these previous histories, the challenge, then, in this section of the chapter is for me to offer insights that both emphasize what appear to be consistent viewpoints on the nature of my research, based on previous auto-biographical statements about my research efforts, and offer to portray these experiences in new ways that do not appear to plagiarize myself (if that is even possible).

I have organized my research into three themes that I believe might capture some sense of my academic scholarship: "Entrepreneurship as Variation," "Entrepreneurship as Organizing," and "Scholarship as Community." I will tell some stories about how specific articles came into existence as exemplars of those themes, and I suggest that readers realize that these stories are a retrospective "theory" (as Du Bois would put it) of these efforts. One issue that comes up for me in offering you this autobiographical effort is my questioning of a "consistent self." I wonder if my goal in telling these stories is to offer a progressive march towards continual enlightenment through particular insights (i.e., "variation," "organizing," "community") or whether the point of this exercise should be to emphasize the continual malleability of the self. Is it possible to say, "Oh, that was Bill Gartner in his twenties, and he isn't that way anymore. He was different then. If I met him on the street now, I would not recognize him." Could I like lemon pie in my twenties and now find that I only want to eat chocolate? Is championing the idea of "variation" merely, then, similar to a preference for lemon pie? I am not sure whether I saw a grand vision in my activities while I was undertaking them. Some ideas I seemed to have fallen in love with. I still wonder why after all of these years.

And, finally, a comment on the nature of the practice of scholarship that I hope underlies the stories that follow: writing is an emotional activity as well as an intellectual one. Sometimes the feelings about a particular idea are more important than the idea itself. The point of the haiku that begins this section hints at that. Rarely have I written a journal article that has been accepted without some major changes. The journal review process, can, at times, be fraught with abusive and unkind reviewers and editors who can write the most malicious and thoughtless comments about a manuscript. If you can visualize that a manuscript is somewhat like your own child, well, then, the review process can seem like a frenzy of faceless marauders who snatch your child from your arms and then proceed to hack the child to death. The process can feel horrific. Early in my career, I received a set of reviews and an editor's comments and "guidance" that led me to tears to the point where I could not look at the manuscript for two years. Every time I opened the file drawer where that manuscript was, I felt like I was driving past the scene of a terrible traffic accident. I eventually put the file of the manuscript in a drawer I rarely used. And, then, with some time passing, I was able to look at the manuscript again and send it out to get hacked up. But by then I was used to the carnage of the process. Here is a haiku I wrote in 2008 after working with some doctoral students in Kolding, Denmark, on their manuscripts and hearing about their hesitancy of sending their manuscripts out for review:

> Love your ideas.
> Care about them enough to
> Give them to others

The practice of academic scholarship requires some generosity of heart and faith in the beauty and insight of one's ideas. Although I have found some satisfaction in seeing words that I have written "in print," I have never found the process of writing easy.

Entrepreneurship as variation

> Never: Either / Or
> Instead "And." Add constraints for
> More rather than less

I assume that my interest in entrepreneurship stems from my studies at the University of Washington (1973 to 1982) where I earned a BA in accounting and an MBA and PhD in business policy (with a dissertation that focused on entrepreneurship). During the second year of my MBA program (1975 to 1977) I took a course in entrepreneurship from Karl Vesper, and it was in that experience of studying individuals involved in creating businesses that I became enamored with the topic.

One particular experience of that course stays in my mind as a harbinger of how entrepreneurship takes many different forms and involves individuals who I would not have ever assumed would be entrepreneurs. As part of the entrepreneurship course, Karl asked me to interview an entrepreneur, and he selected a man who Karl had recently read about in the newspaper: Leonard Tall, who had started Tall's Camera and Supply. What was interesting about Leonard Tall was not his business in selling cameras, but another business he had started (CX Corporation) that grew out of his frustrations with handling camera film that his camera shop developed into photographs for their customers. (For those who have grown up on digital technologies, predigital cameras used celluloid strips of film – negatives – that were developed in chemical baths; then once these rolls of film were processed, machines (or people) would make photographs by magnifying the film images from the rolls of film on to photo paper that was also processed in chemical baths until the images were "set" into the paper.) Although the Kodak Corporation had automated the processes of developing the rolls of film and the printing of the photos, the "front end" – the handling of the film cartridges themselves in a way that could be processed as quickly as the Kodak machines could process the film strips, and the "back end" – the handling of the photograph prints and the negatives used to make the photographic prints in a manner that was easy to handle and provide to customers – was a significant problem. The Kodak machines could process thousands of rolls of film quickly, but the rest of the photofinishing process was all done by hand. In the 1960s as Leonard Tall's camera shop developed more and more film for customers, he formed a company to figure out those problems of automating these front-end and back-end photofinishing issues. By the mid-1970s when I interviewed him, CX Corporation had designed and built machines that were handling over 70% of the photofinishing market in the United States. He was a very unprepossessing person and, in his gentle manner, regaled me with delightful stories of how he had created and built this company. (He eventually sold it to the Ciba-Geigy Corporation for hundreds of millions of dollars.) I left that meeting in awe of a man who did not present himself as a superhero, but rather as someone somewhat ordinary in nature. He had a wonderful sense of humor. He was not self-deprecating; instead, he just came across as smart – like you and me – and insightful, but not a seer. I think this formed the seed of some realization that entrepreneurs are *not* inherently different from other people. Entrepreneurs, indeed, are just like other people (maybe just more fun to be around).

And, then, there was the influence of Karl Vesper as I began my PhD studies.

My dissertation (Gartner, 1982) and the two publications stemming from that effort (Gartner, 1985, 1989) offer a view of entrepreneurship as a phenomenon that involves creating organizations, and this process occurs in a variety of environments, with people who come from different backgrounds and have different kinds of skills and knowledge, who start many different kinds of businesses, and who go about the process of creating these businesses in many different ways. All my subsequent research has its genesis in the experience of the dissertation. The details of this *Bildungsroman* are offered in Gartner (2008). I think anyone who does a close reading of Karl's book *New Venture Strategies* (Vesper, 1980) will be able to make the connections between his way of looking at entrepreneurship in terms of startup strategies, start-up behaviors, and kinds of motivations as serving as the basis for my effort at developing a framework of factors that account for differences among various kinds of new ventures (Gartner, 1985).

Briefly, a synopsis of the dissertation effort: Karl has funding from the National Science Foundation to explore whether university entrepreneurship education courses had an impact on enabling new ventures to come into existence. In surveying instructors of these courses, it became apparent that the names of individuals who attended these courses were often not students in these courses, and the sample of individuals who I had identified were something of a mish-mash of entrepreneurs with various backgrounds that might have some tangential relationship to a university entrepreneurship course (e.g., some entrepreneurs in the sample had been speakers in these classes rather than students in these classes). What to do with this sample? After engaging in in-depth case studies of these individuals, as well as having them fill out a detailed questionnaire about their backgrounds, I then asked for information about how they went about starting their own businesses (based on a case study that they all read and then responded to about how they started their own business using the case as an anchor). I was left with a rather complicated and comprehensive sample of different kinds of business start-ups. I decided to explore whether there were any commonalities among all of the individuals who had been identified as entrepreneurs. The activity of trying to figure out which factors in the stories of these individuals had any commonalities served as the basis for the article "A Framework for Describing and Classifying the Phenomenon of New Venture Creation" (Gartner, 1985). The empirical exploration of the differences among these start-up stories evolved into a quantitative taxonomy of various categories of business start-ups that, at some level, had more similarities than differences compared to other start-ups in the sample. This study appeared as "A Taxonomy of New Business Ventures" (Gartner, Mitchell & Vesper, 1989). Note the lag in years between when the dissertation was completed (1982) and the publication of the framework (1985) and the empirical study (1989). The empirical study was the manuscript that sat in the file cabinet for two years.

In the meantime, a number of other articles emerged that were somewhat on the theme of variation: "Who Is an Entrepreneur? Is the Wrong Question" (Gartner, 1988) and "Properties of Emerging Organizations" (Katz & Gartner, 1988). As mentioned earlier, I have written in some detail about the emergence of the "Who" article in Gartner (2004) and Gartner (2016). Be that as it may, I will re-emphasize that my intention in the "Who" article was to suggest that there was no one specific type of entrepreneur and no one specific set of entrepreneurial motivations that would differentiate between "entrepreneurial" individuals and others. The "Who" article points to the logic of Gartner (1985), with an emphasis on behavior – on the processes of organizing (more on that in the next section). Essentially, then, "Who" suggests that the search for a particular entrepreneurial "type" is likely to be a fruitless search if there are a multitude of various environments, businesses, and activities where entrepreneurial activity occurs. For example, if one were to think of "technology entrepreneurs" as some kind of "type" of entrepreneur, then the problem becomes that of realizing that there are various technologies in technology – pharmaceuticals, chemistry, biology, computer science, etc. And, in each of the previous technology categories, for example, one could divide pharmaceuticals into many different kinds of pharmaceuticals (antihistamines, drugs for cancer, cholesterol, diabetes, etc.), and in each area of pharmaceuticals, there would be specific kinds of pharmaceutical businesses: businesses that develop pharmaceuticals, businesses that test pharmaceuticals, businesses that produce and market pharmaceuticals. To assume that the motivations and abilities of the individuals involved in these various types of technologies would be similar I find rather preposterous. There is no one type of "technology entrepreneur." There is just too much variation in these technology businesses. And then consider all of the other kinds of businesses and organizations that exist. They are all, in most ways, different from each other. We need to pay attention to that. And then the goal is to figure out ways of ascertaining how and why these various "entrepreneurships" are similar to or different from each other. (There is more on the behavioral part of the article in the next section).

The gist of the "Properties" (Katz & Gartner, 1988) article is to provide a framework for making sense of the fundamental characteristics of situations where organizations come into existence. Again, the article is another way of asking scholars to pay attention to the various ways in which organizations emerge. Recently, I have found this article very helpful in providing a scholarly context for making sense of the business model canvas (Osterwalder & Pigneur, 2013). One can categorize activities that students engage in when developing businesses into the various boxes in the canvas and then, show how boxes of the canvas can be linked to the four dimensions of the "Properties" article. I think that this practice of linking activities to the four properties offers important insights into the organization formation process (Brush, Manolova & Edelman, 2008). And, in my imagination, I would also hazard that the "Properties" article can then offer a foundation for considering aspects of how processes of social construction enable organizations to emerge (Fletcher, 2006).

So, I surmise that the foundation of my beliefs about the important of variation, then, stands on three articles written early in my career: Gartner (1985), Gartner (1988) and Katz & Gartner (1988).

Subsequently, then, in a quick tour of my research to look for interesting landmarks that offer insights into variation, I would suggest these articles as places to stop and enjoy the view: Gartner (1989) offers a way to study entrepreneurs based on a belief that the differences among entrepreneurs matter and, therefore, scholars must pay attention to those differences in their research. Gartner (1990) suggests that the language scholars use to talk about entrepreneurship inherently supports a sensibility that the phenomenon varies across such dimensions as kinds of entrepreneurs, the nature of innovativeness (or not), organization creation (or not), the creation of value (or not), profit or nonprofit, growth (or not), uniqueness (or not), and ownership (or not). The challenge, I believe, is that we tend to fixate on a particular entrepreneur, doing a particular set of activities, to create a particular type of business, in a particular type of environment. When you think of entrepreneurship, do your thoughts gravitate towards a particular person? Gartner and Gatewood (1992) introduce a special issue on "Models of Organization Formation" that intended to portray various ways scholars might conceptualize the organization formation process. The key word in the special issue title is "models" – that is, the plural of model – and our introduction offers a lovely riff on Weick's thoughts on requisite variety (Weick, 1979: 188) and the need to pay attention to accurately sensing differences that would occur through the theoretical lenses we use to peer into entrepreneurial phenomenon. And that idea is continued in a coda to this effort (Gartner & Gatewood, 1993) where we offer a number of other ways to consider various aspects of organization formation. And I also provide a specific focus on the creation of voluntary organizations (Gartner, 1993a) as a hint to entrepreneurship scholars that the reasons and purposes of the organization formation process stretch far beyond a specific entrepreneur's intentions and that focusing on aspects of the purposes of "others" who join organizations that do not have overt economic value might offer other ways of seeing the vastness of organizational efforts that encompass entrepreneurship. The story of variation continues in another special issue (Gartner, Shaver, Katz & Gatewood, 1994) that focuses on "Finding the Entrepreneur in Entrepreneurship" where we offer similar ideas about the importance of seeing entrepreneurs rather than "the entrepreneur"; action and thinking are inherent in what an entrepreneur "is"; the nature of entrepreneurship occurs over time (and therefore entrepreneurs themselves are likely to change over time if the process itself changes over time); and that differences among entrepreneurs matter. Is the scenery beginning to the look the same here?

Finally, I would cap off this tour of variation with the monumental edifice of the Panel Study of Entrepreneurial Dynamics – PSED (Gartner, Shaver, Carter & Reynolds, 2004; Reynolds, Carter, Gartner & Greene, 2004; Reynolds, 2007). The history of this effort is a story in itself – see Gartner, Shaver, Carter and Reynolds (2004) for a glimmer of the process; but the outcome of the PSED itself is a generalizable database of individuals in the process of starting businesses in the United States founded at various times between 1998 and 2000 and followed for five years, and there is another follow-on data set, PSED II, that explores individuals starting businesses that were interviewed beginning in 2005 (Reynolds & Curtin, 2008). The kinds of businesses, individuals, activities, and environments that comprise the PSED are vast, multifaceted, and complicated. That is the primary take-away I see when I look at the PSED. We start with "variety" in entrepreneurial phenomenon. Differences matter. So, then, I suggest that thinking in "averages" and using analytical tools that are inherent in linear regression often distract us from seeing the Brobdingnagian proportions of the phenomenon we encounter.

Entrepreneurship as organizing

It could be other –
Wise (Here / There / Then / Now) practice
Comes first for insight[2]

Many of the articles I have identified as exemplars of the idea of variation in entrepreneurship can also be used to champion an idea that the nature of entrepreneurship is inherently process oriented (Steyaert, 2007; Hjorth, Holt & Steyaert, 2015) and that the mechanism by which organizations emerge involves the catch-all term of "organizing" (Weick, 1979). When I look back on how the word "organizing" has been used in various articles I have been involved in, I sense the term has been used, in the end, metaphorically rather than operationally. That is, organizing is seen as a process, as something that occurs over time that involves actions of individuals that result in organizations. Entrepreneurs are organizers, per se, who:

> [unite] all means of production – the labor of one, the capital or the land of the others – and who [find] in the value of the products which result from the employment the reconstitution of the entire capital [they utilize], and, the value of the wages, the interest, and the rent which [they pay], as well as the profits belonging to [themselves].
>
> *(Cole, 1946: 3)*

This idea of organizing as some form of assembly of various factors of production (Say, 1816; Schumpeter, 1934) is embedded in the literature and continues to take on various connotations of this sensibility of "combining and assembly" in such terms as bricolage (Baker & Nelson, 2005) and effectuation (Sarasvathy, 2009). People engage in a variety of activities that result in organizations – that is the aspect of Weick's idea of organizing that, for me, has some resonance. It is both a sense of trying various ways of forming organizations and an emphasis on the "trying." So the idea of an ecological approach to behavior – that is, variation, selection, retention – that is espoused not only in Weick (1979) but is central to foundation texts in the sociology of entrepreneurship (i.e., Aldrich, 1999) should be recognized. Action occurs in the context of a particular situation over time (Welter, 2011).

So the ideas of variation and organizing actually go hand-in-hand down the path of my research efforts. The "framework" article (Gartner, 1985) identifies "process" as a critical dimension of entrepreneurship and suggests that what people do (and "people" is considered broadly to be not only the activities of entrepreneurs, but also the activities of others who could be involved in the process of organizing) matters. The "who" (Gartner, 1988) article champions a behavioral view of entrepreneurship and suggests that one approach to thinking about the nature of behavior is to apply Mintzberg's (1973) study of managers. The suggestion to use Mintzberg (1973) as a touchstone is not to champion his observational study as the only method for identifying the practices of entrepreneurs. I merely point out that observing individuals engaged in forming organizations has great value for understanding the phenomenon of entrepreneurship.

The ways in which researchers might observe entrepreneurs over time are numerous (Stewart & Aldrich, 2015).

In looking back through my resume, I believe there is a case to be made for showing that I have tried to publish a consistent stream of articles to further a behavioral view of entrepreneurship. In 1991 Lanny Herron, Harry Sapienza, and Deborah Smith-Cook organized an "Interdisciplinary Conference on Entrepreneurship Theory" at the University of Baltimore (Herron, Sapienza & Smith-Cook, 1992) where I teamed with Barbara Bird, who had published a book on entrepreneurial behavior two years earlier (Bird, 1989) and who I had collaborated with on efforts to develop the Academy of Management Entrepreneurship Interest Group (see later), and Jennifer Starr, who I had met in my wanderings up from Georgetown University to Wharton to hang around Ian MacMillan and Venkat Venkataraman, and who had just published a very insightful piece on resource acquisition strategies with Ian (Starr & MacMillan, 1990), to develop some ideas around entrepreneurial behavior by differentiating it from organizational behavior, as well as suggest that the field of organizational behavior might provide topics that could be applied to entrepreneurship studies. That article (Gartner, Bird & Starr, 1992) is, I believe, most widely known for the idea of "as if":

> Emerging organizations are thoroughly equivocal realities (Weick, 1979) that *tend* towards non-equivocality through entrepreneurial action. In emerging organization, entrepreneurs offer plausible explanations of current and future equivocal events as non-equivocal interpretations. Entrepreneurs talk and act "as if" equivocal events were non-equivocal. Emerging organizations are elaborate fictions or proposed future states of existence. In the context of the emerging organization, action is taken in expectation of a non-equivocal event in the future.
>
> *(Gartner, Bird & Starr, 1992: 17, original emphasis)*

It is in that space "between" some initial realization that one is in the process of organizing something and the actual organization that interests me – see Gartner (1993) for some thoughts on the process of organizational emergence. What entrepreneurs do to enable organizations to become real is the crux of many subsequent publications. Jennifer and I continued to explore the idea of entrepreneurial work (Gartner & Starr, 1993), and I began to pursue empirical efforts to ascertain the kinds of activities that might lead to on-going viable organizations.

Some highlights of note: Don Duchesneau and I (Duchesneau & Gartner, 1990) expanded on a framework developed in Van de Ven, Hudson and Schroeder (1984) to study differences in how entrepreneurs in the distribution of fresh juice in eight metropolitan areas in the United States organized their firms. Certain activities, such as planning (but not business plans) and seeking information from customers and others, were more likely to lead to viable organizations. Bob Thomas and I (Gartner & Thomas, 1993) explored the ways in which entrepreneurs went about forecasting sales for newly developed software products and services. Insights from that study suggested that emerging markets played havoc on the ability to forecast accurately, but that entrepreneurs who used a variety of forecasting techniques and who had talked to more than fifty potential customers were more likely to generate initial estimates that were subsequently achieved.

Embedded in an article (Gatewood, Shaver & Gartner, 1995) that champions the attributions that entrepreneurs offer for getting into business is an exquisite description of a list of behaviors that were developed to identify what entrepreneurs do over time to create organizations. This study served as one of the anchors to the list of behaviors developed in the PSED (Gartner, Carter & Reynolds, 2004). And, then there was the study that began the entire process of organizing the

PSED (Carter, Gartner & Reynolds, 1996). "Exploring Start-Up Event Sequences" was a longitudinal study of seventy-one new ventures based on a random sample of individuals from the United States with an oversample of individuals from Wisconsin. This study resulted in similar findings to Gatewood, Shaver and Gartner (1995) in that individuals who engage in efforts to make their businesses more tangible to others (formed a legal entity, organized a team, sought and acquired financial support) were more likely to create an on-going organization.

A number of studies stemmed from the PSED that explored various facets of the activities that entrepreneurs engage in when developing their businesses. Jon Liao and I focused on investigations of planning activities in emerging ventures (Liao & Gartner, 2006, 2008; Gartner & Liao, 2007) and we teamed up with Benson Honig on another planning study (Honig, Liao & Gartner, 2009). I am lucky to have a long on-going friendship with Benyamin Lichtenstein in which we corresponded and met often to talk about "emergence." An opportunity developed from these conversations to be involved in ideas from complexity theory to explore start-up events in the PSED (Lichtenstein, Carter, Dooley & Gartner, 2007). I think this article is most intriguing because it shows that the intensity and consistency of entrepreneurial effort matters in the organizing process. Finally, Casey Frid, who was my doctoral student at Clemson University, has spearheaded a number of efforts to explore aspects of financing emerging firms in the PSED (Gartner, Frid & Alexander, 2012; Frid, Wyman & Gartner, 2015).

Besides spotty efforts to keep the idea of behavior as a critical aspect of entrepreneurship studies alive (Gartner & Carter, 2003; Gartner, Carter & Reynolds, 2010), I consider the culmination so far of a way to view the process of organizational emergence as that which is represented in the book chapter with Candy Brush (Gartner & Brush, 2007). This chapter offers a different look at the process of organizing as espoused in Weick (1979) by suggesting that there are processes between the processes of enactment, selection, and retention. That is, between enactment and selection is the process of emergence, and between selection and retention is the process of newness, and between retention and enactment is transformation. Our intention in developing this model was to emphasize where most entrepreneurship scholarship tended to lie: the process of newness, that is, in the space where new organizations already exist and the challenges these new organizations face in establishing themselves. The focus of most entrepreneurship research, therefore, is not on the process of emergence: the creation of organizations. Candy and I used articles that served as the basis for a previous overview of the entrepreneurship field (Busenitz, West, Shepherd, Nelson, Chandler & Zacharakis, 2003) to show that approximately half of those articles in the Busenitz et al. (2003) overview were newness oriented and that 75% of the articles were at the organizational level of analysis. Only about 7% of the articles in Busenitz et al. (2003) concentrated on individuals involved in emergence, the area where studies of entrepreneurial behavior would reside. So, although I would like to believe that the primary focus of entrepreneurship scholarship is on the process of organization creation, it is not.

Now, I would assume that the proportion of scholarship on the process of emergence has increased overall as entrepreneurship researchers have taken up an interest in specific behaviors that entrepreneurs engage in, such as pitching (Chen, Yao & Kotha, 2009; Maxwell, Jeffrey & Lévesque, 2011; Pollack, Rutherford & Nagy, 2012), as well as a reconceptualization of aspects of entrepreneurial behavior through the lens of "entrepreneurship as practice" (De Clercq & Voronov, 2009; Goss, Jones, Betta & Latham, 2011; Johannisson, 2011; García & Welter, 2013).

Finally, my guess as to where the most salient direction for studying "entrepreneurship as organizing" will be is towards a path where scholars immerse themselves in the day-to-day practices of entrepreneurial processes that are gleaned either through ethnographies or autoethnographies, as well as through narrative approaches (Gartner, 2007, 2010a) that attempt to come to terms with the ways that entrepreneurs speak for themselves.

Scholarship as community

> You sail with others
> On the scholarship. We read
> And write together.

Another way to say it: As a scholar, the gist of autobiography is that it is not about me, it is about community. My scholarship is embedded in the context of other scholarship. My publications only make sense through connections to other research. I find academic writing unique as a genre in that scholars attempt to connect to other academic writing through embedded citations in the text that refer to other people's ideas and research. Academic writing is a conversation with other scholars: it is writing about other writing.

This section of the chapter emphasizes the idea that a scholarly community is not only developed intellectually, that is, through what is visible in journal articles, books, book chapters, and the like, but, more importantly, a scholarly community emerges through the creation and nurturing of personal relationships. This autobiographical account of my research could just as well have been an account of the many mentors, champions, colleagues, and friendships that have supported me through my career. So here are a few anecdotes of destiny (Dinesen, 1958/1993).

The year that I write these words (2016) is the thirtieth anniversary of the Academy of Management Entrepreneurship Division. A recent Entrepreneurship Division history (Landstrom & Lindhe, 2016) provides a glimmer into the efforts of a number of individuals to "upgrade" the Entrepreneurship Interest Group that had been founded by Karl Vesper and Arnie Cooper, along with many others, in 1974 to Division status. As chairperson of the Entrepreneurship Interest Group in 1984, I led the charge of many individuals who diligently strove to create the organization structures and processes necessary for the interest group to look and act like any of the other divisions of the Academy of Management. By 1986, through the leadership efforts of Timothy Mescon and John A. Pearce II, the Entrepreneurship Interest Group became the Entrepreneurship Division. The preceding five sentences merely touch on the dozens and dozens of individuals who played critical roles in the formation of the Entrepreneurship Division.

The Entrepreneurship Division history (Landstrom & Lindhe, 2016) mentions the "young Turks," an informal group of scholars (Barbara Bird, Allan Carsrud, Connie Marie Gaglio, William Gartner, Betsy Gatewood, Jerry Katz and Kelly Shaver) who met frequently together, not only for scholarly activities, but also as friends. If you look at my resume you will see that I have published articles with nearly every person on that list. And if you look at the list of Entrepreneurship Division chairpersons, nearly every person on the list of "young Turks" served in that role. Along with the wonderful outcomes of publishing journal articles together and seeing the development of a community of scholars in entrepreneurship, much of the joy for me was in the relationships that developed. Some of the perfect moments in my life have been with these friends. The scholarship that was created was often merely a residual of the time we spent together. The genesis of a journal article or putting together a special issue of a journal had some aspect of asking my friends: "So, what would you like to do now?" Scholarly collaborations are often then just excuses for hanging out and doing something fun.

One important part of the development of the entrepreneurship field involved generating legitimacy for entrepreneurship journals that were either already established (i.e., *Entrepreneurship Theory and Practice*, which grew out of the *American Journal of Small Business*) or new journals (i.e., *Journal of Business Venturing*). An aspect of how this process of legitimizing new journals is done is through (1) showing a correlation between scholars who publish in already established "A" level journals and who also publish in newly emerging entrepreneurship journals, and (2) ensuring that scholars read and cite articles in these emerging journals. I can remember a meeting that was hosted by Ian C. MacMillan and S. Venkataraman about the *Journal of Business Venturing* a few years after the journal was founded in 1985. Their challenge to this budding community of entrepreneurship scholars was to have them divide their research output into two groups: send one article to an "A" level journal, and, the next article (of similar quality) to the *Journal of Business Venturing*. I left that meeting with the goal of sending my articles to only two journals: the *Journal of Business Venturing* and *Entrepreneurship Theory and Practice*. I already had two *Academy of Management Review* articles published, so I bet that other scholars would ensure that they published in the "A" level journals and I would put all of my attention into writing for these two entrepreneurship journals only. I am sure that part of the reason for this decision was my loyalty to both Ian MacMillan, editor at the *Journal of Business Venturing*, and to Ray Bagby, editor at *Entrepreneurship Theory and Practice*. Ian was willing to publish my first article in the *Journal of Business Venturing*, "A Taxonomy. . ." (Gartner, Mitchell & Vesper, 1989) after it had been rejected numerous times at other journals and after the reviewers at the *Journal of Business Venturing* were ambivalent about the manuscript's value. Ray stepped into the review process to accept the "Who. . ." article (Gartner, 1988) after reviewers had given it mixed reviews that leaned toward rejection (see Gartner, 2004 for a more comprehensive story on the process of publishing "Who . . ."). Subsequently, I have published twelve articles in *Entrepreneurship Theory and Practice* and sixteen articles in the *Journal of Business Venturing*.

Both Ian and Ray championed my work at a time in my life when I desperately needed some acknowledgement. I was an untenured assistant professor for ten years (four years at the University of Virginia and six years at Georgetown University) and I had many instances where I thought I was perceived as "damaged goods" by other institutions and unlikely to find another academic job if I did not achieve tenure and promotion at Georgetown University. I needed these publications on my resume. And I needed the gracious evaluations of scholars such as Chuck Hofer, who made a compelling case for granting me tenure at Georgetown University. The trajectory of my career was not obvious to me, so the confidence of tenured senior entrepreneurship scholars had a significant impact on my life.

Finally, I would be remiss if I did not mention Sue Birley and her work with Ian MacMillan to bring together American and European scholars to meet and discuss work in progress at various sites in Europe and the United States. Out of these meetings grew a collaborative effort to showcase qualitative research in entrepreneurship (Gartner & Birley, 2002). And it was in writing the introduction to that special issue that I saw the importance of "facts," that is, the quest for collecting more evidence about the process of organization creation, rather than focusing on theory, as critical to developing insights (Gartner, 2006).

I am sure there are many individuals who have played significant roles in my career that I am not even aware of. Given the "blind review" process in evaluating manuscripts for acceptance at journals and the various ways in which decisions are made for funding projects and in hiring for the many academic positions I have held, I cannot really fathom all of the individuals in this deep ocean of scholars who might have had a positive impact on my career.

Be that as it may, I have written a few articles on the importance of community in entrepreneurship scholarship. Around 2004, at the Babson Entrepreneurship Research Conference in Glasgow, Scotland, Per Davidsson, Shaker Zahra, and I began the development of a special issue on bibliometric analyses of the entrepreneurship field that were composed of working papers we noticed at various conferences we were attending. The articles that comprised that special issue in *Entrepreneurship Theory and Practice* (Volume 30, Issue 3) offered quantitative insights into the relationships entrepreneurship scholars had with each other. And it shouldn't come as a surprise that when Reader and Watkins (2006) studied the citation patterns of scholars in the entrepreneurship field, they found that scholars were more likely to cite people they knew as friends. "Are You Talking to Me?" (Gartner, Davidsson & Zahra, 2006) presents some musings about the emergence of entrepreneurship as a field of scholarship, and we offer some thoughts about the clustering of scholars around particular topic areas. Subsequently, I have made a case for ways the entrepreneurship field might become more inclusive of ideas and methods from other disciplines and research traditions (Gartner, 2010b, 2013, 2014). The practice of scholarship, then, is one part writing (which often is very solitary) and another part relating. Scholarship is essentially a shared experience. You write for others. They write for you.

Impact

The following is a quote I have kept with me for over twenty-five years about my sense of the impact of my scholarship:

> [W]hat you pride yourself on, the things that you think are your insight and contribution . . . no one ever even *notices* them. It's as though they're just for you. What you say in passing or what you expound because you know it too well, because it really bores you, but you feel you have to get through this in order to make your grand point, *that's* what people pick up on. *That's* what they underline. *That's* what they quote. *That's* what they attack, or cite favorably. *That's* what they can use. What you really think you're doing may or may not be what you're doing, but it certainly isn't communicated to others. I've talked about this to other critics, to other writers; they haven't had quite my extensive sense of this, but it strikes an answering chord in them. One's grand ideas are indeed one's grand ideas, but there are none that seem to be useful or even recognizable to anyone else. It's a very strange phenomenon. It must have something to do with our capacity for not knowing ourselves.
>
> *(Bloom, 1991: 232, original emphasis)*

Enough said.

Notes

1   The title refers to Karen Blixen's book *Anecdotes of Destiny and Ehrengard* (Dinesen, 1958/1993) and specifically, to the short story in the book, "Babette's Feast" and, even more specifically, to chapter XI, "General Loewenhielm's Speech." Read his speech. This autobiography is a meditation on his words.
2   A haiku written for Susi Geiger after her keynote presentation, "Practice Accounts" at the VU Amsterdam workshop, "Towards a Social Practice Approach in Entrepreneurship," Amsterdam, 17–19 February 2016.

References

Aldrich, H. (1999). *Organizations Evolving*. Thousand Oaks, CA: Sage.
Baker, T., & Nelson, R. E. (2005). Creating something from nothing: Resource construction through entrepreneurial bricolage. *Administrative Science Quarterly*, 50 (3): 329–366.
Bird, B. J. (1989). *Entrepreneurial Behavior*. Glenview, IL: Scott Foresman & Company.
Bloom, H. (1991). The art of criticism: Interview by Antonio Weiss. *Paris Review*, 33 (Spring): 178–232.
Brush, C. G., Manolova, T. S., & Edelman, L. F. (2008). Properties of emerging organizations: An empirical test. *Journal of Business Venturing*, 23 (5): 547–566.
Busenitz, L. W., West, G. P., Shepherd, D., Nelson, T., Chandler, G. N., & Zacharakis, A. (2003). Entrepreneurship research in emergence: Past trends and future directions. *Journal of Management*, 29 (3): 285–308.
Carter, N. M., Gartner, W. B. & Reynolds, P. D. (1996). Exploring start-up event sequences. *Journal of Business Venturing*. 11 (3): 151–166.

Chen, X. P., Yao, X., & Kotha, S. (2009). Entrepreneur passion and preparedness in business plan presentations: A persuasion analysis of venture capitalists' funding decisions. *Academy of Management Journal*, 52 (1): 199–214.

Cole, A. H. (1946). An approach to the study of entrepreneurship: A tribute to Edwin F. Gay. *The Tasks of Economic History: (Supplement VI of the Journal of Economic History)*, 6: 1–15.

De Clercq, D., & Voronov, M. (2009). Toward a practice perspective of entrepreneurship entrepreneurial legitimacy as habitus. *International Small Business Journal*, 27 (4): 395–419.

Dinesen, I. (1958/1993). *Anecdotes of Destiny and Ehrengard*. New York: Vintage Books.

Du Bois, W. E. B. (1968). *The Autobiography of W. E. B. Du Bois: A Soliloquy on Viewing My Life from the Last Decade of Its First Century*. New York City: International Publishers.

Duchesneau, D. A., & Gartner, W. B. (1990). A profile of new venture success and failure in an emerging industry. *Journal of Business Venturing*, 5 (5): 297–312.

Fletcher, D. E. (2006). Entrepreneurial processes and the social construction of opportunity. *Entrepreneurship and Regional Development*, 18 (5): 421–440.

Frid, C. J., Wyman, D. M., & Gartner, W. B. (2015). The influence of financial 'Skin in the Game' on new venture creation. *Academy of Entrepreneurship Journal*, 21 (2): 1–14.

García, M. C. D., & Welter, F. (2013). Gender identities and practices: Interpreting women entrepreneurs' narratives. *International Small Business Journal*, 31 (4): 384–404.

Gartner, W. B. (1982). An Empirical Model of the Business Startup, and Eight Entrepreneurial Archetypes. Unpublished Doctoral Dissertation. Seattle, WA: University of Washington.

Gartner, W. B. (1985). A framework for describing and classifying the phenomenon of new venture creation. *Academy of Management Review*, 10 (4): 696–706.

Gartner, W. B. (1988). Who is an entrepreneur? Is the wrong question. *American Journal of Small Business*, 12 (4): 11–32.

Gartner, W. B. (1989). Some suggestions for research on entrepreneurial traits and characteristics. *Entrepreneurship Theory and Practice*, 14 (1): 27–38.

Gartner, W. B. (1990). What are we talking about when we talk about entrepreneurship? *Journal of Business Venturing*, 5 (1): 15–28.

Gartner, W. B. (1993a). Organizing the voluntary association. *Entrepreneurship Theory and Practice*, 17 (2): 103–106.

Gartner, W. B. (1993b). Words lead to deeds: Towards an organizational emergence vocabulary. *Journal of Business Venturing*, 8 (3): 231–240.

Gartner, W. B. (2004). The edge defines the (w)hole: Saying what entrepreneurship is (not). In Steyaert, C. & Hjorth, D. (Eds.) *Narrative and Discursive Approaches in Entrepreneurship*. London: Edward Elgar, pp. 245–254.

Gartner, W. B. (2006). A "Critical Mess" approach to entrepreneurship scholarship. In Lundstrom, A. & Halvarsson, S. (Eds.) *Entrepreneurship Research: Past Perspectives and Future Prospects, Foundations and Trends in Entrepreneurship*. Vol. 2 (3): 73–82.

Gartner, W. B. (2007). Entrepreneurial narrative and a science of the imagination. *Journal of Business Venturing*, 22 (5): 613–627.

Gartner, W. B. (2008). Variations in entrepreneurship. *Small Business Economics*, 31: 351–361.

Gartner, W. B. (2010a). A new path to the waterfall: A narrative on the use of entrepreneurial narrative. *International Journal of Small Business*, 28 (1): 6–19.

Gartner, W. B. (2010b). An entrepreneurial jeremiad. In Gartner, William B. (Ed.) *ENTER: Entrepreneurial Narrative Theory Ethnomethodology and Reflexivity*. Clemson, SC: Clemson University Digital Press, pp. 1–14.

Gartner, W. B. (2013). Creating a community of difference in entrepreneurship scholarship. *Entrepreneurship and Regional Development*, 25 (1–2): 5–15.

Gartner, W. B. (2014). Organizing entrepreneurship (research). In Fayolle, A. (Ed.) *Handbook of Research in Entrepreneurship*. Cheltenham, UK: Edward Elgar, pp. 13–22.

Gartner, W. B. (2016). *Entrepreneurship as Organizing: Selected Work of William B. Gartner*. Cheltenham, UK: Edward Elgar Publishing.

Gartner, W. B., Bird, B. J., & Starr, J. (1992). Acting as if: Differentiating entrepreneurial from organizational behavior. *Entrepreneurship Theory and Practice*, 16 (3): 13–32.

Gartner, W. B., & Birley, S. (2002). Introduction to the special issue on qualitative methods in entrepreneurship research. *Journal of Business Venturing*, 17 (5): 387–395.

Gartner, W. B., & Brush, C. B. (2007). Entrepreneurship as organizing: Emergence, newness and transforma-tion. In Habbershon, Tim & Rice, Mark (Eds.) *Praeger Perspectives on Entrepreneurship, Volume 3*. Westport, CT: Praeger Publishers, pp. 1–20.

Gartner, W. B., & Carter, N. M. (2003). Entrepreneurial behavior and firm organizing processes. In Acs, Z. J. & Audretsch, D. B. (Eds.) *Handbook of Entrepreneurship Research*. Boston: Kluwer Academic Publishers, pp. 195–221.

Gartner, W. B., Carter, N. M., & Reynolds, P. D. (2004). Business startup activities. In Gartner, William B., Shaver, Kelly G., Carter, Nancy M., & Paul D. Reynolds. (Eds.) *Handbook of Entrepreneurial Dynamics: The Process of Business Creation*. Thousand Oaks, CA: Sage Publications, pp. 285–298.

Gartner, W. B., Carter, N. M., & Reynolds, P. D. (2010). Entrepreneurial behavior and firm organizing pro-cesses. In Acs, Z. J. & Audretsch, D. B. (Eds.) *Handbook of Entrepreneurship Research, 2nd Edition*. Boston: Kluwer Academic Publishers, pp. 99–128.

Gartner, W. B., Davidsson, P., & Zahra, S. A. (2006). Are you talking to me? The nature of community in entrepreneurship scholarship. *Entrepreneurship Theory and Practice*, 30 (3): 321–331.

Gartner, W. B., Frid, Casey S., & Alexander, J. A. (2012). Financing the emerging business. *Small Business Economics*, 39 (3): 745–761.

Gartner, W. B., & Gatewood, E. (1992). Thus the theory of description matters most. *Entrepreneurship Theory and Practice*, 17 (1): 5–10.

Gartner, W. B., & Gatewood, E. (1993). And now for something completely different. *Entrepreneurship Theory and Practice*, 17 (2): 87–90.

Gartner, W. B., & Liao, J. (2007). Pre-venture planning. In Moutray, C. (Ed.) *The Small Business Economy for Data Year 2006: Report to the President*. Washington, DC: U.S. Small Business Administration Office of Advocacy, pp. 212–264.

Gartner, W. B., Mitchell, T. R., & Vesper, K. H. (1989). A taxonomy of new business ventures. *Journal of Business Venturing*, 4 (3): 169–186.

Gartner, W. B., Shaver, K. G., Katz, J. A., & Gatewood, E. (1994). Finding the entrepreneur in entrepreneur-ship. *Entrepreneurship Theory and Practice*, 18 (3): 5–10.

Gartner, W. B., & Starr, J. A. (1993). The nature of entrepreneurial work. In Birley, Sue & MacMillan, Ian C. (Eds.) *Entrepreneurship Research: Global Perspectives*. Amsterdam: North-Holland, pp. 35–67.

Gartner, W. B., & Thomas, R. J. (1993). Factors affecting new product forecasting accuracy in new firms. *Journal of Product Innovation Management*, 10 (1): 35–52.

Gatewood, E. J., Shaver, K. G., & Gartner, W. B. (1995). A longitudinal study of cognitive factors influencing start-up behaviors and success at venture creation. *Journal of Business Venturing*, 10 (5): 371–391.

Goss, D., Jones, R., Betta, M., & Latham, J. (2011). Power as practice: A micro-sociological analysis of the dynamics of emancipatory entrepreneurship. *Organization Studies*, 32 (2): 211–229.

Herron, L., Sapienza, H. J., & Smith-Cook, D. (1992). Entrepreneurship theory from an interdisciplinary perspective: Volume II. *Entrepreneurship Theory and Practice*, 16 (3): 5–12.

Hjorth, D., Holt, R., & Steyaert, C. (2015). Entrepreneurship and process studies. *International Small Business Journal*, 33 (6): 599–611.

Honig, B., Liao, J., & Gartner, W. B. (2009). Institutional isomorphism, business planning and business plan revision: The differential impact on teams and solo entrepreneurs. In Reynolds, Paul D. & Curtin, Richard T. (Eds.) *New Firm Creation in the U.S.: Initial Explorations with the PSED II Date Set*. New York: Springer, pp. 137–156.

Johannisson, B. (2011). Towards a practice theory of entrepreneuring. *Small Business Economics*, 36 (2): 135–150.

Landstrom, H., & Lindhe, J. (2016). A history of the Entrepreneurship Division of the Academy of Manage-ment. Briarcliff Manor, NY: Academy of Management Entrepreneurship Division.

Liao, J., & Gartner, W. B. (2006). The effects of pre-venture plan timing and perceived environmental uncertainty on the persistence of emerging firms. *Small Business Economics*, 27 (1): 23–40.

Liao, J., & Gartner, W. B. (2008). The influence of pre-venture planning on new venture creation. *Journal of Small Business Strategy*, 18 (2): 1–21.

Lichtenstein, B. B., Carter, N. M., Dooley, K. J., & Gartner, W. B. (2007). Complexity dynamics of nascent entrepreneurship. *Journal of Business Venturing*, 22: 236–261.

Maxwell, A. L., Jeffrey, S. A., & Lévesque, M. (2011). Business angel early stage decision making. *Journal of Business Venturing*, 26 (2): 212–225.

Mintzberg, H. (1973). *The Nature of Managerial Work*. New York: Harper Collins.

Osterwalder, A., & Pigneur, Y. (2013). *Business Model Generation: A Handbook for Visionaries, Game Changers, and Challengers.* New York: John Wiley & Sons.

Pollack, J. M., Rutherford, M. W., & Nagy, B. G. (2012). Preparedness and cognitive legitimacy as antecedents of new venture funding in televised business pitches. *Entrepreneurship Theory and Practice*, 36 (5): 915–939.

Quenk, N. L., & Hammer, A. L. (1998). *MBTI Manual: A Guide to the Development and Use of the Myers-Briggs Type Indicator, Volume 3.* Palo Alto, CA: Consulting Psychologists Press.

Reader, D., & Watkins, D. (2006). The social and collaborative nature of entrepreneurship scholarship: A co-citation and perceptual analysis. *Entrepreneurship Theory and Practice*, 30 (3): 417–441.

Reynolds, P. D. (2007). New firm creation in the United States: A PSED I overview. *Foundations and Trends in Entrepreneurship*, 3 (1): 1–150.

Reynolds, P. D., Carter, N. M., Gartner, W. B., & Greene, P. D. (2004). The prevalence of nascent entrepreneurs in the United States: Evidence from the Panel Study of Entrepreneurial Dynamics. *Small Business Economics*, 23: 263–284.

Reynolds, P. D., & Curtin, R. T. (2008). Business creation in the United States: Panel Study of Entrepreneurial Dynamics II assessment. *Foundations and Trends in Entrepreneurship*, 4 (3): 155–307.

Sarasvathy, S. D. (2009). *Effectuation: Elements of Entrepreneurial Expertise.* Cheltenham, UK: Edward Elgar Publishing.

Say, J. A. (1816). *A Treatise on Political Economy.* London: Sherwood, Neeley and Jones.

Schumpeter, J. A. (1934). *The Theory of Economic Development.* Translated by R. Opie. Cambridge: Harvard University Press.

Starr, J. A., & MacMillan, I. C. (1990). Resource cooptation via social contracting: Resource acquisition strategies for new ventures. *Strategic Management Journal*, 11 (4): 79–92.

Stewart, A., & Aldrich, H. (2015). Collaboration between management and anthropology researchers: Obstacles and opportunities. *The Academy of Management Perspectives*, 29 (2): 173–192.

Steyaert, C. (2007). 'Entrepreneuring' as a conceptual attractor? A review of process theories in 20 years of entrepreneurship studies. *Entrepreneurship and Regional Development*, 19 (6): 453–477.

Van de Ven, A. H., Hudson, R., & Schroeder, D. M. (1984). Designing new business startups: Entrepreneurial, organizational and ecological considerations. *Journal of Management*, 10: 87–107.

Vesper, K. H. (1980). *New Venture Strategies.* Englewood Cliffs, NJ: Prentice-Hall.

Weick, K. E. (1979). *The Social Psychology of Organizing, 2nd Edition.* Reading, MA: Addison Wesley.

Welter, F. (2011). Contextualizing entrepreneurship – Conceptual challenges and ways forward. *Entrepreneurship Theory and Practice*, 35 (1): 165–184.

13

An Austrian perspective on firms and markets

My contributions to entrepreneurship theory

Peter G. Klein

Introduction

My background is unusual for an entrepreneurship scholar. I began my career as an industrial organization economist with little knowledge of the modern entrepreneurship literature (and little experience with entrepreneurship practice). I was trained at Berkeley in the late 1980s and early 1990s by Oliver Williamson, focusing on corporate governance and organizational economics. I was particularly interested in how large firms manage information flows and provide incentives, especially in rapidly changing environments. My dissertation dealt with conglomerate diversification in the 1960s and 1970s from the perspective of transaction cost economics. I was interested in theories of firm behavior and focused on empirical work on firm boundaries and organization. I maintained a general interest in various topics in applied microeconomics, economic growth, and business–cycle theory and did as much popular writing and speaking on economics and economic policy as the tenure clock would allow.

However, I had reservations about "mainstream" neoclassical economics. As an undergraduate economics major I was attracted to Austrian school writers such as Ludwig von Mises, F. A. Hayek, Henry Hazlitt, and Murray Rothbard and eagerly read as many of their books and articles as I could find (with limited understanding). During my graduate studies I was a research fellow of the Mises Institute and developed a personal relationship with Rothbard, the great libertarian polymath and the most dazzling intellectual I have ever known. I also read a lot of Hayek, working at Stanford as a research assistant for W. W. Bartley, III, founding editor of *The Collected Works of F. A. Hayek*. Bartley was also working on intellectual biographies of Hayek and Karl Popper, his own mentor.[1] At seminars and conferences I met leading contemporary practitioners of the Austrian school including Israel Kirzner, Mario Rizzo, Joseph Salerno, Roger Garrison, Gerald O'Driscoll, and Hans-Hermann Hoppe, and I became immersed in the Austrian literature, as well as the neoclassical economics and transaction cost economics that were central to my PhD program. My interests were idiosyncratic, to say the least.

I read Kirzner's *Competition and Entrepreneurship* (1973) as an undergraduate student and studied his works more closely while pursuing my PhD.[2] Like most of Kirzner's contemporaries, I viewed the book as a contribution to microeconomics, not entrepreneurship (Klein and Bylund, 2014: 261). I shared Kirzner's conception of the entrepreneur as an abstract force, not an actual person or group of people acting in real time. As Kirzner (2009: 145–146) later put it,

> [M]y own work has nothing to say about the secrets of successful entrepreneurship. My work has explored not the nature of the talents needed for entrepreneurial success, not any guidelines to be followed by would-be successful entrepreneurs, but, instead, the nature of the market process set in motion by the entrepreneurial decisions.

For Kirzner, the entrepreneur plays a largely instrumental role – entrepreneurship is that which recognizes and exploits profit opportunities existing in a world of disequilibrium, full stop. I, too, viewed the entrepreneur as the central actor in a market system, the agency responsible for moving resources from lower- to higher-valued uses, but had little interest in flesh-and-blood entrepreneurs.[3]

Austrian economics, entrepreneurship, and the theory of the firm

As I have noted elsewhere (Klein, 2008a, 2008b), the Austrian economists, going back to Carl Menger, have differed from their neoclassical economist colleagues in giving the entrepreneur the central position in the analysis of the market. Whereas entrepreneurship played a prominent role in economic theory from the time it emerged as a systematic discipline (Cantillon, 1755), by around World War II the entrepreneur had mostly dropped out of economics journal articles and textbooks. As the language of economics became more formal and stylized, and economists were drawn to highly abstract concepts of markets and competition such as the model of perfectly competitive general equilibrium, it was simply too difficult to incorporate a creative, dynamic, coordinating, or disruptive actor into the analysis. Microeconomics became the description of various equilibrium states (existence, stability, welfare properties), and there was nothing for an entrepreneur to do. For the Austrians, by contrast, the entrepreneur as a speculator, coordinator, allocator, and innovator was always what Mises (1949: 326) called the "driving force of the market." Note that the term "entrepreneur" to most Austrian economists does not mean self-employed person, small-business owner, or technological innovator (though all these persons can act entrepreneurially). Rather, entrepreneurship is a generalized function associated with resource allocation and value creation. For Kirzner, building on Friedrich Wieser and Hayek, that function is alertness to profit opportunities that result from prices that differ from their equilibrium values (Foss and Klein, 2010b). For Mises, Rothbard, and others such as Salerno (1993, 2008) and myself (Klein, 2008b; Foss and Klein, 2012), that function involves acting under conditions of Knightian uncertainty.[4] In either case, entrepreneurship is not uniquely associated with a particular job category (self-employment), firm type (small firm, young firm, high-growth firm), or strategy (R&D-intensive firm) (see Klein, 2008b: 176–178).

I began thinking more carefully about the entrepreneurial function while writing two papers applying Austrian economics to the theory of the firm (Klein, 1996, 1999). The second paper included a section on "Financiers as Entrepreneurs" (Klein, 1999: 36–38) in which I discussed David Scharfstein's (1988) argument that unregulated financial markets will not produce enough disciplinary takeovers, because shareholders in an underperforming target firm will refuse to tender their shares to a raider or acquiring firm for less than their share of the post-takeover value of the firm, leaving no profit for the acquirer. This kind of argument, I realized, assumes that all market participants have the same beliefs about future share prices and are equally willing to bear the uncertainties associated with the restructuring process. In contrast, I saw post-takeover profits (and losses) as returns to exercising the entrepreneurial function.

The analysis of firm governance could not, then, be understood without seeing financial-market participants as entrepreneurs who seek to exploit gaps in the market (à la Kirzner) or specialize in bearing fundamental uncertainties (à la Knight and Mises).[5]

Describing business restructurings as entrepreneurial actions led me to think more systematically about entrepreneurship and to read more widely in the contemporary entrepreneurship literature. I discovered that Kirzner's concept of alertness provides the theoretical foundation for the opportunity-discovery perspective (Shane and Venkataraman, 2000; Shane, 2003), and that Knight's and Schumpeter's ideas play smaller roles. I quickly came to the belief that the entrepreneurship literature had not read Kirzner carefully enough and that many theoretical and applied studies (e.g., surveys asking entrepreneurs or prospective entrepreneurs to list the number of opportunities discovered, evaluated, and exploited) were inappropriately reifying the metaphor of "opportunity" used by Kirzner to explain market coordination.[6]

The judgment-based view

Around that time Nicolai Foss and I were invited to contribute to a *Festschrift* in honor of Kirzner. We assumed that most of the participants would write about entrepreneurial discovery and we wanted to do something different. My wife, also a trained economist, reminded me that Kirzner had written an interesting and underappreciated book on capital theory (Kirzner, 1966). There Kirzner argued, building on earlier work by Ludwig Lachmann (1956), that the nature and value of an asset or resource is determined not by its objective properties (size, weight, location, construction, technical capabilities), but by its imagined place in the subjective production plans of a forward-thinking entrepreneur. Kirzner's capital theory seemed to provide a useful means of integrating the theory of the entrepreneur and the economic theory of the firm, two bodies of literature that had developed largely in isolation, despite much overlap in approach and subject matter.

Developing and extending Kirzner's capital theory led to the *Festschrift* chapter (Foss et al., 2002) and two follow-up papers (Foss et al., 2007; Foss, Foss, and Klein, 2007) and, a few years later, to Foss's and my 2012 book *Organizing Entrepreneurial Judgment: A New Approach to the Firm*. I usually describe my approach here as the "judgment-based view" of entrepreneurship (see Foss and Klein, 2015, for a summary and reflections). The term *judgment* comes from Knight, who described judgment as decision making under uncertainty that cannot be modeled or parameterized as a set of formal decision rules. Judgment is midway between the "rational decision making" of neoclassical economics models and blind luck or random guessing. We sometimes call it intuition, gut feeling, or understanding.[7] In a world of Knightian uncertainty and heterogeneous capital resources with attributes that are subjectively perceived and unknowable ex ante, some agency must bear the responsibility of owning, controlling, deploying, and redeploying these resources in the service of consumer wants. That, in my formulation, is the role of the entrepreneur. The entrepreneur's job is to combine and recombine heterogeneous capital resources in pursuit of profit (and the avoidance of loss). When the entrepreneur is successful in acquiring resources at prices below their realized marginal revenue products – that is, when the entrepreneur exercises good judgment – she earns an economic profit. When her judgments are poor, she earns an economic loss. Competition among entrepreneurs (and those who provide financial capital to entrepreneurs) tends to steer ownership and control of productive resources toward those entrepreneurs with better judgment.

In this model, a firm is an entrepreneur plus the alienable assets she owns and controls. The multiperson firm includes multiple owners and/or employees who may exercise "derived judgment" on the part of the entrepreneur-owner or owners, who exercise judgment in selecting, monitoring, and delegating decision authority to these employees. Organizational character-istics (size, vertical boundaries, diversification, ownership structure, internal organization, etc.) evolve over time as entrepreneurs experiment with different combinations of heterogeneous assets and different strategies and business models. As Lachmann (1956: 16) put it, "We are living in a world of unexpected change; hence capital combinations . . . will be ever changing, will be dissolved and reformed. In this activity, we find the real function of the entrepreneur."

The judgment-based approach plays a distinct role in the current conversation and contro-versy about the nature of entrepreneurship research (Short et al., 2010; Dimov, 2011). The once-dominant opportunity–discovery perspective has come under fire from a variety of perspectives. Alvarez and Barney (2007) kicked off a lively debate by challenging the ontological status of entrepreneurial opportunities, arguing that opportunities are best understood as created subjec-tively, rather than existing outside of entrepreneurial action. The judgment-based view goes a step further, arguing that the construct of opportunity itself is unnecessary at best, misleading at worst.[8] Entrepreneurial action is seen as beginning with the entrepreneur's interpretation of cur-rent (objective) conditions, his beliefs about possible future states of the world (e.g., a profitable product or venture), and his expectations and confidence in his the ability to bring about that possible future. The entrepreneur then acts (or doesn't act), with success or failure determined ex post largely by objective factors.

In this formulation, there is simply no need for the opportunity construct. The discovery view mistakenly implies that opportunities exist independent of human belief and action. The creation view rightly emphasizes human belief and action, but mistakenly implies that profit opportunities, once the entrepreneur has conceived or established them, somehow come into being. I definitely see entrepreneurship is a creative process but say that what entrepreneurs create (or attempt to create) are not opportunities, but new firms, new products, or new markets. When they are successful, their efforts may be recast after the fact in opportunity language. But little or no additional insight is produced by doing so (Foss and Klein, 2016). Moreover, it is extremely awkward to describe entrepreneurial failure – financial loss, bankruptcy, or other forms of unin-tentional exit – in opportunity language. (Kirzner refers to losses as resulting from "mistaken opportunities," but wouldn't it be clearer to refer to them as the results of mistaken actions?)

I see much of my recent work as an attempt to convince entrepreneurship scholars to make action, not opportunities, the unit of analysis for entrepreneurship research, teaching, and out-reach. An action-theoretic perspective helps us (and our students and consulting clients) to remember that action always takes place under conditions of uncertainty (even for mundane activities in established industries!). The language of opportunity may also encourage overcon-fidence by mistakenly conveying the idea that the results of entrepreneurial action exist ex ante, before profits and losses are realized, either because these results were there waiting to be discov-ered, or because the entrepreneur created them through an act of will.

These efforts are bearing some fruit as a judgment-based perspective on entrepreneur-ship is beginning to emerge (Hülsmann, 1997; McMullen and Shepherd, 2006; McCaffrey and Salerno, 2011; Huang, 2012; McCaffrey, 2014, 2015; Halberg, 2015; McMullen, 2015), though its basic claims are often misunderstood (Klein, 2013; Foss and Klein, 2016). Much of this work has been conceptual and theoretical, though we are beginning to see applied work in entrepreneurial cognition, venture formation, and public policy. My hope is that the judgment-based perspective will continue to grow and join the opportunity-discovery, opportunity-creation, and effectuation-bricolage approaches as an alternative (though not nec-essarily mutually exclusive) framework for understanding entrepreneurial action and its role in the economy and in society.

Reflections on Kirzner

Besides seeking to address the entrepreneurship research and teaching communities, I have also continued to engage the contemporary Austrian economics literature. While I continue to have the greatest respect for Israel Kirzner as a scholar and teacher, I am increasingly convinced that his highly influential work on market competition as a process of entrepreneurial discovery (Kirzner, 1997a) – often characterized as "the" Austrian approach to entrepreneurship – has led Austrian microeconomics down the wrong path. It is essentially Walrasian price theory with a twist. Walrasian general equilibrium is seen as the end state toward which the market process is tending, though not quite reaching. Kirzner's entrepreneur is simply an add-on to neoclassical market theory, a disembodied agency making sure that disequilibrium arbitrage opportunities are not too large by acting upon them quickly, if not quite immediately. Kirzner's entrepreneur owns no capital but pursues "pure entrepreneurial profit" by exploiting these arbitrage opportunities, which can be seized at zero risk, moving the economy closer to its hypothetical equilibrium state (Klein, 2008a; Foss and Klein, 2010a).

Along with Salerno (1993, 2008), I have tried to rehabilitate an alternative Austrian theory of the market and the entrepreneur, one based on Cantillon, Menger, Mises, and Rothbard. This conception of the market focuses on day-to-day, real-world market-clearing prices, not hypothetical equilibrium prices, and views the entrepreneur as a capital-owner who invests resources under conditions of uncertainty in pursuit of economic gain. The "market process," in this understanding, is not the continual pressure toward equilibrium in particular markets, but the continual competition among capitalists and entrepreneurs for ownership and control of productive resources that can be used to generate profits. Successful flesh-and-blood entrepreneurs may be particularly alert to changes in market conditions, just as they may be particularly charismatic, creative, and inspirational, but this is not a theoretically necessary component of entrepreneurial action. It is the investment of resources under uncertainty, not alertness to some potential future, that distinguishes the entrepreneurial function from other roles in an economic system (see Klein, 2008a, for a detailed discussion).

This revisionist Austrian perspective has put me at odds with some contemporary Austrian economists and generated some confusion in interactions with entrepreneurship and management scholars with only a passing interest in internecine Austrian controversies. But it shows that there is remarkable diversity within the modern Austrian tradition, as there was in the days of Carl Menger – signs of a healthy and growing movement.

Moving forward

I continue to explore a variety of topics in entrepreneurship theory; the applications of entrepreneurship and innovation; public policy; and related topics in strategy, organization, and governance. I am particularly interested in the effects of public policy on entrepreneurial judgment and in the ways that entrepreneurial judgment, alertness, and innovation can be applied to non market actors, including universities and government officials (Klein et al., 2010, 2013; Kolympiris and Klein, 2016). My sense is that we tend to apply entrepreneurial metaphors too loosely, referring to creative and innovative persons as "entrepreneurs" without fully considering the differences in institutional context (for example, government bureaucrats are investing other people's resources under conditions of uncertainty, not their own resources). But we can gain some insight on the behavior of nonmarket actors, and the emergence and growth of public organizations, by thinking about entrepreneurial processes of resource assembly and recombination.

Underlying these various projects is my continued belief that entrepreneurship is not a separate field of economics or management – the study of self-employment or new-venture formation – but should be integrated more tightly into theories of the firm and market, theories of firm strategy and organization, and theories of public policy and administration.[9] The entrepreneur is at the very heart of a market system, the person who creates and operates firms, who allocates capital across activities, who formulates and executes strategies, who designs and governs organizations. It is my hope that scholars in a variety of academic disciplines will put the entrepreneur back in his proper place.

Notes

1   Bartley died in 1990 before the Hayek or Popper biographies were complete. Before his death he and I were planning to coedit a volume in the Hayek *Collected Works*, and I assumed responsibility for the volume, which appeared in (1992) as *The Fortunes of Liberalism: Essays in Austrian Economics and the Ideal of Freedom* (Hayek, 1992). My first academic publication was an edited book!
2   I applied to NYU's PhD program with thoughts of studying under Kirzner before eventually choosing Berkeley. A long telephone interview with Kirzner was a highlight of my pre-doctoral studies, as was an even longer and livelier telephone conversation with Murray Rothbard as part of my application for a Mises Institute fellowship. Sadly, I never met Hayek, who was alive until 1992 but in poor health during the time I was working on his papers.
3   The same could be said about Schumpeter (1911) and Knight (1921). For Schumpeter, entrepreneurship is that which moves an economy from one equilibrium to another; for Knight, entrepreneurship is that which bears uncertainty.
4   Mises refers not to Knightian uncertainty, but to his brother Richard von Mises's construct of "case probability," which functions in this context much like Knightian uncertainty (see Klein, 2009).
5   I also noted (Klein, 1999: 38): "This account, however, could use further elaboration. For example, how is the bearing of uncertainty distributed among participants in various forms of restructuring? How do regulatory barriers hamper the [entrepreneur's] ability to exercise the entrepreneurial function in this context?"
6   As Kirzner noted in a 1997 interview:

> I do not mean to convey the idea that the future is a rolled-up tapestry, and we need only to be patient as the picture progressively unrolls itself before our eyes. In fact, the future may be a void. There may be nothing around the corner or in the tapestry. The future has to be created. Philosophically, all this may be so. But it doesn't matter for the sake of the metaphor I have chosen . . . Ex post we have to recognize that when an innovator has discovered something new, that something was metaphorically waiting to be discovered. But from an everyday point-of-view, when a new gadget is invented, we all say, gee, I can see we needed that. It was just waiting to be discovered (Kirzner, 1997b).

7   The German word *Verstehen* works better than its English equivalent in conveying a sense of deep, and possibly intuitive or tacit, knowledge or understanding.
8   In this sense, the judgment-based view is closer to the effectuation and bricolage approaches (Baker and Nelson, 2005; Sarasvathy, 2008) in viewing entrepreneurial action, not opportunity, as the unit of analysis – even though effectuation theorists have not always seen this connection (Sarasvathy and Dew, 2013)!
9   This is not to say that entrepreneurship studies should not be contained within separate university departments, published in specialized entrepreneurship journals, and so on. I refer here to the intellectual concept of a distinct field, not the institutional concept.

References

Alvarez, Sharon A., and Jay B. Barney. 2007. "Discovery and Creation: Alternative Theories of Entrepreneurial Action," *Strategic Entrepreneurship Journal* 1(1–2): 11–26.

Baker, Ted, and R. E. Nelson. 2005. "Creating Something from Nothing: Resource Construction through Entrepreneurial Bricolage," *Administrative Science Quarterly* 50: 329–366.

Cantillon, Richard. 1755. *Essai sur la nature du commerce en général*. Henry Higgs, ed. (London: Macmillan, 1931).

Dimov, Dimo. 2011. "Grappling with the Unbearable Elusiveness of Entrepreneurial Opportunities," *Entrepreneurship Theory and Practice* 35: 57–81.

Foss, Kirsten, Nicolai J. Foss, and Peter G. Klein. 2007. "Original and Derived Judgment: An Entrepreneurial Theory of Economic Organization," *Organization Studies* 28(12): 1893–1912.

Foss, Kirsten, Nicolai J. Foss, Peter G. Klein, and Sandra K. Klein. 2002. "Heterogeneous Capital, Entrepreneurship, and Economic Organization," *Journal des Economistes et des Etudes Humaines* 12(1): 79–96.

Foss, Kirsten, Nicolai J. Foss, Peter G. Klein, and Sandra K. Klein. 2007. "The Entrepreneurial Organization of Heterogeneous Capital," *Journal of Management Studies* 44(7): 1165–1186.

Foss, Nicolai J., and Peter G. Klein. 2010a. "Alertness, Action, and the Antecedents of Entrepreneurship," *Journal of Private Enterprise* 25(2): 145–164.

Foss, Nicolai J., and Peter G. Klein. 2010b. "Entrepreneurial Alertness and Opportunity Discovery: Origins, Attributes, Critique," in Hans Landström and Franz Lohrke, eds., *The Historical Foundations of Entrepreneurship Research* (Cheltenham, UK: Edward Elgar, pp. 91–120).

Foss, Nicolai J., and Peter G. Klein. 2012. *Organizing Entrepreneurial Judgment: A New Approach to the Firm* (Cambridge: Cambridge University Press).

Foss, Nicolai J., and Peter G. Klein. 2015. "The Judgment-Based Approach to Entrepreneurship: Accomplishments, Challenges, New Directions," *Journal of Institutional Economics* 11(3): 585–599.

Foss, Nicolai J., and Peter G. Klein. 2016. "Entrepreneurial Discovery or Creation? In Search of the Middle Ground," *Academy of Management Review*, forthcoming.

Halberg, Niklas L. 2015. "Uncertainty, Judgment, and the Theory of the Firm," *Journal of Institutional Economics* 11(3): 623–650.

Hayek, F. A. 1992. *The Fortunes of Liberalism: Essays on Austrian Economics and the Ideal of Freedom,* ed. Peter G. Klein. vol. 4 of *The Collected Works of F. A. Hayek* (Chicago: University of Chicago Press and London: Routledge).

Huang, Laura. 2012. A Theory of Investor Gut Feel: A Test of the Impact of Gut Feel on Entrepreneurial Investment Decisions. Ph.D. dissertation, University of California, Irvine.

Hülsmann, Jörg Guido. 1997. "Knowledge, Judgment, and the Use of Property," *Review of Austrian Economics* 10(1): 23–48.

Kirzner, Israel M. 1966. *An Essay on Capital* (New York: Augustus M. Kelley).

Kirzner, Israel M. 1973. *Competition and Entrepreneurship* (Chicago: University of Chicago Press).

Kirzner, Israel M. 1997a. "Entrepreneurial Discovery and the Competitive Market Process: An Austrian Approach," *Journal of Economic Literature* 35: 60–85.

Kirzner, Israel M. 1997b. "The Kirznerian Way: An Interview with Israel M. Kirzner," *Austrian Economics Newsletter* 17(1): 1–8.

Kirzner, Israel M. 2009. "The Alert and Creative Entrepreneur: A Clarification," *Small Business Economics* 32: 145–152.

Klein, Peter G. 1996. "Economic Calculation and the Limits of Organization," *Review of Austrian Economics* 9(2): 51–77.

Klein, Peter G. 1999. "Entrepreneurship and Corporate Governance," *Quarterly Journal of Austrian Economics* 2(2): 19–42. Reprinted in David B. Audretsch and Erik E. Lehmann, eds., *Corporate Governance in Small and Medium Sized Firms*, 194–217 (Cheltenham, UK: Edward Elgar, 2011).

Klein, Peter G. 2008a. "The Mundane Economics of the Austrian School," *Quarterly Journal of Austrian Economics* 11(3–4): 165–187.

Klein, Peter G. 2008b. "Opportunity Discovery, Entrepreneurial Action, and Economic Organization," *Strategic Entrepreneurship Journal* 2(3): 175–190.

Klein, Peter G. 2009. "Risk, Uncertainty, and Economic Organization," in Jörg Guido Hülsmann and Stephan Kinsella, eds., *Property, Freedom, and Society: Essays in Honor of Hans-Hermann Hoppe* (Auburn, AL: Mises Institute, pp. 325–337).

Klein, Peter G. 2013. "My Response to Shane (2012)," *Organizations and Markets blog*, February 24 (http://organizationsandmarkets.com/2013/02/24/my-response-to-shane-2012/).

Klein, Peter G., Anita M. McGahan, Christos N. Pitelis, and Joseph T. Mahoney. 2010. "Toward a Theory of Public Entrepreneurship," *European Management Review* 7: 1–15.

Klein, Peter G., Joseph T. Mahoney, Anita M. McGahan, and Christos N. Pitelis. 2013. "Capabilities and Strategic Entrepreneurship in Public Organizations," *Strategic Entrepreneurship Journal* 7(1): 70–91.

Klein, Peter G., and Per L. Bylund. 2014. "The Place of Austrian Economics in Contemporary Entrepreneurship Research," *Review of Austrian Economics* 27(3): 259–279.

Knight, Frank H. 1921. *Risk, Uncertainty, and Profit*. Reprinted (1965), New York: Augustus M. Kelley.

Kolympiris, Christos, and Peter G. Klein. 2016. "Universities as Innovators: The Effect of Academic Innovators on Patent Quality," working paper, University of Bath and Baylor University.

Lachmann, Ludwig M. 1956. *Capital and Its Structure* (Kansas City: Sheed Andrews and McMeel, 1978).

McCaffrey, Matthew. 2014. "On the Theory of Entrepreneurial Incentives and Alertness," *Entrepreneurship Theory and Practice* 38(4): 891–911.

McCaffrey, Matthew. 2015. "Economic Policy and Entrepreneurship: Alertness or Judgment?" in Per L. Bylund and David Howden, eds., *The Next Generation of Austrian Economists: Essays in Honor of Joseph T. Salerno* (Auburn, AL: Mises Institute, pp. 183–200).

McCaffrey, Matthew, and Joseph T. Salerno. 2011. "A Theory of Political Entrepreneurship," *Modern Economy* 2(4): 552–560.

McMullen, Jeffrey S. 2015. "Entrepreneurial Judgment as Empathic Accuracy: A Sequential Decisionmaking Approach to Entrepreneurial Action," *Journal of Institutional Economics* 11(3): 651–681.

McMullen, Jeffrey, and Dean A. Shepherd. 2006. "Entrepreneurial Action and the Role of Uncertainty in the Theory of the Entrepreneur," *Academy of Management Review* 31(1): 132–152.

Mises, Ludwig von. 1949. *Human Action: A Treatise on Economics*, Scholar's edition (Auburn, AL: Mises Institute, 1998).

Salerno, Joseph T. 1993. "Mises and Hayek Dehomogenized," *Review of Austrian Economics* 6: 113–146.

Salerno, Joseph T. 2008. "The Entrepreneur: Real and Imagined," *Quarterly Journal of Austrian Economics* 11(3): 188–207.

Sarasvathy, Saras D. 2008. *Effectuation: Elements of Entrepreneurial Expertise* (Northampton: Edward Elgar).

Sarasvathy, Saras D., and Nicholas Dew. 2013. "Without Judgment: An Empirically-based Entrepreneurial Theory of the Firm," *Review of Austrian Economics* 26(3): 277–296.

Scharfstein, David. 1988. "The Disciplinary Role of Takeovers." *Review of Economic Studies*. 55(2): 185–199.

Shane, Scott. 2003. *A General Theory of Entrepreneurship* (Cheltenham, UK: Edward Elgar).

Shane, Scott, and S. Venkataraman. 2000. "The Promise of Entrepreneurship as a Field of Research," *Academy of Management Review* 25: 217–226.

Short, Jeremy C., David J. Ketchen, Christopher L. Shook, and R. Duane Ireland. 2010. "The Concept of 'Opportunity' in Entrepreneurship Research: Past Accomplishments and Future Challenges," *Journal of Management* 36(1): 40–65.

14

Corporate entrepreneurship

A research journey

Donald F. Kuratko

"The journey of 1,000 miles starts with but a single step."

Lao Tzu

The beginning in entrepreneurship

My work as an entrepreneurship scholar began under the tutelage of Richard M. Hodgetts (University of Nebraska and Florida International University), a brilliant management scholar who helped me understand the value of significant research work. He also taught me the art of developing impactful textbooks that could define a field in many ways. I took great pride in co-authoring a number of leading books with Dr. Hodgetts, beginning with *Effective Small Business Management* in 1986 (that book was successful through seven editions culminating in the 2001 version). The other early book was entitled *Management*, published in 1988 and finding successful adoptions through three editions ending with the 1991 version. The development of these books, as well as my early research efforts in small business management issues, provided insights to me about the newly forming discipline of entrepreneurship. Through my research and teaching in this emerging field, I recognized the need for a comprehensive textbook to lead the field. So, in 1986 I set out to write this comprehensive book that would provide a framework for the new field of entrepreneurship. Hence, I wrote *Entrepreneurship: A Contemporary Approach* with Dr. Hodgetts as my co-author. Because this field was so new and seemingly small in development, it took several attempts to convince publishers that this book had an eventual outlet (including my offer to write the first edition for no royalties). I succeeded, and the first edition was published by Harcourt Brace Jovanovich in 1988 and was immediately successful.

Today, that early book is now entitled *Entrepreneurship: Theory, Process, and Practice* (Kuratko, 2017) and is in its tenth edition, translated into seven languages, and is considered one of the leading books on entrepreneurship in the world. The subtitle was changed for two specific reasons, of which one is emotional and the other is logical. As I explain in the preface of that book, I first wanted to honor my former professor, mentor, coauthor, and friend, Richard M. Hodgetts, who passed away in 2001, in selecting a subtitle that he developed for one of his most successful management books decades ago. The second reason I changed the subtitle was to illustrate the actual representation of the book's focus. I believe that students studying entrepreneurship must be exposed to the "theory development" of the field, the "processes" by which we now teach and study entrepreneurship, and the actual "practice" of entrepreneurship by those individuals and organizations that have been successful. Thus, in order to completely understand and appreciate this emerging discipline we call entrepreneurship, students must learn about the theory, the processes, and the practice of this field. This subtitle represents the complete foundation of the discipline.

I mention this beginning with my *Entrepreneurship* book because I wrote an early chapter about "Intrapreneurship" and developing innovative thinking inside established organizations as a contemporary issue that was emerging. As I explain next, there was a reason I included this chapter in my first edition as my research work was transitioning.

The evolution into corporate entrepreneurship

My research efforts evolved from working on the challenges and issues in entrepreneurial ventures to the potential of developing an entrepreneurial mind-set inside of established organizations. When I examined some early research in the 1970s there was a focus on teams and how entrepreneurial activities inside existing organizations could be developed (Hill & Hlavacek, 1972; Peterson & Berger, 1972; Hanan, 1976). Yet, I found this early research to be sparse and mostly focused on marketing aspects of new products. The concept of corporate entrepreneurship (CE) was simply not acknowledged as a strategy within established corporations.

In 1985 there were two seminal books that influenced my thinking on the critical importance of entrepreneurial activity inside organizations. First, Peter Drucker stated in his (1985) groundbreaking book entitled, *Innovation and Entrepreneurship*:

> Entrepreneurship is based upon the same principles, whether the entrepreneur is an existing large institution or an individual starting his or her new venture single-handed . . . The rules are pretty much the same, the things work and those that don't are pretty much the same, and so are the kinds of innovation and where to look for them.
>
> *(p. 143)*

In the same year, Gifford Pinchott released the book *Intrapreneuring* (Pinchott, 1985) in which he coined the term "intra" (within) "preneurship" (derived from entrepreneurship). The gimmick word became a popular representation of corporate entrepreneurship. Pinchott's popular book outlined the guidelines and recommendations for people inside organizations to bring forth and develop new ideas into actual business ventures. His book motivated an executive vice president of a large company in Indiana (Anthem Blue Cross/Blue Shield, which later became Acordia) to approach me about the possibility of teaching employees in a larger entity to "think" like entrepreneurs. I, of course, said it was definitely possible and I took on the challenge of doing it.

In accepting that challenge, I quickly immersed myself into whatever literature was available on the topic so I could create the proper program. In the 1980s some researchers concluded that entrepreneurship and larger entities were mutually exclusive and could not coexist (Morse, 1986; Duncan, Ginter, Rucks, & Jacobs, 1988). However, I found far more researchers who embraced the idea of corporate entrepreneurial activity and conceptualized it as embodying entrepreneurial behavior requiring organizational sanctions and resource commitments for the purpose of developing different types of value-creating innovations (Schollhammer, 1982; Burgelman, 1983a, 1983b, 1984; Kanter, 1985). So, for the most part in the 1980s CE was defined simply as a process of organizational renewal (Sathe, 1989), yet it was acknowledged in the entrepreneurship and strategy literatures.

During the 1990s more comprehensive research of CE began to take place that focused on CE as re-energizing and enhancing the firm's ability to develop the skills through which innovations could be created (Jennings & Young, 1990; Zahra, 1991; Merrifield, 1993; Borch, Huse, & Senneseth, 1999). Developing new ventures within existing organizations and the transformation of on-going organizations through strategic renewal were proposed as two major forms of CE (Guth & Ginsberg, 1990). Corporate entrepreneurship could entail formal or informal activities aimed at creating new businesses in established companies or entrepreneurial innovations through product, process, or market initiatives. These innovations could take place at the corporate, division (business), functional, or project levels (Zahra, 1991). Demonstrating that the two major forms of CE introduced at the beginning of the decade still dominated the landscape, Sharma and Chrisman (1999: 18) suggested that CE "is the process whereby an individual or a group of individuals, in association with an existing organization, create a new organization or instigate renewal or innovation within that organization."

Developing the CEAI

As I continued my work with Acordia (Anthem Blue Cross/Blue Shield), a number of other firms contacted me about the same issue of energizing employees to think more entrepreneurially, including Ameritech, Union Carbide, and AT&T. All of this work provided me and my close friend, colleague and co-author, Jeffrey S. Hornsby, with an inside look at organizations struggling to initiate the entrepreneurial mind-set with their employees. We decided to focus our research efforts on understanding the most effective internal environment for corporate entrepreneurial activity. To do this we used data collected from the companies we had worked with to examine the organizational antecedents to individual entrepreneurial behavior. Most of the research dealing with the impact of organizational antecedents on individual-level entrepreneurial behavior over the years has been based on our empirical work (Kuratko, Montagno, & Hornsby, 1990; Hornsby, Kuratko, & Montagno, 1999; Hornsby, Kuratko, & Zahra, 2002; Kuratko, Hornsby, & Goldsby, 2004; Kuratko, Ireland, Covin, & Hornsby, 2005; Hornsby, Kuratko, Shepherd, & Bott, 2009).

The development of our work in corporate entrepreneurship was very methodical. For example, in our first major study (Kuratko et al., 1990), we attempted to conceive an instrument for measuring the internal organizational antecedents needed for effective individual entrepreneurial behavior. Initially we titled it the IAI (Intrapreneurial Assessment Instrument), and the results from our factor analysis showed that three factors – management support, organizational structure, and reward and resource availability – were important influences on the development of an organizational climate in which entrepreneurial behavior on the part of first- and middle-level managers could be expected. In extending this early study, we conducted further empirical research to explore the effect of organizational culture on entrepreneurial behavior in a sample of Canadian and U.S. firms (Hornsby et al., 1999). In particular, this study sought to determine if organizational culture creates variance in entrepreneurial behavior on the part of managers. The results based on data collected from all levels of management showed no significant differences between Canadian and U.S. managers' perceptions of the importance of five factors – management support, work discretion, rewards/reinforcement, time availability, and organizational boundaries – as antecedents to their entrepreneurial behavior. These findings partially validated those reported by the Kuratko et al. (1990) study and extended the importance of organizational antecedents of managers' entrepreneurial behavior into companies based in a second national culture.

In the Hornsby et al. (2002) study, we officially developed the Corporate Entrepreneurship Assessment Instrument (CEAI) to partially replicate the previous studies and provide a sound instrument for analyzing employee perceptions of the antecedents to an organizational climate conducive for entrepreneurial activity. The instrument featured forty-eight Likert-style questions that were used to assess antecedents of entrepreneurial behavior. Results from factor analyses supported the five stable antecedents of middle-level managers' entrepreneurial behavior. The five antecedents are:

1   Management support (the willingness of top-level managers to facilitate and promote entrepreneurial behavior, including the championing of innovative ideas and providing the resources people require to behave entrepreneurially).
2   Work discretion/autonomy (top-level managers' commitment to tolerate failure, provide decision-making latitude and freedom from excessive oversight and to delegate authority and responsibility to middle- and lower-level managers).
3   Rewards/reinforcement (developing and using systems that reinforce entrepreneurial behavior, highlight significant achievements, and encourage pursuit of challenging work).
4   Time availability (evaluating workloads to ensure that individuals and groups have the time needed to pursue innovations and that their jobs are structured in ways that support efforts to achieve short- and long-term organizational goals).
5   Organizational boundaries (precise explanations of outcomes expected from organizational work and development of mechanisms for evaluating, selecting and using innovations).

The CEAI instrument measures the degree to which individuals within a firm perceive these five elements, which are critical to an internal environment conducive for individual entrepreneurial activity (Kuratko, Hornsby, & Covin, 2014). Through the results of this instrument corporate entrepreneurial leaders are better able to assess, evaluate, and manage the firm's internal work environment in ways that support entrepreneurial behavior, which becomes the foundation for successfully implementing a corporate innovation strategy. A firm's internal entrepreneurial climate should be assessed to evaluate in what manner it is supportive for entrepreneurial behavior to exist and how that is perceived by the managers. When attempting to inventory the firm's current situation regarding the readiness for innovation, managers need to identify parts of the firm's structure, control systems, human resource management systems, and culture that inhibit and parts that facilitate entrepreneurial behavior as the foundation for successfully implementing corporate innovation (Ireland, Kuratko, & Morris, 2006a, 2006b). The CEAI has proven to be an effective instrument not only for significant research in corporate entrepreneurship, but also for the practical assessment of perceived entrepreneurial readiness within organizations.

Insights into managerial levels

In examining the literature we found that the managers at all organizational levels have critical strategic roles to fulfill for the organization to be successful (Ireland, Hitt, & Vaidyanath, 2002). According to Floyd and Lane (2000), senior-, middle-, and first-level managers have distinct responsibilities, which are then associated with particular managerial actions. Applying that to the corporate entrepreneurship realm we found Burgelman (1984) contended that in successful corporate entrepreneurship senior-level management's principal involvement takes place within the strategic and structural context determination processes. Ling, Simsek, Lubatkin, and Veiga (2008) examined 152 firms in regard to "transformational" CEOs' impact on corporate entrepreneurship. Their research demonstrated that the transformational CEOs had a significant role in directly shaping four salient characteristics of top management teams: behavioral integration, risk-taking propensity, decentralization of responsibilities, and long-term compensation. This study provided impetus to the importance of the directing role that top management must embrace. Thus, senior-level managers have critical roles in CE activity in the articulation of an entrepreneurial strategic vision and instigating the emergence of an organizational climate conducive to entrepreneurial activity. In addition, senior-level managers are centrally involved in the defining processes of both the corporate venturing and strategic entrepreneurship forms of CE as they provide leadership to various entrepreneurial initiatives.

In examining the research on managerial roles, we the found evidence that middle-level managers are a hub through which most organizational knowledge flows (Floyd & Wooldridge, 1992, 1994; King, Fowler, & Zeithaml, 2001). This motivated us to delve deeper into examining middle-level managers in the CE process. To interact effectively with first-level managers, middle-level managers must possess the technical competence required to understand the firm's core competencies and, simultaneously, interacting effectively with senior-level executives, middle-level managers must understand the firm's strategic intent and goals. Through interactions with senior- and first-level managers, those operating in the middle of an organization's leadership structure influence and shape their firms' corporate entrepreneurial strategies. From this we developed our specific work on middle-level managers in the corporate entrepreneurship process. In the Kuratko, Ireland, Covin, and Hornsby (2005) study, we argued that middle-level managers' work as change agents and promoters of innovation is facilitated by their positioning in the organization hierarchy. We contended that middle-level managers endorse, refine, and shepherd entrepreneurial initiatives and identify, acquire, and deploy resources needed to pursue those initiatives.

Within our work on middle-level managers (Kuratko et al., 2005), we provided a more detailed breakdown of each role. For example, in the endorsement role, middle-level managers often find themselves in evaluative positions with entrepreneurial initiatives emerging from lower organizational levels. Then middle-level managers must endorse those valued initiatives to the top level of the organization. They must also endorse the top-level initiatives and "sell" their value-creating potential to the primary implementers – first-level managers. In the refinement role, middle-level managers are molding the entrepreneurial opportunity into one that makes sense for the organization, given the organization's strategy, resources, and structure. Middle-level managers must convert potential entrepreneurial opportunities into initiatives that fit the organization. The shepherding role is where middle-level managers champion and guide the entrepreneurial initiative to assure that entrepreneurial initiatives originating at lower organizational levels are not abandoned once their continued development requires higher-level support. With their identification role, middle-level managers must know which resources will be needed to convert the entrepreneurial initiative into a business reality as these initiatives tend to evolve in their scope, content, and focus as they develop (McGrath & MacMillan, 1995). Finally, the acquisition and deployment roles involve middle-level managers being responsible for redirecting resources away from existing operations and deploying them into entrepreneurial initiatives appearing to have greater strategic value for the firm (Burgelman, 1984). In short, it might be argued that the middle management level is where entrepreneurial opportunities are given the best chance to flourish based on the resources likely to be deployed in their pursuit.

Other scholars examined first-level managers and argued that they have experimenting, adjusting, and conforming roles (Floyd and Lane, 2000). The experimenting role is expressed through the initiating of entrepreneurial projects. The adjusting role is expressed through, for example, first-level managers' responding to recognized and unplanned entrepreneurial challenges. Finally, the conforming role is expressed through first-level managers' adaptation of operating policies and procedures to the strategic initiatives endorsed at higher organizational levels. In one empirical examination of managers' relation to employees in the corporate entrepreneurship process,

Brundin, Patzelt, and Shepherd (2008) examined the entrepreneurial behavior of employees in entrepreneurially oriented firms and found a direct relation to managers' emotions and displays. The employees' willingness to act entrepreneurially increased when managers displayed confidence and satisfaction about an entrepreneurial project. It was also shown that the employees' willingness to act entrepreneurially decreased when managers displayed frustration, worry, or bewilderment about an entrepreneurial project.

So, in an effort to study entrepreneurial actions within the context of CE at different levels of management, we conducted an empirical study of 458 managers at different levels in their firms (Hornsby, Kuratko, Shepherd, & Bott, 2009). We found that the relationship between perceived internal antecedents (as measured by the Corporate Entrepreneurship Assessment Instrument mentioned earlier) and corporate entrepreneurial actions (measured by the number of new ideas implemented), differed depending on managerial level. Specifically, the positive relationship between managerial support and entrepreneurial action was more positive for senior and middle level managers than it was for first-level (lower level) managers, and the positive relationship between work discretion and entrepreneurial action was more positive for senior- and middle-level managers than it was for first-level managers. The few studies that have explored managerial-level (primarily conceptual studies) have emphasized the role of first-level managers in a "bottom-up" process of corporate entrepreneurship (Burgelman, 1983a, 1983b, 1984). Our study offered a counterweight to this "bottom-up" process with arguments and empirical support for the notion that given a specific organizational environment more senior managers have greater structural ability to "make more of" the conditions and thus implement more entrepreneurial ideas than do first-level managers. Even with the differences found with levels of management in the Hornsby et al. (2009) study, it reinforced our belief that working jointly, senior-, middle-, and first-level managers are responsible for developing the entrepreneurial behaviors that could be used to form the core competencies through which future competitive success can be pursued (Kuratko, Hornsby, & Bishop, 2005).

Defining the domains of CE

Many of the elements essential to constructing a theoretically grounded understanding of the domains of corporate entrepreneurship can now be identified. Therefore, we attempted to provide a clear understanding of what comprises the concept of corporate entrepreneurship (Kuratko & Audretsch, 2013). Outlining the depiction used in our book entitled *Corporate Entrepreneurship & Innovation* (Morris, Kuratko, & Covin, 2011), we argued that corporate entrepreneurship can be manifested in companies either through corporate venturing or strategic entrepreneurship.

Corporate venturing approaches have as their commonality the addition or development of new businesses (or portions of new businesses via equity investments) within the corporation. This can be accomplished through two implementation modes – internal corporate venturing and external corporate venturing (Miles & Covin, 2002; McGrath, Keil, & Tukiainen, 2006). With internal corporate venturing (ICV), new businesses are created and owned by the corporation. These businesses typically reside within the corporate structure but, occasionally, may be located outside the firm and operate as semiautonomous entities. External corporate venturing refers to entrepreneurial activity in which the firm invests in new businesses created by parties outside the corporation (via the assumption of equity positions) or acquired by the corporation. These external businesses are typically very young ventures or early-growth–stage firms that offer the acquiring corporation access to a new technology or product line that is currently not being pursued internally (Schildt, Maula, & Keil, 2005). In practice, new businesses might be developed through a single venturing mode or a combination of the two venturing modes. Therefore, a firm's total venturing activity is equal to the sum of the ventures enacted through the internal and external modes. With corporate venturing, creating an entirely new business is the main objective (Covin & Miles, 2007).

We conducted specific research on the ICV realm of the corporate entrepreneurship domain because of its relevance to our research with middle-level managers and the internal environment for corporate entrepreneurship. For example, in one study we found that among internal corporate ventures that reside within the firm's organizational boundaries, some may be formed and exist as part of a preexisting internal organization structure and others may be housed in newly formed organizational entities within the corporate structure (Kuratko, Covin, & Garrett, 2009). We then explored the effect on venture performance of the extent to which the ICV's value proposition evolves over the course of the venture's development and the effect the corporate parent's familiarity with the market targeted by the ICV has on this relationship (Covin, Garrett, Kuratko, & Shepherd, 2015). A venture's value proposition is the intended basis on which the ICV will appeal to its target market. We developed a value proposition evolution model of ICV performance and tested it on a sample of 145 ICVs nested within seventy-two parent corporations. We observed how the dynamics of building knowledge stocks among ventures targeting markets unfamiliar to their corporate parents and leveraging knowledge stocks among ventures targeting markets familiar to their corporate parents can influence the relationship between value proposition evolution and ICV performance. We demonstrated the relevance of an ICV's initial founding conditions to the specific shape of the adaptation-performance relationship, showing that initial market familiarity predicts both the extensiveness of venture value proposition evolution and how such evolution relates to ICV performance.

Other streams of research have focused on strategic entrepreneurship which can take one of five forms – strategic renewal (adoption of a new strategy), sustained regeneration (introduction of a new product into an existing category), domain redefinition (reconfiguration of existing product or market categories), organizational rejuvenation (internally focused innovation for strategy improvement), and business model reconstruction (redesign of existing business model), (Covin & Miles, 1999; Hitt, Ireland, Camp, & Sexton, 2001; Ireland, Hitt, & Sirmon, 2003; Ireland & Webb, 2007; Morris, Kuratko, & Covin, 2011).

With these explanations of the currently accepted forms of corporate entrepreneurship, it is clear that a "venturing" focus and a "strategic" focus are the two major lenses through which CE is studied.

Examining control and failure

As our research progressed in CE, we recognized that employees engaging in entrepreneurial behavior are the foundation for "corporate innovation," so organizations must establish a process through which individuals can pursue entrepreneurial opportunities to innovate without regard to the level and nature of currently available resources. However, we also realized that in the absence of proper control mechanisms, firms that manifest corporate innovative activity may tend to generate an incoherent mass of interesting but unrelated opportunities that may have profit potential, but do not move towards positive innovations for the firm (Getz & Tuttle, 2001). Therefore, those factors that drive corporate entrepreneurial activity to produce high levels of innovation performance are likely contingent upon a firm's ability to judiciously use control mechanisms for the proper selection and effective guidance on entrepreneurial actions and initiatives (Goodale, Kuratko, Hornsby, & Covin, 2011).

Although some had emphasized the need to "unleash the entrepreneurial hostages" in organizations simply by removing constraints on behavior, it is clear that, in doing so, they may be ignoring opportunities better to align innovations with organizational interests, which results from encouraging, directing, restricting, and prohibiting behaviors and initiatives. We learned that not all corporate entrepreneurial behavior is good for corporations. Yet the literature in the corporate innovation area tends to implicitly regard such behavior as inherently virtuous. This is an unfortunate and potentially dangerous bias. As we noted in the Kuratko and Goldsby (2004) article, the encouragement of corporate entrepreneurship can and often does result in counterproductive, rogue behavior by organizational members. Thus, the deliberate design and development of organizational systems reflecting the organizational dimensions for an environment conducive to corporate innovation is critical. As such, the senior manager's task is not simply to build an organization whose core qualities are conducive to innovation, but rather to design and develop innovation-facilitating and control-facilitating mechanisms that complement one another such that the innovative potential that resides within the organization is leveraged for the highest and best organizational purposes.

Another area that arose in the entrepreneurship literature was the impact of failure (Shepherd, 2003). As we witnessed the idea of "learning from failure" becoming axiomatic in the corporate entrepreneurial literature and practice, dealing with the failure on a personal level was something that was not fully examined. Therefore building on the work of Dean Shepherd, we examined the importance of managing grief that results from project failures in the corporate entrepreneurship setting (Shepherd & Kuratko, 2009). Grief, which triggers behavioral, psychological, and physiological symptoms, is a negative emotional response to the loss of something important. Therefore, we found that managing grief represents a particularly salient task in the context of corporate entrepreneurship practice, because the amount of commitment essential to project success is often matched by corresponding levels of grief when projects fail. Organizational routines and rituals are likely to influence the grief recovery of those involved in failed projects. To the extent that an organization's social support systems can effectively channel negative emotions, greater learning and motivational outcomes from project failures are certainly possible. The inevitability of project failure tests social support mechanisms and failure-related coping skills of corporate managers, giving dedicated innovation units with adequate social supports for dealing with grief an operational edge that also strengthens coping self-efficacy of individuals (Shepherd, Covin, & Kuratko, 2009).

Framing a corporate entrepreneurial strategy

Coming back full circle, my earlier work with Acordia (Anthem Blue Cross/Blue Shield) provided an interesting academic study (Kuratko, Ireland, & Hornsby, 2001). We used insights from the academic literature, the business press, and my own experiences inside the company as the framework for the story of how one company was able to use entrepreneurial actions as the foundation for its successful corporate entrepreneurship strategy. However, we realized that the actual definition of such a strategy was elusive at that time. So, over the next few years, we began to formulate the concepts and framework that could define a corporate entrepreneurial strategy.

We began by reviewing the work on entrepreneurial orientation (EO). My close friend, colleague and co-author, Jeffrey G. Covin, was one of the pioneers of this entire concept. In the Covin and Slevin (1991) study, he introduced the concept of EO that consisted of three underlying dimensions: innovativeness, risk-taking, and proactiveness, with different combinations of these dimensions possible. EO, a firm's strategic posture towards entrepreneurship, has become the predominant construct of interest in strategic entrepreneurship research. Despite the ever-increasing volume of nomological research on EO, there remain ongoing conversations regarding its ontology. Drawing from measurement theory, we outlined an EO reconceptualization addressing the likely prevalence of type II nomological error in the EO literature stemming from measurement model misspecification. Focusing on the question of whether EO is an attitudinal construct, a behavioral construct, or both, we proposed a formative construction of EO viewing the exhibition of entrepreneurial behaviors and of managerial attitude towards risk as jointly necessary dimensions that collectively form the higher-order EO construct (Anderson, Kreiser, Kuratko, Hornsby, & Eshima, 2015).

Based on the work developed in EO, we introduced the concept of "entrepreneurial intensity," which refers to the overall level of the degree and frequency of entrepreneurial actions demonstrated by an individual or organization. In the Morris, Kuratko, and Covin (2011) book, we created a two-dimensional matrix ("entrepreneurial grid") with the frequency (number of entrepreneurial events) on the vertical axis, and the degree (extent of innovativeness, risk, and proactiveness) on the horizontal axis. Because there are no absolute standards for degree or frequency of entrepreneurial actions, the results are relative meaning that different points on the grid at different periods in time could be applied to the same organization or person depending on their activity. However, a firm's "entrepreneurial intensity" does provide some measure of an organization's entrepreneurial activity at any point in time that could then form the basis for what constitutes a corporate entrepreneurial strategy.

All of this work on EO and entrepreneurial intensity helped us to formulate a specific definition of a corporate entrepreneurial strategy. In the Ireland, Covin, and Kuratko (2009) article, we stated that a corporate entrepreneurship strategy is "a vision-directed, organization-wide reliance on entrepreneurial behavior that purposefully and continuously rejuvenates the organization and shapes the scope of its operations through the recognition and exploitation of entrepreneurial opportunity" (p. 21). As companies have found themselves continually redefining their markets, restructuring their operations, and modifying their business models, this definition lends a framework to what they are trying to accomplish. It is clear that learning the skills to think and act entrepreneurially has become a major source of competitive advantage for organizations today.

Achieving entrepreneurial actions is not something that management can simply decide to do. Corporate entrepreneurship does not produce instant success. It requires considerable time and investment, and there must be continual reinforcement. By their nature, organizations impose constraints on entrepreneurial behavior. To be sustainable, the entrepreneurial spirit must be integrated into the mission, goals, strategies, structure, processes, and values of the organization. Flexibility, speed, innovation, and entrepreneurial leadership are the cornerstones. The managerial mindset must become an opportunity-driven mindset, where actions are never constrained by resources currently controlled (Morris, Kuratko, & Covin, 2011). This entrepreneurial mind-set becomes the essence of corporate entrepreneurship. Today there is a greater understanding and respect for the strategy of corporate entrepreneurship.

The journey continues

Through the passing years I have truly enjoyed focusing my research on corporate entrepreneurship. Today I continue to research and write in this field because I believe in the impact it will continue to have for organizations in a global economy (Kuratko, Hornsby, & Hayton, 2015). Corporate entrepreneurship and innovation is the greatest challenge facing leaders in the current economic landscape. The challenge of leadership today has more to do with entrepreneurial thinking than ever before. An entrepreneurial revolution has taken hold in a global economic sense, and the entrepreneurial mind-set is the dominant force. If leadership means the capacity to lead and entrepreneurship means assuming risks beyond security, then entrepreneurial leadership combines the capacity to lead and the capacity to take risks. The combination of these two terms may be one of the most significant phrases in the twenty-first century because the current global entrepreneurial revolution is more impactful than the industrial revolution was for earlier centuries (Kuratko & Morris, 2013).

As entrepreneurial thinking is about searching for opportunities and driving innovation, it has become the standard by which true leadership is now measured (Kuratko, Goldsby, & Hornsby, 2012). It is leadership in discovering new possibilities, opening up new horizons, promulgating a new vision, combining resources in new ways, and inspiring others to create new venture concepts (Kuratko & Morris, 2013). The ability to trigger entrepreneurial action is a cornerstone of entrepreneurial leadership (McMullen & Shepherd, 2006). However, because it is essentially disruptive, as it introduces change to organizations, markets, industries, and individuals, it may also be considered threatening. As I point out in one of my latest articles, there are numerous obstacles to the implementation of such action (Kuratko, Covin, & Hornsby, 2014). The willingness to take on the risks associated with entrepreneurial action and the courage to address the obstacles and sources of resistance represent the essence of entrepreneurial leadership (Kuratko, 2016).

With this in mind, the journey continues!

Acknowledgements

In sharing this research journey, it is important for me to recognize the significant scholars who have affected my work in this field. As one can see by the numerous publications with co-authors, there were scholars who not only helped to shape the research on corporate entrepreneurship, but also helped to shape me as a scholar. Here are those great scholars who I am proud to call my close friends:

Richard M. Hodgetts, Florida International University
Jeffrey S. Hornsby, UMKC
Jeffrey G. Covin, Indiana University
Michael H. Morris, University of Florida
Dean A. Shepherd, Indiana University
R. Duane Ireland, Texas A&M University
David B. Audretsch, Indiana University
Jeffery S. McMullen, Indiana University
Michael G. Goldsby, Ball State University

There are also some young scholars that I have had the privilege to work with in recent years. They are bright minds that have demonstrated their abilities to shape the next generation of our field. Here are just a few of the rising stars that I have had the privilege to co-author with and whom I greatly admire:

Robert P. Garrett, University of Louisville
Brian S. Anderson, University of Colorado
Patrick M. Kreiser, Iowa State University
Greg Fisher, Indiana University

References

Anderson, B.S., Kreiser, P.M., Kuratko, D.F., Hornsby, J.S., & Eshima, Y., (2015), Reconceptualizing entrepreneurial orientation. Strategic Management Journal, 36 (10), 1579–1596.

Borch, O.J., Huse, M., & Senneseth, K., (1999), Resource configuration, competitive strategies, and corporate entrepreneurship: An empirical examination of small firms. Entrepreneurship Theory & Practice, 24 (1), 49–70.

Brundin, E., Patzelt, H., & Shepherd, D.A., (2008), Managers' emotional displays and employees' willingness to act entrepreneurially. Journal of Business Venturing, 23 (2), 221–243.

Burgelman, R.A., (1983a), A process model of internal corporate venturing in the major diversified firm. Administrative Science Quarterly, 28 (2), 223–244.

Burgelman, R.A., (1983b), Corporate entrepreneurship and strategic management: Insights from a process study. Management Science, 23, 1349–1363.

Burgelman, R.A., (1984), Designs for corporate entrepreneurship in established firms. California Management Review, 26 (3), 154–166.

Covin, J.G., Garrett, R.P., Kuratko, D.F., & Shepherd, D.A., (2015), Value proposition evolution and the performance of internal corporate ventures. Journal of Business Venturing, 30 (5), 749–774.

Covin, J.G. & Miles, M.P., (1999), Corporate entrepreneurship and the pursuit of competitive advantage. Entrepreneurship Theory & Practice, 23 (3), 47–64.

Covin, J.G. & Miles, M.P., (2007), Strategic use of corporate venturing. Entrepreneurship Theory & Practice, 31 (2), 183–207.

Covin, J.G. & Slevin, D.P., (1991), A conceptual model of entrepreneurship as firm behavior. Entrepreneurship Theory & Practice, 16 (1), 7–25.

Drucker, P.F., (1985), Innovation and entrepreneurship (New York: Harper & Row).

Duncan, W.J., Ginter, P.M., Rucks, A.C., & Jacobs, T.D., (1988), Intrapreneuring and the reinvention of the corporation. Business Horizons, 31 (3), 16–21.

Floyd, S.W. & Lane, P.J., (2000), Strategizing throughout the organization: Managing role conflict in strategic renewal. Academy of Management Review, 25, 154–177.

Floyd, S.W. & Wooldridge, B., (1992), Middle management involvement in strategy and its association with strategic type. Strategic Management Journal, 13, 53–168.

Floyd, S.W. & Wooldridge, B., (1994), Dinosaurs or dynamos? Recognizing middle management's strategic role. Academy of Management Executive, 8 (4), 47–57.

Getz, G. & Tuttle, E.G., (2001), A comprehensive approach to corporate venturing, in handbook of business strategy. (New York: Thompson Financial Media).

Goodale, J.C., Kuratko, D.F., Hornsby, J.S., & Covin, J.G., (2011), Operations management and corporate entrepreneurship: The moderating effect of operations control on the antecedents of corporate entrepreneurial activity in relation to innovation performance. Journal of Operations Management, 29 (2), 116–127.

Guth, W.D. & Ginsberg A., (1990), Corporate entrepreneurship. Strategic Management Journal, 11 (Special Issue), 5–15.

Hanan, M., (1976), Venturing corporations – Think small to stay strong. Harvard Business Review, 54 (3), 139–148.

Hill, R.M. & Hlavacek, J.D., (1972), The venture team: A new concept in marketing organizations. Journal of Marketing, 36, 44–50.

Hitt, M.A., Ireland, R.D., Camp, S.M., & Sexton, D.L., (2001), Strategic entrepreneurship: Entrepreneurial strategies for wealth creation. Strategic Management Journal, 22 (Special Issue), 479–491.

Hodgetts, R.M. & Kuratko, D.F., (1991), Management, 3rd ed. (New York, NY: Dryden/Harcourt Brace).

Hodgetts, R.M. & Kuratko, D.F., (2001), Effective small business management, 7th ed. (San Diego, CA: Wiley & Sons).

Hornsby, J.S., Kuratko, D.F., & Montagno, R.V., (1999), Perception of internal factors for corporate entrepreneurship: A comparison of Canadian and U.S. managers. Entrepreneurship Theory and Practice, 24 (2), 9–24.

Hornsby, J.S., Kuratko, D.F., Shepherd, D.A., & Bott, J.P., (2009), Managers' corporate entrepreneurial actions: Examining perception and position. Journal of Business Venturing, 24 (3), 236–247.

Hornsby, J.S., Kuratko, D.F., & Zahra, S.A., (2002), Middle managers' perception of the internal environment for corporate entrepreneurship: Assessing a measurement scale. Journal of Business Venturing, 17, 49–63.

Ireland, R.D., Covin, J.G., & Kuratko, D.F., (2009), Conceptualizing corporate entrepreneurship strategy. Entrepreneurship Theory and Practice, 33 (1), 19–46.

Ireland, R.D., Hitt, M.A., & Sirmon, D.G., (2003), A model of strategic entrepreneurship: The construct and its dimensions. Journal of Management, 29 (6), 963–989.

Ireland, R.D., Hitt, M.A., & Vaidyanath, D., (2002), Strategic alliances as a pathway to competitive success. Journal of Management, 28, 413–446.

Ireland, R.D., Kuratko, D.F., & Morris, M.H., (2006a), A health audit for corporate entrepreneurship: Innovation at all levels – Part I. Journal of Business Strategy, 27 (1), 10–17.

Ireland, R.D., Kuratko, D.F., & Morris, M.H., (2006b), A health audit for corporate entrepreneurship: Innovation at all levels – Part 2. Journal of Business Strategy, 27 (2), 21–30.

Ireland, R.D. & Webb, J.W., (2007), Strategic entrepreneurship: Creating competitive advantage through streams of innovation. Business Horizons, 50, 49–59.

Jennings, D.F. & Young, D.M., (1990), An empirical comparison between objective and subjective measures of the product innovation domain of corporate entrepreneurship. Entrepreneurship Theory and Practice, 15 (1), 53–66.

Kanter, R.M., (1985), Supporting innovation and venture development in established companies. Journal of Business Venturing, 1, 47–60.

King, A.W., Fowler, S.W., & Zeithaml, C.P., (2001), Managing organizational competencies for competitive advantage: The middle-management edge. Academy of Management Executive, 15 (2), 95–106.

Kuratko, D.F., (2016), The challenge of corporate entrepreneurial leadership. In R. Harrison & C.M. Leitch (Eds.) Research handbook on entrepreneurship and leadership (London: Edward Elgar).

Kuratko, D.F., (2017), Entrepreneurship: Theory, process, practice, 10th ed. (Mason, OH: Cengage/South-Western Publishing).

Kuratko, D.F. & Audretsch, D.B., (2013), Clarifying the domains of corporate entrepreneurship. International Entrepreneurship & Management Journal, 9 (3), 323–335.

Kuratko, D.F., Covin, J.G., & Garrett, R.P., (2009), Corporate venturing: Insights from actual performance. Business Horizons, 52 (5), 459–467.

Kuratko, D.F., Covin, J.G., & Hornsby, J.S., (2014), Why implementing corporate innovation is so difficult. Business Horizons, 57 (5), 647–655.

Kuratko, D.F. & Goldsby, M.G., (2004), Corporate entrepreneurs or rogue middle managers? A framework for ethical corporate entrepreneurship. Journal of Business Ethics, 55 (1), 13–30.

Kuratko, D.F., Goldsby, M.G., & Hornsby, J.S., (2012), Innovation acceleration: Transforming organizational thinking (Upper Saddle River, NJ: Pearson/Prentice Hall).

Kuratko, D.F., Hornsby, J.S., & Bishop, J.W., (2005), Managers' corporate entrepreneurial actions and job satisfaction. International Entrepreneurship & Management Journal, 1 (3), 275–291.

Kuratko, D.F., Hornsby, J.S., & Covin, J.G., (2014), Diagnosing a firm's internal environment for corporate entrepreneurship. Business Horizons, 57 (1), 37–47.

Kuratko, D.F., Hornsby, J.S., & Goldsby, M.G., (2004), Sustaining corporate entrepreneurship: A proposed model of perceived implementation/outcome comparisons at the organizational and individual levels. International Journal of Entrepreneurship and Innovation, 5 (2), 77–89.

Kuratko, D.F., Hornsby, J.S., & Hayton, J., (2015), Corporate entrepreneurship: The innovative challenge for a new global economic reality. Small Business Economics, 45 (2), 245–253.

Kuratko, D.F., Ireland, R.D., Covin, J.G., & Hornsby, J.S., (2005), A model of middle level managers' entrepreneurial behavior. Entrepreneurship Theory & Practice, 29 (6), 699–716.

Kuratko, D.F., Ireland, R.D., & Hornsby, J.S., (2001), The power of entrepreneurial outcomes: Insights from Acordia, Inc. Academy of Management Executive, 15 (4), 60–71.

Kuratko, D.F., Montagno, R.V., & Hornsby, J.S., (1990), Developing an entrepreneurial assessment instrument for an effective corporate entrepreneurial environment. Strategic Management Journal, 11 (Special Issue), 49–58.

Kuratko, D.F. & Morris, M.H., (2013), Entrepreneurship and leadership (Cheltenham, UK: Edward Elgar).

Ling, Y., Simsek, Z., Lubatkin, M.H., & Veiga, J.F., (2008), Transformational leadership's role in promoting corporate entrepreneurship: Examining the CEO-TMT interface. Academy of Management Journal, 51 (3), 557–576.

McGrath, R.G., Keil, T., & Tukiainen, T., (2006), Extracting value from corporate venturing. MIT Sloan Management Review, 48 (1), 50–56.

McGrath, R.G. & MacMillan, I.C., (1995), Discovery-driven planning. Harvard Business Review, 73 (4), 4–12.

McMullen, J.S. & Shepherd, D.A., (2006), Entrepreneurial action and the role of uncertainty in the theory of the entrepreneur. Academy of Management Review, 31 (1), 132–152.

Merrifield, D.B., (1993), Intrapreneurial corporate renewal. Journal of Business Venturing, 8, 383–389.

Miles, M.P. & Covin, J.G., (2002), Exploring the practice of corporate venturing: Some common forms and their organizational implications. Entrepreneurship Theory and Practice, 26 (3), 21–40.

Morris, M.H., Kuratko, D.F., & Covin, J.G., (2011), Corporate entrepreneurship & innovation, 3rd ed. (Mason, OH: South-Western/Thomson Publishers).

Morse, C.W., (1986), The delusion of intrapreneurship. Long Range Planning, 19(6), 92–95.

Peterson, R. & Berger D., (1972), Entrepreneurship in organizations. Administrative Science Quarterly, 16, 97–106.

Pinchott, G., (1985), Intrapreneurship (New York: Harper & Row).

Sathe, V., (1989), Fostering entrepreneurship in large diversified firm. Organizational Dynamics, 18 (1), 20–32.

Schildt, H.A., Maula, M.V.J., & Keil, T., (2005), Explorative and exploitative learning from external corporate ventures. Entrepreneurship Theory & Practice, 29 (4), 493–515.

Schollhammer, H., (1982), Internal corporate entrepreneurship. In C. Kent, D. Sexton, & K. Vesper (Eds.) Encyclopedia of entrepreneurship (Englewood Cliffs, NJ: Prentice-Hall), 209–223.

Sharma, P. & Chrisman, J.J., (1999), Toward a reconciliation of the definitional issues in the field of corporate entrepreneurship. Entrepreneurship Theory & Practice, 23 (3), 11–28.

Shepherd, D.A., (2003), Learning from Business Failure: Propositions about the Grief Recovery Process for the Self-Employed. Academy of Management Review, 28, 318–329.

Shepherd, D.A., Covin, J.G., & Kuratko, D.F., (2009), Project failure from corporate entrepreneurship: Managing the grief process. Journal of Business Venturing, 24 (6), 588–600.

Shepherd, D.A. & Kuratko, D.F., (2009), The death of an innovative project: How grief recovery enhances learning. Business Horizons, 52 (5), 451–458.

Zahra, S.A., (1991), Predictors and financial outcomes of corporate entrepreneurship: An exploratory study. Journal of Business Venturing, 6, 259–286.

15

From integrating functions to integrating ideas

Albert N. Link

What was in that residual?

Math was my thing. I was fortunate to go to a high school in Virginia that offered advanced courses in calculus and matrix algebra, and I did well in those classes. So, majoring in math at the University of Richmond seemed like the logical path to follow. However, math was about all that I was interested in when I started college. By the end of my sophomore year I had completed my major requirements in math as well as my minor requirements in physics. The next step was to satisfy the university's core requirements; U of R is a liberal arts college. By my junior year I had grown an appreciation for the humanities and social sciences, so I began to dabble across the spectrum, constrained only by area requirements and a four-year time constraint. These explorations ranged from Pavlov to production possibilities and from the New Testament to neoclassical thought. In my senior year, with only a rudimentary understanding of supply and demand under my belt, I decided to give graduate studies in economics a try at Tulane University in New Orleans. Perhaps in the back of my mind was that a break from math would be a nice change. Little did I know at the time how useful my math background would prove to be.

The core course work at Tulane was traditional, yet there were few field courses from which to choose because of the small size of the faculty. Production theory immediately captured my attention, and that interest led me to read the 1957 article by Robert Solow on technical change and the aggregate production function and then to ask the question: What was in that residual?[1] My dissertation attempted to address that question, and it focused me on static investments in research and development (R&D) as an initial answer.

After graduation, Southern roots took my wife and me to Auburn University. The interests of the faculty there were broader than the faculty at Tulane, and I took full advantage of that fact. One such step was to sit in on Bob Hébert's graduate class on the history of economic thought. I knew little about the history of economic thought at that time, save selected mentions about the classical economists in the margins of Samuelson's principles textbook back when. I remember being intrigued by one of Bob's lectures on Joseph Schumpeter, and afterwards at lunch I asked him about the origin of the concept of the entrepreneur. Well, that got it all started.

My fondness for New Orleans cuisine and Bob's Louisiana heritage and culinary skills were the glue (or perhaps the gumbo) that bonded us together on our quest toward understanding from an historical perspective who an entrepreneur is and what he or she does. This was quite an adventure; our quest began with Aristotle and has yet to end. Cantillon, Baudeau, Knight, and Kirzner, among others, were friendly acquaintances along the way. What resulted from this quest was *The Entrepreneur: Mainstream Views and Radical Critiques* (1982, revised 1988).[2]

It is interesting to think about now, in the afternoon of my research career, how an event here and event there has influenced my path. In my case, or so I think retrospectively, there was a confluence of relationships and events in the early 1980s that has indeed influenced the evolution of my scholarship to date.

I first met David Audretsch at a conference at Middlebury College in April 1981. We later reconnected at a conference at INSEAD, the European Business School in Fontainebleau, France, in June 1986. Perhaps it was those meetings, or perhaps it was my 1982 book with Bob, or perhaps it was both, but David was kind enough to invite Bob and me to write a paper for the inaugural issue of *Small Business Economics*.[3] Preparing that paper caused Bob and me to integrate the history of ideas about the entrepreneur in a way that we had not previously done. We are grateful for that challenge and have benefitted from it many times over. It was that reintegration of thought that eventually led us to rethink *Mainstream Views*, and that process culminated a decade later with *A History of Entrepreneurship* (2009).[4]

Public–private research partnerships

The other person I spent time with at the Middlebury conference was Ed Mansfield. He and I had met the previous December at the International Institute of Management Science in Berlin. We were talking the evening before the Middlebury conference started, and I confessed to him that I had been one of the referees on his 1980 paper in the *American Economic Review* (AER) on the returns to basic research, and he responded that he was one of the referees on my rejoinder to his paper.[5] It turned out that my paper would also appear in the AER later that year.[6] Small world. Obviously, the discussion during the rest of the evening went in the direction of: "What are you working on now?" It turned out that we both were working on similar topics. More accurately, that which was consuming my time overlapped with a small segment of Ed's encompassing and forward-looking research agenda. One topic was what the literature has come to call public/private research partnerships, and the other topic was firm-with-university research partnerships.

There are a few more pieces of the puzzle that need to be put into place, keeping in mind that I am putting this puzzle together with both a well-intended memory and a retrospective eye. The paper that I presented at the INSEAD conference where I reconnected with David was on voluntary standards and the role of the public sector to provide a framework for such technology infrastructure.[7]

My research landscape by the mid-1980s looked like this. At the center was my appreciation for the historical roots of entrepreneurship. Over time both Bob and I came to the conclusion that an entrepreneurial effort – that is an effort by an individual, a firm, or even a public organization – can be described with reference to the attendant historical literature as encompassing both the perception of an opportunity and the ability to act on that perception. The conjunction *and* is important; perception *and* action. From that core are several branches. One branch leads to private-sector investments in R&D, another branch leads to public-sector investments in R&D, another branch leads to university research, and yet a fourth branch leads to public-sector investments in technology infrastructure. The vine that connects these branches is the notion of research partnerships.

Timing is everything. In the mid-1980s, the National Cooperative Research Act (NCRA) of 1984 gained the attention of theoretical and empirical researchers. The coincidental timing of this legislation, as well as the National Science Foundation's interest in funding my exploratory research on research joint ventures, fit nicely within the landscape of my unfolding research agenda.[8] The NRCA was not to be viewed in isolation of other post-productivity slowdown policy initiatives, and so I became interested in related policies such as university technology transfer through the Bayh-Dole Act of 1980. Thus, the linkage among the research areas of private- and public-sector R&D, university research activity, and public support of technology were tightly in place in the mid-1980s within my research agenda, and they were in place within the literature by the late 1980s.

These interests brought about some influential research partnerships. One of the longest lasting and, from a friendship perspective, most important was with John Scott. He and I first met at a National Bureau of Economic Research (NBER)conference in the fall of 1981. It was not the focus of the conference, but rather our later mutual interest in the NCRA and in cooperative R&D that were the seeds that grew into more than a three-decade research partnership. From there, our independent and mutual interest in cooperative R&D expanded into our study of public/private partnerships. We were fortunate to have been invited to study a number of such partnerships that were supported by the National Institute of Standards and Technology (NIST) and its Advanced Technology Program (ATP), and those experiences evolved into our theory about program evaluation. This focus of our research partnership continued for nearly two decades.[9]

The *Journal of Technology Transfer*

It was my research with John on the activities at NIST that fueled my interest in technology transfer activities. That interest, however, remained dormant for a number of years until a door unexpectedly opened for me to become the editor of the *Journal of Technology Transfer* (JTT). In 1996 that journal was little more than a practitioner vehicle for communicating ideas among the members of the Technology Transfer Society (which at that time was dominated by members from the Federal Laboratory Consortium). My challenge was to transform the journal into an academic vehicle for scholars. That was a slow, uphill process, but one aided initially through the help of Don Siegel at the University at Albany, SUNY and later through the help of Barry Bozeman at Arizona State University. I am proud of what the JTT has become, but more visible times are yet to come.

Public-sector entrepreneurship

There is one more piece of the puzzle to describe before I explain how my research agenda has come full circle. In 2007, I began a benefit-cost study for the Department of Energy (DOE) on their improved vehicle combustion engine R&D investments.[10] During that project, which concluded in 2010, I was thinking about the sources of ideas that originally led to the creation of the advanced combustion engine R&D program and the impetus for its on-going funding. What gelled was that this program was an example of government as entrepreneur – the DOE perceiving an opportunity to fulfill a dimension of its mission and then having the ability to act on that perception. Before the project ended, I realized that my research endeavors had indeed come full circle. My early work with Bob Hébert on this historical origin of entrepreneurship and our synthesized definition of entrepreneurship as perception *and* action illuminated how I began to think about selected public policies, especially technology-based public policies.

In 2008, I began a retrospective look at a large segment of my prior research, especially my research on NIST-funded projects, and I arrived at the following definition (Link and Link, 2009, p. 4):

> Government acts as entrepreneur in the provision of technology infrastructure when its involvement is both innovative and characterized by entrepreneurial risk.

Here I was, back in Bob's lecture on Schumpeterian entrepreneurs!

The circle is now complete. My research career related to entrepreneurship began with my work with Bob and with *Mainstream Views*. Events and personal relationships developed my interest in public- and private-sector R&D; university research relationships[11]; public/private research collaborations; and technology-based policies, especially those related to technology infrastructure. Over time these threads became connected through an understanding of entrepreneurship. As a culmination, all of these threads are present in my most recent work with my colleague Dennis Leyden as evident through what we wrote in *Public Sector Entrepreneurship* (Leyden and Link, 2015a, p. 14)[12]:

> [P]ublic sector entrepreneurship is a variant of the more general notion of entrepreneurship [in a private sector setting] . . . What makes public sector entrepreneurship different is not its fundamental *modus operandi* but rather its observable behaviors that are due . . . to the different institution environment in which it operates. Thus, the public sector entrepreneur, like his private sector counterpart, seeks to identify and exploit heretofore unexploited opportunities, and this means that the public sector entrepreneur engages in a process of innovation whose outcome is uncertain.

Therein we discuss not only the NCRA but also attendant public policies that were designed from an entrepreneurial perspective to affect public-sector as well as private-sector R&D.

What next? Chronically, I am in the afternoon of my academic career, but I hope I am not yet there in terms of that segment that represents my research career.

Notes

1 See Solow (1957).
2 See Hébert and Link (1982, 1988).
3 See Hébert and Link (1989).
4 See Hébert and Link (2009).
5 See Mansfield (1980). For those unfamiliar with the journal publication process, the time from submission to publication can easily approach a two-year time period.
6 See Link (1981).
7 See Link and Tassey (1987).
8 See Link and Bauer (1989) and Link and Tassey (1989).
9 See Hall et al. (2001, 2003) and Link and Scott (1988, 2005, 2011).
10 See Gallaher et al. (2012) and Link (2010) .
11 See Link (2015).
12 See Leyden and Link (2015b) for a more formal theory of the ideas in Leyden and Link (2015a).

References

Gallaher, Michael P., Albert N. Link, and Alan O'Connor (2012). *Public Investments in Energy Technology*, Northampton, MA: Edward Elgar Publishers.

Hall, Bronwyn H., Albert N. Link, and John T. Scott (2001). "Barriers Inhibiting Industry from Partnering with Universities: Evidence from the Advanced Technology Program," *Journal of Technology Transfer* 26: 87–98.

Hall, Bronwyn H., Albert N. Link, and John T. Scott (2003). "Universities as Research Partners," *Review of Economics and Statistics* 85: 485–491.

Hébert, Robert F. and Albert N. Link (1982). *The Entrepreneur: Mainstream Views and Radical Critiques*, New York: Praeger.

Hébert, Robert F. and Albert N. Link (1988). *The Entrepreneur: Mainstream Views and Radical Critiques*, 2nd edition, New York: Praeger.

Hébert, Robert F. and Albert N. Link (1989). "In Search of the Meaning of Entrepreneurship," *Small Business Economics* 1: 39–49.

Hébert, Robert F. and Albert N. Link (2009). *A History of Entrepreneurship*, London: Routledge.

Leyden, Dennis Patrick and Albert N. Link (2015a). *Public Sector Entrepreneurship: U.S. Technology and Innovation Policy*, New York: Oxford University Press.

Leyden, Dennis Patrick and Albert N. Link (2015b). "Toward a Theory of the Entrepreneurial Process," *Small Business Economics* 44: 475–484.

Link, Albert N. (1981). "Basic Research and Productivity Increase in Manufacturing: Additional Evidence," *American Economic Review* 71: 1111–1112.

Link, Albert N. (2010). "Retrospective Benefit–Cost Evaluation of U.S. DOE Vehicle Combustion Engine R&D Investments: Impacts of a Cluster of Energy Technologies," final report for the Energy Efficiency and Renewable Energy (EERE) Program, Washington, DC: U.S. Department of Energy.

Link, Albert N. (2015). "Capturing Knowledge: Private Gains and Public Gains from Universities Research Partnerships," *Foundations and Trends in Entrepreneurship* 11: 139–206.

Link, Albert N. and Gregory Tassey (1987). "The Impact of Standards on Technology-Based Industries: The Case of Numerically-Controlled Machine Tools in Automated Batch Manufacturing," in *Product Standardization and Competitive Strategy*, edited by L. Gabel, pp. 217–238, Amsterdam: North-Holland.

Link, Albert N. and Gregory Tassey (1989). *Cooperative Research and Development: The Industry, University, Government Relationship*, Norwell, MA: Kluwer Academic Publishers.

Link, Albert N. and Jamie R. Link (2009). *Government as Entrepreneur*, New York: Oxford University Press.

Link, Albert N. and John T. Scott (1988). *Public Accountability: Evaluating Technology-Based Institutions*, Norwell, MA: Kluwer Academic Publishers.

Link, Albert N. and John T. Scott (2005). *Evaluating Public Research Institutions: The U.S. Advanced Technology Program's Intramural Research Initiative*, London: Routledge.

Link, Albert N. and John T. Scott (2011). *Public Goods, Public Gains: Calculating the Social Benefits of Public R&D*, New York: Oxford University Press.

Link, Albert N. and Laura L. Bauer (1989). *Cooperative Research in U.S. Manufacturing: Assessing Policy Initiatives and Corporate Strategies*, Lexington, MA: D.C. Heath.

Mansfield, Edwin (1980). "Basic Research and Productivity Increase in Manufacturing," *American Economic Review* 70: 863–873.

Solow, Robert M. (1957). "Technical Change and the Aggregate Production Function," *Review of Economics and Statistics* 39: 312–320.

16

Location matters

Olav Sorenson

Introduction

More than once, I heard Jim March utter, with just a hint of disdain, "I will not commit auto-biography." Although I never inquired into the rationale behind his commitment, I suspect that he considered such self-accounts problematic in at least two regards. For starters, they require a certain level of vanity, believing that strangers want to learn about your life. Although I suppose that one could claim that an autobiography allows the author to explore his or her own history for personal reasons, much as one would write a diary, the introduction of an audience tends to change both the topics that one covers and the way in which one writes about them.

Autobiography also runs the risk of revisionism. Despite the best of intentions – perhaps because of them – authors want to tell coherent stories about their lives. Uninformed choices turn into plans and strategies. Serendipitous events become fated. In the kind light of retrospection, we appear cleverer, more ambitious, and more independent than our actual selves.

This chapter feels precariously close to committing autobiography. I have tried to avoid the most egregious sins. My selection of ideas of interest has been guided almost entirely by the extent to which others have cited particular papers rather than by my own feelings about them. My recollection of the origins and evolution of these ideas, meanwhile, has been aided by revisiting the earliest drafts of these papers. But, despite these attempts at inoculation, I would hardly consider myself immune from either hubris or retrospective rationalization. Readers should therefore approach my story with caution: The history described next almost certainly has more coherence and credits fewer influences than one would find in a truly objective account of the evolution of these ideas.

Stanford University

I do not believe that I really gave entrepreneurship much thought before entering the second year of the doctoral program in sociology at Stanford. As an undergraduate at Harvard, I had expected to become a management consultant. That seemed the tried and true path for predecessors who had little idea what they wanted to do but had a taste for variety. But when a recession hit in the fall of my senior year, I decided that I should stay in school. With little in the way of direction beyond that, I began the program in sociology at UNC. I am sure that I benefited in ways that I have never fully appreciated from exposure there to Howard Aldrich, Peter Bearman, and Arne Kalleberg, but I never quite felt at home in Chapel Hill. So, I moved on.

I arrived at Stanford in the fall of 1993. It seemed a paradise to me, with its combination of perfect weather, country club–like athletic facilities, and close proximity to nature. I spent thirty to forty hours per week playing tennis and volleyball, hiking, running, sailing, and skiing. It also offered an unusually stimulating intellectual environment for someone interested in organizations, with a faculty that included Mike Hannan, Jim March, Dick Scott, John Meyer, Jim Baron, Bill Barnett, Joel Podolny, and Steve Barley. Its location meant that I ended up immersed in the high-tech industries that had been fueling Silicon Valley's economy.

At Stanford, three faculty members in particular heavily influenced me. Although I never took a regular class from Mike Hannan, for four years, I attended the Workshop of Organizational Ecology that he led every Thursday afternoon, in which we would discuss the various analyses that participants had done over the previous week. I took two classes from Jim March, one on leadership and one on organization theory, and benefited from numerous conversations with him. Mike and Jim also served as the co-chairs of my dissertation committee. Bill Barnett, meanwhile, hired me to help him assemble a data set on computer manufacturers. That employment freed me from more distracting teaching assistantships and meant that I had the opportunity to spend dozens of hours with Bill discussing research and academia.

My dissertation, however, had nothing to do with entrepreneurship. In it, I developed a theory of how vertical integration would constrain the ability of organizations to learn and how it would influence the intensity of competition between organizations in a population. It combined some of March's ideas about learning with Hannan's ecological perspective on organizational populations (Sorenson, 2003).

My path into studying entrepreneurship nevertheless began at roughly the same time as a consequence of another interest: economic geography. Living in the heart of Silicon Valley's high-tech agglomeration, I had become quite interested in why industries clustered in certain cities and had therefore begun reading many of the recent writings on industrial agglomeration, most notably Saxenian (1994), Krugman (1991), and Arthur (1988, 1990), as well as a few of the classics on location choice, such as Weber (1928).

Soong Moon Kang, a graduate student in the Engineering Economic Systems program, shared these interests, and we ended up spending hours discussing them, usually over noodles from the Thai cafe in the Psychology department or sandwiches from the Political Science cafe. We concluded that the basis for location choice had probably changed over time, from focusing on physical inputs – such as coal and iron ore – to social inputs – such as the availability of specialized suppliers – and decided to pursue a research project that would allow us to explore that idea.

After months of discussion, we settled on multimedia manufacturers as the population for our study. Those firms never really matured into an industry because technological changes soon allowed anyone with a home computer to produce their own CD-ROMs but, in the early 1990s, the machines used to press CD-ROMs could cost hundreds of thousands of dollars. A number of firms therefore began to enter the business of "publishing" CD titles – copying, selling, and distributing discs. The population seemed perfect to us because it had begun recently – allowing us to avoid left-censoring in our data collection – and it had a small enough number of firms that it seemed feasible to survey all of the founders.

We planned to ask the founders of these firms which locations they had considered for their firms and to use the information on where they actually located to reveal the factors that appeared to matter to their choices. With generous financial support from Bill Miller, through his grant from the Alfred P. Sloan Foundation, we sent surveys to roughly 500 founders of multimedia firms, receiving responses from more than 100 of them. After coding the question-naires, however, we discovered an unexpected problem: almost no one had moved to found their firms; 94% stayed in the location in which they had been living. We had no leverage for analyzing their "choice" of location.

To try to understand better what went wrong, we set up some in-person interviews with the respondents. I recall one vividly. We arrived at the house to find the quintessential founder in a garage, his utilitarian desk stacked with floppy discs in colorful cases. A large CD-pressing machine sat behind him. A few minutes into the interview, we asked him why he had started his firm where he did. His response: "My wife did not want the mess in the kitchen." He thought we had meant why the garage, not why Sunnyvale. When we pressed him further, it became clear that he had never even considered location to be a choice variable. He just founded his firm where he had been living. Our other interviewees told similar stories.

Industrial clusters

The insight that entrepreneurs might not choose locations influenced significantly my thinking about industrial clusters. Both the classic and the more recent literatures on economic geography had approached the choice of firm locations from the perspective of an omniscient and unconstrained social planner. What if one thought about the problem from the perspective of the entrepreneur?

If entrepreneurs simply began businesses in the places that they lived and most entrepreneurs came from prior employment in the industries that they entered (or in closely related ones), then geographic agglomeration could persist simply because the places with the most firms and employees in an industry would also have the largest pools of nascent entrepreneurs. Clusters might initially emerge, moreover, simply from stochastic arrival processes that become self-rein-forcing as they influence the geographic distribution of employees in the industry. Locating near competitors need not provide any economic benefits for clusters to emerge and persist.

Although I had that basic idea in 1995, I did not have the data to test it. But I had a sense of what I would need: longitudinal information on a population of organizations with detailed information about the location of each one. When I met Pino Audia a few months later at a poster session at the Academy of Management in Vancouver, I discovered that he had just such a data set. After several months of correspondence, we agreed to collaborate and began to test these ideas in Pino's data on the footwear industry in the United States, 1940–1989.

Pino and I found that footwear manufacturers located in close proximity to other footwear manufacturers failed at substantially higher rates than those in more remote regions. But, because entrepreneurs entered these crowded regions at even higher relative rates, the industry remained geographically concentrated despite these economic disadvantages (Sorenson and Audia, 2000). Although the differential failure rates meant that the industry had been diffusing slowly over time, as those few founders arriving in out-of-the-way places had firms that survived much longer, our calculations indicated that the system would not reach equilibrium for nearly a century.

When I presented my paper with Pino to my colleagues at the University of Chicago in 1998, Toby Stuart suggested that we could investigate the same processes using his data on the biotech industry. Although that paper began as a replication, Toby and I ended up building out the theory around how the need for entrepreneurs to use their social networks to mobilize resources, such as financial and human capital, would constrain them to locate their businesses in close proximity to their prior employers. Because few firms in the biotech industry failed, we used IPO valuations as our measure of performance. But once again, entrepreneurial entry maintained the geographic clustering of firms in spite of the fact that co-location led to lower performance (Stuart and

Sorenson, 2003). Although both of these papers have been highly cited, my sense has been that those reading them have only extracted a portion of the message. People usually cite these papers (1) for the idea that spin-off processes play an important role in the creation and maintenance of geographic clusters, (2) for the idea that entrepreneurs rely on their social networks to mobilize resources to build their firms, (3) for the idea that regions rich in financial and human capital spawn more startups, and (4) for the spatially weighted density measure that I introduced. But they rarely appear to engage the more radical idea – also supported consistently by the analyses – that clusters do not provide any performance advantages per se.

Those papers had a side benefit of introducing me to Steve Klepper (who the community sadly lost in 2013). I first met Steve in 2002 when he invited me to present as part of a panel that he organized for the International Schumpeter Society. There, I discovered that he, too, had come to believe that spinoffs played an important role in agglomeration. However, whereas I had been focusing on why entrepreneurs would remain local, Steve had been primarily interested in why most successful entrepreneurs had prior experience in the industry (Klepper, 2001, 2007). Over the course of the next four years, I ended up seeing Steve at a dozen conferences and had many debates with him over the importance of prior industry experience versus social capital in the spinoff and agglomeration processes. Those discussions influenced my next round of papers on the location choices of entrepreneurs.

Home sweet home

As I continued to think about these issues, I realized that I needed more information about the entrepreneurs themselves. Jesper Sørensen had introduced me to the Danish employer–employee data, which had the information that I wanted. But Jesper did not seem interested in pursuing the project and I did not have access to the data myself. Fortunately, when talking about some other research ideas with Michael Dahl, I discovered that he had access to the Danish data. Thus another productive collaboration began.

We began, in large part, to demonstrate empirical support for the assumptions made in my earlier papers on agglomeration. Our original paper therefore first demonstrated that entrepreneurs had a tendency not to move to found their ventures and that when they did move that they did not move far. We then showed that entrepreneurs who stayed in the regions in which they had been living performed better than those who moved, but that locating near rivals hurt firm performance. These results implied that as regions became increasingly crowded with competitors, entrepreneurs from the cluster would eventually maximize their performance by moving away from their rivals.

But, a couple of months after the paper had been submitted to a journal, Michelacci and Silva (2007) came out in the *Review of Economics and Statistics*. That paper essentially demonstrated the same fact – that entrepreneurs exhibit less geographic mobility than employees – as the first half of our original paper. The reviewers therefore felt that our paper primarily replicated these results, and the editor offered us a very difficult revise and resubmit opportunity.

After considerable consternation, we decided to split the paper into two. The first half, on which we had been scooped, became Dahl and Sorenson (2009). Splitting this half off gave us sufficient space to do something more interesting than simply demonstrating geographic inertia. We could estimate the extent to which entrepreneurs actually appeared to respond to social factors, such as the proximity of family and friends, and to industry conditions, such as competition, in their choices of locations. We found a couple of interesting patterns: First, entrepreneurs appeared far, far more sensitive to the proximity to family and friends in their choices of locations than to local industry conditions. Second, to the extent that they did respond to industry conditions, they seemed systematically attracted to places with more intense competition, the opposite of what one would generally expect (cf. Sørensen and Sorenson, 2003).

The second half of the paper took much longer for us to develop, though it eventually appeared in *Management Science* (Dahl and Sorenson, 2012). Once again, having more pages available allowed us to push far beyond our original analyses of performance. We demonstrated that the beneficial effects of having deep roots in a region held not only for firm failure rates, but also for firm profits and total returns to the entrepreneur, and that these results held even when using an instrumental variable to account for the potential endogeneity of the choice of locations. Interestingly, the magnitude of the value of prior experience in the region ended up being almost the same as the magnitude of the value of prior experience in the industry. In the end, it would appear that Steve (Klepper) and I had both been highlighting important aspects of the overall story.

The splitting of the paper did, however, have one casualty: in the interest of presenting as clean and as convincing an analysis as possible of the benefits of being embedded in the region, we adjusted for industry conditions in the *Management Science* paper through industry-region fixed effects rather than by including variables to capture the attributes of the local industry. That meant that the paper no longer demonstrated the micro-level equivalent of the industry agglomeration papers – that locating in regions dense with rivals hurts firm performance.

University of Toronto

I spent the first eight years of my career teaching business and corporate strategy, first at the University of Chicago (1997–1999), then at UCLA (1999–2005), and finally at London Business School (2005–2006). But when I moved to the University of Toronto's Rotman School of Management in 2006, they already had plenty of people who could teach strategy. They did, however, need someone to cover a course on venture capital and, having written one paper on the subject, I knew more about it than anyone else.

Syndication networks

Let me backtrack to 1999 to provide some background on the one paper that I had written on venture capital. Interestingly, the paper began as a footnote in my paper with Toby Stuart on geographic agglomeration in the biotech industry, though that footnote ended up being deleted in one of the rounds of revisions (Stuart and Sorenson, 2003).

In the process of writing the agglomeration paper, Toby felt that we could not simply show that biotech firms entered in the locations that had the largest concentrations of resources – universities, venture capital, and scientists and engineers – but that we needed to provide some direct evidence that entrepreneurs did indeed mobilize resources locally. We therefore acquired data on venture capital investments and used it to demonstrate that venture capitalists tend to invest locally.

Someplace along the way, however, we decided that we could turn the footnote into a paper. The paper essentially takes the fact that venture capitalists invest locally as a given. Sorenson and Stuart (2001) then explores the extent to which venture capitalists deviate from that baseline, investing at greater distances, and demonstrates that expansions in geographic reach appear to come primarily from having built an extensive network in the venture capital industry through syndication (i.e., co-investment).

Despite such humble beginnings, it has ended up becoming my most highly cited paper!

Venture capital and economic growth

Fast-forward back to 2007. Three events conspired to renew my interest in venture capital. First, to develop a syllabus and to prepare to teach the course on venture capital, I ended up reviewing most of what academics had written about the industry. Second, around the same time, the province of Ontario announced that it planned to design and implement a program to subsidize the venture capital industry. Third, and perhaps most importantly, I reconnected with Sampsa Samila.

I had originally met Sampsa around 2004 at one of the Academy of Management meetings, I believe in New Orleans. Sampsa proposed collaborating on a project – on organizational learning – and we even began estimating some models, but both of us ended up being distracted by other projects. I had lost track of him after that, but it turned out that he had moved to Toronto to join the faculty of Brock University. When I arrived at Toronto, I ran into him at a seminar and we began discussing research ideas again on a regular basis.

At some point, we ended up talking about the stimulus for the venture capital industry proposed by the provincial government, and we realized that almost nothing in the academic literature could inform policy makers as to the wisdom of the program or its ideal design. The academic literature had largely looked at venture capital from the perspective of the investor, examining its returns. But the policy question depended not so much on whether the investors earned money but on whether venture capital had implications for the real economy.

We therefore began by asking a straightforward question: Does the local supply of venture capital influence the number of startups, the number of jobs, and the incomes of regions? We found that it did, using a variety of identification strategies. Depending on the estimation procedure used, a doubling in the supply of venture capital increased the entrepreneurship rate by 0.3% to 2.1%, resulted in a 0.2% to 1.2% increase in the number of jobs in the region, and raised aggregate income by 0.5% to 3.8% (Samila and Sorenson, 2011). To put that into more concrete figures, the funding of one additional startup by venture capitalists appeared to lead to the creation of two to six businesses, around 350 jobs, and nearly $35 million in income.

Our estimates even proved robust to estimation with an instrumental variable, based on the number of institutional investors in the region and their probable returns. One of the advantages of spending a great deal of time getting to know the institutional details of a setting is that it can often help you develop better empirical designs. Recall that a valid instrument should have a strong association with the (potentially) endogenous variable but have no effect on the dependent variable except through the endogenous regressor. In this case, that meant we needed something that would increase the supply of venture capital without having any direct effect on the local economy (and without being the result of reverse causality – something about the strength of the local economy influencing the amount of capital available). Because institutional investors generally manage their portfolios to maintain ideal asset allocation ratios, differential returns across asset classes – such as higher returns in public equities or in debt – create a demand for investments in venture capital due to their value for diversification rather than for their expected returns. We could therefore use those returns in other asset classes as an instrument.

The fact that the typical venture capital investment ends up producing more than one start-up also interestingly suggests that "demonstration" effects – seeing similar others engaged in entrepreneurship – plays an important role in regional entrepreneurship rates. When doing research for the first paper on industrial agglomeration, I sought out and read every biography that I could find of someone who started a company in the shoe industry. In nearly every one, the author would describe a eureka moment, in which the person in question – who had often been a foreman or plant manager in an existing shoe plant – saw someone like him, perhaps the manager of a rival plant, start a company. An observation which would lead them to ask, "If they can do it, why not me?" (Sorenson and Audia, 2000)

These demonstration effects probably operate primarily at the local level because they require that the would-be entrepreneurs see the person starting a firm as similar to them. Those beliefs seem most likely to occur for friends and acquaintances, people known personally. People can easily dismiss the accomplishments of entrepreneurs in distant places as due to the imagined superhuman qualities of those heroes. Although I have never attempted to explore it empirically, I also suspect that these effects may account for much of what people mean when they say that a place has an entrepreneurial culture.

Business schools

Since receiving my PhD in sociology from Stanford, I have essentially spent my entire career in business schools: two years at the University of Chicago's Graduate School of Business (now the Booth School of Business), six years at UCLA's Anderson Graduate School of Management, one year at London Business School, three years at the University of Toronto's Rotman School of Management, and more than six years so far at the Yale School of Management.

Being located in a business school has a number of implications. It means that not only do I study organizations and entrepreneurship but also I interact with investors, entrepreneurs, and managers on a regular basis. Although I try to base my courses on rigorous research, it means that the courses themselves have a practical orientation. And it means that my students ask questions not just as a means of understanding the ideas, but also to inform decisions relevant to their professional lives.

That engagement with practice keeps those in business schools firmly rooted in the phenomenon. Many of the ideas that I have had for papers over the last decade have come not from reading the academic literature but from questions or ideas that have arisen through the course of teaching or interacting with students. That, too, has been the inspiration for my latest foray into entrepreneurship research.

Entrepreneurship and inequality

Over the years, many a student has come to me seeking career advice. It's one thing to compare an offer from BCG to one from McKinsey. It's quite another to try to consider completely different career paths. For example, I recall one student who came to me trying to decide which of three offers to accept: one to join McKinsey; another to become the personal assistant to a billionaire, managing his far-flung business empire; the third to become employee number three at a start-up Internet retailer.

If anything, it has become more and more common over the years for MBA students to find themselves choosing between a tried-and-true career path firm and a job at a start-up. In an attempt to offer more informed advice, I therefore have scoured the academic literature more than once to see what I could find on how joining a start-up as an employee might affect the student's life and career. It turns out that a fair amount of research considers the implications of founding a firm for the entrepreneur, but almost nothing had been done from the perspective of the employee.

Together with Diane Burton (a friend from graduate school), Michael Dahl, Rodrigo Canales (a colleague at Yale), and Marco Huesch (a former student), I have therefore begun to explore the implications of joining a start-up as an employee. Our initial investigations have focused on income.

We have found that individuals suffer a small wage penalty when they join a start-up, primarily because most start-ups are small and small firms tend to be less productive and to pay less (Sorenson et al., 2015). More surprisingly, this differential grows over time. In fact, those who join a start-up never recover in terms of earning as much as their peers who went to more established firms (Burton et al., 2015). We want to continue to explore the effects of being employed by a start-up on other outcomes, such as family life and health, to see whether other factors might compensate for these wage losses.

More broadly, however, this project begins to address a largely unexplored question: Does an entrepreneurial economy have a downside? There has been a tendency for policy makers and academics studying entrepreneurship alike to view it with rose-colored glasses, a panacea to ailing economies and stultifying careers. But entrepreneurship may have a dark side as well.

In particular, high rates of entrepreneurship might lead to increasing levels of societal inequality. A common theme in many of the literatures on entrepreneurship has been the high variance in outcomes. Investors either win big or lose almost everything (Cochrane, 2005). The self-employed earn less than they would as employees, on average, but those in the long right- hand tail do far better (Hamilton, 2000). Seemingly similar individuals have more varied wages in small firms (Sørensen and Sorenson, 2007). Although investors might have the ability to diversify these risks away, entrepreneurs and employees generally do not – they have but one job.

References

Arthur, W. Brian. 1988. The Economy as an Evolving Complex System. New York: Wiley.

Arthur, W. Brian. 1990. "Silicon Valley locational clusters: When do increasing returns imply monopoly?" Mathematical Social Sciences 19:235–251.

Burton, M. Diane, Michael S. Dahl, Olav Sorenson, and Rodrigo Canales. 2015. "The career consequences of working for a startup." Working paper, Cornell University.

Cochrane, John H. 2005. "The risk and return of venture capital." Journal of Financial Economics 75:3–52.

Dahl, Michael S. and Olav Sorenson. 2009. "The embedded entrepreneur." European Management Review 6:172–181.

Dahl, Michael S. and Olav Sorenson. 2012. "Home sweet home? Entrepreneurs' location choices and the performance of their ventures." Management Science 58:1059–1071.

Hamilton, Barton H. 2000. "Does entrepreneurship pay? An empirical analysis of the returns to self-employment." Journal of Political Economy 108:604–631.

Klepper, Steven. 2001. "The evolution of the U.S. automobile industry and Detroit as its capital." Working paper, Carnegie Mellon University.

Klepper, Steven. 2007. "Disagreements, spinoffs, and the evolution of Detroit as the capital of the U.S. automobile industry." Management Science 53:616–631.

Krugman, Paul. 1991. "Increasing returns and economic geography." Journal of Political Economy 99:483–499.

Michelacci, Claudio and Olmo Silva. 2007. "Why so many local entrepreneurs?" Review of Economics and Statistics 89:615–633.

Samila, Sampsa and Olav Sorenson. 2011. "Venture capital, entrepreneurship, and economic growth." Review of Economics and Statistics 93:338–349.

Saxenian, Annalee. 1994. Regional Advantage. Cambridge, MA: Harvard, University Press.

Sørensen, Jesper B. and Olav Sorenson. 2003. "From conception to birth: Opportunity perception and resource mobilization in entrepreneurship." Advances in Strategic Management 20:89–117.

Sørensen, Jesper B. and Olav Sorenson. 2007. "Corporate demography and income inequality." American Sociological Review 72(5): 766–783.

Sorenson, Olav. 2003. "Interdependence and adaptability: Organizational learning and the long-term effect of integration." Management Science 49:446–463.

Sorenson, Olav, Michael S. Dahl, and M. Diane Burton. 2015. "Do startups create good jobs" Working paper, Yale School of Management.

Sorenson, Olav and Pino G. Audia. 2000. "The social structure of entrepreneurial activity: Geographic concentration of footwear production in the United States, 1940–1989." American Journal of Sociology 106:424–462.

Sorenson, Olav and Toby E. Stuart. 2001. "Syndication networks and the spatial distribution of venture capital investments." American Journal of Sociology 106:1546–1588.

Stuart, Toby E. and Olav Sorenson. 2003. "The geography of opportunity: Spatial heterogeneity in founding rates and the performance of biotechnology firms." Research Policy 32:229–253.

Weber, Alfred. 1928. Theory of the Location of Industries. Chicago, IL: University of Chicago Press.

17

Visions of the past
Wish you had been there

Roy Thurik

Some introduction

It is the kind of request that simultaneously thrills and induces panic: colleagues – nay, friends – approaching you, claiming that you are "one of the indisputable pioneers leading scholarship and thinking in entrepreneurship," then, in the next breath, ask you to write something that "clearly articulates what were your most important ideas about entrepreneurship, what led you to develop those ideas into the literature, and what has been the impact of those ideas."

A thirty-five-year-long career in entrepreneurship research has led to many ideas: some well matured, others hardly ripened; some well cited, others completely overlooked; some hopelessly off the mark, others getting right to the heart of the matter; and some the result of hours spent alone in my office, others more a result of an evening pondering the world with wine and friends.

With these marching orders, my first inclination was to plunder my own website in order to list the published scholarly contributions that I have (co-)authored over the years. My spreadsheet is nearly 200 rows long. Starting with a 1984 publication in *Journal of Retailing* about part-time labor in various shop types, it ended with a 2016 publication in *Applied Psychology* about ADHD and entrepreneurial orientation.

At first glance, I was startled: these contributions appear to be completely unrelated – the only common thread that came to mind when I first reviewed the list was one Roy Thurik: "me, myself, and I." Yet, there had to be more – my research had evolved. Would it be possible to identify chapters in my professional life? Playing with the spreadsheet, I tried to make it as perfect as possible: uniformity in the referencing system typically has a calming effect on me. But it did not in this case, so I resorted to doing what any one of the "indisputable pioneers leading scholarship and thinking in entrepreneurship" – would do: I started typing.

Thus the panic turned into a sense of reward: the forced introspection allowed me to realize that my professional life has bled into my personal life, with colleagues becoming friends. Looking at each row brought back memories as I found the research that stands out, as well as uncovered long-forgotten papers and projects. As the rows scrolled by, memories built, and I quickly arrived at a major conclusion: I have been very lucky in choosing fields, colleagues, work environments, networks and employers.

But would I now want to have done things differently? Maybe I should have tried to write fewer texts of a higher caliber. But developing a field often goes together with multiple attempts. Working with young PhDs – which I like tremendously – requires guiding them through the swampy morass that is peer review. Thus, aiming at lower-ranked journals may be helpful. Also, there was often so much data available, waiting to be analyzed, and since journals attach no value to "internal replication," I would have quickly have abandoned the higher-caliber strategy.

Some more introduction

With the advantage of having "lived" a scientific career, I can see that there are three principle approaches, each with its own pros and cons: (1) one can fill in gaps in an existing field; (2) one can extend an existing field by introducing new concepts and/or connecting it to another one; or (3) one can try to discover new fields. With the benefit of hindsight, it is clear that my career business model is to try and discover new fields, but then move on after the really clever people take it over.

I hope that I contributed to retail economics and small business economics, to connecting entrepreneurship and macroeconomics, to economic behavior and biology (such as genes and hormones) and to using neurocognitive mechanisms (such as hyperactivity, addictive behaviors, hypomania) and psychopathological symptoms (such as motivational drive, preference for reward, inhibitory control) for economic behavior. Using neurocognitive mechanisms and psychopathological symptoms for economic behavior is more a promise than a reality. Still, I can already point to decent progress. In the connection between entrepreneurship and the macroeconomy, I feel that I did not do a good enough job. I could never convince my macroeconomics colleagues that entrepreneurship was a serious contribution to their models. A manuscript that I count as being one of the best I ever contributed to has been rejected numerous times, is still not published and – consequently – is not part of my spreadsheet. It is about adding an entrepreneurship measure to several families of existing models explaining total factor productivity (TFP) for countries over time. Maybe here lies yet another reason why a high-caliber strategy is not always compatible with the quest for a new field. After reading multiple rejection letters, I got the feeling that referees never quite appreciated the novelty of our introduction of entrepreneurship into the existing models. They were more concerned about whether the latest models and techniques of their macroeconomics world were applied.

The same thing happened when I was involved in a series of papers connecting attention-deficit/hyperactivity disorder (ADHD) and entrepreneurial behavior [192, 200]. Referees of the top journal were overly concerned about the definition and treatment of our concepts of entrepreneurship behavior – which is known material – but barely commented upon the newness of ADHD as a factor linked to entrepreneurial behavior. The frustration of a lifetime happened with our papers on genes and entrepreneurship [138, 146, 149, 160, 179, 184], which I tried to bind together in my "gentreprenomics" paper [195]. Indeed, we never found the entrepreneurial gene, but the scholarly management/entrepreneurship community pretended to be blind to the newness of our approach. Ultimately we moved to management and entrepreneurship journals not ranked among the highest to publish our results. This is a clear example of having to abandon the high-caliber strategy.

So, I started typing and – Accio! – my life's professional chapters appeared as if summoned by Harry Potter waving his wand. The many rows naturally reduced to several distinct chapters. Ex post self-documentation is inherently intriguing; hopefully not just for me, but also for my old and new colleagues. With the benefit having written and rereading the text that follows, I noticed that streaming through the inevitable self-congratulatory element, the loose ends are often stressed more than the solid contributions. I cannot wait for my colleagues to comment here. For the general reader, I am not so sure that the text brings much. Or maybe it brings a general lesson: work hard, be nice, be generous, and also be sure to stay lucky and healthy. Another lesson? I never put much value on contributing to finding and describing a central paradigm in the field of small business economics or that of entrepreneurship economics. I rarely tried to contribute to the endless and fruitless battles over the definition of entrepreneurship [74, 147]. Generations of students were startled when I announced that I would not begin my entrepreneurship course with a long deliberation of its definition. Instead I concentrated on its causes and consequences, always leaving its definition somewhat open. It is much more fun and effective to look at small business and entrepreneurship as phenomena having a meaning in other fields of scientific discovery, such as industrial organization, macroeconomics, epidemiology and psychiatry, and to trying to find out what that meaning is for them. By venturing out to other fields, my work seems to be hopelessly spread out. Still, it is fascinating and motivating to stick one's nose in someone else's field — in my case bringing my entrepreneurship construct to the table and seeing how they respond to it.

In the following I will often use "I," but for the reasons described earlier I have very few single-authored products or solitary initiatives. So, the "I" represents some form of "we," but since I am the only constant within this "we" over the last thirty-five years, it is easiest to use "I."

In the beginning there was productivity and pricing

How could I resist? I had just finished my studies of econometrics at Erasmus University Rotterdam (EUR), which was — and still is — a separate curriculum, with no clue how to apply my newly acquired knowledge. And then my professor of statistics, Johan Koerts, offered me a job at an independent research institute for small- and medium-sized businesses, EIM, which much later became Panteia. An abundance of data for many of these businesses was available at the institute, but only tables of descriptive data were actually printed and made public. Although differences in productivity across different-sized businesses were well documented, the question of why such differences existed remained unasked. Instead, the reports resorted to storytelling. This called for some applied micro-economic cross-sectional analyses. My senior colleague at the institute, Bart Nooteboom, helped me a lot. Analyzing retail business labor productivity was fun and easy. Scale effects [5, 13, 14, 19], part-time labor [1], French hypermarkets [22], Japanese stores [49, 32, 38], opening hours [53, 20] and degree of affiliation [7] were analyzed, and journals were eager to print our results. I only remember two journal rejections of my early productivity work. Similar studies were done on the hotel and catering business [2], the wholesale business [28, 34], and comparing sectors [23]. After analyzing individual businesses, the road opened to also look at the development of productivity for entire small business sectors [3] and across time [16].

When my professor of operations research heard that I was working on projects explaining productivity differences in the retail sector he reacted in his very own style: "What do I hear, Roy, you are now calculating grocery shops? Hahaha. And you were always so smart and promising?" This lack of understanding with a mild twist of contempt convinced me that I was on the right track: presumed adversity can be a stimulating starting point for an endeavor.

Amazingly, retail floor space productivity was often analyzed independently of labor productivity [4, 11, 30]. Only sometimes substitution played a role in our modeling [8, 21]. There were so many stylized facts to be discovered in this area of scale economies of small businesses and other factors determining productivity differences that several years passed before more sophisticated modeling produced papers in such journals like the *Journal of Econometrics* [9] and *European Journal of Operational Research* [35]. My PhD thesis, which I defended in 1984, consisted of eight chapters analyzing productivity differences in retailing [6]; each was published in an internationally recognized journal.

It was some time before pricing became a part of my endeavors [54, 15, 29]. It was a great inspiration to be able work with Bart Nooteboom on retail mark-up pricing and the role of costs, expectations and environmental determinants [17, 25, 27, 10, 24, 36, 39, 46, 52]. It not only led to similar analyses in other sectors, such as the hotel and catering sector [18, 51] and manufacturing [26], but also to the realization that these type of studies belong to an already existing scholarly field called industrial organization.

The day after I defended my PhD thesis and while I was recuperating from too much alcohol celebrating it, I suddenly realized that I had missed the whole point of all my projects on retail productivity. What I had found was that larger shops were always more productive than smaller ones, but I never asked why smaller shops exist, given that the scale effect is so pervasive. This question is one of the focal questions of a field called small business economics, but its time had not yet come.

Embedment, encounters and economics

The pioneer phase of my career happened at the Econometric Institute of Erasmus University of Rotterdam (EUR). Discipline-free empirical investigations were encouraged as long as their statistics were done in the right, rigorous, fashion. In the early days of the applied microeconomic analyses of retail firms, we found some publication shelter in areas such as marketing or retailing itself: in the *International Journal of Research in Marketing* [12, 21, 28] and *Journal of Retailing* [1, 11, 15]. Later I started to realize that industrial organization seemed to provide a better environment [37, 43, 47, 50].

Undoubtedly, the most important encounter of my entire career was meeting David Audretsch at the 15th EARIE (European Association for Research in Industrial Organization) conference in Rotterdam in 1988. He had just trained up from Dordrecht, where he had signed a contract with Kluwer Publishers to establish a new journal to be called *Small Business Economics Journal*. I had just made a deal with my dean at the Erasmus School of Economics to name the part-time chair to which I had been appointed to the year before as "small business economics." Since then, David and I have written about forty articles together. At the same time, I have co-authored nearly thirty articles in *Small Business Economics Journal*, and I refereed at least a hundred articles, all while taking on the shadow editor role at *Small Business Economics Journal* assisting David Audretsch and Zoltan Acs. But most importantly, I have slept many nights in the "famous economist guest room" at Audretsch residences on both sides of the Atlantic.

Slowly my work became recognized in general interest economics journals like *European Economic Review* [24], *Economics Letters* [10, 26, 40], *De Economist* [18, 37, 42, 51], *Southern Economic Journal* [83], *Journal of Economic Behavior and Organization* [68], *Weltwirtschaftliches Archiv* [46], *Journal of Institutional and Theoretical Economics* [56] and *Applied Economics* [67]. Not the highest journals in economics, but these initiatives helped small business economics become an accepted part of the economics discipline. It also helped me get a full chair in small business economics at the Erasmus School of Economics in the early 1990s.

The field of industrial organization, with journals such as *Review of Industrial Organization* [47, 59, 60, 85, 110] and *International Journal of Industrial Organization* [75, 91], provided an interesting testing ground of our ideas. Martin Carree, my only PhD student to receive cum laude and who became full professor fairly quickly afterwards, played a big role here. Our studies of entry and exit behavior of businesses were well received [55, 48, 60, 75]. I still regret that we never used the discrepancy between replacement (businesses entering because others exited) and displacement (businesses exiting because others entered) as a measure of competition in an industry. I similarly regret that I abandoned writing a paper called "Storming the Minimum Efficient Scale (MES)." Businesses can and do survive at a level of output below the MES by offering a different product or using a different production factor [85, 91] than their larger scaled counterparts. Alternatively, their existence can be understood from the standpoint that they have only limited time to survive below the MES and hence "must storm it."

The organizers of the EARIE conferences were quick to understand the role of small businesses for the organization of industries. In 1985 our paper was rejected for the 12th EARIE conference in Cambridge because, in the words of the referees, "it was about small business and we were meant to know that small businesses were no part of the scholarly field of industrial organization." With that in mind, the word *small business economics* was only conspiratorially whispered between David and me at the 15th edition in Rotterdam. There were a dozen or so small business papers at the 16th edition in Budapest, all well quarantined in separate sessions. At the 17th edition in Lisbon in 1990, empirical small business papers were an integral part of the entire program, despite the fact that the theoretical game theory papers dealing with the struggles of large businesses were considered to be the promising future of industrial organization.

Discovering small business economics

I have always held a small part-time position at the research institute for small- and medium-sized businesses, EIM, now called Panteia, located in Zoetermeer in the so-called "green heart of Holland." While I was fully employed by the institute from 1977 onward, I generally spent two days a week at the Econometrics Institute of EUR as a visitor. From 1987 I did so while having a part-time chair in small business economics at EUR. In getting this chair I was lucky: at the time the Erasmus School of Economics – of which the Econometrics Institute was part – was looking for scientifically coherent research programs with a well-defined problem area. The then Ministry of Science and Education wished to better organize academic research, and one way to do this was called "conditional research financing." There was no financing involved. Hence, it was certainly not conditional, but the term had some attraction value and it meant that universities had to identify coherent programs. After defending my PhD thesis in 1984, I was dissatisfied with my research methodology despite the fact that I managed to publish all eight chapters. So, I started to look for colleagues at the Econometrics Institute who could help me do a better job by going over my work and applying more sophisticated methods. Many showed interest, and the resulting initiative, called "retail econometrics," was the ideal example of a "conditional research financing" program. Because someone not on the payroll of the Econometrics Institute, since he was only a visitor, could not be leader of such a program, a part-time chair was established for me.

From 1992 my main employer was EUR, although one day a week was devoted to EIM, which I will call Panteia from here on. Peter van Hoesel, the Panteia director at the time, wanted me to stick around, so he offered me a "fellow" contract. This meant that I could do whatever I felt had to be done, which is exceptional and generous for a commercial institute. My role at Panteia evolved from being a young researcher showing that applied econometric techniques may help discriminate between the determinants of productivity in small businesses to that of scientific advisor for an entire research program on small business. In the latter role I served as trait-d'union between the scientific research of academia and the applied research of a commercial institute like Panteia. This role determined my view of doing scientific work and how to organize it. Without Panteia, its mission and its data sources, I would never have been able to show my colleagues at EUR and elsewhere that there is actually a field called small business economics and that I could contribute developing this field. On the other hand, without the implicit support of EUR and the wider academic world, Panteia would never have been able to keep carrying out its famous "research program on entrepreneurship and small business," financed by the Dutch ministry of economic affairs. Unfortunately, this program was terminated in 2015, and I stopped working as a Panteia scientific advisor in 2016. It was the end of an era.

My golden days at Panteia were without any doubt the closing years of the previous century and the first decade of the present one, from 1997 onwards, when Sander Wennekers was director of the "research program on entrepreneurship and small business," and I was his right-hand man. This coincided with a series of stimulating and productive visits to the Institute of Development Strategies (IDS) at the School of Public and Environmental Affairs of Indiana University Bloomington. The IDS director was the young man I first met in 1988: David Audretsch. As a research fellow, I contributed to investigations of how geographical places perform, how to identify what needs to be done to make them better, and what the role of entrepreneurship may be [92, 144, 163]. IDS is also the place where I met Adam Lederer who was meant to play such a big role as managing editor of *Small Business Economics Journal*. A few years later, David Audretsch reappeared in Europe, this time as directing the Entrepreneurship, Growth and Public Policy group at the Max Planck Institute of Economics in Jena, Germany, from 2004 through 2010. There I served as a visiting research professor, participating in the three Kauffman-Max Planck-Ringberg conferences, in 2006, 2007 and 2008. These were clear highpoints for scholars of entrepreneurship, economic development and public policy [145], defining markers of an era.

The Erasmus School of Economics also had an important role in creating the field of small business economics. I founded a small research group called CASBEC (Centre for Advanced Small Business Economics), I had my chair, and there were close contacts to Panteia and *Small Business Economics Journal*. Moreover, two important conferences were held in cooperation with the Tinbergen Institute at EUR. They were called the third and the fourth "Global Conference on Small Business Economics." It was never revealed whether there had ever been a first or a second conference, or when and where they had been held. The first of the two Rotterdam conferences resulted in two special issues of *Small Business Economics Journal* [57, 58] and one in *Review of Industrial Organization* [59]. The second conference resulted in an edited volume with Cambridge University Press [81]. Thus, my scientific positioning moved from an orientation toward retailing, marketing [64, 69] and industrial organization to that of issues of smallness, such as structural change of industries and size distribution [45, 12, 33], specific elements of smallness such as exports [41], R&D [42, 56], competitive position [72, 91], debt ratios [61, 44], survival [79, 85], efficiency [76], productivity [84], and innovation [65]. In the adapted version of my inaugural lecture of 1989 [31] I volunteered some thoughts about what, in fact, constituted small business economics. It could and should be executed at all levels of aggregation: firms, industries and economies. I stressed the role the entrepreneur should play in small business research. And, finally, I provided several reasons why small business economics is a relevant and important discipline. Today they seem to be a series of obvious statements.

The E of SBE

Still more importantly, I arrived at what would become a main theme for at least fifteen years: the interplay between small firms – and what was later termed as entrepreneurship – and the macro economy. It started off with a series of empirical publications in obscure journals like *Atlantic Economic Journal* [70] in edited book volumes published by Basil Blackwell, JAI Press, Cambridge University Press and Edward Elgar Publishing [63, 62, 77, 78, 88]. These studies show with simple means that smallness can positively affect economic performance at aggregate levels. They provided the roots for four approaches. The first approach was a conceptual one about the role of small firms – which was more and more frequently referred to as entrepreneurship – in the macro economy and in particular for economic growth [102, 124, 153, 74, 93, 95]. My publication, with Sander Wennekers, in *Small Business Economics Journal*, called "Linking Entrepreneurship and Economic Growth" [74], would prove to be my best-cited with nearly 1,800 Google Scholar hits in 2016. It also ranks first among the most highly cited articles ever published in *Small Business Economics Journal*.

The second approach consisted of a series of empirical single equation studies, often based on aggregate panel data, on the role of small firms for economic growth and development [166, 94, 96, 111, 112, 113, 127, 135, 147]. In particular, the two *Small Business Economic Journal* publications [112, 113] using material from the Global Entrepreneurship Monitor received many citations.

The third approach was again conceptual and coupled the changing role of small business and entrepreneurship with a larger change in the economic system, which was coined the switch from the managed to the entrepreneurial economy [132, 73, 86, 90, 107, 109, 183]. David Audretsch played a crucial role in helping me understand this switch and writing up the analyses. These analyses also helped better understand the role the second ICT (information and communication technology) revolution played in developed modern and developing [164] economies. It provided important material for the foundation of courses in small business economics for both students and entrepreneurs with a distinct societal flavor that I gave at the Free University of Amsterdam and at Erasmus University Rotterdam. Martin Carree and I had great fun bringing together material for the *Handbook of Entrepreneurship and Economic Growth* [125, 124], but again the economics flavor dominated.

The fourth approach was based upon a stylized fact: in many OECD countries, U-shaped entrepreneurship rates (business owners per workforce) can be observed over time as well as over the level of economic development [147]. This U-shape results from the fact that the entrepreneurship rate has declined since there is economic life, but this decline stopped in the early 1990s and a reversal has even set in. The resulting trough marks the beginning of the entrepreneurial economy [86, 90]. I never managed to theoretically derive this U-shape from the many interplays between entrepreneurship and macroeconomic phenomena, such as unemployment or economic growth, which separately have all been well documented [140]. However, we did some work on the U-shape or L-shape as a normative development, while deviations consequently lead to growth penalties [94, 96, 127].

Policy and the business cycle

My studies on the changing role of small business and entrepreneurship in the economy and society inevitably led to policy contemplations. The so-called eclectic theory of entrepreneurship [97] provided a basis with many off shoots [80, 92, 98, 103, 133, 144, 163, 161, 188]. This model is not based on real theory because it is highly eclectic in that it borrows many stylized facts from diverse fields showing the complex effects different policies may have on entrepreneurship and how then entrepreneurship influences the structure of the economy [186]. It should have provided the basis for a contemplation that entrepreneurship policy does not exist, per se, but that policies in general have entrepreneurship effects, but I never wrote this up. My "entreprenomics" paper, a combination of the "from the managed to the entrepreneurial economy" view and the eclectic theory never caught much attention [145], whereas the simple analysis of the effect of business regulations of nascent and young entrepreneurship did catch considerable attention [128]. I tried to improve my view on regulation and compliance by contributing to an edited volume [142, 141] as well as my view on job flows in traditional service industries by contributing to another edited volume [87]. Differences between the United States and Europe concerning determinants of entrepreneurship and the role of policy were laid out in a Kluwer Publishers edited volume [99], while I kept struggling with whether entrepreneurship policy existed in an Edward Elgar volume [134].

While thinking about the interface of entrepreneurship and policy, one is bound to start exploring the role of culture. This fascinating area was investigated in many publications [156, 175, 104, 154, 165, 108, 129, 130, 131]. Dissatisfaction, uncertainty avoidance and post-materialism are among the phenomena taken into account in these studies. The publications in the special issue of *Journal of Evolutionary Economics* [129, 130, 131] are particularly remarkable because one would hardly look for the role of sluggish culture effects in a journal on economic dynamics. They were well received, and subsequently Springer devoted an edited volume to the full content of this special issue [154, 155]. Some studies on social entrepreneurship [173, 150] are closely linked to my portfolio of culture studies.

The investigations of entrepreneurship and the economy culminated in a later phase with studies on the interplay between self-employment and unemployment using a vector autoregression (VAR) model for 23 OECD countries for the period 1974–2002 [140] and in specific countries like the United Kingdom [100], Spain [120] and Portugal [122, 126]. In the *Journal of Business Venturing* [140], the many alleged effects between self-employment and unemployment and their lag structure are dealt with from many angles. André van Stel played a big role in getting these and other aggregate growth studies on the road, not only because of his econometric expertise, but also because he is the mastermind behind the famous Compendia (COMparative Entrepreneurship Data for International Analysis) data set. Some studies of Gibrat's law on the disproportionate effect of firm size on growth [121, 101, 110] should have been built into the macro determinants of self-employment, but never were.

When the economy went in a recession in 2008, my colleague Phillip Koellinger suggested looking beyond the interplay between changes or levels of self-employment, unemployment and aggregate output, going to the heart of the matter by examining the interplay between their cyclical effects [172]. This publication in the *Review of Economics and Statistics* led to some spin-offs [189, 193, 194]. The main conclusion is that indeed there is a self-employment cycle and that it is affected by the unemployment cycle. Although it received many citations, few were in the world of macroeconomics.

Finally, some entrepreneurship research

Through my many contacts with the European Commission, I met Isabel Grilo, who pointed me to the Eurobarometer Entrepreneurship. Together with her and many others, I wrote a series of papers about the determinants of entrepreneurship, but not in the traditional way. Instead of explaining whether or not people become an entrepreneur – in other words what the likelihood is that they become an entrepreneur – instead we set up what we termed the *entrepreneurship ladder model* discriminating between successive engagement levels [123, 115, 117, 137, 151, 152, 157, 162, 168, 169, 178]. I really like this series of papers: many data sets were analyzed using similar models or methodologies with minor variations in the phenomenon to be explained, all covering a wide range of determinants and countries. Such an approach calls for an umbrella text binding it all together. I never wrote that text for a simple reason: despite the many and coherent findings suggesting that the ladder approach makes sense, the effect sizes of the usual suspects among the determinants, such as age, education, experience and risk averseness, remained small. My sense was that in terms of modeling we were on the right track, but in terms of determinants we missed the point. Life intervened – as is often the case – and showed me where to look for the missing link.

But before I elaborate on this, let me first devote some words to my endeavors in the world of hard-core entrepreneurship research. This is not the place to define what hard-core entrepreneurship research is. It is a relatively new and productive field that has fought its way into the ranks of management sciences. However, it is obsessed by new theory and consequently attaches a low value to replication of results. It is vulnerable to data and theory mining. However, it has made immense progress in terms of academic results and respectability in the last two decades mainly thanks to journals like *Journal of Business Venturing*, *Entrepreneurship Theory and Practice*, *Small Business Economics Journal*, and *Strategic Entrepreneurship Journal*. Although I have been employed as an entrepreneurship researcher for decades, my contribution in this area is limited. I did some gender work [89, 114, 119, 143], some technical work on endogeneity and instruments [170, 171, 182], some work on practices and performance [82, 106, 116, 118, 158], on finance [89, 44] on entrepreneurial aspiration and motivation [136, 139], location decisions [187, 198] and start-up modes [185]. There was never a technical follow-up of the one-pager in *Harvard Business Review* [148] on Blue Ocean, although this would have been fun: it ties in directly with my early retail work of thirty years ago.

What I could have done, and what I probably will do in the years to come, is to simply ignore the fixation on new theory of the main journals in entrepreneurship and focus on replication and testing the experiments and the investigations of my colleagues. At my age I have the liberty to ignore what is in vogue and concentrate on what is reproducible. For those seeking to inspire entrepreneurs and who aim to support them – whether it be politicians, financiers or family members – it is crucial to know whether scholarly ideas work or not. Recent large-scale survey work in medicine and psychology that attempt to reproduce earlier results have had truly disappointing results. There is no obvious reason to assume that duplication results would be different in entrepreneurship. A parallel approach is to do research based upon multiple data sets, applying "internal replication." In my own work I try to do so, and in my editorial work I try to encourage it. Here I learned a lot from my colleagues and friends in medicine, with whom I tried to conquer the rocky terrain of entrepreneurship and biology.

Hello, biology

Entrepreneurship is hereditary. This follows directly from the sign and the significance of the "entrepreneurial parents" variable, which is one of the usual suspects in the determinants of the entrepreneurship literature. I am inclined to say that I never saw a nonsignificant effect here. But how this works remained obscure until recently: Is it nature or nurture? Twin studies now show that it is both. And if it is nature, which bit of DNA is responsible for the nature effect? Or in layman's terms: which genes are responsible? Given the spectacular progress in DNA research, it is now straightforward to connect DNA to diseases and physical properties of human beings. Ten years ago it took my frustration with the progress of entrepreneurship research, despite – or thanks to – the ladder approach, to think that DNA might be the missing link. So, when I approached Bert Hofman, the principal investigator of a large research initiative at the Erasmus Medical Centre investigating the links between DNA and horrid diseases, with the question of whether he could make his DNA material available so that I could research the link with the entrepreneurial choice, he probably thought of entrepreneurship as yet another horrible disease. But he said yes, let's do it. This was the beginning of a fascinating, still ongoing, research project. Bert and I immediately understood that analyzing DNA and economic behavior, such as the entrepreneurial choice, is a big and risky adventure and we surrounded ourselves with many talented people like Philipp Koellinger, Patrick Groenen, and André Uitterlinden. The entrepreneurial gene was never found [195, 146, 160, 179], but we did find some of the genes connected to educational attainment and subjective well-being and reported about it in *Science* [181], *Nature* [197] and *Nature Genetics* [199]. The collaboration between my Erasmus School of Economics and the Erasmus Medical Centre culminated in the creation of the Erasmus University Rotterdam Institute for Behavior and Biology (EURIBEB). I contributed to some of its many publications of which like the ones in *Journal of Economic Perspectives* [159] and *Physiology and Behavior* [180] the most.

The EURIBEB initiative started by investigating the links between DNA and economic behavior, but quickly broadened its scope toward the role of satisfaction and health [177, 191]. Other studies connecting entrepreneurial behavior with hormones [180], electroencephalography [190], and attention-deficit/hyperactivity (ADHD) [192, 200] followed. EURIBEB received two significant grants from my EUR: one for research on the interface between genes and economic behavior and the second on the neurocognition – a blend of neurocognitive mechanisms and psychopathological symptoms – of economic behavior. As a test – or rather as a proof of concept – behavior we used entrepreneurship in its many manifestations like the intention, choice, orientation, success, etc. The social sciences are at the eve of a major regime switch. The so-called social science standard model (SSSM) dominated the social sciences since they came into existence. This model dictates that human decision making is explained using determinants like environment, socialization, demographics, traits and other behaviors. The model left no room for biological determinants. Currently, biology is making its way into the social sciences at a rapid pace. By biology we mean neuroimaging, hormones and genetic information. It is precisely here that EURIBEB is contributing. In particular, in using genetic information it is ahead of the worldwide pack. It is also contributing in the area of using determinants originally developed to assess symptoms derived from the field of clinical and neuropsychology – in other words psychiatric scales – for nonclinical purposes. I am determined to devote my scientific life of the next five years or so to these new developments as a director of EURIBEB.

Looking back and ahead

My work at EURIBEB in Rotterdam on the discovery of the entirely new field of economics and biology seems not compatible with that of "directeur de la recherche" at the Montpellier Business School in France, which is largely organizational. But wait: Isn't combining the two entirely different fields of economics and biology just like combining two strikingly different cultures, like the (horizontal) Dutch and (vertical) French ones? And is that not similar to combining the scientific research of academia and the applied research of a commercial institute like Panteia, which I have been doing for nearly forty years now? And being "directeur de la recherche" will not prevent me from doing research with a biology or psychiatry saveur in partnership with my French colleagues to extend my modest French language output [17, 156, 167, 174, 175, 188, 196]. I do not anticipate increasing my Dutch language output in the years to come: it will probably remain at the level of two edited handbooks [71, 105], a booklet on small firms and jobs [66], 27 contributions for the Dutch (bi)-weekly ESB, and an assorted collection of newspaper column–type offerings.

Like many fellow researchers I learn more from my students than they do from me. I was thrilled to take over the small business course of Professor Jan van der Wilde at Free University Amsterdam in the late 1980s: I did so out of my respect for him because he had supported me when I was a young, ill-informed, economic researcher with the idea of changing the field of small business from an institutional to a scholarly one, at a time when it was dominated by vested and institutional interests. I already had this part-time chair at the Econometrics Institute EUR without any teaching obligation. So, why teach in Amsterdam? Taking on this teaching activity proved valuable when EUR upgraded my chair from a part-time temporary to a full time fixed position. I did not have to develop courses from scratch and my beginner's mistakes were left behind in Amsterdam. Setting up my first small business course in Rotterdam was one of the most hilarious episodes of my entire career, which I am happy to share with anybody over a beer or two. Over the years I set up a bachelor's major "Organization and Entrepreneurship" for third year economics students, a bachelor's minor "Entrepreneurship in the Modern Economy" for third year students of all backgrounds and a master's program "Entrepreneurship and Strategy Economics." As far as I am aware, my Erasmus School of Economics is the only school of economics in the world with such a variety of entrepreneurship programs.

The Centre for Advanced Small Business Economics (CASBEC) was established in 1987 and started as a placeholder for those working in the "conditional research financing" group on "retail econometrics." Gradually it began showing to those involved and to the world that it was not just about inventing the field of "retail econometrics" but also about small business economics. Most importantly it was a joint effort between Panteia and the Erasmus School of Economics (ESE): a platform for the collaboration between Panteia, which brought in research questions and data sets, and ESE, which provided human capital. It is a platform coupling societal relevance and scientific rigor. There's no document explicitly stating any regular financial support or the goals of CASBEC; rather it has always been entirely virtual. Which probably explains its longevity. It has been of great value to both partners in terms of its scholarly output, the number of PhD students who defended successfully and national and international visibility for the two partners.

The Erasmus Centre for Entrepreneurship (ECE) offers a learning environment where both students and companies nurture their entrepreneurship skills, gaining new insights and turning ideas into innovations. It supports them with a combination of a strong academic environment and a community filled with experienced entrepreneurs. The ECE campus is now home to more than fifty innovative companies and is the stage for many entrepreneurship events. Furthermore, it built an infrastructure fostering ambitious entrepreneurship and empowering a global community of 20,000 entrepreneurs who can help solve global challenges – creatively and effectively. Currently, I am scientific director of ECE, which is mainly ornamental. But when I go there, I observe and always leave the place in an optimistic mood. It is filled with many young people, who are talented and driven, all with vision for a great future. But getting it off the ground was a gigantic exercise. I invested at least the equivalent of a full professional year in its gestation and its fragile nascent state. It was fully worth it.

The Erasmus School of Economics has always been tolerant and even generous with my field and with me. It invested in PhD students and education programs. It supported my eclectic approach of economics and went along with my lifelong campaign based on my alleged lack of management genes. It never gave me any managerial duties and allowed me to live far away from the organizational power center. My field, my small group and I have survived three reorganizations. The last which took place was really big and, when it was over, the size of the school appeared to have been halved from 2004 to 2006. Practically alone – but with the help of colleagues funded by external financing – I established the "Entrepreneurship and Strategy Economics" master's degree. Some students called it the "Roy Thurik and friends" master's, and it was the most rewarding teaching that I've ever engaged in, with incredibly involved and thankful students. External financing also played a big role for my small research group CASBEC until some ten years ago. The Dutch Ministry of Economic Affairs; VBS Schiedam Vlaardingen, a big philanthropic foundation; the Foundation for the Economic Organization of the Construction Industries; the Dutch Retail Trade Board; and many others invested in our research. A big bank and an accounting firm invested in a spinoff of CASBEC, the European Family Business Institute, but unfortunately that proved to be "too much and too early."

Somehow we even started making money by organizing the Erasmus Master Class for Entrepreneurship and the Erasmus Master Class for Family Business. Advertised as a "Master Class for Entrepreneurs who do not need a Master Class," the entrepreneurial course was a huge success – with entrepreneurs coming to me, I learned a lot. As did the handsomely paid professors hired to participate in the Master Class: They lost their innate inclination to see entrepreneurship as a frivolity for serious schools. However, at the time, actually being entrepreneurial and making money was not necessarily seen as a virtue. So we abandoned the initiative.

Erasmus University Rotterdam has been even more supportive than my own school. Since 2000, it has given me four major grants to develop "Small Business Economics," the "Erasmus Centre for Entrepreneurship," the "Erasmus University Rotterdam Institute of Behavior and Biology," and the "Neuro-cognition of the Entrepreneur" project. These four grants amount to at least 2M euros. Without them I would have led a marginal existence at EUR and beyond.

My PhD students have played, and will continue to play, a focal role in my professional life. I always tried to recruit candidates who I thought were far cleverer than I. I hear the reader think: "That is not a strong statement in your case, Roy!" I had few drop out. I very much acknowledge the collaboration with Ben Bode, Jan van Dalen, Jeroen Potjes, Yvonne Prince, Luuk Klomp, Martin Carree, Jan de Kok, Marco van Gelderen, André van Stel, Ingrid Verheul, Sander Wennekers, Armenio Bispo, Jolanda Hessels, Hugo Erken, Haibo Zhu, Peter van der Zwan, Brigitte Hoogendoorn, Matthijs van der Loos, Niels Rietveld and Wim Rietdijk. I am confident that my current PhD students, Aysu Okbay, Pourya Darnihamedani, Ronald de Vlaming, Indy Bernoster, Christian Fisch and Plato Leung, will all successfully defend.

Ultimately, though, there are four key colleagues: two unaware of the impact that they have had on me (at least until now, that is), and two on speed-dial. David Storey [196] and Simon Parker are the two caught unawares: David Storey's superb presentation style and fine-tuned feel for what policy needs is reflected in how I approach the application of my research. Simon Parker has benefitted financially – each of the three times I bought his book, *The Economics of Entrepreneurship*, because I'd been foolish enough to loan the previous copy of this important book to friends. On speed-dial are my ultimate collaborators, conspirators and friends, Johan Koerts, my supervisor, and David Audretsch [176], my co-author. They have two things in common. They discouraged me from moving out of the field, and we seldom talked about the field, instead focusing on the personal things that make life inside and outside the office enjoyable: walking along the River Maas, drinking a pint in a beer garden and savoring the best things in life.

Acknowledgements

David Audretsch, Martin Carree, Adam Lederer and Sander Wennekers gave helpful comments. All references can be found in a document available at www.thurik.com.

References

1 Thurik, R. and N. van der Wijst (1984), Part-time labour in retailing, Journal of Retailing, 60(3): 62–80.
2 Van der Hoeven, W.H.M and A.R. Thurik (1984), Labour productivity in the hotel business, Service Industries Journal, 4(2): 161–173.
3 Thurik, A.R. and J.A.C. Vollebregt (1984), A generalized labour cost relation for French retailing, Annales de l' Insee, 53: 93–106.
4 Thurik, A.R. and J. Koerts (1984), Analysis of the use of retail floorspace, International Small Business Journal, 2(2): 35–47.

5 Thurik, A.R. (1984), Labour productivity, economies of scale and opening time in large retail establishments, Service Industries Journal, 4(1): 19–29.

6 Thurik, A.R. (1984), Quantitative Analysis of Retail Productivity, (W.D. Meinema: Delft).

7 Thurik, A.R. and J.A.C. Vollebregt (1985), Degree of affiliation and retail labour productivity in France, The Netherlands and the U.K., International Small Business Journal, 3(4): 65–71.

8 Thurik, A.R. and J. Koerts (1985), Behaviour of retail entrepreneurs, Service Industries Journal, 5(3): 335–347.

9 Kooiman, P., H.K. van Dijk and A.R. Thurik (1985), Likelihood diagnostics and Bayesian analysis of a micro-economic disequilibrium model for retail services, Journal of Econometrics, 29(1–2): 121–148.

10 Nooteboom, B. and A.R. Thurik (1985), Retail margins during recession and growth, Economics Letters, 17: 281–284.

11 Thurik, R. and P. Kooiman (1986), Modelling retail floorspace productivity, Journal of Retailing, 62(4): 431–445.

12 Nooteboom, B., A.R. Thurik and J.A.C. Vollebregt (1986), An international comparison in the general food trade: cases of structural change, International Journal of Research in Marketing, 3(4): 243–247.

13 Thurik, A.R. (1986), Productivity in small business: an analysis using African data, American Journal of Small Business, 11(1): 27–42.

14 Thurik, R. (1986), Transaction per customer in supermarkets, International Journal of Retailing, 1(3): 33–42.

15 Bode, B., J. Koerts and R. Thurik (1986), On storekeeper's pricing behaviour, Journal of Retailing, 62(1): 98–110.

16 Thurik, A.R. and A.J.M. Kleijweg (1986), Procyclical retail labour productivity, Bulletin of Economic Research, 38(2): 169–175.

17 Nooteboom, B., A.R. Thurik and J.A.C. Vollebregt (1986), Les marges de la distribution de détail différent-elles entre les pays européens? Revue Française du Marketing, 106(1): 63–74.

18 Hoeven, W.H.M. van der and A.R. Thurik (1987), Pricing in the hotel and catering sector, De Economist, 135(2): 201–218.

19 Thurik, A.R. (1987), La produttivita del lavoro nel commercio al dettaglio: alcone implicazioni ed applicazioni della curva lineare dei costi, Commercio: Rivista di Economia e Politica Commerciale, 25: 101–118.

20 Thurik, A.R. (1987), Optimal trading hours in retailing, International Journal of Retailing, 2(1): 22–30.

21 Bode, B., J. Koerts and A.R. Thurik (1988), On the measurement of retail marketing mix effects in the presence of different economic regimes, International Journal of Research in Marketing, 5(2): 107–123.

22 Thurik, A.R. (1988), Les grandes surfaces en France: étude de la relation ventes/surface du magasin, Recherche et Applications en Marketing, 3(3): 21–37.

23 Kleijweg, A.J.M. and A.R. Thurik (1988), Determinants of aggregate employment: an example of the food retail and hotel and catering sectors, Service Industries Journal, 8(1): 91–100.

24 Nooteboom, B., A.J.M. Kleijweg and A.R. Thurik (1988), Normal costs and demand effects in price setting: a study of retailing, European Economic Review, 32(4): 999–1011.

25 Nooteboom, B., J.A.C. Vollebregt and A.R. Thurik (1988), Do retail margins differ among European countries?, A comparative study, in Transnational Retailing, E. Kaynak (ed.), (Walter de Gruyter: Berlin and New York): 155–166.

26 Thurik, A.R. and W.H.M. van der Hoeven (1989), Manufacturing margins: differences between small and large firms, Economics Letters, 29(4): 353–359.

27 Dijk, V. van, A.J.M. Kleijweg and A.R. Thurik (1989), Retail purchasing prices: theoretical and empirical viewpoints, in Retail and Marketing Channels, L. Pellegrini and S.K. Reddy (eds.), (London and New York: Routledge Publishers): 73–83.

28 Dalen, J. van, J. Koerts and A.R. Thurik (1990), Measurement of labour productivity in wholesaling, International Journal of Research in Marketing, 7(1): 21–34.

29 Bode, B., J. Koerts and A.R. Thurik (1990), Market disequilibria and their influence on small retail store pricing, Small Business Economics, 2(1): 45–57.

30 Potjes, J.C.A., Y. Suzuki and A.R. Thurik (1990), A floorspace productivity relationship for Japanese convenience stores, Aoyama Business Review, 15: 31–44.

31 Thurik, A.R. (1990), Small business economics: a perspective from the Netherlands, Small Business Economics, 2(1): 1–10.

32 Potjes, J.C.A. and A.R. Thurik (1991), Japanese supermarket chains and labour costs, Part 1: differing marketing strategies among chains, Journal of Marketing Channels, 1(2): 53–73.

33 Carree, M.A. and A.R. Thurik (1991), Recent developments in the Dutch firm-size distribution, Small Business Economics, 3(4): 261–268.

34 Dalen, J. van and A.R. Thurik (1991), Labour productivity and profitability in the Dutch flower trade, Small Business Economics, 3(2): 131–144.

35 Frenk, J.B.G., A.R. Thurik and C.A. Bout (1991), Labour costs and queueing theory in retailing, European Journal of Operations Research, 55: 260–267.

36 Hertog, R.G.J. den and A.R. Thurik (1992), Expectations and retail price setting, The International Review of Retail, Distribution and Consumer Research, 2(3): 263–282.

37 Prince, Y.M. and A.R. Thurik (1992), Price-cost margins in Dutch manufacturing: effects of concentration, business cycle and international trade, De Economist, 140(3): 310–335.

38 Potjes, J.C.A. and A.R. Thurik (1992), Japanese supermarket chains and labour costs, Part 2: comparison with French variety stores, supermarkets and hypermarkets, Journal of Marketing Channels, 1(3): 97–113.

39 Potjes, J.C.A. and A.R. Thurik (1993), Profit margins in Japanese retailing, Japan and the World Economy, 5(4): 337–362.

40 Carree, M.A., J.C.A. Potjes and A.R. Thurik (1993), Small store presence in Japan, Economics Letters, 41(3): 329–334.

41 Thurik, A.R. (1993), Exports and small business in the Netherlands: presence, potential and performance, International Small Business Journal, 11(3): 47–58.

42 Hertog, R.G.J. den and A.R. Thurik (1993), Determinants of internal and external R&D: some Dutch evidence, De Economist, 141(2): 279–289.

43 Prince, Y.M. and A.R. Thurik (1993), Firm-size distribution and price-cost margins in Dutch manufacturing, Small Business Economics, 5(3): 173–186.

44 Wijst, D. van der and A.R. Thurik (1993), Determinants of small firm debt ratios: an analysis of retail panel data, Small Business Economics, 5(1): 55–65.

45 Thurik, A.R. (1993), Recent developments in firm-size distribution and economies of scale in Dutch manufacturing, in Small Firms and Entrepreneurship: An East-West Perspective, Z. Acs and D. Audretsch (eds.), (Cambridge: Cambridge University Press): 78–109.

46 Hertog, R.G.J. den, Potjes, J.C.A. and A.R. Thurik (1994), Retail profit margins in Japan and Germany, Weltwirtschaftliches Archiv, 130(2): 375–390.

47 Prince, Y.M. and A.R. Thurik (1994), The intertemporal stability of the concentration-margins relationship in Dutch and U.S. manufacturing, Review of Industrial Organization, 9(2): 193–209.

48 Carree, M.A. and A.R. Thurik (1994), The dynamics of entry, exit and profitability: an error correction approach for the retail industry, Small Business Economics, 6(2): 107–116.

49 Potjes, J.C.A., M.A. Carree and A.R. Thurik (1994), Japanese retail stores: regulation, demand and the dual labour market, in SMES, Internationalization, Networks and Strategy, J.M. Veciana (ed.), (Avebury: Aldershot): 222–236.

50 Prince, Y.M. and A.R. Thurik (1995), Do small firms price-cost margins follow those of large firms?, Bulletin of Economic Research, 47(4): 321–327.

51 Dalen, J. van and A.R. Thurik (1995), Wholesale pricing in a small open economy, De Economist, 142(1): 55–76.

52 Hertog, R.G.J. den and A.R. Thurik (1995), A comparison between Dutch and German retail price-setting, Service Industries Journal, 15(1): 66–73.

53 Thurik, A.R. (1995), Labour productivity, economics of scale and opening time in large retail establishments, in Retail Employment, G. Akehurst and N. Alexander (eds.), (Frank Cass: London): 139–149.

54 Hertog, R.G.J. den and A.R. Thurik (1995), A comparison between Dutch and German retail price-setting, in Retail Marketing, G. Akehurst and N. Alexander (eds.), (Frank Cass: London): 196–203.

55 Carree, M.A. and A.R. Thurik (1995), Profitability and number of firms: their dynamic interaction in Dutch retailing, in Studies in Industrial Organization: Market Evolution: Competition and Cooperation, A. van Witteloostuijn (ed.), (Boston and Dordrecht: Kluwer Academic Publishers): 257–266.

56 Audretsch, D.B., A.J. Menkveld and A.R. Thurik (1996), The decision between internal and external R&D, Journal of Institutional and Theoretical Economics, 152(3): 519–530.

57 Thurik, A.R. (1996), Introduction: economic performance and small business, Small Business Economics, 8(5): 327–328.

58 Thurik, A.R. (1996), Introduction: innovation and small business, Small Business Economics, 8(3): 175–176.

59 Audretsch, D.B. and A.R. Thurik (1996), Introduction: the dynamics of industrial organization, Review of Industrial Organization, 11(2): 149–153.

60 Carree, M.A. and A.R. Thurik (1996), Entry and exit in retailing: incentives, barriers, displacement and replacement, Review of Industrial Organization, 11(2): 155–172.

61 Wijst, D. van and A.R. Thurik (1996), Determinants of small firm debt ratios: an analysis of retail panel data, in Small Firms and Economic Growth, Vol 1, Z.J. Acs (ed.), (Edward Elgar: Cheltenham): 639–649.

62 Thurik, A.R. (1996), Small firms, entrepreneurship and economic growth, in Small Business in the Modern Economy, Z. Acs, B. Carlsson and A.R. Thurik (eds.), (Basil Blackwell Publishers: Oxford): 126–152.

63 Acs, Z., B. Carlsson and A.R. Thurik (eds.) (1996), Small Business in the Modern Economy, (Basil Blackwell Publishers: Oxford).

64 Farris, P., A.R. Thurik and W. Verbeke (1997), The acid test of brand loyalty: a consumer response to out of stocks for their favorite brands, Journal of Brand Management, 5: 43–52.

65 Dijk, B. van, R. den Hertog, B. Menkveld and R. Thurik (1997), Some new evidence on the determinants of large- and small-firm innovation, Small Business Economics, 9(4): 335–343.

66 Klomp, L. and A.R. Thurik (1997), Kleine Bedrijven als Banenmotor? (Van Gorkum: Assen).

67 Bode, B., J. Koerts and A.R. Thurik (1998), On the use of disequilibrium models in applied microeconomic research and the value of sample separation information, Applied Economics, 30: 1511–1530.

68 Dalen, J. van and A.R. Thurik (1998), A model of pricing behavior: an econometric case study, Journal of Economic Behavior and Organization, 36: 177–195.

69 Verbeke, W., P. Farris and A.R. Thurik (1998), Consumer response to the preferred brand out-of-stock situation, European Journal of Marketing, 32(11–12): 1008–1028.

70 Carree, M.A. and A.R. Thurik (1998), Small firms and economic growth in Europe, Atlantic Economic Journal, 26(2): 137–146.

71 Scherjon, D.P. and A.R. Thurik (eds.) (1998), Handboek Ondernemers en Adviseurs in het MKB, (Kluwer Bedrijfsinformatie: Deventer).

72 Audretsch, D.B., Y.M. Prince and A.R. Thurik (1999), Do small firms compete with large firms? Atlantic Economic Journal, 27(2): 201–209.

73 Audretsch, D.B. and A.R. Thurik (1999), La nuova organizzazione industriale: Dalla economia gestita all'economia imprenditoriale, L'Industria: Revista di Economia e Politica Industriale, 20(4): 637–656.

74 Wennekers, S. and R. Thurik (1999), Linking entrepreneurship and economic growth, Small Business Economics, 13(1): 27–55.

75 Carree, M.A. and A.R. Thurik (1999), Carrying capacity and entry and exit flows in retailing, International Journal of Industrial Organisation, 17(7): 985–1007.

76 Menkveld, B. and A.R. Thurik (1999), Firm size and efficiency in innovation, Small Business Economics, 12(1): 97–101.

77 Thurik, A.R. (1999), Entrepreneurship, industrial transformation and growth, in The Sources of Entrepreneurial Activity: Vol. 11, Advances in the Study of Entrepreneurship, Innovation, and Economic Growth, G.D. Libecap (ed.), (JAI Press: Stamford, CT): 29–65.

78 Carree, M.A. and A.R. Thurik (1999), Industrial structure and economic growth, in Innovation, Industry Evolution and Employment, D.B. Audretsch and A.R. Thurik (eds.), (Cambridge: Cambridge University Press): 86–110.

79 Audretsch, D.B., L. Klomp and A.R. Thurik (1999), The post-entry performance of firms in Dutch services, in Innovation, Industry Evolution and Employment, D.B. Audretsch and A.R. Thurik (eds.), (Cambridge: Cambridge University Press): 230–252.

80 Audretsch, D.B. and A.R. Thurik (1999), Introduction, in Innovation, Industry Evolution and Employment, D.B. Audretsch and A.R. Thurik (eds.), (Cambridge: Cambridge University Press): 1–12.

81 Audretsch, D.B. and A.R. Thurik (eds.) (1999), Innovation, Industry Evolution and Employment, (Cambridge University Press).

82 Gelderen, M. von, M. Frese and R. Thurik (2000), Strategies, uncertainty and performance of small startups, Small Business Economics, 15(3): 165–181.

83 Carree, M.A. and A.R. Thurik (2000), The life cycle of the US tire industry, Southern Economic Journal, 67(2): 254–278.

84 Carree, M.A., L. Klomp and A.R. Thurik (2000), Productivity convergence in OECD manufacturing industries, Economics Letters, 66(3): 337–345.

85 Audretsch, D.B., P. Houweling and A.R. Thurik (2000), Firm survival in the Netherlands, Review of Industrial Organization, 16(1): 1–11.

86 Audretsch, D.B. and A.R. Thurik (2000), Capitalism and democracy in the 21st century: from the managed to the entrepreneurial economy, Journal of Evolutionary Economics, 10(1–2): 17–34.

87 Klomp, L. and A.R. Thurik (1999), Job flows in traditional services, in Entrepreneurship, Small and Medium-Sized Enterprises and the Macro Economy, Z. Acs, B. Carlsson and Ch. Karlson (eds.), (Cambridge: Cambridge University Press): 310–326.

88 Carree, M.A. and A.R. Thurik (2000), Market structure dynamics and economic growth, in Regulatory Reform and Competitiveness in Europe no. 1: Horizontal Issues, G. Galli and J. Pelkmans (eds.), (Edward Elgar Publishing: Cheltenham, UK): 430–460.

89 Verheul, I. and R. Thurik (2001), Start-up capital: 'does gender matter?', Small Business Economics, 16(4): 329–345.

90 Audretsch, D.B. and A.R. Thurik (2001), What is new about the new economy: sources of growth in the managed and entrepreneurial economies, Industrial and Corporate Change, 10(1): 267–315.

91 Audretsch, D.B., G. van Leeuwen, B.J. Menkveld and A.R. Thurik (2001), Market dynamics in the Netherlands: competition policy and the response of small firms, International Journal of Industrial Organisation, 19(5): 795–821.

92 Audretsch, D.B. and A.R. Thurik (2001), Globalization and the strategic management of regions, in Globalization and Regionalization: Challenges for Public Policy, D.B. Audretsch and C.F. Bonser (eds.), (Kluwer Academic Publishers: Boston and Dordrecht): 49–70.

93 Wennekers, A.R.M., L. Uhlaner and A.R. Thurik (2002), Entrepreneurship and its conditions: a macro perspective, International Journal of Entrepreneurship Education, 1(1): 25–64.

94 Carree, M., A. van Stel, R. Thurik and S. Wennekers (2002), Economic development and business ownership: an analysis using data of 23 OECD countries in the period 1976–1996, Small Business Economics, 19(3): 271–290.

95 Thurik, A.R., S. Wennekers and L.M. Uhlaner (2002), Entrepreneurship and economic performance: a macro perspective, International Journal of Entrepreneurship Education, 1(2): 157–179.

96 Audretsch, D.B., M.A. Carree, A.J. van Stel and A.R. Thurik (2002), Impeded industrial restructuring: the growth penalty, Kyklos, 55(1): 81–97.

97 Verheul, I., A.R.M. Wennekers, D.B. Audretsch and A.R. Thurik (2002), An eclectic theory of entrepreneurship: policies institutions and culture, in Entrepreneurship: Determinants and Policy in a European-US Comparison, D.B. Audretsch, A.R. Thurik, I. Verheul and A.R.M. Wennekers (eds.), (Kluwer Academic Publishers: Boston and Dordrecht): 11–81.

98 Audretsch, D.B., A.R. Thurik, I. Verheul and S. Wennekers (2002), Understanding entrepreneurship across countries and over time, in Entrepreneurship: Determinants and Policy in a European-US Comparison, D.B. Audretsch, A.R. Thurik, I. Verheul and A.R.M. Wennekers (eds.), (Kluwer Academic Publishers: Boston and Dordrecht): 1–10.

99 Audretsch, D.B., A.R. Thurik, I. Verheul and S. Wennekers (eds.) (2002), Entrepreneurship: Determinants and Policy in a European-US Comparison, (Kluwer Academic Publishers: Boston and Dordrecht).

100 Thurik, A.R. (2003), Entrepreneurship and unemployment in the UK, Scottish Journal of Political Economy, 50(3): 264–290.

101 Piergiovanni, R., E. Santarelli, L. Klomp and A.R. Thurik (2003), Gibrat's law and the firm size/firm growth relationship in Italian services, Revue d'Economie Industrielle, 102: 69–82.

102 Carree, M.A. and A.R. Thurik (2003), The impact of entrepreneurship on economic growth, in Handbook of Entrepreneurship Research, D.B. Audretsch and Z.J. Acs (eds.), (Kluwer Academic Publishers: Boston and Dordrecht): 437–471.

103 Audretsch, D.B. and A.R. Thurik (2003), Entrepreneurship, industry evolution and economic growth, in Austrian Economics and Entrepreneurial Studies: Advances in Austrian Economics, R. Koppl (ed.), (JAI/Elsevier Science: Oxford): 39–56.

104 Hofstede, G., N.G. Noorderhaven, A.R. Thurik, A.R.M. Wennekers, L. Uhlaner and R.E. Wildeman (2003), Culture's role in entrepreneurship: self-employment out of dissatisfaction, in Innovation, Entrepreneurship and Culture: The Interaction between Technology, Progress and Economic Growth, J. Ulijn and T. Brown (eds.), (Edward Elgar Publishing Limited: Cheltenham, UK and Brookfield, US): 162–203.

105 Risseeuw, P.A. and A.R. Thurik (eds.) (2003), Handboek Ondernemers en Adviseurs: Management en Economie van het Middenen Kleinbedrijf, (Kluwer Bedrijfsinformatie: Deventer).

106 Bosma, N., M. van Praag, R. Thurik and G. de Wit (2004), The value of human and social capital investments for the business performance of startups, Small Business Economics, 23(3): 227–236.

107 Audretsch, D.B., P. Houweling and A.R. Thurik (2004), Industry evolution: diversity, selection and the role of learning, International Small Business Journal, 22(4): 331–348.

108 Noorderhaven, N.R. Thurik, S. Wennekers and A. van Stel (2004), The role of dissatisfaction and per capita income in explaining self-employment across 15 European countries, Entrepreneurship Theory and Practice, 28(5): 447–466.

109 Audretsch, D.B. and A.R. Thurik (2004), A model of the entrepreneurial economy, International Journal of Entrepreneurship Education, 2(2): 143–166.

110 Audretsch, D.B., L. Klomp, E. Santarelli and A.R. Thurik (2004), Gibrat's Law: are the services different?, Review of Industrial Organization, 24(3): 301–324.

111 Thurik, R. and S. Wennekers (2004), Entrepreneurship, small business and economic growth, Journal of Small Business and Enterprise Development, 11(1): 140–149.

112 Wennekers, S., A. van Stel, R. Thurik and P. Reynolds (2005), Nascent entrepreneurship and the level of economic development, Small Business Economics, 24(3): 293–309.

113 Stel, A. van, M. Carree and R. Thurik (2005), The effect of entrepreneurial activity on national economic growth, Small Business Economics, 24(3): 311–321.

114 Verheul, I., L. Uhlaner and R. Thurik (2005), Business accomplishments, gender and entrepreneurial self-image, Journal of Business Venturing, 20(4): 483–518.

115 Grilo, I. and R. Thurik (2005), Entrepreneurial engagement levels in the European Union, International Journal of Entrepreneurship Education, 3(2): 143–168.

116 Gelderen, M. van, R. Thurik and N. Bosma (2005), Success and risk factors in the pre-startup phase, Small Business Economics, 24(4): 365–380.

117 Grilo, I. and A.R. Thurik (2005), Latent and actual entrepreneurship in Europe and the US: some recent developments, International Entrepreneurship and Management Journal, 1(4): 441–459.

118 Kok, J.M.P. de, L.M. Uhlaner and A.R. Thurik (2006), Professional HRM practices in family-owned enterprises, Journal of Small Business Management, 44(3): 441–460.

119 Verheul, I., A. van Stel and A.R. Thurik (2006), Explaining female and male entrepreneurship at the country level, Entrepreneurship and Regional Development, 18(2): 151–183.

120 Verheul, I., A. van Stel, A.R. Thurik and D. Urbano (2006), The relationship between business ownership and unemployment in Spain: a matter of quantity or quality? Estudios de Economía Aplicada, 24(2): 105–127.

121 Santarelli, E., L. Klomp and A.R. Thurik (2006), Gibrat's Law: an overview of the empirical literature, in Entrepreneurship, Growth, and Innovation: The Dynamics of Firms and Industries: International Studies in Entrepreneurship, Enrico Santarelli (ed.), (Springer Science: Berlin): 41–73.

122 Baptista, R., A. van Stel and A.R. Thurik (2006), Entrepreneurship, industrial restructuring and unemployment in Portugal, in Entrepreneurship, Growth, and Innovation: The Dynamics of Firms and Industries: International Studies in Entrepreneurship, Enrico Santarelli (ed.), (Springer Science: Berlin): 223–241.

123 Grilo, I. and A.R. Thurik (2006), Entrepreneurship in the old and new Europe, in Entrepreneurship, Growth, and Innovation: The Dynamics of Firms and Industries: International Studies in Entrepreneurship, Enrico Santarelli (ed.), (Springer Science: Berlin): 75–103.

124 Carree, M. and R. Thurik (2006), Understanding the role of entrepreneurship for economic growth, in The Handbook Entrepreneurship and Economic Growth (International Library of Entrepreneurship Series), M.A. Carree and A.R. Thurik (eds.), (Edward Elgar Publishing Limited: Cheltenham, UK and Northampton, MA): ix-xix.

125 Carree, M.A. and A.R. Thurik (eds.) (2006), The Handbook of Entrepreneurship and Economic Growth (International Library of Entrepreneurship), (Edward Elgar Publishing Limited: Cheltenham, UK and Northampton, MA).

126 Baptista, R. and A.R. Thurik (2007), The relationship between entrepreneurship and unemployment: is Portugal an outlier?, Technological Forecasting and Social Change, 74(1): 75–89.

127 Carree, M.A., A. van Stel, A.R. Thurik and S. Wennekers (2007), Economic development and business ownership revisited, Entrepreneurship and Regional Development, 19(3): 281–291.

128 Stel, A. van, D. Storey and A.R. Thurik (2007), The effect of business regulations on nascent to young business entrepreneurship, Small Business Economics, 28(2–3): 171–186.

129 Freytag, A. and A.R. Thurik (2007), Entrepreneurship and its determinants in a cross-country setting, Journal of Evolutionary Economics, 17(2): 117–131.

130 Wennekers, S., R. Thurik, A. van Stel and N. Noorderhaven (2007), Uncertainty avoidance and the rate of business ownership across 23 OECD countries, 1976–2004, Journal of Evolutionary Economics, 17(2): 133–160.

131 Uhlaner, L.M. and A.R. Thurik (2007), Post-materialism: a cultural factor influencing total entrepreneurial activity across nations, Journal of Evolutionary Economics, 17(2): 161–185.

132 Audretsch, D.B. and A.R. Thurik (2007), The models of the managed and the entrepreneurial economy, in The Elgar Companion to Neo-Schumpeterian Economics, H. Hanusch and A. Pyka (eds.), (Edward Elgar Publishing Limited: Cheltenham, UK and Northampton, MA): 211–231.

133 Audretsch, D.B., I. Grilo and A.R. Thurik (2007), Explaining entrepreneurship and the role of policy: a framework, in The Handbook of Research on Entrepreneurship Policy, D.B. Audretsch, I. Grilo and A.R. Thurik (eds.), (Edward Elgar Publishing Limited: Cheltenham, UK and Northampton, MA): 1–17.

134 Audretsch, D.B., I. Grilo and A.R. Thurik (eds.) (2007), The Handbook of Research on Entrepreneurship Policy, (Edward Elgar Publishing Limited: Cheltenham, UK and Northampton, MA).

135 Carree, M.A. and A.R. Thurik (2008), The lag structure of the impact of business ownership on economic growth in OECD countries, Small Business Economics, 30(1): 101–110.

136 Hessels, J., M. van Gelderen and A.R. Thurik (2008), Drivers of entrepreneurial aspirations at the country level: investigating the role of start-up motivations and social security, International Entrepreneurship and Management Journal, 4(4): 401–417.

137 Grilo, I. and A.R. Thurik (2008), Determinants of entrepreneurial engagement levels in Europe and the US, Industrial and Corporate Change, 17(6): 1113–1145.

138 Groenen, P., A. Hofman, Ph. Koellinger, M. van der Loos, F. Rivadeneira, F. van Rooij, A.R. Thurik and A. Uitterlinden (2008), Genome-wide association for loci influencing entrepreneurial behavior: the Rotterdam study, Behavior Genetics, 38(6): 628–629.

139 Hessels, J., M. van Gelderen and A.R. Thurik (2008), Entrepreneurial aspiration, motivation and their drivers, Small Business Economics, 31(3): 323–339.

140 Thurik, A.R., M.A. Carree, A. van Stel and D.B. Audretsch (2008), Does self-employment reduce unemployment? Journal of Business Venturing, 23(6): 673–686.

141 Nijsen. A., J. Hudson, K. van Paridon, Chr. Mueller and R. Thurik (2008), The world of regulation and compliance, in Business Regulation and Public Policy: The Costs and Benefits of Compliance, A. Nijsen, J. Hudson, K. van Paridon, Chr. Mueller and R. Thurik (eds.), (Springer, Intl Studies in Entrepreneurship Series: New York): vii–xxv.

142 Nijsen, A., J. Hudson, K. van Paridon, Chr. Mueller and R. Thurik (eds.) (2008), Business Regulation and Public Policy: The Costs and Benefits of Compliance, (Springer, International Studies in Entrepreneurship Series: New York).

143 Verheul, I., M.A. Carree and A.R. Thurik (2009), Allocation and productivity of time in new ventures of female and male entrepreneurs, Small Business Economics, 33(3): 273–291.

144 Audretsch, D.B. and A.R. Thurik (2009), Globalization, entrepreneurship and the strategic management of regions, in The Role of SMEs and Entrepreneurship in a Globalized Economy, A. Lundström (ed.), (The Globalization Council: Sweden): 14–40.

145 Thurik, A.R. (2009), Entreprenomics: entrepreneurship, economic growth and policy, in Entrepreneurship, Growth and Public Policy, Z.J. Acs, D.B. Audretsch and R. Strom (eds.), (Cambridge University Press: Cambridge, UK): 219–249.

146 Loos, M. van der, P. Groenen, Ph. Koellinger and A.R. Thurik (2010), A genome-wide association study of entrepreneurship, European Journal of Epidemiology, 25(1): 1–3.

147 Wennekers, A.R.M., A.J. van Stel, M.A. Carree and A.R. Thurik (2010), The relation between entrepreneurship and economic development: is it U-shaped? Foundations and Trends in Entrepreneurship, 6(3): 167–237.

148 Burke, A., A.J. van Stel and A.R. Thurik (2010), Blue ocean vs. five forces, Harvard Business Review, May: 28.

149 Koellinger, Ph.D., M.J.H.M. van der Loos, P.J.F. Groenen, A.R. Thurik, F. Rivadeneira, F.J.A. van Rooij, A.G. Uitterlinden and A. Hofman (2010), Genome-wide association studies in economics and entrepreneurship research: promises and limitations, Small Business Economics, 35(1): 1–18.

150 Hoogendoorn, B., E. Pennings and A.R. Thurik (2010), What do we know about social entrepreneurship? An analysis of empirical research, International Review of Entrepreneurship, 8(2): 71–112.

151 Zwan, P. van der, A.R. Thurik and I. Grilo (2010), The entrepreneurial ladder and its determinants, Applied Economics, 42(17): 2183–2191.

152 Stam, E., A.R. Thurik and P. van der Zwan (2010), Entrepreneurial exit in real and imagined markets, Industrial and Corporate Change, 19(4): 1109–1139.

153 Carree, M.A. and A.R. Thurik (2010), The impact of entrepreneurship on economic growth, in Handbook of Entrepreneurship Research, D.B. Audretsch and Z.J. Acs (eds.), (Springer Verlag: Berlin and Heidelberg): 557–594.

154 Freytag, A. and A.R. Thurik (2010), Introducing entrepreneurship and culture, in Entrepreneurship and Culture, A. Freytag and A.R. Thurik (eds.), (Springer Verlag: Berlin and Heidelberg): 1–8.

155 Freitag, A. and R. Thurik (eds.) (2010), Entrepreneurship and Culture, (Springer Verlag: Berlin and Heidelberg).

156 Dejardin, M. and R. Thurik (2010), Nature ou culture, quelle est la source de l'esprit d'entreprendre? Revue Louvain, 183(avril–mai): 35–36.

157 Hessels, J., I. Grilo, A.R. Thurik and P. van der Zwan (2011), Entrepreneurial exit and entrepreneurial engagement, Journal of Evolutionary Economics, 21(3): 447–471.

158 Gelderen, M. van, A.R. Thurik and P. Pankaj (2011), Encountered problems and outcome status in nascent entrepreneurship, Journal of Small Business Management, 49(1): 71–91.

159 Beauchamp, J.P., D. Cesarini, M. Johannesson, M.J.H.M. van der Loos, Ph.D. Koellinger, P.J.F. Groenen, J.H. Fowler, J.N. Rosenquist, A.R. Thurik and N.A. Christakis (2011), Molecular genetics and economics, Journal of Economic Perspectives, 25(4): 57–82.

160 Loos, M.J.H.M. van der, Ph.D. Koellinger, P.J.F. Groenen, C.A. Rietveld, F. Rivadeneira, F.J.A. van Rooij, A.G. Uitterlinden, A. Hofman and A.R. Thurik (2011), Candidate gene studies and the quest for the entrepreneurial gene, Small Business Economics, 37(3): 267–275.

161 Leitao, J., F. Lasch and A.R. Thurik (2011), Globalization, entrepreneurship and regional environment, International Journal of Entrepreneurship and Small Business, 12(2): 129–138.

162 Zwan, P. van der, I. Verheul and A.R. Thurik (2011), Entrepreneurial ladder in transition and non-transition economies, Entrepreneurship Research Journal, 1(2): article 4.

163 Audretsch, D.B., I. Grilo and A.R. Thurik (2011), Globalization, entrepreneurship and the region, in Handbook of Research on Entrepreneurship and Regional Development, M. Fritsch (ed.), (Edward Elgar Publishing Limited: Cheltenham, UK and Northampton, MA): 11–32.

164 Thurik, A.R. (2011), From the managed to the entrepreneurial economy: considerations for developing and emerging economies, in Entrepreneurship and Economic Development, W. Naudé (ed.), (Palgrave McMillan: Houndmills, Basingstoke, England): 147–165.

165 Thurik, A.R. and M. Dejardin (2011), Entrepreneurship and culture, in Entrepreneurship in Context, M. van Gelderen and E. Masurel (eds.), (Routledge: London): 175–186.

166 Stam E., Ch. Hartog, A. van Stel and A.R. Thurik (2011), Ambitious entrepreneurship, high-growth firms and macro-economic growth, in The Dynamics of Entrepreneurship: Theory and Evidence, M. Minniti (ed.), (Oxford University Press: Oxford): 231–249.

167 Thurik, A.R. (2011), Préface de La Croissance de l'Entreprise: une Obligation pour le PME? Frank Janssen, (De Boeck: Bruxelles): 11–15.

168 Zwan, P. van der, I. Verheul and A.R. Thurik (2012), The entrepreneurial ladder, gender and regional development, Small Business Economics, 39(3): 627–643.

169 Verheul, I., A.R. Thurik, I. Grilo and P. van der Zwan (2012), Explaining preferences and actual involvement in self-employment: new insights into the role of gender, Journal of Economic Psychology, 33(2): 325–341.

170 Block J., L. Hoogerheide and A.R. Thurik (2012), Are education and entrepreneurial income endogenous? A Bayesian analysis, Entrepreneurship Research Journal, 2(3).

171 Hoogerheide, L., J. Block and A.R. Thurik (2012), Family background variables as instruments for education in income regressions: a Bayesian analysis, Economics of Education Review, 31(5): 515–523.

172 Koellinger, Ph.D. and A.R. Thurik (2012), Entrepreneurship and the business cycle, Review of Economics and Statistics, 94(4): 1143–1156.

173 Hoogendoorn, B., H.P.G. Pennings and A.R. Thurik (2012), A conceptual overview of what we know about social entrepreneurship, in The Community Development Reader, J. DeFilippis and S. Saegert (eds.), (Routledge: New York): 117–124.

174 Thurik, A.R. (2012), Préface de Ecosystèmes d'affaires et PME, Michaël Géraudel et Annabelle Jaouen, (Lavoisier: Cachan): 13–15.

175 Dejardin, M. and R. Thurik (2012), L'impact de la culture sur l'entrepreneuriat, Reflets et Perspectives de la Vie Economique, 2012(2): 75–81.

176 Thurik, A.R. (2013), Valuing an Entrepreneurial Enterprise by D.B. Audretsch and A.N. Link, Oxford University Press, 2012, (book review), Journal of Economic Literature, 51(1): 202–204.

177 Millan, J.M., J. Hessels, R. Aguado and A.R. Thurik (2013), Determinants of job satisfaction across the EU-15: a comparison of self-employed and paid employees, Small Business Economics, 40(3): 651–670.

178 Zwan, P. van der, I. Verheul, A.R. Thurik and I. Grilo (2013), Entrepreneurial progress: climbing the entrepreneurial ladder in Europe and the US, Regional Studies, 47(5): 803–825.

179 Loos M.J.H.M. van der, C.A. Rietveld, N. Eklund, P.D. Koellinger, F. Rivadeneira, et al. (2013), The molecular genetic architecture of self-employment, PLoS ONE, 8(4): e60542.

180 Loos, M.J.H.M. van der, R. Haring, C.A. Rietveld, S.E. Baumeister, P.J.F. Groenen, A. Hofman, F.H. de Jong, Ph.D. Koellinger, T. Kohlmann, M.A. Nauck, F. Rivadeneira, A.G. Uitterlinden, F.J.A. van Rooij, H. Wallaschofski and A.R. Thurik (2013), Serum testosterone levels in males are not associated with entrepreneurial behavior in two independent observational studies, Physiology and Behavior, 119: 110–114.

181 Rietveld, C.A., et al. (2013), GWAS of 126,559 individuals identifies genetic variants associated with educational attainment, Science, 340(21 June): 1467–1471.

182 Block, J., L. Hoogerheide and A.R. Thurik (2013), Education and entrepreneurial choice: evidence from an instrumental variables regression, International Small Business Journal, 31(1): 23–33.

183 Thurik, A.R., D.B. Audretsch and E. Stam (2013), The rise of the entrepreneurial economy and the future of dynamic capitalism, Technovation, 33(8–9): 302–310.

184 Koellinger, Ph., M. van der Loos, C. Rietveld, D. Benjamin, D. Cesarini, N. Eklund, S. Williams, P. Groenen, A. Uitterlinden, A. Hofman and R. Thurik (2013), GWA studies on entrepreneurship: the trade-off between phenotype accuracy and sample size, Behavior Genetics, 43(6): 526.

185 Block, J., A.R. Thurik, P. van der Zwan and S. Walter (2013), Business takeover or new venture start? Individual and environmental determinants from a cross-country study, Entrepreneurship Theory and Practice, 37(5): 1099–1121.

186 Block, J., A.R. Thurik and H. Zhou (2013), What turns inventions into innovative products? The role of entrepreneurship and knowledge spillovers, Journal of Evolutionary Economics, 23(4): 693–718.

187 Lasch, F., F. Robert, F. LeRoy and A.R. Thurik (2013), The start-up location decision and regional determinants, in Cooperation, Clusters, and Knowledge Transfer: Universities and Firms Towards Regional Competitiveness, J.J.M. Ferreira, M. Raposo, R. Rutten and A. Varga (eds.), (Springer Verlag: Berlin and Heidelberg): 3–17.

188 Messeghem, K., S. Sammut, D. Chabaud, C. Carrier and R. Thurik (2013), L'accompagnement entrepreneurial, une industrie en quête de leviers de performance? Management International, 17(3): 65–71.

189 Thurik, A.R. (2014), Entrepreneurship and the business cycle, IZA World of Labor, 90: (doi: 10.15185/izawol.90).

190 Rietdijk, W.J.R, I.H.A. Franken and A.R. Thurik (2014), Internal consistency of event-related potentials associated with cognitive control: N2/P3 and ERN/Pe, PloS ONE, 9(7).

191 Rietveld, C.A., H. van Kippersluis and A.R. Thurik (2015), Self-employment and health: barriers of benefits?, Health Economics, 24(10): 1302–1313.

192 Verheul, I., J. Block, K. Burmeister-Lamp, R. Thurik, H. Tiemeier and R. Turturea (2015), ADHD-like behavior and entrepreneurial intentions, Small Business Economics, 45(1): 85–101.

193 Sanchis Llopis, J.A., J.M. Millán, R. Baptista, A. Burke, S.C. Parker and A.R. Thurik (2015), Good times, bad times: entrepreneurship and the business cycle, International Entrepreneurship and Management Journal 11(2): 243–251.

194 Scholman, G., A. van Stel and A.R. Thurik (2015), The relationship among entrepreneurial activity business cycles and economic openness, International Entrepreneurship and Management Journal, 11(2): 307–319.

195 Thurik, A.R. (2015), Determinants of entrepreneurship: the quest for the entrepreneurial gene, in Concise Guide to Entrepreneurship, Technology and Innovation, D.B. Audretsch, Ch.S. Hayter and A.N. Link (eds.), (Edward Elgar Publishing Limited: Cheltenham, UK): 28–38.

196 Landström, H., R. Thurik and F. Lasch (2015), David Storey: un point entre recherche et politique en faveur des petites entreprises, en Les Grands Auteurs en Entrepreneuriat et PME, dirigé par Karim Messeghem et Olivier Torrès (eds.), (Editions EMS: Cormelles-le-Royal): 387–408.

197 Okbay, A., J.P. Beauchamp, M.A. Fontana, J.J. Lee, T.H. Pers, et al. (2016), Genome-wide association study identifies 74 loci associated with educational attainment, Nature, 533, 539-542 (doi:10.1038/nature17671).

198 Ferreira, J., C. Fernandes, M. Raposo, R. Thurik and J. Faria (2016), Entrepreneur location decisions across industries, International Entrepreneurship and Management Journal, (doi:10.1007/s11365-015-0370-7).
199 Okbay, A. et al. (2016), Genetic associations with subjective well-being also implicate depression and neuroticism, Nature Genetics, (doi:10.1038/ng.3552).
200 Thurik, A.R., A. Khedhaouria, O. Torrès and I. Verheul (2016), ADHD symptoms and entrepreneurial orientation of small firm owners, Applied Psychology, (doi:10.1111/apps.12062).

18

A place for entrepreneurship

Mary Lindenstein Walshok

Introduction: early career

My journey as a student of entrepreneurship differs from many traditional academics and business school professors with an interest in innovation, entrepreneurship and the phenomenon of start-up enterprises. As a woman born in 1942, I received mixed messages about what to be when I grew up. I encountered significant barriers to my intellectual and career development. However, I was also the beneficiary of some unique opportunities to pioneer new territory, in particular in helping to build what is today one of Americas great research universities, UC San Diego, and, with that, contribute to the evolution of what today is one of America's most dynamic innovation economies, San Diego, California.

Born in 1942 before the end of World War II, I was shaped by the phenomenal period of economic growth and scientific breakthroughs during the postwar decades in the United States. The phenomena of Sputnik and the Cold War led the state of California in the 1950s to reengineer many of its public schools in order to assure "fast tracks" for students in math, science and precollegiate disciplines in order to compete with the putative, superior science education in the Soviet Union. By the eighth grade I was placed in such an advanced cohort. I had the experience of being encouraged to excel academically at the same time that prevailing social norms undervalued the professional and intellectual commitments women, as opposed to men, could potentially make.

Fortunately, my undergraduate career at an exceptional liberal arts institution, Pomona College, further encouraged the development of my intellectual interests and capabilities. Urged on by professors to do something more than become a public school teacher, which was what many gifted young women did at that time, I decided to pursue a PhD in sociology. However, I hedged my bets by selecting Indiana University for graduate work rather than a higher-profile West Coast university so that I could have an opportunity to simultaneously explore a potential career in music. I did so during the first two years of my PhD studies in the Sociology Department where a mere three of the ninety grad students were women.

These facts are important because they suggest how my gender and eclectic interests affected my approach to very limited career options once I was awarded my PhD in sociology at Indiana University, in 1969 at the age of twenty-six. My dissertation topic focused on the cultural and social characteristics influencing the career choices of high-achieving women – essentially a sociology of work and occupations emphasis. And even though I excelled and finished "fast", none of the professors at that time expected a woman to seriously pursue an academic career. I felt a bit like an orphan and began my career without any sponsors or advocates. Mid-summer after I was awarded my PhD an opportunity to teach at one of the California State University campuses arose just as my new husband, who was a political scientist, was negotiating for a position in the School of Public Administration at San Diego State University. In the fall of 1969 we both took jobs in California and it was at that point that my journey into entrepreneurship truly began.

By 1969 America was "on fire" in terms of various human rights movements: civil rights, anti–Vietnam War demonstrations and the rapid growth of the women's movement. As one of the few female professors in that pre–affirmative action era who also was doing significant research on women and work, I found myself in my late twenties being invited to speak at a variety of nonacademic meetings and conferences, providing commentary to journalists both in broadcast and print media, being both a resource about the dynamics that had shaped women's options in the past and a commentator on how those dynamics were changing in the present. It was a time when whole new career options were opening up for women along with the desire among women to better utilize their education and talents.

It sounds like an odd way perhaps to develop a deep interest in how businesses are birthed, grow and eventually plateau. However, it was because of my interest in new jobs and how the growth in jobs created the demand for workers that exceeded the supply of men available that I developed an interest in business incubation and growth. For nearly a decade I did work on women and careers, publishing my first book with Anchor/Doubleday in the early 1980s, *Blue Collar Women*. The book examined the effects of the federal affirmative action legislation on the entry of women into a wide variety of skilled trades across America and was one of the few serious works on this topic at the time. It propelled me into a world of companies, employers and national media attention that I had in no way anticipated as a graduate student.

By the early 1970s I had left the state university system to join the still young University of California campus in La Jolla, UC San Diego, to be director of Women's Programs. At the time I didn't even realize that this activity was anchored in the university's Extension Division, which was not a traditional academic department on the campus. Nonetheless, as I met the people associated with the program, drawn by the prospects of driving five miles rather than seventy miles to work and most especially, the opportunity to become embedded in the community in which I lived, I took a leave of absence from Cal State University, Fullerton, where I was teaching to spend two years at UC San Diego to see if it would be a good fit. Forty-four years later I am still there. That is because I discovered that the Extension platform was perfectly suited to the combination of intellectual and practical interests I had always had. Understanding 1) how companies get started and grow, 2) how employers think about talent issues as well as gender and race issues vis-à-vis talent recruitment and development and 3) ultimately how communities grow diverse sectors of employment that both need and value a diverse talent pool has been my life's work.

In 1972, when I joined UC San Diego, the region was on the cusp of beginning what was to be a twenty-five-year transition from a primarily tourism, military and defense contracting economy to one that today is characterized by multiple clusters of globally competitive science and technology-based industries: IT and wireless, pharmaceuticals, medical devices, renewable energy, software, cybersecurity, aerospace, robotics and sporting goods. Fortuitously, from my perch in Extension at a young campus, with a sociology background, fieldwork experience and ease with interviewing employers and interests in tracking employment opportunities I was able to become a critical partner in the campus' growth over a fourteen-year period, under the leadership of Richard C. Atkinson.

Atkinson arrived at UCSD in 1980 after six years as director of the National Science Foundation where he had helped craft the Bayh-Dole Act, as well as launch Small Business Innovation Research (SBIR) and Small Business Technology Transfer (STTR), initiatives, which enabled universities to more rapidly patent, license and commercialize promising technologies. Prior to that, Atkinson had been a professor and protégé of Frederick Terman at Stanford University. He brought to UC San Diego a desire to "connect" with business and industry in a manner similar to what he had observed during the early growth of the Silicon Valley. The radical 1960s and 1970s had led to profound disconnections between universities and their regional economies particularly in conservative, military communities such as San Diego. Atkinson's goal was to reconnect the university with its regional economy, in particular, the defense contracting and burgeoning entrepreneurial science-based companies clustering around the university on the Torrey Pines Mesa. Lacking a business school or a school of engineering at the time and granting primarily science PhDs in traditional disciplines, my background ended up being an asset to him in addressing these needs.

I was made the dean of the Extension Division in the early 1980s shortly after Atkinson's arrival, about the same time my first highly visible book, *Blue Collar Women*, was published by Anchor/Doubleday. The combination of my academic credibility in the arena of companies and employers combined with my position now as dean of the Extension Division, represented the tipping point in my career. It was at this point in time that I developed a much more focused approach to the world of work and industry, one that zeroed in on company creation, on innovative science and technology-based companies, how they get started and what helps them succeed so that they in turn can generate high-value–added jobs for the region. Critical to that was also understanding the skills and competencies such companies needed at every stage of development in order to successfully navigate the early commercialization stage, as well as build the talent pool (often through specialized education and training) that they needed to grow into large and profitable enterprises. A three-year fellowship from the Kellogg Foundation in the mid-1980s allowed me to research emergent innovation regions such as the Silicon Valley and in turn focus my research and writing on regionally anchored innovation dynamics.

Regional transformation through innovation and entrepreneurship

Since the 1980s, my research and writing has focused primarily on the contributions of research universities to regional economic growth and transformation, understanding the commercialization and innovation dynamics of successful companies and regions and understanding the knowledge, skills, and competencies needed to start and grow successful entrepreneurial, science-based companies. My book *Knowledge Without Boundaries* published in 1995 was extremely well received by practitioners', university leaders, trustees and deans tasked with building community outreach and service. In that book, I formulated a way of thinking about the value of research universities to both regional prosperity and civic capacity that has shaped my research and writing ever since. The book was built around the notion that in a knowledge economy the value of research universities is multidimensional. Increasingly university research represents the "seed corn" of the new products and services, which become new businesses and often new clusters of economic activity, creating jobs and wealth for regions. It argued that universities had to take a more assertive role in partnering with regional economic and business leadership in identifying promising technologies, supporting proof of concept and translational research, as well as incubating enterprises in order to launch new companies in high-value–added sectors that would contribute to regional prosperity. In the case of San Diego, these sectors were originally in aeronautics, wireless communications, medical devices and pharmaceuticals.

The second major point the book underscored was the need for new kinds of skills and competencies in the workforce in order to build and grow science and technology-based companies. A completely new configuration of skills and competencies is often required because of the complexity of science-based companies, their foundation in breakthrough technologies and the necessity of reaching national, even global markets, from day one. Thus the book introduced a variety of new models of education and training that were appropriate to this new reality.

Finally, the book addressed the problem of civic culture and civic education, once again through the lens of rapid changes in science and technology and the increasing globalization of not only the production, but also the consumption, of goods and services. It asserted a continuing need for strong arts, humanities and social science programs to once again play that translational role in helping local communities understand new political realities, deal with increasingly diversified populations due to the increased migration and immigration of talent and help to address issues related to health, the environment and education in an era of rapid changes in technology. The book offered case studies of "best practices" in universities and communities around the United States that were addressing one or more of these issues.

By the time I wrote *Knowledge Without Boundaries*, we had facilitated some early entrepreneurial successes at UC San Diego by being the catalyst for a regional networking organization, which helped build the ecosystem that today enables high levels of innovation and entrepreneurship across the diversity of sectors driving San Diego's economy. An innovative program was launched in 1985 to partner UCSD with the larger community and to create conversations across academic disciplines and between the academy and diverse business services and industrial and technology company leaders. Known as UCSD CONNECT, it has gone on to be an internationally recognized model for regionally anchored networking, education and capacity building whose purpose is to enhance knowledge flows and trust development among all the diverse players in a regional innovation system. That book, the success of CONNECT and a number of subsequent publications describing the dynamics of emerging innovation regions eventually pulled me into a much wider set of conversations, initially among policy makers, but eventually among serious academics such as many of the colleagues who have contributed to this volume.

What I discovered early in my journey to both enhance and document the innovation dynamics in San Diego is that the traditional literature on innovation and entrepreneurship at that time had two characteristics that made it essentially useless to the work I was doing at the intersection of ideas and practice: 1) It focused primarily on the dynamics of single large firms and as of the 1980s, the innovation challenges of companies such as 3M or General Electric, or IBM, with very little attention being paid to the dynamics of start-up science and technology enterprises spinning out of university research or out of larger tech-companies. 2) The entrepreneurial literature also focused heavily on the characteristics and skills of individual entrepreneurs. This individualistic approach, not unlike the "great man" theories that dominated much historical scholarship at the time, implied that it was individuals fighting against all odds to innovate who were the key to understanding entrepreneurship when I kept bumping into entrepreneurial "teams". My hands-on experience in the San Diego region and my frequent interactions with entrepreneurial hubs such as the Silicon Valley suggested that neither of these dominant themes was at the heart of what enabled communities to grow robust clusters of entrepreneurial, science-based companies. Early work by many of the authors in this volume critically informed my thinking by the mid-1980s. And thus, I began both a practical and intellectual journey to try to elucidate the extent to which the environment, the ecosystem, the dynamics of entrepreneurial teams are at the heart of successful clusters, not just the internal dynamics of specific firms or the characteristics of individual entrepreneurs.

The books, research papers, journal articles and book chapters that I have written over the last twenty years have each in their own way sought to elucidate the extent to which entrepreneurship is inspired, enabled and ultimately successful when embedded in knowledge rich, diverse and nurturing social environments, which today we refer to as innovation ecosystems. Ecosystems provide access to diverse forms of knowledge and competencies as well as capital and human resources, all of which can be aggregated and mobilized quickly to seize often unplanned for market opportunities. They also enable relationships to form based on mutual respect and shared knowledge enabling the levels of trust needed to venture into uncertain arenas with high levels of risk. At the heart of this dynamic is the fact that science and technology-based companies typically succeed not because of an individual entrepreneur, but because of entrepreneurial teams who bring complementary skills to the enterprise. I have observed this phenomenon and written about this phenomenon over many years. And I have come to feel quite strongly that research in the field of entrepreneurship needs to better define, operationalize and measure the value of "connected entrepreneurial teams" to ultimate business success. It is in this arena where my current work is focused, and I would like to zero in on two critical issues related to why and where innovation occurs, which in my view are not well understood nor properly researched: 1) the distinctive dynamics of regional innovation ecosystems, which 2) enable the development of powerful entrepreneurial teams.

Lessons learned from a dynamic innovation economy

The importance of culture and social dynamics to successful regional innovation ecosystems

In my 2014 book for Stanford University Press co-authored with Abe Shragge a social historian, *Invention and Reinvention: The Evolution of San Diego's Innovation Economy*, we offered a list of key ingredients that appear to enhance the capacity of regions to grow innovative, entrepreneurial start-ups. They are productive of the kind of enabling culture and social dynamics, which generate connected entrepreneurial teams and incubate start-up and growth companies in the "new economy". Our analysis of San Diego's evolution over a century and especially its phenomenal shift in economic focus over a thirty-year period revealed the important ways in which a civic culture that recognizes the value of "talent" and supports collaborative mechanisms can facilitate regions' creating "new economy" clusters, which become national and international magnets for inventors and entrepreneurs across the globe.

Over a fifty-year period, for example, the migration of science and technology professionals to the San Diego region from across the United States and around the globe has increased the percentage of the population with engineering and technical know-how significantly. And San Diego's innovation ecosystem has become highly robust, thanks to collaborative mechanisms locally, which stimulate the growth of entrepreneurial teams and enterprises. The region has both gotten better at retaining the talent it has, as well as attracting the talent it needs. More than 5,000 technology and life science employers are resident in San Diego representing 20 billion dollars a year in economic impact and 140,000 new high-wage jobs. In our book, we identified five social dynamics that were essential to the transformation of San Diego from a military hub to an innovation and entrepreneurship hub. We also suggested that these may represent dynamics that likely shape how other communities might go about building an ecosystem supportive of not only individual entrepreneurs, but also of those essential entrepreneurial teams who create durable companies and eventually clusters.

Knowing how to leverage the natural advantages of "place"

All cities begin with geographical advantages and disadvantages which shape their early economic horizons. Harbors, rivers, forests, coal, oil, climate and arable land were all essential components of those places where the agricultural and/or industrial revolutions initially took hold. The great cities of the Northeast and the Middle West leveraged those natural advantages for both the production and distribution of goods and services: the New York and New Jersey harbors; coal in West Virginia; steel in Pennsylvania; the Great Lakes and the Mississippi River waterways; forests in Wisconsin, Western Michigan and the Pacific Northwest; the plains of the agricultural Midwest; oil in Texas and California; gold in the Sierras, and California's year-round sunshine for the early movie industry. In a knowledge economy, where information and brain power drive innovation rather than the exploitation of these sorts of natural assets, it is being a place where talented people want to work, live and play that becomes essential. That may be an important reason why previously underdeveloped geographical and ecological settings such as the Southeast and the Far West have been able to support the growth of new economy clusters. Most have been able to combine amenities of place with research, development and entrepreneurial opportunities. Climate and lifestyle matter to the new economy in ways they did not during the great agricultural and industrial ages. People can now live and find meaningful work in environments where they can ski or surf, listen to country music or go to opera, run marathons or enjoy national sports teams, sip coffee in outdoor cafes or crawl local breweries and wine bars.

Recognizing the embedded cultural values early settlers bring

If one looks at the various cities across America and the character of their economic achievements, it is important to understand historically who the early settlers were and what sorts of values they brought to their early "place making". Agriculture based on slavery, industries built upon noneducated assembly line workers, prospectors and explorers looking for oil, gold or uranium, each represent a different kind of mentality – people with different kinds of values who often are the first to define the core character and the social norms of a given place. Grand Rapids, Michigan, was shaped by the values and skills of Dutch Reform furniture makers who migrated to the forests of Western Michigan in order to build furniture for the wealthy industrialists building great cities such as Chicago, St. Louis and Cleveland during the nineteenth century. Cities such as Denver and Phoenix and San Diego were shaped during a period of anti-industrialism in the United States and established with the migration of health seeking migrants fleeing the industrial Midwest plagued by respiratory diseases such as tuberculosis, asthma and rhinitis, all chronic diseases of the Industrial Age. The automobile industry centered in Ohio, Northern Indiana and Michigan quite deliberately hired non–English-speaking Eastern Europeans as assembly line workers. The Gold Rush benefited enormously from trade with Mexico and Latin America for agricultural and consumer products, at the same time that it relied on non–English-speaking, poor Chinese immigrants (coolies) for a wide variety of low-skill, low-paid jobs, all of which contributed to the unique forms of diversity and tolerance one sees in California today. This is an important issue because many regional economies shaped by the Agricultural or the Industrial Revolution were shaped by different demographics and evolved different kinds of business culture, a by-product of which are often more "closed" hierarchical social dynamics based on inherited wealth or large company practices. In some cities where small businesses have been at the heart of their early and developing economies, such as in the "Wild West", social institutions tend to be more open, potentially more collaborative and thus more enabling of the kinds of interactions that drive the new economy.

How citizens organize to achieve economic prosperity and growth

Building on the point just made, in many cities in the West and Southwest in particular, where there traditionally have been fewer wealthy and influential multigenerational families, the talent and connections of key local citizens and the pooled resources of multiple business organizations of necessity have been relied upon to pursue new economic opportunities. The collaborative dynamics that drove the growth of many of these sorts of communities at the turn of the last century turn out to be very hospitable to the dynamics that enable nimble, regional adaptation to contemporary changing economic opportunities, as well as the collaborative platforms essential to growing innovation ecosystems.

What resources and talents a community chooses to cultivate

Here again, economies dominated by large industrial clusters such as automobiles, appliances or mining, which stimulate management practices, and public policies supportive of an industrial economy also can create barriers to the nimbleness and change required by the new economy. Communities adept at growing "new economy" clusters differ significantly with regard to the sorts of talent strategies they've utilized to grow their economies. Agricultural workers and assembly line workers represent different skill sets than doctors and medical professionals needed in regions that initially grew based on their "health-giving" attributes. Similarly, the engineering and technical know-how that was essential to cities in America where military-focused aviation, naval and national security enterprises shaped early economic development such as San Francisco and San Diego gave rise to a context where technical talent is highly valued. In cities where you find robust ecosystems supportive of innovation and entrepreneurship, you also find a higher percentage of college grads in the population and, especially, workers with competence in science, technology, engineering and math. Valuing this kind of talent is likely built on a 100-year history of attracting high-level expertise to grow the local economy rather than attracting field laborers for agriculture or assembly line workers for industrial manufacturing.

How citizens choose to define and promote their "place" to the wider world

Different cities leverage different assets in order to attract investors and workers. These attraction strategies vary – in some places going back hundreds of years and in others merely decades. Thus, how people identify and describe a place is affected by all of the factors just identified. This is something social scientists and marketers refer to as "branding". Pittsburg, St. Louis and Detroit had powerful brands at the height of the Industrial Age. Thanks to incredible family wealth they established museums, symphony orchestras, zoological societies and botanical gardens, all of which created a notion of what a city is and should be. In other regions of the United States building on different economic histories, regional geographies and amenities of place, cities have often branded themselves differently. They tend to leverage monikers that appeal to people who value outdoor activities, clean air and natural beauty, as well as entrepreneurial opportunities and hip lifestyles, rather than venerable cultural institutions such as museums and symphony orchestras: Austin City Limits, skiing in Denver, San Diego's weather promoted as technology's perfect "climate". These efforts at promoting and sustaining a regional economy based on its amenities as well as its opportunities can shape what kinds of people and key industries become anchored there. They affect over the long haul the extent to which inventors, innovators and entrepreneurs are drawn to specific places. Older cities often end up being perceived as "stodgy", whereas newer cities can feel more "hip" and inclusive.

These regional dynamics, both cultural and social, are important because they shape to what extent an ecosystem supportive of innovation and entrepreneurship can develop. Without such an ecosystem a region is unlikely to harness the diverse assets and connected entrepreneurial teams who grow the critical mass of clustered companies, which create large numbers of high-value–added jobs and new forms of regional wealth.

The power of connected entrepreneurial teams

The importance of entrepreneurial teams composed of diverse skills and connections in contrast to the lone entrepreneur for science-based companies cannot be overstated. Entrepreneurship today is increasingly about ecosystems that enable open and fluid processes whereby resources can be developed and teams can be built, even reconstituted, as needed to increase the probabilities that a technology-based enterprise in a highly competitive global marketplace can achieve success. Individual ideas and potentially breakthrough technologies exist in abundance. However, the ability to execute in a marketplace, particularly one that is fraught with financing, marketing, legal and global positioning challenges, requires a range of competencies and connections beyond what any single individual entrepreneur is likely to possess. What it takes to commercialize and build a product, much less a business, especially one that can be globally competitive, means that many, many resources and activities are essential to success. Start-up companies that can flexibly access resources and navigate business development essentials because of access to diverse competencies and connections locally are likely to have better outcomes.

Based on my experience in a dynamic entrepreneurial ecosystem, as well as comparative research I have been funded to do over multiple decades, I have concluded there are six critical capabilities teams of "connected entrepreneurs" bring to successful companies.

Opportunity recognition

Opportunism and imagination are informed by a variety of experiences and points of view. The ability to recognize a need or articulate the promise represented by a new market, a new technology or a new solution to an old problem is not the exclusive purview of the research scientist or engineer. It can be a characteristic of inventors, marketers, IP attorneys or investors. Market intelligence is multidirectional, and connected teams are likely to be able to connect innovative ideas with a broader range of potentially valuable applications, jump on an idea quickly, assess market opportunities and develop a business strategy before others do.

Building the founding team

The ability to put together a founding team to both leverage unique but essential competencies and to synthesize the diverse forms of input that they can effectively provide also allows a start-up to quickly navigate a wide range of legal and operational issues along with fine-tuning their technology and securing financial support more rapidly. This involves enrolling team members early who can address the diverse range of issues companies inevitably face, as well as connecting with potential investors and partners where needed.

Creating a winning strategy

Teams also accelerate the ability to turn a not-well-articulated opportunity into reality, defining a strategy forward, or determining it is best to pass on a given opportunity. The ability to honestly evaluate the uniqueness of the technology, the opportunity in the marketplace and the various financing, production, marketing and distribution skills and competencies it will take to get from A to Z is greatly enhanced by teams with distinctive experiences, abilities and independent connections from which they can gather information and insight.

Inspiring confidence among investors/partners

To successfully innovate requires self-confidence and the ability to inspire and articulate needs, opportunities and outcomes in a way that enrolls not only potential investors, but also strategic partners and allies, to join with the team in taking the risk. When an enterprise can draw upon a wide range of skills such as engineering know-how, marketing and finance intelligence, legal savvy, cash flow management intelligence or innovative compensation practices, it can be buoyed by small wins while building the business even though the "big splash" is still on the horizon.

Listening to the marketplace and continuously adapting

Knowing how to listen and to many voices is important. The capacity to listen is an absolutely essential characteristic in innovative enterprises where outcomes are uncertain. It requires all members of the team to harvest disparate information from multiple places and bring it back to the enterprise to inform strategy, which is constantly being revised based on interim results and continuous feedback. This in turn can affect momentum, which often means that an initial battle plan may not survive, but new strategies and tactics are quickly incorporated thanks to continuous input on multiple fronts. Where speed to market is important, this can make an enormous difference.

Navigating setbacks while retaining momentum

The ability to deal with adversity and setbacks relates to the earlier point about confidence and the importance of a well-tuned team. When there are major setbacks, either in the quality of the technology or the results of clinical trials or early-stage marketing efforts, this adversity can be processed collectively, minimizing the chances of negative feedback and creating a lack of confidence. It can be transformed into valuable strategic input that allows the team to do a better job moving forward. Adaptive firms are more likely to succeed. Teams also allow for forward momentum, with some of the players being "up" even while others feel "down".

Conclusion: research needs to better document cultural factors and social dynamics

As a sociologist and practitioner in a dynamic innovation region, I have observed science and technology-based companies across America, Europe and increasingly Asia and Latin America. I am struck by how important teams with these six characteristics are to successful companies. However, building entrepreneurial teams is enabled/dependent on that regional ecosystem out of which the diverse pool of expertise and know-how described in the previous section can be mobilized. Without that a few entrepreneurial companies may emerge in any given community, but the critical mass of companies and services making up whole new clusters of economic activity are unlikely to be established

My journey through both the practice of entrepreneurship and my approach to research on entrepreneurship admittedly has been unconventional. This is largely because of my emergence as a young female sociologist at a time when very few women were encouraged, much less supported, to pursue "high-powered" careers. The emergence of what initially seemed like marginal professional opportunities in my early career paradoxically enabled me to be at the very center of one of the most dynamic innovation regions in the United States. My academic background allowed me to not only be an observer, but also a documenter and, increasingly, an analyst of how innovation and entrepreneurship processes work "on the ground".

In this chapter, I have attempted to identify two important themes that, based on my experience, are essential to teasing out why it is that some places rather than others are more adaptive, more nimble, more conducive to building the collaborative platforms and nurturing the social and cultural values that enable networking, knowledge flows, trust building and risk taking. Understanding ecosystems and all the component parts of those systems represents an essential first step in understanding differences in regional innovation and entrepreneurship outcomes. This ecosystem is important because knowledge-based industries developing uncertain products, processes or services for national and international markets need to draw upon a diversity of skills and competencies from day one. An ecosystem represents an aggregation of these multiple skills and competencies.

This ecosystem also represents a variety of social mechanisms and institutional platforms through which interdisciplinary and cross-functional conversations can take place and professional relationships can develop. These connections are made in a social milieu that puts an enormous amount of emphasis on relationships, especially trustworthiness and adaptability, as opposed to transactions between unknown partners. The preexisting relationships that grow out of highly networked ecosystems end up giving rise to the connected entrepreneurial teams, who in turn end up founding and growing dynamic knowledge-based companies.

This is what I have observed throughout my professional life working at the intersection of scholarship and practice. It is what I have attempted to write about in a variety of descriptive and occasionally data analytic ways. What my experience and community-anchored work suggest is that in the field of entrepreneurship there is a need for more theoretical and analytical attention to be paid to industrial history, regional amenities of place, cultural legacies and embedded social dynamics. These forces represent the assets and liabilities shaping the entrepreneurial potential of any region. They need to be clearly understood and inform strategy as cities and regions attempt to build momentum towards new entrepreneurial opportunities. They also influence the development of the collaborative, inclusive platforms, which enable the knowledge flows, relational networks and competency "bundling" one sees in entrepreneurial teams.

In a knowledge age, understanding entrepreneurship and entrepreneurial outcomes in the context of these broader contextual issues is essential. It is critical to accurately assess the key environmental factors that enable new forms of job and wealth creation. It is also essential to spend more time examining the founding teams, especially the characteristics and competencies of the team's starting and growing companies. Most companies end up having individual team members who become the "face" of the company, often the driver of its momentum. However, it would be a terrible mistake to assume that a company lives or dies on just that one individual. Again, in my experience such individuals typically are part of a well-tuned team that is helping move the ball forward by being engaged with the multiple issues that can make or break in particular technology-based entrepreneurial companies.

More research needs to be done on such teams and more case studies need to be written about successful companies such as we have witnessed in San Diego: Linkabit and Qualcomm, Life Technologies and Illumina, Hybritech and Biogen Idec, General Atomics, SAIC and Titan Industries. In each instance these companies were enabled by the connections and the complementary skills and competencies of their early founding teams. Companies such as these are emerging in the Silicon Valley, in Seattle, Chicago, Indianapolis, New York City, Atlanta and across the

Southwest. It behooves social scientists, and in particular, professors in business schools interested in entrepreneurship, to dissect through careful case studies the characteristics and dynamics of the teams that start these companies and the extent to which the environments in which they are founded and grow facilitate or inhibit their success.

In the twenty-first century when more and more nations are developing scientific and technical know-how as well as a commitment to nurturing innovation and entrepreneurships, we need to revisit conventional thinking about entrepreneurs and entrepreneurial enterprises. A central issue today is not only what it takes to create a product or a single business. Creating dynamic regional innovation systems that are continually birthing and growing new companies is a central question. The benefits of established companies are shorter lived than in the past. Companies rise and fall at accelerated rates in a knowledge economy. The Schumpeterian dynamic is alive and well in the twenty-first century. It is simply more complex. It also is faster and perhaps even more uncertain than in the Agriculture or the Industrial Age. If we are to create the sorts of products that will benefit humankind along with the kinds of companies and opportunities that will employ large numbers of individuals, we need to better understand how regional ecosystems and the dynamics of entrepreneurial teams help grow robust clusters of hundreds, even thousands, of new companies, which in turn create high-wage employment opportunities and wealth for their regions.

19

Wandering between contexts

Friederike Welter

Introduction: it's all about context!

As I sat down to reflect on my contributions to entrepreneurship research and what motivated them, I quickly realized that I needed to examine my own academic upbringing and early research activities. Looking back, my research ideas have been formed both by what I studied and by the variety of contexts to which my subsequent work has taken me. And my context ideas have also been formed by all the scholars, practitioners and policy makers from around the world I have been fortunate enough to be inspired by and to work with. Across what otherwise seems a diverse – perhaps even too diverse – list of research interests, the notion of context provides a common thread and unifying theme.

I believe it is the great variety of contexts in which I had the opportunity to work that has greatly sensitized me to the role of context in creating the differences that make both the world and good theory interesting. The great variety of contexts has also made me intolerant of "universalizing" claims that endorse the belief that entrepreneurship is the same as we move through time or across places. My work has tried to appreciate that understanding differences are important both for building both theory and policy. In the following, I will relate in more detail how the context theme started to emerge throughout my studies and early research career and how a whole array of different research streams over time have fed into my understanding and appreciation of that, how and why context matters and what to do with this insight.

How it all started

The beginnings of a SME researcher

At the universities of Wuppertal and Bochum, I studied economics and business administration, combining these with economic and social history. I also included a few other subjects on the side, such as two years studying Chinese language, culture and economy along with courses in sociology, Russian, Italian and Spanish. What I took away from these years was an appreciation for different disciplines, always with an eye to seeing what they had to offer for my own research and a desire to work beyond disciplinary boundaries. I suppose that this is also what attracted me to the entrepreneurship community later on. Add to the drive to move between disciplines my desire to move across geographic boundaries inherited from my mother's family. During my study years this took me to Ghana for a student internship and to Nigeria to collect data for my doctoral thesis and later on to most countries of the former Soviet Union and formerly social-ist Europe – and I'd say it is no surprise that context dominates as my most important research theme.

However, what may not come across clearly in some of my entrepreneurship research is that both in my heart and by my academic upbringing, I am a small business researcher. Recently, as head of the Institut für Mittelstandsforschung (IfM) Bonn, I have returned to what I see as both my passion and my calling – allowing me to feed my passion by bringing together my theo-retical interests in entrepreneurship and my practical research interests in small business. Having wandered for many years, I have now come full circle – I started my research career in a policy-oriented economic research institute, the Rheinisch-Westfälisches Institut für Wirtschaftsforsch-ung (RWI) Essen, and since 2013, I head one: I am fortunate to lead the oldest such institute in Germany that is solely focused on small business and entrepreneurship topics.

I became hooked on SME research while at university from 1983–1989. In 1984 or 1985 I attended a seminar on the "Informal Sector in Developing Countries", given by Dr. von Wedel-Parlow, which I still vividly remember, because it first triggered my lasting interest in small and medium-sized enterprises (SMEs). Until then, I had never given a thought to whether there are differences between small and large companies or why this could be interesting. I quickly learned about a whole new set of theories to explain why some firms stay small and why some of them are informal. Those explanations pointed to institutions, regulatory, and cultural differences as important influences: it was clearly impossible to understand what we observed without a deep appreciation for context!

The series of experiences I relate next showed me the importance of context over and over again. First came an internship in a small manufacturing business in Ghana (1986), followed by my *diplomarbeit* (master's thesis) on the informal sector in African countries (1987). Then, a nearly year-long internship in 1988 with the German State Company for Technical Assistance (GTZ) headquarters, which placed me in the Handicraft, SMEs, Informal Sector and Microfinancing department. Just imagine my pleasure in getting hands-on experiences in assisting SMEs! I co-designed a project for informal micro-businesses, the so-called *jua kali*, in Kenya; learned about the challenges of microfinancing, heard from consultants how difficult it is to set up functioning rotating savings associations in practice, came into touch with programmes fostering women entrepreneurs, was responsible for setting up a training-of-trainers in new venture creation and many more exciting tasks. But at the same time I came to realize that academia is too often far, far away from practice and started questioning what I had learned in school about small businesses, their characteristics and structures and their behaviour.

At the GTZ, I also had my first ever exposure to scholarly academic discussions around SMEs. This occurred one day in summer 1988 over lunch. Wolfgang Schneider-Barthold, whose research on micro-enterprises in developing countries (Schneider-Barthold 1984) had been the basis for my master thesis (and later for my doctoral dissertation), and who had just moved from a research institute to the GTZ, questioned me about my master thesis. Also, for the first time, I encountered entrepreneurship as something that seemed (though I no longer think it should be!) in contrast to small business management and SMEs. The late Rainer Kolshorn, my internship supervisor, was well known in the development community for the course on "New Business Creation" he had set up with Nepali colleagues, which at the time I joined the GTZ started to develop into a larger initiative (that still exists today as CEFE). And just as an aside, many of today's discussions around how to teach entrepreneurship at higher education institutions were already reflected in the action-oriented approach of the course: Rainer and his colleagues were far ahead of the curve.

In retrospect, I see an important pattern emerging here, which reflects both my motivation – why I do research – and also the ways I think about disseminating my results. From early on, I moved between academia and the "real world" of entrepreneurs and those supporting them. The differences in audiences sparked my ongoing interest in searching for means to best communicate research results both to scholars and to practice. To me, there is one set of "truths" I am trying to point towards, but communicating and discussing what is true differs greatly between the context of scholarly research and that of entrepreneurship practice.

Scholarly communities in Europe and beyond

My second encounter with entrepreneurship was in 1994. After my dissertation, I had left academia and, in 1993, started working in the RWI Essen. Our research group "Crafts and SMEs" received an invitation to participate in the RENT conference (Researching Entrepreneurship). For those not familiar with RENT, it started out as a small research workshop in 1987, with fifty attendees, and today is the largest entrepreneurship conference in Europe with around 200 scholars. My colleague, the head of our group, asked the newcomer to attend the conference only to hear from me: "This is an entrepreneurship conference, and I don't know what that is about. I am a small business researcher. I don't think we need to go there." In contrast, I was honoured to be invited to the Rencontre-de-St-Gall, the oldest conference on small businesses, where since 1948 approximately fifty SME researchers from all over the world meet biannually in Switzerland. This was a wonderful opportunity for me to personally meet the people whose work I knew and loved from the SME literature and a first step toward becoming a part of the German-speaking and European community of SME researchers. Needless to say, as I came to understand the close symbiotic relationship between small business and entrepreneurship research, I welcomed the opportunity to participate in RENT, and from 1999 on I have turned into a regular attendee. Over the years, these conference communities helped me to find a strong footing in the entrepreneurship field, initially in Europe, and since 2000 also in the wider international community, with my first attendance at the Babson-Kauffmann Entrepreneurship Research Conference, which is the oldest and most renowned entrepreneurship conference internationally.

Many of the most interesting European entrepreneurship scholars originally came from small business research (Blackburn and Smallbone 2008; Schmude, Welter and Heumann 2008). And many of these scholars have had a strong influence on my own thinking and research. David Storey's books on small firms helped me to gain a much deeper understanding of their behaviour and structures (Atkinson and Storey 1994; Storey 1994); David Smallbone's writings on small business survival, failure and growth and support policies were an eye-opener for me (Smallbone 1990; Smallbone, Leigh and North 1995; Smallbone and North 1995); Allan Gibb's early writings on starting small firms and on their strategic awareness (Gibb and Ritchie 1982; Gibb and Scott 1985), together with his call to rethink our research on SMEs in Central and Eastern Europe (Gibb 1993), inspired me over and over again. All three of them also helped to nurture my interest in policy issues around small firms and entrepreneurs. With the late José Veciana I shared an interest in what institutional theory could tell us about entrepreneurship and what entrepreneurship could contribute to institutional theory. He recruited me as a visiting teacher to the European Doctoral Programme (EDP) at Universidad Autonoma Barcelona (UAB), the first ever European entrepreneurship training program for doctoral students. Here I first realized the need for contextualized entrepreneurship teaching: When I began teaching in the EDP in 2002, using lots of personal examples from a non-Western context and, increasingly, from women entrepreneurs, I was surprised by how strongly this resonated with the international doctoral students. All of a sudden they could relate our teaching about entrepreneurship to their own experiences. And at one of the EDP conferences, I met Bengt Johannisson, whose great ideas on entrepreneuring in context (Johannisson 1991; Johannisson et al. 1994) I already knew from the literature – many years later, in 2009, he joined my first doctoral course on context and entrepreneurship at JIBS.

Now that I am asked by the editors of this book to reflect upon my intellectual journey, I realize that I always have been a wanderer between many different worlds – research communities, national and international contexts, research and practice, academia and policy-oriented research institutes. Looking back, I think that my moving around between these contexts – notwithstanding the challenges in having to find my place both in the German and the international research communities – has formed me as researcher. Can it come as any surprise that context became one of my major research themes and that I am currently engaged in efforts to help other scholars see how important and exciting – and perhaps ironically, how universally important – this theme can be!

Institutions matter

In the field for the first time: small business owners in Nigeria and public support

I finished my university studies in 1989 and by then found SMEs in developing countries such a fascinating topic that I wanted to conduct my own empirical study in one of the West African countries – not least because I really had loved my three-month internship in Ghana. I finally settled on Nigeria because my supervisor, the late Professor Karlernst Ringer, knew that country. Can you imagine that as an empirical researcher I completed my university education without doing a single empirical project? I did not learn how to design questionnaires, how to analyze data or how to avoid even the most common traps in empirical research. I find it hard to believe myself – but this was the situation in which I found myself when I embarked on my doctoral studies. At that time, in the universities I attended, these techniques were taught in sociology or psychology and not in economics or business administration. Moreover, doctoral studies in Germany then weren't nearly as structured and elaborated as today – I basically had no course work or further classroom training. I had only my motivation: I really wanted to get out into the field and interview informal businesses in an African country. Lucky for me, I had just won a two-year scholarship from the state government for a proposal supporting this desire. My idea was to study small business owners and their support needs in comparison to the support policies offered by the Nigerian government and/or international donors. Although my master's thesis had set the ground, that work had been limited to a review of the literature and theories and an analysis of secondary data.

When I went to Nigeria in 1991 to collect data for my doctoral dissertation, I had a mammoth task ahead of me – looking back I believe I was fortunate not to have known this upfront. I arrived with nothing but my ideas regarding the sorts of questions I wanted to study, some practical advice from senior researchers who had been to Nigeria on what to do and what not to do, and my supervisor's essential contacts to two of his former PhD students, both professors at Nigerian universities. On the Nsukka campus in Eastern Nigeria, I shared a house with two empirically well-versed agricultural economists from Katholieke Universiteit (KU) Leuven. Luckily for me, Stefaan and Peter trained me on the spot in empirical techniques: After throwing up their hands in despair about my ignorance, they provided tips on how to properly identify my respondents (I'd never heard of snowball sampling!) as well as how to do the interviews. They checked through my questionnaire, helped me learn from the initial results . . . and became good friends, as we played darts and travelled around the country. Since then, I really have cherished working in international teams because of the fun and the learning experiences cross-cultural research provides, which goes far beyond the results from the projects themselves (though my darts playing has not much improved since this time).

Anyway, I conducted fifty interviews with business owners in the informal sector in Nsukka and Port Harcourt plus almost forty expert interviews with government officials, donors and business associations and I discussed my results with researchers from SME institutes at the Universities in Ibadan and Ile-Ife. This was a good reality check (clearly informing the assumptions I use to understand and interpret the world to this day!) for my initially oversimplified explanations. I also collected statistical publications on Nigerian SMEs and those few SME studies that existed at that time (that I didn't have to pay for excess luggage on my way back was just pure luck . . .). There was much I liked about field work once I became used to rejections from potential interviewees – in particular I cherished all the stories my interviewees told me of how they dealt with problems and with the constraints of their business environment. Today I often wish I had written those down as well instead of just reporting their answers to my questions! Oftentimes, instead of the series of interviews I had planned, I spent whole days with one or two entrepreneurs and their customers – all of them curious about me, my country and why I wanted to study them (and, of course, about German soccer teams – which forewarned by my internship in Ghana, I had learnt by heart before coming to Nigeria. . .) and with me learning a lot about how the business worked by just sitting, listening and observing their interactions.

Back in Germany, I sat down to analyze my data – again, like so many in our community, self-taught on working with field data. My results confirmed, on the one hand, the existing research on SMEs in the developing world. Most of the public policies and support did not reach the small business owners, mainly due to the inefficiencies of public administrations, a lack of proper regulations and guidelines on how to disseminate donor money and many other incoherent policies at the intersection of people who wanted to help and those running small businesses. On the other hand, I was surprised by the creativity of the entrepreneurs I interviewed in finding solutions to pretty much all of the myriad constraints they faced. But, few of their "strategies" resembled the textbook strategic behaviour I had been taught in business administration, which forced me to search for adequate theoretical explanations – not that I found them at that time, I have to admit in retrospect. Looking back today, these findings clearly highlighted the role of institutions for entrepreneurs and their behaviour. And that in turn paved the way for later work in which we started to explicitly apply an institutional theory perspective in order to explain entrepreneurial behaviour in a hostile and unstable context (Welter and Smallbone 2003, 2011a, 2012), alongside others like Mike Wright and Mike Peng (Hoskisson et al. 2000; Peng 2000; Wright et al. 2007). For better or for worse, much of my own research on institutional theory in relation to entrepreneurship was much less visible, not least because David Smallbone and I initially mainly published in books, which I strongly believe should be a more important outlet than it turns out to be in our field.

The distinctiveness of entrepreneurship in a transition context

Most of my initial work from 1993 onwards was contract research for national or international organizations – and in retrospect, I am surprised to see that even here, context has been an underlying theme from the beginning. The first large-scale research project I was involved in, commissioned by the German Federal Ministry of Economics, was to analyze the emergence and development of new and small ventures in Poland, Hungary, the Czech and Slovak Republics

(Lageman et al. 1994). In 1993, little was known about SMEs and new businesses in formerly socialist countries (Acs and Audretsch 1990). I jumped onto this topic, not least because it allowed me to continue the research interest from my doctoral thesis, but in different country contexts than I originally imagined. What greater gift could I have been handed? We combined large-scale surveys in the four countries with expert interviews, documentary analysis and secondary data analysis. In other words, we did everything we could to understand both theoretically and in very local terms, what was going on. And I got to travel over these two years. During the project, I studied the development, nature and extent of entrepreneurship; I looked at the background of new entrepreneurs and found out how much of what they did today was influenced by their socialist upbringing, that and how both historical and current external conditions affected the nature and extent of small business development in these countries. My first "external" journal publication on entrepreneurs in Central Europe (Welter 1996b) stems from that project, as did my first keynote address given in English in 1994 to the OECD Expert Group on "Entrepreneurial Development in Economies in Transition" (which I was invited to join afterwards) and my first paper in English (Welter 1995) – a huge step as I had until then solely presented and published in German.

Little did I know at that time that this would be the start of my sustained research interest in entrepreneurship in transition economies, a theme that most entrepreneurship researchers in Central and Eastern Europe associate with me (and my partner in writing David Smallbone). In 2005, one particularly nice recognition for this research was the endowed professorship I was awarded by the Stockholm School of Economics (SSE) Riga. Over the next two decades I accumulated a strong track record in conducting international research projects, together with a similar strong track record in evaluating business associations and chambers of commerce, which were supported by the German government all over Central and Eastern Europe and Central Asia. Looking back at the list of countries I have worked in since 1994 only the Caucasus region and Turkmenistan are missing. And the large and deep differences in what it meant to engage in entrepreneurship in all these places I researched and worked in have made a strong and indelible impression on how I think about the world: context matters and it matters much more than most entrepreneurship scholars can see, believe or care to acknowledge.

Something else I really cherish from all my work in these countries is the close network of researchers (and friends) I can easily draw on when new research opportunities arise: in Belarus Anton Slonimski and Anna Pobol; Urve Venessar in Estonia, Elena Aculai from Moldova and Alexander Chepurenko from Russia, in the Ukraine Nina Isakova, in Uzbekistan Natalia Schakirova, plus all the junior researchers we trained in our projects, later in Latvia Arnis Sauka, my former doctoral student, and Ruta Aidis, herself a wanderer between different worlds. And not to forget, David Smallbone, who I first met in Bulgaria in 1995: Both of us were invited as keynote speakers to a conference – my first ever keynote at a scholarly international event! This was definitely a turning point for my research career: Not only was David the best mentor I could have wished for as a young postdoc researcher. He and I also had many research interests in common, and since then, we have collaborated in several research projects and writing adventures. One highlight is definitely our co-authored book on entrepreneurship and small business development in postsocialist economies (Smallbone and Welter 2009); another is our edited book on entrepreneurship policies in the same contexts (Welter and Smallbone 2011b).

What all our research that we conducted in the so-called transition economies showed sounds pretty obvious nowadays, but it wasn't so obvious in the literature then: context matters – and entrepreneurship is not the same across contexts, but is distinctive because of context. In our most-cited paper (Smallbone and Welter 2001a), which also was my first paper I presented at a RENT conference in 1999 and my first paper that underwent a review process in *Small Business*

Economics, we discussed this distinctiveness of entrepreneurship in relation to countries in different stages of transition. Interestingly enough, we already rather implicitly highlighted the importance of the historical context as reflected in the socialist heritage and its impact on entrepreneurs as well as the wider business environment. Where entrepreneurship and small businesses were part of the country's history as, for example, in Poland, or where communism allowed for experiments with private business forms as, for example, in Hungary, entrepreneurship flourished once market reforms began. Also, we identified the different strategies entrepreneurs used to deal with institutional constraints, thus adding to the typology developed by Peng (2000).

The nature of entrepreneurship and entrepreneurial behaviour under different contextual conditions became one of my major research foci. In the early 2000, the Global Entrepreneurship Monitor came up with the distinction between opportunity- and necessity-driven ventures, arguing that opportunity-driven ventures were better for economic growth. But these concepts simply did not apply to the reality of entrepreneurship in those countries I had done research in! I remember discussing this with Paul Reynolds, probably at the Babson Conference in 2003, where David Smallbone and I presented a paper in which we investigated the meaning and appropriateness of necessity and opportunity-driven entrepreneurship in early-stage transition economies – countries like Belarus, Ukraine and Russia, where market reform has been slow and institutional deficiencies make the environment for productive entrepreneurship difficult (Smallbone and Welter 2003). We argued that these concepts were overly simplistic, had limited value outside their social context and paid insufficient attention to dynamic influences, such as the learning capacity of individuals, particularly in postsocialist economies where entrepreneurs typically possess considerable human capital.

By the way, this is a paper I wish we had been able to see through to publication – it is my most cited conference paper, but never appeared in a journal. We indeed submitted a version to *Entrepreneurship Theory and Practice* and received a "high-risk R&R". Very encouraging was the editor's note that ". . . the topic is of great interest" and ". . . that you have collected some valuable data which has the potential to yield some unique insights and conceptual contributions", as it confirmed that we were right in arguing for a more complex and dynamic conceptualization. Nevertheless, we made the decision to pull the paper because at that time both of us had too many contract research projects with tight deadlines going on that simply left no room to cope with a high-risk revise and resubmit. This is definitely one of the downturns of being a researcher in an organization that relies on external funding and where pressing project deadlines and the next funding proposal to write regularly got in the way of writing papers.

Context matters

Entrepreneurs as change agents

In Nigeria, I had discovered my interest in the people behind the businesses and the impact of their contexts on how they act and why they solve business problems in a particular way. And my research in transition economies and elsewhere continued to highlight the strong link between entrepreneurial behaviour and the contexts it takes place in – in which ways entrepreneurs are bounded by institutions and in which ways they attempt to overcome institutional and spatial boundaries. Drawing on Douglass North's concept of formal and informal institutions (North 1981, 1990), David and I were able to explain entrepreneurial behaviour in a post-Soviet context as adaptation to the specific external environmental conditions, in particular to the mismatch between formal and informal institutions (Welter and Smallbone 2003): Entrepreneurs evaded inadequate laws by, for example, (partly) working informally. Where they had no access to bank credits, they used portfolio and serial entrepreneurship as well as unrelated diversification to obtain working capital or the capital required to start their business. Trust, in particular personal trust between individuals who had been through the same hardships in socialist times, played an important role in a context where regulations did not work properly: entrepreneurs relied on connections they had from socialist times as well as on extensive networking to get things done (Welter and Smallbone 2006). Thus, what may constitute, at first glance to be 'irrational' behaviour from an economist's point of view emerged as rational behaviour in the contexts we observed in Central and Eastern Europe (Welter 2005; Welter and Smallbone 2003).

One particular interesting example of entrepreneurial behaviour we observed is 'shuttle trading', with individuals exporting and importing all types of goods, often illegally. Some researchers see this as simple arbitrage (Scase 1997). However, our results from two projects on cross-border entrepreneurship in the EU and neighbouring postsocialist countries, where we conducted around 800 case studies in a total of nine countries and around twenty border regions (Smallbone and Welter 2012a; Smallbone, Welter and Xheneti 2012), confirmed our hunch that this again was a strategy made necessary by a deficient institutional environment, but without restricting individuals to simple arbitrage behaviour. Instead, our cases showed several small business owners progressing from informal shuttle trading, which provided them with financing, to more substantial businesses (Welter et al. 2014; Welter and Smallbone 2009), thus confirming the development potential of some informal ventures.

These results drove us to further develop our conceptualization of entrepreneurship in a transition context, and that brought me yet another step closer to theorizing the role of contexts in entrepreneurship. We argued for paying more attention to the interplay of institutional contexts, temporal dynamics and individual learning over time (Smallbone and Welter 2006; Welter and Smallbone 2009), with trust being an important element of these contexts, both as glue and as constraint (Höhmann and Welter 2005; Welter 2012a). Next, we suggested that informal entrepreneurship ,which recently has gained importance in the management literature, is a "missing piece in the entrepreneurship jigsaw puzzle" (Welter, Smallbone and Pobol 2015) – too much research focuses on a very small part of the entrepreneurship population (the high flyers and the growth-oriented ones), and our research has confirmed again and again that many more ventures than we want to acknowledge have development potential, however small that may be.

And we revisited our ideas on entrepreneurial behaviour in turbulent institutional contexts. For a while now, I had felt uncomfortable using institutional theory to examine and explain entrepreneurial behaviour in relation to hostile contexts because of its pretty deterministic stance (Welter and Smallbone 2011a), which can be summarized in short as "Institutions influence the entrepreneur, but the entrepreneur does not influence institutions". In fact, we had voiced such concerns already right from the beginning (Welter and Smallbone 2003), but without taking this further then. With more and more empirical evidence accumulating over the years (e.g., Aidis and Welter 2008a; Aidis and Welter 2008b; Smallbone and Welter 2009), we noticed many instances where entrepreneurs did not simply avoid institutions, but rather ingeniously used institutional holes, such as a misfit of laws with administrative practices, to create novel business models (Smallbone et al. 2010). When searching for adequate explanations from institutional theory, I came across the concept of institutional entrepreneurship, which had rapidly gained importance in the entrepreneurship literature. Here was a concept I initially thought could explain entrepreneurial action that pushed boundaries and re-created institutions, or, in other words, re-created and changed contexts. But I quickly discovered that institutional entrepreneurship did not fit what most of our interviewees were doing, because they weren't intentionally changing and re-creating institutions. We have since been talking about "institutional change agents" by which we mean individuals whose actions unintentionally may have contributed to changes in their contexts, both to the benefit of the wider economy or society and to themselves (Welter 2012b; Welter and Smallbone 2015).

Women entrepreneurship in and across different contexts

Younger researchers frequently are surprised to learn that my most important research ideas emerged out of commissioned research. That was certainly the case with the entrepreneurship-transition theme, but also with my research on women's entrepreneurship, and both strands drove me constantly towards the more general context idea. The first study on women entrepreneurs a colleague from the RWI and I conducted was commissioned by the then Ministry of Women, Youth, Family and Health of North-Rhine Westphalia (Rudolph and Welter 2000). We compiled international good practices in fostering women entrepreneurs as preparation for a large international conference in Düsseldorf in 2000 – where, by the way, I first met Sara Carter, whose writings on women entrepreneurs I had devoured (Carter and Rosa 1998; Rosa, Carter and Hamilton 1996), and I met Paul Reynolds again.

In 2000 followed the first large-scale study on women entrepreneurs in Germany, funded by the Federal Ministry of Research and Education. René Leicht, a sociologist from University of Mannheim, and I, together with a fantastic team of junior researchers, set out to map the structure of women enterprises and the factors influencing business development. We looked at the background of the entrepreneurs and the factors influencing their interest in entrepreneurship, and, not surprisingly perhaps, my task also was to describe and assess the institutional context in Germany (Leicht and Welter 2004; Welter, Lageman and Stoytcheva 2003). This was an eye-opener for me as I realized the huge impact the interplay of regulatory and normative institutions could have on women and that in an environment I thought I was familiar with! Whereas in East Germany (the former socialist part of Germany) women always had been an accepted part of the labour market, which partly explained a higher share of women entrepreneurs, in West Germany laws that until the 1970s outright forbade women to enter the labour market without their husband's permission still have an impact today, contributing to a societal image of working mothers who neglect their family responsibilities and children that only changes very slowly (Welter 2002, 2006).

With all those studies on women entrepreneurs, I achieved expert status, similar to my research on transition economies, and invitations started to pour in: keynote speaker at high-level policy conferences and at international conferences, membership of advisory boards at various institutions or – a highlight – the invitation to join the government committee selecting the best model for a national agency fostering women entrepreneurs in Germany. Quite a new experience for me at that time, but one through which I learnt much about how to communicate my results and implications to practitioners, in this case policy makers.

This research also brought me into contact with the Diana group, which in 2003 organized its first international conference on women's entrepreneurship in Stockholm – an intensive workshop with researchers from all over the world, and, of course, the Diana project founders Candy Brush, Nancy Carter, Betsy Gatewood, Patti Greene and Myra Hart. In Candy Brush and Anne de Bruin I found new international collaborators (and friends), and in 2006 and 2007 we were guest editors for the first ever special issues on women entrepreneurs in *Entrepreneurship Theory and Practice* – both introductory papers are still widely cited and used. In de Bruin, Brush and Welter (2006), we set out to explain the low interest of researchers in women's entrepreneurship, identifying three challenges: the research approach – with researchers having a pronounced tendency to assume homogeneity of the entrepreneurship population instead of recognizing its diversity and contextual differences; social perceptions about women as entrepreneurs rendering them less visible; and the then lack of incentives and institutional support in academia for those interested in studying women's entrepreneurship. In de Bruin, Brush and Welter (2007), we went a step further in discussing whether we needed a separate theory for women's entrepreneurship, concluding that we better look to broaden our existing concepts. We offered some elements of a gender-specific framework, which indeed, as we had hoped for at that time, inspired more research on women's entrepreneurship in the next years. Re-reading what we have written at that time, I recognize the influence of my own context thinking as we argued for a framework that paid attention to the "embeddedness and context-specificity of entrepreneurship" (p. 331), going on to outline the contextual elements that would need to be taken into account. More research on women's entrepreneurship followed, centring around different aspects of regulatory or normative institutions and their influence on the extent and nature of women's entrepreneurship (Achtenhagen and Welter 2011; Aidis et al. 2007; Diaz Garcia and Welter 2013).

From my research on women's entrepreneurship I see a typical pattern for my research in countries or fields, where little was known beforehand: Map the phenomenon first in order to get a grip on what's going on, often by simply describing structures and characteristics and the contexts something takes place in. Then move on to more complex research questions and discuss how your own research results can inform existing theories. For example, our project researching women's entrepreneurship in Ukraine, Moldova and Uzbekistan in 2002–2004 was one of the first large-scale research efforts focusing on women entrepreneurs in the context of formerly planned economies (Welter, Smallbone and Isakova 2006). Our findings illustrated the strong embeddedness of women in their institutional, social and spatial contexts, showing how contexts could be at the same time a constraint and an enabler for women entrepreneurs (Welter et al. 2006; Welter and Smallbone 2008, 2010). In building on our proposed framework from 2007, Candy Brush, Anne de Bruin and I pulled these insights together in a theoretical model to explain different levels of embeddedness of women's entrepreneurship (Brush, de Bruin and Welter 2009). This paper was published in the inaugural issue of a new journal devoted to gender and entrepreneurship issues and has since received wide attention – it's amongst my top four papers. And my ideas are in constant flux – Candy, Anne and I currently are refining our initial model by more strongly paying attention to my context ideas in relation to gender (Brush, de Bruin and Welter 2014; Welter, Brush and de Bruin 2014).

Contextualizing entrepreneurship research

Moving back to academia and on to Sweden

In 2002, I was appointed deputy head of our research group at the RWI Essen and at the same time I finalized my "habilitation" at the University of Lüneburg, which then was still required to qualify for a full professorship. With approval from the University of Lüneburg, I received my *venia legendi* ("permission to lecture") and acquired the status of unpaid private docent. Since 1998, I had chipped away at my *Habilitationsschrift* (the professorial thesis to prove independent scholarship) during weekends and long evenings – still a more-than-welcome break amongst the ongoing projects at the RWI and all the proposals we had to write to bring in more external funding! I revisited the results from my research projects, searching for adequate theoretical interpretations of the behaviour of entrepreneurs in their respective contexts. I further refined my institutional theory approach to entrepreneurial behaviour, but also looked into processual theories, evolutionary approaches (Aldrich 1999 – by now, I have re-read Howard's book many times from cover to cover, and each time I discover something new in relation to my research ideas) and complexity science, in particular emergence concepts, inspired by Benyamin Lichtenstein's ideas (Lichtenstein 2000a; Lichtenstein 2000b) and Ted Fuller's work (Fuller and Moran 2001). What came out of this was another book, which won an award from the Lüneburg-Wolfsburg Chamber of Commerce and Trade (Welter 2003), a nomination by the Leibniz-Society for the renowned Science Prize "Society needs Academia" of the Stifterverband – and to my big surprise, I made it onto their shortlist – and the professorship in Siegen.

In October 2004, I took over a chaired professorship for small business management at the University of Siegen. I stayed four years – busy years with lots of data input for my research! The context theme continued to dominate my research, as is reflected in two large-scale and European Union–funded projects on cross-border entrepreneurship (Smallbone, Welter and Xheneti 2012) and another European project on entrepreneurship within a regional context, which involved several regional stakeholders (Bugge et al. 2010; Welter and Kolb 2006) – quite a new experience and today business associations and policy makers in Siegen still associate me with this project. We also won a large contract to develop entrepreneurship education in the engineering and the social science departments of the university; I tested interactive approaches to teaching small business management; I built, for the first time, my own team of student assistants and doctoral researchers – and I remember a constant struggle to secure sufficient funding for their contracts.

That left me with very little time to further develop my research ideas. Looking into my electronic folders I can still identify a few conference papers from those years that never made it into journals. Together with Ted Fuller and Lorraine Warren, I worked on incorporating the emerging ideas into entrepreneurship research – but abandoned the idea after a few conference presentations (Fuller et al. 2008; Fuller, Warren and Welter 2007, 2008). And there's the unpublished conference paper with a colleague from SSE Riga, Vyacheslav Dombrovsky, in which we took a closer look at the family antecedents of entrepreneurship in a transition context based on Latvian data from a study on nascent entrepreneurs (Dombrovsky and Welter 2006).

In autumn 2008, for the first time in my life, although I always had been an avid traveller, I moved countries, joining Jönköping International Business School (JIBS) in Sweden as full professor. Per Davidsson, who I knew from the Rencontre-de-St-Gall, had lured me to JIBS. In 1998 I attended his workshop on "The Future of Entrepreneurship Research" and since 2004 I had been a visiting professor. This move gave my research much-needed new impetus. Finally, I sat down and refined my ideas on context, which had been around for such a long time that despite my plans and promises to my husband Robert to focus on research, it took the dean only a month to persuade me to join the school's management team as associate dean of research as well. JIBS definitely was a great place to be with all those visiting entrepreneurship scholars, and I had so much more time to write up my research ideas than I ever had before (and probably will have in the future).

Moving the context idea forward

By now, my context idea was definitely ripe to get out into the community. I had presented some of my thinking already in 2005, when Mike Wright invited me to the Babson Showcase Symposium "Entrepreneurship in Transition and Emerging Economies" and I talked about context and trust. Next, I wrote a review paper on "Entrepreneurship in its Context(s)" for a workshop on "Contextualising Economic Actions", organized by the German Research Foundation (DFG) together with the National Science Foundation (NSF) and held in New York in 2008. This was a highlight for me, not only because this was my first visit to the "Big Apple", but also because of the interdisciplinary set-up with psychologists, economists, sociologists and entrepreneurship researchers, all discussing a common theme. Howard Aldrich, who commented on my paper draft, strongly recommended that I should reduce my bashing of mainstream entrepreneurship, although I found it difficult to let go of the critique. From the workshop discussions, I took away many more suggestions on why context mattered, how it was tackled in different disciplines and what that could mean for entrepreneurship theories as well as for methodologies, but I also increasingly saw the challenges we would face in realizing this.

The same year, I presented my ideas in Sweden at a workshop on "The Future of Entrepreneurship", organized by Charlie Karlsson, Per Davidsson, Johan Wiklund and David Audretsch and with a great bunch of entrepreneurship scholars attending: Erkko Autio, Sara Carter, Dimo Dimov, Gerry George, Jeff McMullen, Saras Sarasvathy, Dean Shepherd. I received excellent feedback, confirming my hunch that I seemed to have something interesting to say. Yet another revision that I submitted to the special issue that resulted from the workshop – and one of the main comments from the first review round (besides that I was attempting too much) – was "Please contextualize the paper." You should have seen my face when I read that, with me thinking: "What? But the whole paper speaks about nothing else than context!" So, what happened? By now, I was so familiar with the contexts I had drawn from (transition countries), that I had left out most of the explanation of why this is distinctive and what context has to do with this distinctiveness and how that could further entrepreneurship research and theory building. The paper took a few more review rounds, which helped me to refine and develop my argumentation (thanks to the reviewers and to Per as editor!) and was finally published in early 2011 (Welter 2011).

Looking back, this has been an important paper to write – when I re-read it today, it comes across as a paper where I took stock of what I had learned from all those research projects since the early 1990s and condensed that into a few ideas how to further entrepreneurship research. Its main idea is to show why context mattered, what context is and how to contextualize. I set out by reviewing the multiplicity and intersectionality of contexts beyond the business context, which had dominated entrepreneurship research: social contexts as reflected in households, families and community; the spatial context of neighbourhoods, communities and regional cultures and, of course, the institutional contexts. In a very simple and obvious way, contextualization is about recognizing differences instead of searching for similarities. Those differences could be differences between countries and business environments, regions, ventures, individuals and their actions. In other words, a contextualized understanding of entrepreneurship questions our tendency for an "all-are-alike" approach, which is nonsense anyway (Aldrich 2009) – identical twins are alike, but ventures created at the same time in the same location are definitely not, and not least because the founders are different.

And, as a bonus, the paper also provided a justification for all the research I had done in, as someone once said to me, "weird" environments such as the rural parts of Uzbekistan or authoritarian-governed Belarus and many others – not that I needed one. But in discussions with Per as to why I included all those examples from transition economies in my context paper, I finally realized that we see something novel much better in a context we are not familiar with. In our own context we take things for granted. Culture is a very good example of that: we all follow unwritten rules guiding our behaviour, but most of us only recognize those when they move to another culture and conflicts arise.

The context article has been a well-received paper (my top 2 paper after Smallbone and Welter 2001a), although the context theme by no means was that new in the entrepreneurship field (Ucbasaran, Westhead and Wright 2001). Since then, I have discussed my context ideas at several workshops and given a few keynotes on "Contextualizing Entrepreneurship" at international conferences. Currently, David Smallbone and I are revisiting entrepreneurship research on transition economies with a context lens. We argue that the growing interest in contextualizing entrepreneurship over the past few years provides a route for transition economy research (or any "minority issue" research) to be fed into existing theories in order to extend them so that they can include a wide range of different contexts (Smallbone and Welter 2014; Smallbone, Welter and Ateljevic 2014). And Mirela Xheneti and I have started to bring together context and resourcefulness (Welter and Xheneti 2013). We illustrate how in hostile environments individuals use resourcefulness to change and influence their social, institutional and spatial contexts – thus adding theoretical insights to my previous work on entrepreneurial behaviour in unstable environments. Currently, we are studying how entrepreneurs create value in and for their contexts, for example, for their communities (Welter and Xheneti 2015).

And now? Contextualising entrepreneurship theory and policy

Context is such a huge theme. There is so much more I am interested in – and I am delighted to see that there's a conversation developing around the context idea. The same year my context paper came out, Shaker Zahra and Mike Wright published theirs (Zahra and Wright 2011). Since then there have been several more (Chalmers and Shaw 2015; van Gelderen and Masurel 2012; Watson 2013; Welter and Xheneti 2013; Zahra, Wright and Abdel-Gawad 2014) and the first special issue (Wright et al. 2014). Add to that the book Bill Gartner and I currently are editing, which focuses on developing a research agenda for entrepreneurship and context (Gartner and Welter 2016, forthcoming).

For me, my different research ideas work like a context puzzle. Over time, more and more pieces are falling into place, also as I pick up ideas from others and vice versa – I just hope that the puzzle will never be finished. One of the context ideas I am pursuing is theory development related to context and entrepreneurship. Shaker has pointed out that contextualizing research means "the effective linking of theory and research objectives and sites." (Zahra 2007: 445). This is a first step, but I believe there's more theory development required. In my experience, many of our theories have been designed based on evidence from market economies or looking at one particular group of entrepreneurs. This is exactly why such theories may fall short in explaining the same phenomenon in a different context – as in an emerging market economy or when studying micro ventures in the informal sector. So do we need a separate theory? Or can we stretch existing ones to incorporate different contexts? But exactly how do we incorporate different contexts into our theories and also into empirical research? I don't think that we need new theories, but it is important to consider the implications of different contexts for existing entrepreneurship theory. Theories of entrepreneurship need to be robust enough to accommodate the various forms of entrepreneurship that emerge in a variety of circumstances. This can be traced back to what Bill Gartner had said in 1985 (Gartner 1985): entrepreneurship is not about similarities, but about differences. It is the variations between entrepreneurs that count and that make contextualized theories a necessity – a fascinating avenue for more research!

For me, this questions whether we still need those ghettos on women entrepreneurs, minority entrepreneurs, youth entrepreneurs, senior entrepreneurs. For example, in relation to women's entrepreneurship, our special issue from 2012 clearly demonstrated that today's studies are so much richer in theory and contributing to theory building (Hughes et al. 2012) than when I started with this theme. Over the years, I have seen research on women's entrepreneurship maturing, and my own ideas on this topic also have changed. Today, I am much more interested in seeing whether and how the lessons we have acquired from studying a particular population (such as women and their businesses) can inform entrepreneurship theories and research in general. Just another jigsaw piece in my context puzzle because the underlying question is one of how we can better contextualize our existing entrepreneurship theories – something both Ted Baker, who I have met more than a decade ago at my first Babson conference in 2000, and I are currently interested in. In Baker and Welter (2015) we have started to discuss the (future) nature of entrepreneurship scholarship as scholarship that is alert to variations and differences and thus is contextualized and relevant to practitioners and policy makers.

And there's more: context is not static, but it changes over time and it has roots in history. This also interests me a lot, not least because it allows me to go back to history; and again, there's a community evolving, with business historians like Dan Wadhwani working on similar issues. Currently, Dan, David Kirsch, Geoff Jones, Bill Gartner and I have put out a call on "Historical Approaches to Entrepreneurship Research: Investigating Context, Time, and Change in Entrepreneurial Processes" (see: http://sej.strategicmanagement.net/conf-dl/sej-historical-approaches-to-entrepreneurship-research.pdf). Once that's published we hopefully know much more about the historical, temporal and processual facets of context. And here's yet another idea to follow up, namely, linking the context and the process theme (McMullen and Dimov 2013).

On a more policy-related level and linking this theoretical discussion back to my current job, I am interested in contextualizing entrepreneurship and SME policies: What does context mean for policy making? David Smallbone and I have touched upon that in some of our work on entrepreneurship and SME policies in transition economies (Smallbone and Welter 2001b, 2012b; Welter and Smallbone 2011b). My recent investigations into what constitutes the *Mittelstand* (owner-managed businesses) in Germany, which have clearly illustrated the huge diversity and heterogeneity of that segment of the economy, definitely question current policy approaches – and we just started a project to look into what more contextualized policies could mean in Germany. And I am sure there's more to come. In November 2015, Ted Baker and I convened a workshop on the "Future of Entrepreneurship (Research)" at the University of Siegen, together with Sara Carter and Bill Gartner, and the most interesting food for my context thinking came from the junior researchers attending. My "context" thinking definitely benefits from working with so many different people from very varied contexts!

Moving on: who are the makers of future entrepreneurship?

That brings me to the next generation of (context) researchers. My research journey would not be complete without a look at those junior researchers who I had the pleasure to work and co-author with. Seeing junior researchers growing up is so much fun – and for me, it is a decisive part of my identity as researcher. This all started back in 1998 and in 2001, when we won two large research grants: one came from the DFG for a project on nascent entrepreneurship in Germany – research inspired by Paul Reynolds – and another grant was from the Volkswagen Foundation for research on trust and entrepreneurship in a West-East Europe comparison. Those were my first opportunities to work with and supervise junior researchers who today are themselves established in the research world: Heiko Bergmann is project leader at the University of St. Gallen; Matthias Peistrup, student assistant in our project on nascent entrepreneurship, is professor for economics; Teemu Kautonen, with whom I share a longstanding interest in trust and its impact on entrepreneurial behaviour stemming from the Volkswagen Foundation project, now is professor at Aalto University. And Kerstin Ettl I have known and worked with for a long time: She joined my team as student assistant in 2004, wrote both her master and doctoral theses under my supervision; we worked on a few research projects together, combining some of my context ideas with her interest in gender and learning (Ettl and Welter 2010a, 2010b). Kerstin joined my team again as postdoctoral researcher once I came back to Germany in early 2013. Currently she is developing her own research ideas around entrepreneurial diversity.

So, are the makers of future entrepreneurship amongst them? For someone to be able to push entrepreneurship further, their research would add a new perspective to well-known questions, maybe allowing us to see a phenomenon in a different way, or bridging different perspectives.

The future maker's impact could also lie in questioning research questions we have taken for granted and pushing the boundaries beyond what we have known so far. There's a whole bunch of upcoming researchers whose research ideas and approach I like because of their somewhat unusual take on well-known phenomena. Amongst them are, for example, Cristina Diaz, Sameeksha Desai, Kerstin Ettl, Eva Kasperova, Steffen Korsgaard, René Mauer, Karl Wennberg, Mirela Xheneti. Plus some of the doctoral students I have met recently at JIBS, coming from Rwanda and Ethiopia, and elsewhere – all of them with very inquisitive and curious minds. Well, who among them will be the makers of future entrepreneurship? That definitely is not for me to decide, but for the future reader.

Acknowledgements

Many thanks to Ted Baker, Kerstin Ettl, and Bill Gartner for their helpful and constructive comments on an earlier version.

Note

1 When I started out as researcher in the early 1990s, the usual publication language in German academia, especially in business administration, was still German, and for me the more so as I worked in a research institute that advised German policy makers. My first publications were a working paper (my master thesis) and a book (my dissertation), both in German (Welter 1989, 1993); my first ever article, analyzing the bankruptcy laws in Central European countries was published in German in the institute's journal (Welter 1994); it earned me an unlimited work contract. My first solely authored publications in English were write-ups of keynote presentations to policy makers and to a scholarly audience (Welter 1995, 1996a). Today, English is an accepted language in German academia, thus making it easier for early career scholars because they can serve both the national and international markets with one publication. Whether the trend towards solely publishing in English is good or bad because we may lose some of the refinements in developing argumentations that we would have in our mother tongue is a difficult question! I enjoy writing in both German and English, and I have done so more or less consistently since the start of my research career.

References

Achtenhagen, L. and Welter, F. (2011) '"Surfing on the ironing board" – the representation of women's entrepreneurship in German newspapers', Entrepreneurship & Regional Development 23 (9–10): 763–786.

Acs, Z. J. and Audretsch, D. B. (1990) 'Small Firms and Entrepreneurship: A Comparison between West and East Countries', WZB Discussion Papers, Vol. FS IV 90–13. Berlin: WZB.

Aidis, R. and Welter, F. (eds.) (2008a) The cutting edge: innovation and entrepreneurship in New Europe, Cheltenham: Edward Elgar.

Aidis, R. and Welter, F. (eds.) (2008b) Innovation and entrepreneurship: successful start-ups and businesses in emerging economies, Cheltenham: Edward Elgar.

Aidis, R., Welter, F., Smallbone, D. and Isakova, N. (2007) 'Female entrepreneurship in transition economies: the case of Lithuania and Ukraine', Feminist Economics 13 (2): 157–183.

Aldrich, H. E. (1999) Organizations evolving, London: Sage.

Aldrich, H. E. (2009) 'Lost in space, out of time: why and how we should study organizations comparatively', in King, B. G., T. Felin and D. A. Whetten (eds.), Studying differences between organizations: comparative approaches to organizational research, Bingley: Emerald Group Publishing Limited, 21–44.

Atkinson, J. and Storey, D. J. (1994) Employment, the small firm and labour market, London: Routledge.

Baker, T. and Welter, F. (2015) 'Bridges to the future', in Baker, T. and F. Welter (eds.), The Routledge companion to entrepreneurship, London: Routledge, 3–17.

Blackburn, R. and Smallbone, D. (2008) 'Researching small firms and entrepreneurship in the U.K.: developments and distinctiveness', Entrepreneurship Theory and Practice 32 (2): 267–288.

Brush, C. G., de Bruin, A. and Welter, F. (2009) 'A gender-aware framework for women's entrepreneurship', International Journal of Gender and Entrepreneurship 1 (1): 8–24.

Brush, C. G., de Bruin, A. and Welter, F. (2014) 'Advancing theory development in venture creation: sign-posts for understanding gender', in Lewis, K. V., C. Henry, E. J. Gatewood and J. Watson (eds.), Women's entrepreneurship in the 21st century: an international multi-level research analysis, Cheltenham: Edward Elgar Publishing, 11–31.

Bugge, K. E., O'Gorman, B., Hill, I. and Welter, F. (2010) 'Regional sustainability, innovation and welfare through an adaptive process model', in Sarkis, J., D. V. Brust and J. J. Cordeiro (eds.), Facilitating sustainable innovation through collaboration: a multi-stakeholder perspective, New York: Springer, 77–96.

Carter, S. and Rosa, P. (1998) 'The financing of male- and female-owned businesses', Entrepreneurship & Regional Development 10 (3): 225–241.

Chalmers, D. M. and Shaw, E. (2015) 'The endogenous construction of entrepreneurial contexts: a practice-based perspective', International Small Business Journal. Online early. DOI: 10.1177/0266242615589768.

de Bruin, A., Brush, C. G. and Welter, F. (2006) 'Introduction to the special issue: towards building cumulative knowledge on women's entrepreneurship', Entrepreneurship Theory and Practice 30 (5): 585–593.

de Bruin, A., Brush, C. G. and Welter, F. (2007) 'Advancing a framework for coherent research on women's entrepreneurship', Entrepreneurship Theory and Practice 31 (3): 323–339.

Delmar, F. and Wiklund, J. (2008). 'The effect of small business managers' growth motivation on firm growth: A longitudinal study,' Entrepreneurship Theory and Practice. 32 (3): 437–457.

Diaz Garcia, C. and Welter, F. (2013) 'Gender identities and practices: interpreting women entrepreneurs' narratives', International Small Business Journal 31 (4): 384–403.

Dombrovsky, V. and Welter, F. (2006) 'The role of personal and family background in making entrepreneurs in a post-socialist environment (Summary)', Frontiers of Entrepreneurship Research 26 (6): article 8.

Ettl, K. and Welter, F. (2010a) 'Gender, context and entrepreneurial learning', International Journal of Gender and Entrepreneurship 2 (2): 108–129.

Ettl, K. and Welter, F. (2010b) 'How female entrepreneurs learn and acquire (business-relevant) knowledge', International Journal of Entrepreneurship and Small Business 10 (1): 65–82.

Fuller, T. and Moran, P. (2001) 'Small enterprises as complex adaptive systems: a methodological question?', Entrepreneurship & Regional Development 13 (1): 47–63.

Fuller, T., Warren, L., Argyle, P. and Welter, F. (2008) 'A complexity perspective on entrepreneurship: a new methodology for research in high velocity environments', paper presented at the British Academy of Management Conference, Harrogate.

Fuller, T., Warren, L. and Welter, F. (2007) 'Towards an emergence perspective on entrepreneurship', paper presented at the RENT XXI, Cardiff.

Fuller, T., Warren, L. and Welter, F. (2008) 'An emergence perspective on entrepreneurship: processes, structure and methodology', Centre for Operational Research, Management Science and Information Systems, Working Papers CORMSIS-08–02, Southampton University: School of Management.

Gartner, W. B. (1985) 'A conceptual framework for describing the phenomenon of New Venture Creation', Academy of Management Review 10 (4): 696–706.

Gartner, W. B. and Welter, F. (eds.) (2016, forthcoming) A research agenda for entrepreneurship and context, Cheltenham: Edward Elgar.

Gibb, A. A. (1993) 'Small business development in central and Eastern Europe – opportunity for a Rethink', Journal of Business Venturing 8 (6): 461–486.

Gibb, A. A. and Ritchie, J. (1982) 'Understanding the process of starting small businesses', European Small Businesses Journal 1 (1): 26–48.

Gibb, A. A. and Scott, M. (1985) 'Strategic awareness, personal commitment and the process of planning in the small business', Journal of Management Studies 22 (6): 597–631.

Höhmann, H. H. and Welter, F. (eds.) (2005) Trust and entrepreneurship: a west-east perspective, Cheltenham, UK, and Northampton, MA: Edward Elgar.

Hoskisson, R. E., Eden, L., Lau, C. M. and Wright, M. (2000) 'Strategy in emerging economies', Academy of Management Journal 43 (3): 249–267.

Hughes, K. D., Jennings, J. E., Brush, C. G., Carter, S. and Welter, F. (2012) 'Extending women's entrepreneurship research in new directions', Entrepreneurship Theory and Practice 36 (3): 429–442.

Johannisson, B. (1991) 'Unternehmertum in unterschiedlichen organisatorischen und gesellschaftlichen Kontexten', Internationales Gewerbearchiv 39 (3): 192–200.

Johannisson, B., Alexanderson, O., Nowicki, K. and Senneseth, K. (1994) 'Beyond anarchy and organization: entrepreneurs in contextual networks', Entrepreneurship & Regional Development 6 (4): 329–356.

Lageman, B., Friedrich, W., Döhrn, R., Brüstle, A., Heyl, N., Puxi, M. and Welter, F. (1994) Aufbau mittelständischer Strukturen in Polen, Ungarn, der Tschechischen Republik und der Slowakischen Republik, Untersuchungen des Rheinisch-Westfälischen Instituts für Wirtschaftsforschung, Heft 11, Essen: RWI.

Leicht, R. and Welter, F. (eds.) (2004) Gründerinnen und selbstständige Frauen: Potenziale, Strukturen und Entwicklungen in Deutschland, Karlsruhe: von Loeper.

Lichtenstein, B. B. (2000a) 'Self-organized transitions: a pattern amid the chaos of transformative change', Academy of Management Executive 14 (4): 128–141.

Lichtenstein, B. M. B. (2000b) 'Emergence as a process of self-organizing – new assumptions and insights from the study of non-linear dynamic systems', Journal of Organizational Change Management 13 (6): 526–544.

McMullen, J. S. and Dimov, D. (2013) 'Time and the entrepreneurial journey: the problems and promise of studying entrepreneurship as a process', Journal of Management Studies 50 (8): 1481–1512.

Markowska, M. Saemundsson, R. and Wiklund, J. (2010) Contextualizing business model development in Nordic rural gourmet restaurants. In Alsos, G., Carter, S., Ljunggren, E. & Welter, F. (Eds.) The Handbook of Research on Entrepreneurship in Agriculture and Rural Development. Cheltenham: Edward Elgar.

North, D. C. (1981) Structure and change in economic history, New York and London: Norton.

North, D. C. (1990) Institutions, institutional change, and economic performance, Cambridge: Cambridge University Press.

Peng, M. W. (2000) Business strategies in transition economies, Thousand Oaks, CA; London: Sage.

Rosa, P., Carter, S. and Hamilton, D. (1996) 'Gender as a determinant of small business performance: insights from a British study', Small Business Economics 8 (6): 463–478.

Rudolph, A. and Welter, F. (2000) Mehr Erfolg für Gründerinnen: wie junge Unternehmen gefördert werden – ein internationaler Vergleich, Schriften und Materialien zu Handwerk und Mittelstand, 5, Essen: RWI.

Scase, R. (1997) 'The role of small businesses in the economic transformation of Eastern Europe: real but relatively unimportant', International Small Business Journal 16: 113–121.

Schmude, J., Welter, F. and Heumann, S. (2008) 'Entrepreneurship research in Germany', Entrepreneurship Theory and Practice 32 (2): 289–311.

Schneider-Barthold, W. (1984) Industrie und Grundbedürfnisbefriedigung in Afrika: zur Förderung von Handwerk und Kleinindustrie in afrikanischen "least developed countries" am Beispiel, Obervoltas: Campus-Verlag.

Smallbone, D. (1990) 'Success and failure in new business start-ups', International Small Business Journal 8 (2): 34–47.

Smallbone, D., Leigh, R. and North, D. (1995) 'The characteristics and strategies of high growth SMEs', International Journal of Entrepreneurial Behaviour & Research 1 (3): 44–62.

Smallbone, D. and North, D. (1995) 'Targeting established SMEs: does their age matter?', International Small Business Journal 13 (3): 47–64.

Smallbone, D. and Welter, F. (2001a) 'The distinctiveness of entrepreneurship in transition economies', Small Business Economics 16 (4): 249–262.

Smallbone, D. and Welter, F. (2001b) 'The role of government in SME development in transition economies', International Small Business Journal 19 (4): 63–77.

Smallbone, D. and Welter, F. (2003) 'Entrepreneurship in transition economies: necessity or opportunity driven?', paper presented at the Babson-Kauffman Entrepreneurship Research Conference (BKERC), Babson College. http://fusionmx.babson.edu/entrep/fer/Babson2003/XXV/XXV-S8/XXV-S8.html; www.researchgate.net/publication/235966724_Entrepreneurship_in_transition_economies_Necessity_or_opportunity_driven?ev=prf_pub

Smallbone, D. and Welter, F. (2006) 'Conceptualising entrepreneurship in a transition context', International Journal of Entrepreneurship and Small Business 3 (2): 190–206.

Smallbone, D. and Welter, F. (2009) Entrepreneurship and small business development in post-socialist economies, London: Routledge.

Smallbone, D. and Welter, F. (2012a) 'Cross-border entrepreneurship', Entrepreneurship and Regional Development 24 (3–4): 95–104.

Smallbone, D. and Welter, F. (2012b) 'Entrepreneurship and institutional change in transition economies: the commonwealth of independent states, central and Eastern Europe and China compared', Entrepreneurship and Regional Development 24 (3–4): 215–233.

Smallbone, D. and Welter, F. (2014) 'Revisiting entrepreneurship in a transition context', paper presented at the RENT XXVIII, Luxembourg. www.researchgate.net/publication/273000201_REVISITING_ ENTREPRENEURSHIP_IN_A_TRANSITION_CONTEXT

Smallbone, D., Welter, F. and Ateljevic, J. (2014) 'Entrepreneurship in emerging market economies: contemporary issues and perspectives', International Small Business Journal 32 (2): 113–116.

Smallbone, D., Welter, F., Voytovich, A. and Egorov, I. (2010) 'Government and entrepreneurship in transition economies: the case of small firms in business services in Ukraine', Service Industries Journal 30 (5): 655–670.

Smallbone, D., Welter, F. and Xheneti, M. (eds.) (2012) Cross-border entrepreneurship and economic development in Europe's border regions, Cheltenham: Edward Elgar.

Storey, D. J. (1994) Understanding the small business sector, London: Routledge.

Ucbasaran, D., Westhead, P. and Wright, M. (2001) 'The focus of entrepreneurial research: contextual and process issues', Entrepreneurship Theory & Practice 25 (4): 57–80.

van Gelderen, M. and Masurel, E. (eds.) (2012) Entrepreneurship in context, Abingdon: Routledge.

Watson, T. J. (2013) 'Entrepreneurship in action: bringing together the individual, organizational and institutional dimensions of entrepreneurial action', Entrepreneurship & Regional Development 25 (5–6): 404–422.

Welter, F. (1989) Der informelle Sektor in Entwicklungsländern: dargestellt an Beispielen in Afrika, Materialien und kleine Schriften des Instituts für Entwicklungsforschung und Entwicklungspolitik, 125, Bochum: Institut für Entwicklungsforschung und Entwicklungspolitik der Ruhr-Universität Bochum.

Welter, F. (1993) Eigeninitiative im Kleingewerbe und staatliche Förderprogramme: eine empirische Untersuchung am Beispiel Nigerias, Bremer Afrika-Studien, 6, Münster: LIT Verlag.

Welter, F. (1994) 'Bedeutung des Konkursrechts im Transformationsprozeß der ostmitteleuropäischen Länder', RWI-Mitteilungen 45 (4): 325–344.

Welter, F. (1995) 'Development of small and medium enterprises and entrepreneurship promotion in the Central European Economies in Transition', in Elsässer, J., J. Brhel and M. Forst (eds.), The Role of Intermediary Organisations in Entrepreneurship Promotion. OECD Expert Group on Entrepreneurial Development in Economies in Transition. Workshop, Bratislava, 3.-4.10.1994, Bratislava: NARMSP, 20–48.

Welter, F. (1996a) 'Internal and External Actors in the Restructuring Process of Former State Enterprises: 'Helpful' or 'Harmful' Networks?', in Dimitrov, M. and K. Todorov (eds.), Industrial organisation and entrepreneurship in transition. Proceedings of International Conference, Varna–Albena, Bulgaria, June 5–8, 1995, Sofia: Informa Intellect 17–25.

Welter, F. (1996b) 'Unternehmer in Osteuropa', Berliner Debatte INITIAL (3): 100–107.

Welter, F. (2002) 'The environment for female entrepreneurship in Germany', Journal of Small Business and Enterprise Development 11 (2): 212–221.

Welter, F. (2003) Strategien, KMU und Umfeld: Handlungsmuster und Strategiegenese in kleinen und mittleren Unternehmen, RWI: Schriften, Heft 69, Berlin: Duncker und Humblot.

Welter, F. (2005) 'Entrepreneurial behaviour in differing environments', in Audretsch, D. B., H. Grimm and C. W. Wessner (eds.), Local heroes in the global village, international studies in entrepreneurship, Vol. 7, New York, NY: Springer, 93–112.

Welter, F. (2006) 'Women's entrepreneurship in Germany: progress in a still traditional environment', in Brush, C. G., N. Carter, E. J. Gatewood, P. G. Greene and M. M. Hart (eds.), Growth-oriented women entrepreneurs and their businesses, Cheltenham, UK, and Northampton MA: Edward Elgar, 128–153.

Welter, F. (2011) 'Contextualizing entrepreneurship – conceptual challenges and ways forward', Entrepreneurship Theory and Practice 35 (1): 165–184.

Welter, F. (2012a) 'All you need is trust? A critical review of the trust and entrepreneurship literature', International Small Business Journal 30 (3): 193–212.

Welter, F. (2012b) 'Breaking or making institutions? – A closer look at (institutional) change agents', paper presented at the Rencontres de St-Gall 2012 "In Search of a dynamic Equilibrium: Exploring and Managing Tensions in Entrepreneurship and SMEs", St. Gallen.

Welter, F., Brush, C. G. and de Bruin, A. (2014) 'The gendering of entrepreneurship context', Working paper 1/14, Bonn: Institut für Mittelstandsforschung Bonn.

Welter, F. and Kolb, S. (2006) How to make regions RTD success stories?: good practice models and regional RTD, Beiträge zur KMU-Forschung, Vol. 2, Siegen: PRO KMU.

Welter, F., Lageman, B. and Stoytcheva, M. (2003) Gründerinnen in Deutschland: Potenziale und institutionelles Umfeld, Untersuchungen des Rheinisch-Westfälischen Instituts für Wirtschaftsforschung, Heft 41, Essen: RWI.

Welter, F. and Smallbone, D. (2003) 'Entrepreneurship and enterprise strategies in transition economies: an institutional perspective', in Kirby, D. and A. Watson (eds.), Small firms and economic development in developed and transition economies: a reader, Aldershot: Ashgate, 95–114.

Welter, F. and Smallbone, D. (2006) 'Exploring the role of trust in entrepreneurial activity', Entrepreneurship Theory and Practice 30 (4): 465–475.

Welter, F. and Smallbone, D. (2008) 'Women's entrepreneurship from an institutional perspective: the case of Uzbekistan', International Entrepreneurship and Management Journal 4: 505–520.

Welter, F. and Smallbone, D. (2009) 'The emergence of entrepreneurial potential in transition environments: a challenge for entrepreneurship theory or a developmental perspective?', in Smallbone, D., H. Landström and D. Jones-Evans (eds.), Entrepreneurship and growth in local, regional and national economies: frontiers in European entrepreneurship research, Cheltenham, UK, and Northampton, MA: Edward Elgar, 339–353.

Welter, F. and Smallbone, D. (2010) 'The embeddedness of women's entrepreneurship in a transition context', in Brush, C. G., A. De Bruin, E. Gatewood and C. Henry (eds.), Women entrepreneurs and the global environment for growth: a research perspective, Cheltenham, UK, and Northampton, MA: Edward Elgar, 96–117.

Welter, F. and Smallbone, D. (2011a) 'Institutional perspectives on entrepreneurial behavior in challenging environments', Journal of Small Business Management 49 (1): 107–125.

Welter, F. and Smallbone, D. (eds.) (2011b) Handbook of research on entrepreneurship policies in central and eastern Europe, Cheltenham: Edward Elgar.

Welter, F. and Smallbone, D. (2012) 'Institutional perspectives on entrepreneurship', in Hjorth, D. (ed.), Organizational entrepreneurship handbook, Cheltenham: Edward Elgar, 64–78.

Welter, F. and Smallbone, D. (2015) 'Creative forces for entrepreneurship: The role of institutional change agents', Working Paper 1/15, Bonn: Institut für Mittelstandsforschung Bonn.

Welter, F., Smallbone, D. and Isakova, N. B. (eds.) (2006) Enterprising women in transition economies, Aldershot: Ashgate.

Welter, F., Smallbone, D., Mirzakhalikova, D., Schakirova, N. and Maksudova, C. (2006) 'Women entrepreneurs between tradition and modernity–the case of Uzbekistan', in Welter, F., D. Smallbone and N. Isakova (eds.), Enterprising women in transition economies, Aldershot: Ashgate, 45–66.

Welter, F., Smallbone, D. and Pobol, A. (2015) 'Entrepreneurial activity in the informal economy: a missing piece of the entrepreneurship jigsaw puzzle', Entrepreneurship & Regional Development, 27 (5-6): 292–306.

Welter, F., Smallbone, D., Slonimski, A., Linchevskaya, O., Pobol, A. and Slonimska, M. (2014) 'Enterprising families in a cross-border context: the example of Belarus', in Thai, M. T. T. and E. Turkina (eds.), Internationalization of firms from economies in transition, Cheltenham: Edward Elgar, 276–302.

Welter, F. and Xheneti, M. (2013) 'Reenacting contextual boundaries – entrepreneurial resourcefulness in challenging environments', in Corbett, A. C. and J. Katz (eds.), Entrepreneurial resourcefulness: competing with constraints, advances in entrepreneurship, firm emergence and growth, Vol. 15, Bingley: Emerald, 149–183.

Welter, F. and Xhencti, M. (2015) 'Value for whom? exploring the value of informal entrepreneurial activities in post-socialist contexts', in McElwee, G. and R. Smith (eds.), Exploring criminal and illegal enterprise: new perspectives on research, policy and practice, Bingley: Emerald, 253–275.

Wiklund J., Davidsson P., Audretsch, D. and Karlsson, C. (2011) ‚The future of entrepreneurship research,' Entrepreneurship Theory and Practice. 35 (1): 1–9.

Wiklund, J. and Shepherd, D. (2011). 'Where to from here: EO-as-experimentation, failure and distribution of outcomes,' Entrepreneurship Theory and Practice. 35 (5): 925–946.

Wiklund, J. Yu, W., Marino, L. and Tucker, R. (2016) ADHD, impulsivity and entrepreneurship,' Academy of Management 2016 Anaheim Conference. Anaheim, CA, August, 2016.

Wright, M., Chrisman, J. J., Chua, J. H. and Steier, L. P. (2014) 'Family enterprise and context', Entrepreneurship Theory and Practice 38 (6): 1247–1260.

Wright, M., Filatotchev, I., Hoskisson, R. E. and Peng, M. W. (2005) 'Strategy research in emerging economies: challenging the conventional wisdom', Journal of Management Studies 42 (1): 1–33.

Friederike Welter

Zahra, S. A. (2007) 'Contextualizing theory building in entrepreneurship research', Journal of Business Venturing 22 (3): 443–452.

Zahra, S. A. and Wright, M. (2011) 'Entrepreneurship's next act', Academy of Management Perspectives 25 (4): 67–83.

Zahra, S. A., Wright, M. and Abdel-Gawad, S. G. (2014) 'Contextualization and the advancement of entrepreneurship research', International Small Business Journal 32 (5): 479–500.

20

Re-search = me-search

Johan Wiklund

Introduction: why and how it all started

I have always advocated prospective real-time data collection instead of retrospective accounts. In part, this is because people suffer from memory decay and recall bias and have difficulties remembering events as they actually took place. The task of recounting my academic career is therefore somewhat ironic because it relies solely on my recollection. I don't keep a diary and my memory is not great. With this caveat, I will attempt to provide a summary of my academic journey, some lessons I've learned, and possible implications of my work. In writing this, I have come to realize that it is essentially impossible to understand anything about the kind of research a person conducts unless we also know something about the context in which this research arose.

The family business was an integral part of our family when I grew up. Started by my great-grandfather and operated by my mother and uncle when I grew up, it remained in the family for over a century. When I was about ten, my mother started bringing home work that the family would complete around the dining table at night. Although the actual work was tedious, working together as a family was enjoyable. Since then, I was engaged off and on in the business throughout my upbringing. While studying supply chain management for my engineering degree, I was bothered by the fact that all examples and guest speakers concerned Fortune 500 companies, although the supply chain challenges were indeed applicable to the small business context I was familiar with. After a short stint at Swedish Telecom, I ended up at a new venture, alone with the founder, consulting with small firms. This was something that felt much more familiar and meaningful.

My starting a PhD was a haphazard event and not at all planned. At the time I was not actively considering social science research. One day, my master's thesis advisor called me at work out of the blue. He had received a large grant and was starting supply chain research at the university college in Jonkoping where I lived. He needed research assistance and asked if I could help him on a part-time basis. I kindly turned down the offer. I was simply too busy with a full-time job and two little kids. My boss overheard the conversation and curiously asked about it. To my great surprise, he encouraged me to take up the offer and actively helped make it happen. Nothing came out of this project. But I got a taste for the academic world and went on to administrative work, becoming international director for the newly founded Jonkoping University and later its new International Business School (JIBS). When Per Davidsson moved there, we soon connected on a personal level. A year later, I left my administrative duties and became a full-time PhD student, working with Per on the growth of small firms. It was a wonderful time. I was researching small firms, which were largely absent from popular debate in Sweden and from the academic conversation at the time. Through my upbringing I felt that small firms were important; I felt connected to and knowledgeable about them. It also allowed me to connect with my mother. I wrote parts of the dissertation at her summer house. During our afternoon walks I would tell her about my hypotheses and findings, and she would reflect upon them based on her experience. That was a very rewarding experience. It strengthened the bond between us and also made me reflect on my research. At this time my wife once walked past me as I was working on the computer late at night. She stopped in the middle of her stride and said – "Johan, you're like a fish back in water." Surprised, I looked up, not knowing what she was talking about. When she explained that she meant that I seemed engaged in this work to an extent she had never seen before, I agreed. I knew I had found what I wanted to do. Since then, I have never looked back at my career choice.

I mention this at some length because I think it illustrates one of my strong beliefs related to academic success. I believe we do best when we engage in research that is deeply meaningful to us. That signifies all of my scholarship and is the reason for the title of this chapter. There is a common saying that we should "seek out our passions". Although I don't disagree with this notion, I believe that it runs deeper than that. Just as artists may engage in art that relates to traumas or identity crises rather than passions, I believe that scholars can engage in issues that are deeply meaningful to them without being passionate about them. The concern for and understanding of small business were engrained in me since childhood. But I wouldn't say I have been passionate about them. I even believe that my engagement in this research to some extent was a compensation because I did not take over the family business so it could be passed on to a fourth generation.

Dissertation research on the growth of firms

In my actual dissertation research (Wiklund, 1998), I surveyed over 600 small businesses through annual waves of telephone interviews and mail questionnaires. The study went on for four years; data from the first two years were included in the actual dissertation. Assisted by my advisor, I made some important insights into survey research during the study – insights that I rarely see communicated in research handbooks and the like. First, it makes a great deal of sense on many levels to conduct a telephone interview before sending out a questionnaire. For example, it ensures that you get in touch with the right person and that she or he (or the business) is actually part of the relevant sampling frame. By explaining the purpose of the study and asking relevant questions, you can actually get the respondent interested in the study, increasing the willingness to take part. You can also end the interview by asking them to fill out the questionnaire. Out of the original sample, 78% responded to the phone interview, and 75% of those also filled out the questionnaire. The second insight is that if you provide something in return, people will be much more likely to respond the next time you call them. About a year after the first interview, I sent all the participants a nice booklet with interesting findings discussed in ways that would be meaningful to managers. The response rate to the mail questionnaire I sent out shortly thereafter was an astounding 96%.

The main focus of the dissertation was on the growth of small firms. When I set out as a PhD student, I naively thought that methodological and theoretical issues had already been settled and that the possibility of making a contribution was confined to finding some new aspect of a phenomenon. I soon realized that this assumption was incorrect. As I learned more about the topic, I also confronted small and large theoretical and methodological issues. One such issue related to the dominating approach of using cross-sectional data. Although cross-sectional data pose a challenge for any causal analyses, because, by definition, a cause is supposed to precede its effect and there is no way of empirically controlling this using cross-sectional data, it poses a particular problem in the study of firm growth. Growth is a process that unfolds over time. Thus, with a cross-sectional design, the growth process ends at the time of data collection. Independent variables collected at the same time thus explain a process of the past. This is particularly bothersome when people use independent variables that may change as a result of growth, such as, e.g., any variables related to strategy. When I reviewed the literature for my dissertation some twenty years ago, the majority of studies used this approach. I decided against it and ensured to collect information about independent variables and initial size at one point of time and final size at a later time. I have noted this problem in a number of publications and have strongly advocated the use of longitudinal data in research on firm growth. I note with satisfaction that the field has moved in that direction.

During my dissertation, I also noted that growth as such was typically poorly conceptualized. What does it actually mean that a firm grows, and what assumptions do we make about this phenomenon when we study it empirically? I found that the work by Edith Penrose was very different in this regard. To me, it represented the only serious attempt to conceptualize firm growth, or at least the only successful attempt to do so. I became very inspired and influenced by Penrose's work. Like good poetry, her theory of the growth of the firm is quite ambiguous and open to different interpretations. Further, her theory is presented as a narrative and is not formalized. Although this is the case, it is possible to extract specific testable hypotheses from her work and to test them empirically. This is something which I have done. In a number of papers, I have dealt with various aspects of her theory, using my dissertation data or other data sets to test and to further develop the theory (e.g., Bradley, Wiklund & Shepherd, 2011; Locket, Wiklund & Davidsson, 2011; Nason & Wiklund, Forthcoming; Shepherd & Wiklund, 2009; Wiklund & Shepherd, 2009). In recent years, we have seen a surge of resource-based theorizing and empirical studies. Very little of this research, however, relates to Penrose's resource-based approach. I believe that it is important to also consider and develop the Penrosean branch of resource-based theorizing.

One conceptual aspect of growth that has received virtually no attention in the literature, Penrose included, is that growth does not represent one homogenous phenomenon, but several different phenomena. For example, expanding sales, employees, or assets are different processes, with different underlying motives, strategies, and outcomes. Despite this, scholars tend to interchangeably use one or the other, depending on what data they have access to. Similarly, expanding a business organically by developing new products or markets is completely different from expanding it by acquiring a major competitor, but most research tends to not separate organic from acquired growth, but lumps them together. In my research I have shown empirically that these distinctions are important and that failing to acknowledge that growth is a multifaceted concept has substantial negative consequences for our ability to understand growth and to move this research field forward. I have also proposed methodological and theoretical approaches for dealing with them (e.g., Davidsson & Wiklund, 2013; McKelvie & Wiklund, 2010; Nason & Wiklund, Forthcoming; Shepherd & Wiklund, 2009). Firm growth continues to be a topic that interests me, and I keep returning to it although several years may pass between papers (e.g., Delmar & Wiklund, 2008; Wiklund & Shepherd, 2003b). I hope that through the work I have done and continue to do, I am helping to move this important research field forward.

Entrepreneurial orientation

During my first weeks as a PhD student in 1995 – this was before everything was online – Per Davidsson pulled two big binders full of entrepreneurship papers out of his bookshelf and asked me to read them to get some insights into the field. I did. Admittedly, I found most of it relatively uninteresting and, frankly, boring. But I came across one paper that stood out head and shoulders above the rest. It was Danny Miller's (1983) "The Correlates of Entrepreneurship in Three Types of Firms". For reasons I could not articulate, the paper made a big impression on me. It just spoke to me in a way that the others didn't. At least in part, I believe I was attracted by the idea that different types of firms, small and large, in different industries, and with different types of managers could be entrepreneurial. I also liked the notion that entrepreneurship (or entrepreneurial orientation [EO] as it is commonly called today) was a matter of degree manifested in behavior related to risk taking, innovation, and proactiveness. Some firms can be very entrepreneurial and introduce novelty before others, whereas other firms are more cautious and wait to see what others do before they change. It rung true. I could see our how our family business fit that description – how my mother with great pride spoke about how we were the first in Sweden to introduce a certain new technology and how profitable it had turned out. During my time as a consultant, I have visited tons of mundane small businesses in various industries and had noticed that some of them appeared innovative and entrepreneurial in ways that others didn't, although they largely engaged in the same types of activities. As with our family business, it appeared that novelty and innovativeness often paid off.

At this time, I had also located the works of Covin and Slevin (e.g., Covin & Slevin, 1989). Whereas Miller had examined the antecedents of EO, Covin and Slevin were interested in the consequences of EO in terms of performance outcomes. In a series of papers, they provided thoughts and empirical evidence of how EO influenced performance. Among other things, they contended that the performance implications of EO varied across different types of environments. I thought that both sets of ideas were very interesting – that the level of EO could be determined by a set of factors, but that EO also had varying effects on growth and performance. On the basis of these insights, I developed a rather complex model for my dissertation research, which included EO as a mediator between a set of antecedents and outcomes in terms of growth and performance.

As a result of enjoying Miller's paper so much, I made sure to read all his papers. I was not disappointed. They were all interesting and presented novel ideas. As a bonus it turned out that several of the papers he had written included the actual measurement scales that he used to measure EO, or "entrepreneurship" as he called it in the 1983 paper, as well as other important constructs. When it was time for me to design my dissertation study, I made sure to include several of Miller's scales, in particular his measure of EO.

My first round of data collection for my dissertation took place in 1996, the same year as Lumpkin and Dess (1996) published their conceptual paper on EO. It seems that their paper set off a stream of publications into EO that continues to this day. Following my dissertation defense in 1998, I published a number of papers related to EO. Judging by citation numbers, it seems that they have influenced many others who do research in the interface of strategy and entrepreneurship. To some extent I believe this is a coincidence. For reasons beyond my control, scholars around the world started paying increased attention to this line of research at about the same time as I did. But I also hope that it is somewhat a function of the actual research presented in these papers. To some extent I believe it has to do with data quality. All my papers were based on large, carefully selected probability samples, high response rates, and longitudinal research designs, which was helpful for the validity of the findings. This was a step above what was typical at the time. Each paper also attempts to move beyond simply examining some new antecedent or outcome of EO. Some papers introduce more solid and novel theoretical framing of EO (e.g., Naldi, Nordqvist, Hellerstedt & Wiklund 2007; Perez-Luño, Wiklund & Valle, 2011; Wales, Wiklund & McKelvie, 2013; Wiklund, Patzelt & Shepherd, 2009). For example, one paper that has received particular attention frames EO within the resource-based view of the firm (Wiklund & Shepherd, 2003a). In this paper, my coauthor Dean Shepherd and I suggest that although knowledge-based resources can be valuable, rare, and inimitable, EO reflects the extent to which these resources are also organized in a way that allows the firm to reap the performance potential associated with these resources.

Other papers address unexpected and/or unexplored relationships between EO and outcomes. I believe that Wiklund and Shepherd (2003a) do that. Moreover, inspired by Danny Miller's work on configuration, in another collaboration with Dean Shepherd, I propose that studying EO as an element of a larger configuration of factors related to internal resources and the external environment provides a better understanding of the performance implications of EO (Wiklund & Shepherd, 2005). In this paper we show that EO has the largest performance implications for firms operating in impoverished environments with limited resources. This finding ran counter to much of the established logic at the time and appeared somewhat counterintuitively. However, we argued, and I still believe, that it makes sense that an entrepreneurial orientation is most important when there are few other means of competition. The saying 'necessity is the mother of invention' seems to apply.

A meta-analysis of the EO-performance relationship pinpointed the status of the field at the time, showing that the effect size of EO (and its dimensions) on performance was actually strongly positive, which showed promise for the future (Rauch, Wiklund, Lumpkin & Frese, 2009). In a version of the paper, we noted that the effect size was comparable to the effect size of sleeping pills on improved sleep. I enjoyed that comparison, but believe the editor encouraged us to take it out in the final version of the paper. Thanks to the fact that we reviewed the whole body of literature on EO, we were also able to conduct a qualitative assessment of the standing of the field. On the basis of this, we developed extensive suggestions for moving the field forward. This paper has received lots of attention. It recently received the Greif Award for being the most cited entrepreneurship papers of all published in 2009.

The longitudinal research design of my dissertation study was beneficial in terms of safeguarding against reverse causality by using a lagged dependent variable. But this research design also allowed me to lag the performance implications of EO for a longer or shorter period of time, showing that the implications of EO seemed to grow rather than shrink as I extended the lag of performance relative to EO (Wiklund, 1999).

One advantage of collecting data in Sweden is that all incorporated companies have to report their annual statements to the authorities by law. This information becomes public. Through these official registers, I was able to collect additional secondary performance data many years after the dissertation study. Importantly, these databases also include information of firms that have ceased to exist and the cause for exit. Although I had written several papers on the performance advantages of EO and conducted a meta-analysis finding very strong support for the notion that EO has positive performance implications, it had always bothered me to assume that firms taking bold risks would perform better. Theory would suggest that risk taking is associated with performance variance. If things turn out well, firms that take risks will do better than those that don't. But if things do not turn out well, they will perform worse, even to the extent that they will fail. As we had noted in our meta-analysis of EO and performance, no study took possible firm failure into account. Thus, we knew that EO was associated with higher performance among surviving firms but not how EO affected survival. With these new data I hypothesized that EO would indeed be associated with higher performance among surviving firms, which was what I found. But I also hypothesized that EO would increase the probability of bankruptcy. That was also supported by the data (Wiklund & Shepherd, 2009). This is an important empirical finding that has large implications for EO in research as well as practice – when telling an entrepreneur that the business will likely perform better if it pursues more of an entrepreneurial orientation, adding the caveat 'if it survives' is important to say the least. But it also has implications for how we think about and conceptualize EO. Rather than solely improving performance as associated with a competitive advantage, it seems that EO has an influence on performance variance. With this series of papers, I hope that I have helped move this research field forward in terms of methodological and theoretical rigor, while also opening up new avenues of research that others have later explored in greater depth.

Looking back, it seems remarkable how a single paper that I more or less stumbled across could have such a substantial impact on the work that I have done. Miller's paper triggered a series of events that unfolded in me publishing a number of papers, the most recent published almost twenty years after I first read his paper as a very fresh PhD student. More importantly, I believe that it illustrates the importance of trusting your gut feeling, even as a student who has barely entered the PhD program. Even if we can't articulate why certain papers or scholars attract our attention, I believe we benefit from taking these signals seriously. I am very happy and thankful that I did. Hopefully we are admitted to PhD programs because we have reasonably good academic acumen and somewhat of a judgment. We should apply that judgment where it really matters, namely in the kind of research we carry out. Many years later, I met Miller and then got to know him, realizing that we have many things in common, way beyond EO or other academic interests. I firmly believe that I picked up on that kinship the first time I came across his writings.

Stockholm

After graduating in 1998, a postdoc in Queensland University of Technology in Australia, and a research fellowship at JIBS, I moved on to Center for Entrepreneurship and Business Creation at Stockholm School of Economics in 2002, which was headed by Carin Holmquist. The center had received a very generous grant from H&M owner Stefan Persson. Thanks to this and the leadership of Carin, I could focus on research and supervision of PhD students with a teaching load of one course per year. Together with Frederic Delmar and four newly recruited PhD students, I started building large employer–employee matched databases. Through our contacts with international scholars, we had learned that in Sweden we had access to high-quality secondary data in a way that scholars in other countries could only dream of. Working with Statistics Sweden and three PhD students in a very laborious process, we were able to construct some high-quality panels of the entrepreneurial activities of the whole population of the science and technology labor force in Sweden, that is, everybody with a college degree in science, medicine, or engineering. Essentially, we had information on every individual and his or her labor market activities – if and when they entered and exited entrepreneurship and how successful they were as entrepreneurs. I believe that in terms of size and data quality the databases we generated were unique in the entrepreneurship field at the time. It allowed us to answer some new research questions, but also to address established research questions in a much more precise and appropriate manner. To the best of my knowledge, nobody had constructed these kinds of employer–employee data panels at the time. In that sense we were pioneers. For reasons of computer power and financial restrictions, we limited ourselves to examining the part of the labor market that we deemed most interesting, that is, the science and technology labor force. Since then, in particular in Denmark, data panels containing the whole labor force have been constructed. These databases have also been linked to several other registers, including, for example, medical records.

Given that we had these unique data and that I have made a huge time investment into building the databases, I felt as if I could potentially crank out high-quality publications for the rest of my career. On the basis of these data, I managed to generate some interesting and well-cited papers in collaboration with some great scholars (e.g., Bradley, Aldrich, Shepherd & Wiklund, 2011; Bradley, Shepherd & Wiklund, 2010; Wennberg, Wiklund, DeTienne & Cardon, 2010; Wiklund, Baker & Shepherd, 2010). Truth be told, however, I soon got tired of endless hours spent on cleaning and organizing data and running analyses and felt the lure of more exciting and interesting endeavors. Some other scholars made better use of the data and still do. Frederic and some of the PhD students initially recruited into the project have been able to publish a number of interesting papers on the basis of these data. Their interests and mind-sets are likely different from mine. That is also one of the beauties of working in academia – people are attracted to academia for a wealth of different reasons, and the academic freedom allows us to seek out the research that we find must interesting and rewarding. That contributes to diversity.

I believe that a data set in and of itself, regardless of quality, does not have sufficient appeal to me to warrant the long work hours put in for extensive periods of time that are needed to generate high-quality research output. Simply put, the generation and exploration of these large data sets did not feel deeply meaningful to me in the sense that the other research that I had been involved in. It was time to move on.

Wining and dining

In the fall of 2004, I moved back to JIBS for an entrepreneurship chair. I soon realized that being part of a large management department had severe drawbacks. At about this time, I became member of the advisory board to the Director General for the Swedish Department of Agriculture. Thanks to EU's extensive agricultural subsidies, this department handles large sums of money. They asked me to join because the EU was redirecting its funding to support rural entrepreneurial activities rather than just agriculture and believed I may have some insights. This turned out to be a very rewarding experience. Not only the Department of Agriculture, but other organizations, were interested in rural entrepreneurship. As such, through a number of different sources, I was able to raise large sums of money, including a chair, for research on rural entrepreneurship. Eventually, I had enough funding to start a research center on the topic and move myself and a group of other scholars away from the department into our own building away from campus. That independence felt great.

Since I was a child, cooking, eating, and drinking has always been among my greatest passions in life. With the newfound connections and money related to rural entrepreneurship, I realized that I could combine my passion for food with my passion for research. So I started a research project on fine dining in rural locations. The overarching idea was that these restaurants could serve as local engines of development. Within this market segment, there was a strong push for locally grown, high-quality ingredients. But Swedish farming was generally poor at serving the fine dining restaurants with these kinds of ingredients, because it was geared towards large-scale production of standardized products. It wasn't hard to convince colleagues to engage in the project, in particular because we would do case studies of these restaurants, including trying out their food. It led to a pan-Scandinavian project where I worked together with scholars in Norway, Finland, Sweden, and Iceland to collect data from these four countries. We interviewed and observed prestigious rural restaurateurs in these four countries, and also their suppliers and other collaborators, in order to get an understanding of the sense in which these restaurants were important to the local economy and local development. To date, I have not published any academic articles on the basis of the project. Not so much because of lack of trying – there have been multiple journal rejections. Output has been limited to a couple of book chapters (e.g., Markowska, Saemundsson & Wiklund, 2010) and a joint report for the Nordic Council. Despite this relative lack of academic success, I believe that the research has been important in other ways, including for rural policies in Sweden. It is also a good illustration of conducting research that is deeply meaningful. I am still engaged in related research, but now focusing on wineries rather than restaurants (e.g., Brannon & Wiklund, Forthcoming).

Working with PhD students

In January 2008 I moved to the Whitman School at Syracuse University. To a large extent, I was recruited to build a PhD program in entrepreneurship. Although the school had a PhD program on paper, there was only one student and no permanent PhD seminars. As I arrived, we admitted five new PhD students over the next two years, and I became the supervisor for all of them. I also wrote a PhD program handbook and developed and delivered three new PhD seminars in entrepreneurship. I found these tasks extremely stimulating and enjoyable.

I had started supervising PhD students almost as soon as I received my PhD, and during my time in Stockholm, I started doing so in a more extensive and systematic fashion. During this time, I came to realize that I really enjoyed it and that I had a certain talent for it. The supervision of PhD students is as much an art and a craft as it is a science. My knowledge of how to do it consisted mainly of my own experience as a PhD student. Per Davidsson was an excellent supervisor for me, and I tried to apply what I could learn from him. I also spoke at several doctoral consortia and similar activities, often under the title "Managing Your Committee". As a PhD student in management, I felt that I should take a management approach to my committee and I communicated that to the students. In articulating this approach and receiving feedback and viewpoints from the PhD students taking part in the consortia, I learned a lot that I could then plug into my supervision. I have come to realize that working with PhD students is one of the aspects of academic life that I enjoy the most. I feel that it is rewarding from a number of viewpoints. First, in a way, passing knowledge on to the next generation is the essence of the academic 'business model'. Research is a difficult task that requires lots of tacit knowledge. This knowledge is passed on through a master and apprentice system. It is most evident in the actual relationship between a professor and a PhD student, but the same system essentially applies in the peer review system or in tenure evaluations, where experienced and accomplished scholars use their judgment to assess the quality of other people's work and provide insights into how the work can be improved. I feel extremely thankful to those who came before me and helped me by passing their knowledge and experience on to me. The way of paying back is not to help them in return, but instead to help those who come after me. We are like fish that swim upstream towards the well of knowledge. We continue getting closer to the well and can learn from those that are ahead of us, but whatever we learn from them we pass on to those that are behind us. This is also the reason why I have engaged as journal editor for three journals, editorial board member of over a dozen journals, ad hoc reviewer for others, numerous evaluations for tenure and promotion, and of research applications, evaluation of doctoral dissertations, and so on. Each of these activities certainly provides some new insights and learning. But from a utilitarian viewpoint, it is not time well spent.

Further, working with PhD students allows me to widen my horizons as well as theirs. In H. C. Andersen's "The Emperor's New Clothes" it is the innocent and inexperienced child who reveals that the emperor is naked. Somewhat similarly, those who are new to a research field approach it and question assumptions in a way that those who have been in it for a long time don't because they have been socialized into certain ways of thinking. My PhD students have introduced me to using entrepreneurs' blogs for establishing real-time longitudinal data, the importance of the sharing economy, and self-determination theory as valuable in the entrepreneurship context, just to mention a few examples. The enthusiasm and vitality of those who are just starting their academic journey are also contagious and help revitalize those of us who are further down the line. PhD students graduating and building an academic career is very tangible evidence of the impact of our scholarship.

Entrepreneurship and mental health: still crazy after all these years

For the most part, the transition to the United States and Syracuse went smoothly for the whole family. However, I had reason to seek out mental health professionals, which was a new experience. As an academic, I immediately started consulting the literature on the topic. As I did, I soon came across books published on the fringes of research with titles such as *The Dyslectic Advantage*, *The ADHD Advantage*, and *Neurodiversity: Discovering the Extraordinary Gifts of Autism, ADHD, Dyslexia, and Other Brain Differences*. These books were written by people with medical and/or research degrees and seemed credible. The essence of all these books is the idea that conditions we normally consider mental disorders can actually convey certain advantages. For example, people with ADHD and dyslexia have been credited for high creativity. I found these ideas fascinating, and they resonated with my own experiences. Therefore, I confronted these books with clinical psychologists and medical doctors that I know who have extensive experiences with these mental disorders. I simply asked them if these books made any sense. They responded that based on their own personal experiences, the ideas indeed seem plausible, but there has been limited research focusing on possible advantages of mental disorders. Given the many thousands articles on all sorts of negative consequences of mental disorders generated by scholars in medicine, sociology, education, economics, neuroscience, and so on, at first, I was very surprised by this. I later understood that the very fact that they are mental disorders, as defined by the medical profession, leads to the focus on the negative consequences as opposed to possible strengths and advantages. As I read more about the disorders, I started making connections to entrepreneurship. It seemed that certain aspects of the actual psychiatric diagnosis (e.g., sensation seeking among people with ADHD) or 'side effects' like the creativity of dyslexics, could be advantageous in entrepreneurship. As I conducted more systematic searches, looking for research connecting mental disorders to entrepreneurship, I found that there were very few papers. Probably less than a handful. Was there a good reason for this? Maybe it is simply not a very interesting or promising line of research. As I thought more about it, I became more and more convinced that research on the link between entrepreneurship and mental disorders would meet several of the criteria that makes research interesting to me. First, I have a personal relationship to the topic. From firsthand experience, I can see that what we usually regard as deficits associated with mental disorders can actually be strengths in the appropriate contexts. Second, the topic itself and theorizing around it runs counter to the received wisdom in mental health research. In his famous article "That's Interesting", Murray Davis (1971: 309) notes that it is the counterintuitive that is interesting "Question: How do theories that are generally considered interesting differ from theories that are generally considered non-interesting? Answer: Interesting theories deny certain assumptions of their audience, while non-interesting theories affirm certain assumptions of their audience." I certainly agree with this statement. For example, there is absolutely nothing wrong in hypothesizing and showing that people with more work experience perform better as entrepreneurs, or that those who have stronger confidence in their own entrepreneurial abilities are more likely to form entrepreneurial intentions. It just isn't that exciting or interesting. It seems far more exciting to explore if certain aspects of mental disorders could be positively associated with entrepreneurship and its outcomes.

Third, this research could have extensive real-world implications. The negative personal, social, and economic implications of mental health problems are very far reaching. Research that focuses on strengths and possibilities as opposed to deficits and problems has the potential of changing the conversation and providing productive avenues for people who suffer. It is certainly possible to do meaningful and impactful research in other areas. For example, I have done and continue to do research on university spinoffs and incubators and have also engaged with policy makers regarding these and other issues. Although such research can be potentially influential, it certainly does not have the same potential at the individual level. People who start university spinoffs or start their businesses in incubators usually belong to the more fortunate in life. In my encounters with entrepreneurs diagnosed with mental disorders, it is clear that they immediately connect with the essential message and are genuinely thankful that I carry out this research. That is greatly and immediately rewarding in a way than none of my previous research has been.

Fourth, it is a new and novel research field. Only a small group of scholars is starting to get interested in this line of research. When a research field is new, there is greater opportunity to make a substantial contribution. There are also fewer established rules and standards, which makes it feasible to seek out new research questions, research designs, and theoretical approaches, something which I find very stimulating.

One of the challenges in carrying out this research has been the access to relevant data. Information about mental health is sensitive and private. Mental health is also highly stigmatized. I have conducted research on entrepreneurial failure, which is also stigmatized. Apart from entrepreneurs who had later become widely successful, people were generally unwilling to share information about their failures. The same applies to mental health, but it is even rarer that entrepreneurs share their experiences with mental health. There are few entrepreneurs outside of superstars such as Richard Branson or David Neeleman who openly speak about their diagnoses.

I had previously worked with data combined from public Swedish records and thought it may provide a way forward. Linking such data to mental health records is a different matter and not something that is typically done. Epidemiologists at Swedish Karolinska Institutet (KI) had amazing data on people with mental diagnoses, their medications, and other details. Linking this to labor market data would be easy. The main obstacle would be receiving the permissions to generate the databases and the funding to pay for them. After over a year of fruitless attempts to establish contacts at KI and Swedish authorities, I realized that this would not be a productive avenue. At the same time, I contacted support organizations and clinical psychologists around Syracuse in order to get in touch with practicing entrepreneurs with mental disorders that I could interview. Again, nothing came out of it. I then contacted and met with support organizations in Sweden. Primarily through becoming a member of and posting messages on the Facebook page of Swedish support organizations, I was able to get in touch with and interview around twenty practicing entrepreneurs who also had a formal diagnosis of ADHD, autism, or dyslexia (Wiklund, Patzelt & Dimov, 2014).

Looking back, I am very happy that I started with this kind of research. In my earlier research on firm growth and EO, I think I had a relatively good understanding of the phenomena I was interested in through my family background and consulting experience. Thus, I don't think that interviews or case studies were necessary to reach fundamental understanding. This research was different. I did not know how mental health symptoms would pan out in entrepreneurship, and neither did other scholars. The case studies gave me broad insights into and intuitive understanding of how mental health symptoms and entrepreneurship can be entwined. As I have said throughout this chapter, I strongly believe that we should conduct research that is deeply meaningful to us. One advantage is that it means that we have some fundamental insights into the phenomena that we study. I am therefore baffled by the large number of scholars that I encounter, in particular PhD students, who have had little or no personal encounters with the phenomena that they study. I find it worrying because I think it severely reduces their ability to make sense of the results. How will they be able to tell the interesting findings from nonsensical correlations if they lack the fundamental understanding of the phenomena they study? As an editor and reviewer, it seems I come across several papers that completely misinterpret findings or present utterly meaningless results.

The case studies made me realize that ADHD was potentially the most interesting mental diagnosis to study. Being a neurodevelopment disorder, it is pervasive. It is also very common, and the number of diagnoses is increasing worldwide. Today, no less than 11% of all American children have a formal ADHD diagnosis. Most importantly in this context, however, it seems that the actual symptoms of the condition are directly associated with entrepreneurial behavior. In particular, it seems that impulsivity manifested in risk taking, innovativeness, and proactiveness within their businesses (see Wiklund et al., 2014). Put simply, it seems that impulsivity drives EO. Much more research is needed to establish if this is the case. However, if it is, with the knowledge we have about EO and performance, it would provide for an important mechanism related to how ADHD potentially translates into positive entrepreneurial outcomes. Being able to establish such a mechanism can potentially have vast implications for research on entrepreneurship in mental health (see also Wiklund, Yu, Tucker & Marino, 2016). It would also be an interesting and surprising way of tying together two streams of research that caught my interest for completely different reasons. I guess that it is a consequence of conducting research that I find deeply meaningful. We only have a limited repertoire of issues that we find truly interesting, and these things tend to remain relatively stable over time.

At the current time, I am involved in several data collection efforts related to ADHD and entrepreneurship, examining entrepreneurial intentions among entrepreneurs, as well as behavior among practicing entrepreneurs. I am also working on other papers related to mental health and entrepreneurship while also trying to get more people onboard this interesting and exciting line of research by organizing workshops at international conferences and organizing special issues dedicated to the topic in our leading academic journals.

In closing

The title of this chapter is Re-search = Me-search. I hope I have been able to explain what I mean by that title. I also hope that I have made it plausible that conducting research that we find deeply meaningful at a personal level has many advantages in terms of keeping us motivated and having a fundamental understanding and interest in the phenomena that we study. I also think that if we are lucky, we can realize something about ourselves in the process. We become academics for our own personal and very idiosyncratic reasons. The academic freedom allows us to explore those personal interests and idiosyncrasies on ways that is impossible in most other professions. That is a blessing of our profession.

What I have described here comes across as a straightforward and deliberate process. Of course, it has been much more random and haphazard than this. For example, the possibility to work with people I like has guided some of the projects that I have engaged in. Through lucky circumstances or particular opportunities, I have become involved in other projects or papers. I do believe, however, that the way I have approached these projects, the things that I have found interesting about the phenomena studied, and the way I have written these papers reflect who I am and what I find important.

Over the years, I have encountered several texts with the mission of how we conduct entrepreneurship research and/or increasing the academic legitimacy of the field. I believe I have written some such texts myself. A relatively recent trend has been the call for doing more theory-driven rather than phenomenon-driven research (e.g., Wiklund, Davidsson, Audretsch & Karlsson, 2011). There is certainly nothing wrong with such recommendations. We can set out to do our research on the basis of theories we like, methods we believe are interesting and promising, or phenomena that seem relevant and important. Alternatively, as I advocate here, we can start by asking who we are and what is important to us. If we do, I believe that we can come up with important research that will keep us going for a long, long time!

References

Bradley, S., Aldrich, H., Shepherd, D., & Wiklund, J. (2011). Resources, environmental change, and survival: Asymmetric paths of young independent and subsidiary organizations. Strategic Management Journal, 32(5): 486–509.

Bradley, S., Shepherd, D., & Wiklund, J. (2010). The importance of slack for new organizations facing "tough" environments. Journal of Management Studies, 48(5): 1071–1097.

Bradley, S., Wiklund, J., & Shepherd, D. (2011). Swinging a double-edged sword: The effect of slack on entrepreneurial management and growth. Journal of Business Venturing, 26(5): 537–554.

Brannon, D.L. & Wiklund, J. (forthcoming). An analysis of business models: Firm characteristics, innovation and performance. Academy of Entrepreneurship Journal.

Covin, J. G. & Slevin, D. P. (1989). Strategic management of small firms in hostile and benign environments. Strategic Management Journal, 10(1): 75–87.

Davidsson, P. & Wiklund, J. (2013). New Perspectives on Firm Growth. Cheltenham, UK: Edward Elgar Publishing.

Davis, M. S. (1971). That's interesting: Towards a phenomenology of sociology and a sociology of phenomenology. Philosophy of the Social Sciences, 1(4): 309.

Locket, A., Wiklund, J., Davidsson, P., & Girma, S. (2011). Organic and acquisitive growth: Re-examining, testing and extending Penrose's growth theory. Journal of Management Studies, 48(1): 48–74.

Lumpkin, G. T. & Dess, G. G. (1996). Clarifying the entrepreneurial orientation construct and linking it to performance. Academy of Management Review, 21(1): 135–172.

McKelvie, A. & Wiklund, J. (2010). Advancing firm growth research: A focus on growth mode instead of growth rate. Entrepreneurship Theory and Practice, 34: 261–288.

Miller, D. (1983). The correlates of entrepreneurship in three types of firms. Management Science, 29(7): 770–791.

Naldi, L., Nordqvist, M., Hellerstedt, K., & Wiklund, J. (2007). Entrepreneurial orientation, risk taking, and performance in family firms. Family Business Review, 20(1): 33–47.

Nason, R. & Wiklund, J. (forthcoming). An assessment of resource-based theorizing on firm growth and suggestions for the future. Journal of Management.

Perez-Luño, A., Wiklund, J., & Valle, R. (2011). The dual nature of innovative activity: How entrepreneurial orientation influences innovation generation and adoption. Journal of Business Venturing, 26(5): 555–571.

Rauch, A., Wiklund, J., Lumpkin, T., & Frese, M. (2009). Entrepreneurial orientation and business performance: Cumulative empirical evidence. Entrepreneurship Theory and Practice, 33(3): 761–787.

Shepherd, D. A. & Wiklund, J. (2009). Are we comparing apples with apples or apples with oranges? Appropriateness of knowledge accumulation across growth studies. Entrepreneurship Theory and Practice, 33(1): 105–123.

Wales, W., Wiklund, J., & McKelvie, A. (2013). What about new entry? Examining the theorized role of new entry in the entrepreneurial orientation–performance relationship. International Small Business Journal, 33(4): 351–373.

Wennberg, K., Wiklund, J., DeTienne, D., & Cardon, M. (2010). Reconceptualizing entrepreneurial exit: Divergent exit routes and their drivers. Journal of Business Venturing, 25: 361–375.

Wiklund, J. (1998). Small Firm Growth and Performance: Entrepreneurship and Beyond. Doctoral dissertation. Jönköping: Jönköping International Business School.

Wiklund, J. (1999). The sustainability of the entrepreneurial orientation performance relationship. Entrepreneurship Theory and Practice, 24(1): 37–48.

Wiklund, J., Baker, T., & Shepherd, D. A. (2010). The age effect of financial indicators as buffers against the liability of newness. Journal of Business Venturing, 25: 423–437.

Wiklund, J., Patzelt, H., & Dimov, D. (2014). Entrepreneurship and Psychological Disorders. Babson College Entrepreneurship Research Conference, London, ON, Canada. June 2014.

Wiklund, J., Patzelt, H., & Shepherd, D. A. (2009). Building an integrative model of small business growth. Small Business Economics, 32: 351–374.

Wiklund, J. & Shepherd D. A. (2003a). Knowledge-based resources, entrepreneurial orientation, and the performance of small and medium-sized businesses. Strategic Management Journal, 24(13): 1307–1314.

Wiklund, J. & Shepherd, D. A. (2003b). Aspiring for and achieving growth: The moderating role of resources and opportunities. Journal of Management Studies, 40(8): 1919–1941.

Wiklund, J. & Shepherd, D. A. (2005). Entrepreneurial orientation and small firm performance: A configurational approach. Journal of Business Venturing, 20(1): 71–79.

Wiklund, J. & Shepherd, D. A. (2009). The effectiveness of alliances and acquisitions: The role of resources combination activities. Entrepreneurship Theory and Practice, 33(1): 193–212.

Wiklund, J. & Shepherd, D. A. (2011). Where to from here: EO-as-experimentation, failure and distribution of outcomes. Entrepreneurship Theory and Practice, 35(5): 925–946.

21

The conquest of interestingness
Entrepreneurial ownership mobility

Mike Wright

Introduction

> "Mike, if you want to continue looking at management buyouts, go ahead, but you're wasting your academic career".

Such was the advice of my soon to be head of the department after we co-organized the first conference on management buyouts in 1981. Some thirty-four years, several millions dollars of research funds and many journal papers and books later, I'm still wasting my career on this topic. While still including management buyouts, my work has evolved to embrace a wider agenda involving different forms of entrepreneurship. Although there is an old strand of the literature that sees residual ownership as a central part of entrepreneurship (e.g., Hawley, 1907), little of the mainstream recent literature seemed to recognize this, and even less was concerned with changes in ownership, or what I shall refer to as entrepreneurial ownership mobility. I illustrate my contribution with reference to several papers that cover the development and scope of my research. I have provided elsewhere some suggestions for sustaining a publications career (Wright and Sharma, 2013; Wright et al., 2016).

My back pages

My road to entrepreneurship was a circuitous one involving a number of seemingly unconnected byways. I subsequently connected many of these byways in ways that at the outset I did not envision.

Following an undergraduate degree in economics, which also included a number of accounting and finance courses, I was employed for almost three years doing market research for a regional, at the time state-owned, gas corporation. I say employed by rather than worked for because not a great deal of work was done. This was the mid-1970s when state-owned enterprises were overmanned and highly inefficient. In 1976 I left to take up a two-year research assistant post at Durham University working on a project on the impact of competition (antitrust) policy on cartels under the wonderful supervision of Denis O'Brien, an expert on cartels and also the greatest living historian of economic thought. This provided me with a great research training experience, not the least of which involved traveling to distant parts of the country in the depths of winter to hand-collect accounting data from obscure little trawler companies and the like whose historical accounts going back some twenty-odd years were not otherwise available. The results of the project were published in a book (O'Brien et al., 1979).

In parallel, I undertook to earn a master's degree. Fortunately, it was possible to do a two-year part-time MA by thesis, which made it feasible alongside the demands of the cartels project. Building on my experience of the gas industry, which had kindled in me an interest in the challenges of achieving efficiency in state-owned enterprises, I focused my thesis on developing new ways of measuring efficiency. This was that far-off time of rampant inflation and equally rampant debate about how to adjust accounts to reflect the effects of inflation. Accordingly, my thesis was on inflation accounting and measuring efficiency in state-owned enterprises, with particular reference to the gas industry, and resulted in two journal articles (Wright, 1979, 1980). I gained some interesting insights by talking to the corporation's finance director rather than simply going through the accounts, not least of which was that this multibillion-dollar corporation, which was a pioneer in inflation-adjusted accounts, did not have a complete asset register.

By the time I left Durham to take up a lectureship (assistant professor) in industrial economics and accounting at Nottingham University, I had begun two research trajectories that were seemingly unrelated.

Maggie's farm

The Industrial Economics Department at Nottingham, which subsequently metamorphosed into the Business School, had a particularly interesting and refreshing ethos. Not only were colleagues publishing in top academic journals, they were also interacting with practice and policy.

It also was a great environment for 'water-cooler' conversations, one of which with Brian Chiplin led to some initial work on corporate parent-to-parent divestments (Chiplin and Wright, 1980) because we saw it as an interesting nonsymmetrical decision and counterpart to corporate acquisition activity. Although it eventually led to some journal articles (Thompson and Wright, 1986; Wright and Thompson, 1987) and merger policy–related publications (Chiplin and Wright, 1987), this work proved to be the precursor to the management buyout work. In thinking about how we might take the divestment work further and raise some research funding, we visited the local office of the private equity firm 3i (then ICFC). Talking to them it became clear that they were beginning to be actively involved in deals where incumbent managers, rather than other corporations, were acquiring divested divisions and subsidiaries. Initially, the term management buyout was not used, but we did decide to jointly hold what was to be the first conference on management buyouts, with the help of Ron Arnfield then the university's Industrial and Business Liaison officer. This took place in March 1981. Because this was in the depths of the 'Thatcher Recession', much of the focus was on management buyouts as a way to save firms from closure and how to handle employment and industrial relations issues, although one case study presented did involve a growth-oriented service business in the oil sector (Arnfield et al., 1981). Although over 120 delegates participated in the conference, many listed themselves along the lines of 'Donald Duck' and 'Mickey Mouse' because they were afraid of being summarily fired if their employers found out.

It was after this conference that Brian Chiplin gave me the advice in the quotation at the start of this chapter. His view was that the management buyout (MBO) was a nine-day wonder that would disappear as soon as the recession was over. I was faced with a situation of entrepreneurial uncertainty regarding information about what was going to happen to MBO activity and career advice not to go there. Weighing against this, I had now passed through probation and had a permanent position, but promotion seemed a very distant and slim prospect. This was also a time before the UK's five-year Research Assessment Exercise/Research Excellence Framework was in place. I also had been developing some further work on efficiency audits in state-owned firms and newer work on management control systems. So the downside risk was small. More importantly, the MBO phenomenon seemed to me to be a fascinating one, but it took some time to recognize the scope of the entrepreneurial research opportunity and to connect it to debates in the literature. Discussions with another colleague, John Coyne, led to us obtaining a very small grant from the ESRC (then SSRC) to conduct a systematic survey of the effects of management buyouts, which eventually led to the first book in the area (Wright and Coyne, 1985) and articles principally on effects on employee relations (Wright et al., 1984), vertical disintegration, and changes to the make-buy decision (Wright, 1986) and deconglomerization (Thompson and Wright, 1987). A substantial portion of this work was combined to form my PhD dissertation.[1]

Meanwhile following the conference and the extensive press coverage it received, I was being contacted quite regularly by the *Financial Times* for data on the extent of management buyout activity. Although this press coverage had no direct pay-off career-wise,[2] it did turn out to have a very important effect in that it brought us to the attention of the PR agent for what was then Spicer and Pegler, an accountancy firm now part of Deloitte. Following a lunch meeting to discuss possible projects that they might support, it was decided to create a center to monitor trends in management buyouts. Eighteen months later in March 1986, the Center for Management Buyout Research (CMBOR) was born, with what is now Equistone Partners Europe (previously the private equity arm of Barclays Bank) coming on board as the second funder and remaining a sponsor for the next thirty years (so much for the short termism of private equity). Besides developing a database that now stands at over 30,000 deals over a period stretching back to the 1970s, CMBOR undertook regular surveys of enterprises that had gone through a management buyout.[3]

Much of the early debate, especially in the United States, was dominated by the hypothesis that leveraged buyouts (LBOs) of listed corporations took place in order to resolve agency cost problems that were due to managers in large corporations holding little, if any, equity not being adequately monitored (Jensen, 1986).

From my work in the United Kingdom dating from the beginning of the 1980s I struggled to reconcile this view with what I was seeing on the ground. In many detailed interviews with managers, I was struck by the frequency with which they were saying that they had identified opportunities for new markets and products but were prevented from pursuing these opportunities by the prevailing ownership and governance regime in which they found themselves (Wright and Coyne, 1985). This perception was reinforced in some later work on product development following buyout (Wright et al., 1992) and on the longevity of management buyouts, where case studies again demonstrated that those deals that subsequently were sold or came to IPO engaged in significant entrepreneurial activities (Wright et al., 1984, 1995).[4]

These observations prompted me to try to develop a paper that critiqued the agency perspective and advanced an alternative entrepreneurial perspective (Wright et al., 2000). Those readers wondering how long it might take to get a theory paper published look away now because I was about to embark on a seven-year journey.

I set out some initial thoughts around 1993 in a 'mud draft'. At one point I thought about framing it around a US vs. European perspective because some of the differences seemed to emanate from different deal types in the two continents. However, I put it to one side because I couldn't immediately see a way forward with a red thread of a story line. The paper languished for some time until I mentioned the idea to Bob Hoskisson, who was visiting Nottingham to give a paper. Bob thought that there was a germ of an idea here and that we should try to develop it.

Subsequently, in early 1997 I visited with Bob, at that time at Texas A&M, to work on developing the paper. While there, Bob introduced Jay Dial, who was also working on LBOs. After many iterations, we finally had a draft long after I had departed from College Station. We submitted this paper to *Journal of Management* as a review article and received a major revise and resubmit. By this time Bob had moved to Oklahoma, so in the late fall of 1998 I went over to work on it with him. Discussing how we might address the reviewers' comments we decided that there was something more here than a review piece. We decided to withdraw it from *Journal of Management* with a view to developing a theory paper for AMR. We duly repositioned it, again after many iterations, as a theory article on an entrepreneurship view of buyouts. We received a risky revise and resubmit and duly spent a lot of time revising it, but the paper was rejected. Key problems we were facing were (1) that we came up against reviewers with strong agency perspectives who did not like the entrepreneurial perspective as an alternative to the agency view and (2) we didn't really have a strong conceptually framing of the entrepreneurial perspective.

We continued to work on the paper and noticed that AMR announced a special issue call on privatization and entrepreneurship. This was interesting because I had been doing a lot of work on the role of management buyouts and privatization in the United Kingdom (Thompson et al., 1990; Wright et al., 1993), Austria (Wright et al., 1997), and Central and Eastern Europe (Karsai and Wright, 1994; Wright et al., 1994). We thought that this might offer an opportunity to take the paper forward if we repositioned it. After checking with the special issue editors that they would be open to a substantially reworked paper, given that it had previously been rejected by the regular AMR process, we submitted the paper. Again, we received a risky R&R, and again the problems were agency reviewers and lack of a clear entrepreneurial conceptual framework. At this point, we brought Lowell Busenitz on board, who was a colleague of Bob's at Oklahoma and who worked on cognitive aspects of entrepreneurial behavior. At last, we had identified an alternative conceptual framework. But in reworking the paper, reflecting my earlier comments, we built it on the heterogeneity of buyout types and contexts. This enabled us to treat agency and cognitive perspectives as complementary explanations of different types of buyouts and managerial behavior. This did the trick, and the paper was subsequently accepted and appeared in the special issue published in June 2000. Subsequently, I have used the framework developed in the paper to frame in MBA and MSc class discussion of cases of different types of buyouts.

Subsequent work on MBOs partly focused on exploring the efficiency buyout quadrant in the paper by examining productivity effects, linking back to my long-standing interest in enterprise efficiency, but also stimulated by the arrival of Don Siegel as a colleague in Nottingham who had done work on LBO productivity in the United States. The result of this collaboration was Harris et al. (2005). Subsequent work involved attempts to explore the quadrant concerned more with entrepreneurial aspects of buyouts, involving growth and the role of private equity firms (Meuleman et al., 2009; Wervaal et al., 2013).

Sustaining the research agenda on management buyouts also required being alert to changes that were taking place in the market. Hence, research evolved from exploring MBOs of divisions to include the taking private of listed corporations, MBOs involving distressed firms and management buy-ins. The second wave of buyouts from 2005 to 2008 drew considerable media and policy critique of the role of private equity firm funding these deals. Having built a comprehensive database covering the full range of private equity–backed buyouts, it was feasible with a group of collaborators, notably Kevin Amess, Nick Bacon, Hans Bruining, Miguel Meuleman, Don Siegel and Nick Wilson, to provide systematic evidence that pointed to the positive aspects regarding on employment (Amess and Wright, 2007); employee relations (Bacon et al., 2012); longevity, distress and failure (Wilson and Wright, 2014); and growth and financial performance (Meuleman et al., 2009; Wilson et al., 2012) as well as being able to provide a more fine-grained analysis of the heterogeneity of the market in terms of deal types and funders. This evidence was able to influence the parliamentary and media debate, which had been largely based on unrepresentative anecdotal examples of small numbers of large deals. The evident woeful lack of knowledge among commentators and policy makers about private equity, the deliberations of the UK Treasury Select Committee being a case in point, led to a collaboration with a former MBA student of mine, John Gilligan, to produce an accessible guide. The book, now in its third edition and published by the Institute of Chartered Accountants in England and Wales (ICAEW), brought together a practitioner's ability to explain the private equity process with an overview of the academic evidence (Gilligan and Wright, 2014).

In the postfinancial crash period, research opportunities have emerged that involve examining the relative financial performance and survival of private equity–backed buyouts during and after the crash. But also, as the market has evolved and new primary deals become more difficult to find, attention focuses on the impact of secondary buyouts. Buyouts of family firms have always been an important part of the market, but have generally not attracted the same level of attention as divisional and public to private buyouts, perhaps because the agency issues involved have not been seen as important as those in other forms of buyout. Yet, there are agency issues in buyouts of family firms, and this is a promising area for further research to explore the implications for entrepreneurship, innovation and survival of family firms that undertake the ownership mobility involved in a buyout as a form of succession route (Howorth et al., 2004; Scholes et al., 2007).[5]

As the scope for returns due to efficiency improvements alone has become more challenging in buyouts, my attention is shifting to examine further the entrepreneurial activities of buyouts, notably with respect to innovation through patenting (Amess et al., 2015). Combined with the entry of cross-border private equity firms, attention to the entrepreneurial aspects of buyouts also needs to explore their internationalization activities. Finally, although much of the recent debate about the social effects of private equity has been shown to be misplaced, it has rekindled a need for research on ethical and corporate social responsibility (CSR) dimensions.

Fourth time around

Much of the early literature on entrepreneurship focused heavily on new venture start-ups and seemed to assume, at least implicitly, that entrepreneurs only ever undertook one entrepreneurial act. My work on habitual entrepreneurs sought to explore entrepreneurial ownership mobility in terms of entrepreneurs who create multiple ventures, either moving to the next one having exited the previous one (serial entrepreneurs) or owning them concurrently (portfolio entrepreneurs).

My initial work on serial entrepreneurs was sparked by a side comment at a meeting of the sponsors of CMBOR about entrepreneurs who were being refunded to do further deals, especially management buy-ins (Robbie and Wright, 1996) and the challenges faced by these entrepreneurs in obtaining venture capital finance.[6] This was becoming a pertinent issue in practice because of the increase in exits from VC-backed firms as matured, creating a pool of entrepreneurs with the potential for reinvestment and for researchers because of potential insights regarding recontracting and due diligence.

The study used a questionnaire survey of venture capital firms, which at the time generated a very high response rate, something that is no longer possible (Wright et al., 1997a). The review process was notable for the need for us to conduct a follow-up survey to collect data on aspects omitted from the first survey but which were demanded by reviewers. Fortunately, we were able to do this, and the response rate remained high. The study revealed something of a puzzle and some policy insights for VCs in that although venture capitalists did not make extensive use of serial entrepreneurs from their own portfolio, they frequently used entrepreneurs who have exited from other venture capitalists' portfolios. Venture capitalists rarely assessed entrepreneurs formally at the time of exit, and it was unusual to maintain formal links with entrepreneurs' after they had exited.

This study focused on the venture capitalist's perspective, and it was evident that there was a need to explore the perspective of the serial entrepreneur. The first attempt in this direction involved a qualitative study, interviewing a small number of serial entrepreneurs, which enabled some initial propositions to be developed (Wright et al., 1997b). The study generated some insights that serial entrepreneurs were heterogeneous in their motivations and their behavior.

I've also found that research ideas can come from unexpected places and times, not least of which when I've been doing something else. The extension of this initial work to look at habitual entrepreneurs in more depth was sparked on my regular Saturday morning off-road cycle ride. Thinking about serial entrepreneurs as I struggled to avoid the worst of the mud, it became clear that the next step needed to be a large-scale study. I recalled that Paul Westhead, who I barely knew at the time, had published some preliminary work in this area. Returning home, I contacted him to ask what further data he had and would he be interested in developing this further. He was interested and we began a collaboration which resulted in Westhead and Wright (1998) and a special issue of *Entrepreneurship Theory and Practice* on this topic. This work was novel in that it was the first to provide quantitative evidence on the assets and liabilities of different types of habitual entrepreneurs as well as novice entrepreneurs and has become well cited.

This initial work, led subsequently to funding by Scottish Enterprise, enabled us to design a specific study that would enable us to explore more deeply with more rigorous measures the behavior of habitual entrepreneurs, which had not been possible in the initial study, but which would also enable us to develop some policy insights. It also enabled us to compare habitual entrepreneurs with novice entrepreneurs and to examine the heterogeneity of habitual entrepreneurs. Specifically, we were able to identify behavior relating to opportunity identification and pursuit, human capital resource differences and behavior relating to success and failure of different ventures (Ucbasaran et al., 2008, 2009, 2010). Subsequent work explored the creation of innovative opportunities by portfolio, serial and novice entrepreneurs (Robson et al., 2012) as well as accessing financial resources by these entrepreneurs with different extent and nature of experience (Mueller et al., 2012; Robson et al., 2013). The agenda continues with longitudinal qualitative work exploring in depth the crucial question that we do not understand, which is how do portfolio entrepreneurs orchestrate their resources over time to learn from prior ventures how to develop subsequent ones in their portfolio (Baerts et al., 2015).

The world of research has gone berserk

I believe strongly that researchers should also be serious about teaching. Teaching offers opportunities to convey one's research to a wider audience and challenges in conveying it in a way that is accessible without dumbing it down. Interactions with students can also be another way of generating ideas and developing a research agenda. Steve Franklin, a student in my 1998 MBA class, held a PhD in biotechnology but was also working for a technology transfer incubator. He brought the idea for his three-month capstone dissertation to explore the challenge faced by technology transfer offices (TTOs) as to how to recruit commercially oriented entrepreneurs to complement or supplement academic scientists in running spin-off ventures based on their research. We came up with the idea of surveying TTOs for their perspectives and achieved a respectable response rate because it was an issue they were facing and they had not been inundated with survey requests. Steve passed his MBA with distinction and obtained some insights that he could take back to his day job. Partly because of pursuing the other research avenues outlined in this chapter, and partly because at the time academic spin-offs had not particularly registered with me, I left it there. However, it was retrieved over a year later when I began to discuss with a new colleague, Don Siegel, academic entrepreneurship and spin-offs which were then beginning to attract research and policy attention. The results were reworked and papers published on surrogate entrepreneurs (Franklin et al., 2001) and university strategy and spin-offs (Lockett et al., 2003).

An indirect benefit from having corporate funding for the MBO research was that it made me eligible for a Realizing Our Potential Award (ROPA) from the ESRC. Exploring academic spin-outs was ideal because it met the criterion of a topic that was disconnected from the work funded by industry. The award enabled us to employ a research assistant and to extend the initial work more rigorously with both a survey of universities regarding their spin-off activity and qualitative analysis of how spin-offs did or did not develop the resources and capabilities to become viable. In essence, part of the initial intention was to replicate the monitoring idea behind CMBOR, although in the event that aspect did not materialize. Nevertheless, the survey did provide a university-level database of spin-off and licensing activity that enabled us to analyze the relationships between the resources and capabilities of TTOs and the quality of spin-offs created (Lockett and Wright, 2005) and of the efficiency of TTOs (Chapple et al., 2005).

The qualitative data relating to spin-offs enable us to gain insights into the resources and capabilities that spin-offs needed to develop in order to overcome a number of critical junctures in their development (Vohora et al., 2004). This paper won an Academy of Management Entrepreneurship Division best paper award. The review process at *Research Policy* was notable for one reviewer taking a complete dislike to it, primarily because they did not like qualitative work. Thankfully, an appeal to the then-editor Chris Freeman elicited the response that we should ignore this reviewer.

Around this time I also became involved in collaborative research with Bart Clarysse who was also working in this area as part of a European Commission–funded project, providing scope for more comparative work on the role of TTOs as incubator mechanisms for spin-offs (Clarysse et al., 2005, 2007). Extending this work in a subsequent European Commission project widened further the collaborative network to include Philippe Mustar and Massimo Colombo, among others, which further extended the analysis to consider the effects on spin-off activity of institutional differences between countries and universities. This work had important policy implications because it pointed to the dangers of trying to apply one-size-fits-all lessons from places like MIT to universities elsewhere, many of which had neither the infrastructure nor research environment to support spin-offs that could become global leaders but which nevertheless had scope to generate viable businesses that could contribute to growth (Wright et al., 2008). These insights were brought together in a book (Wright et al., 2007), while editing a series of journal special issues provided fora to debate the scope and impact of academic entrepreneurship.

More recently, the focus has been on assessing the impact of academic entrepreneurship (Grimaldi et al., 2011; Link et al., 2015; Siegel and Wright, 2015) and on understanding the dimensions of the evolving contexts for innovative entrepreneurship (Autio et al., 2014). Skepticism about the direct impact of university spin-offs by academic scientists (Wennberg et al., 2011) is opening up a new research agenda that encompasses the development of an ecosystem for student and alumni entrepreneurship. An important aspect of such ecosystems concerns the need to explore the role, variety and efficacy of new forms of incubators and finance providers, especially accelerator programs (Pauwels et al., 2015).

No direction home

The work on returnee entrepreneurs arose as an outgrowth of the research program associated with the restructuring of emerging economies. In turn, my initial work in this area began as a development of the research on MBOs. As the state-owned firms whose efficiency I had been studying began to be privatized from the early 1980s, this research agenda would clearly need to adapt if it were to continue. I noticed that despite the huge attention attracted by the IPOs of the largest corporations, a large number of activities were being bought by their managers and employees. This provided an opportunity to link my state-owned–sector work with my MBO work in ways that were unexpected at the outset. It raised interesting questions about the rationale for these forms of privatization, their differences from other forms of buyout and expectations about drivers of performance changes post buyout. Asymmetric information issues were a particular problem for sellers seeking to maximize the sale price. As privatization diffused worldwide, it became possible to extend the scope of our agenda to explore how privatization MBOs differed in other contexts.

As Central and Eastern Europe began to transition from communism, some scholars in those countries began to take an interest in privatization and specifically in the scope for management and employee buyouts (MEBOs). First contacts with Tea Petrin from Slovenia led to a joint paper and an invitation to make a presentation to the outgoing government in January 1990 on privatization through MEBOs at which the interpreter famously was unable to translate the word entrepreneurship. Second, through an indirect route I learned of interest from a Russian scholar by the name of Igor Filatotchev and conveyed some papers to him through my colleague Trevor Buck who was taking a party of students to Moscow on a field trip. A couple of years later we recruited Igor as a full-time member of our department and produced a series of papers on privatization, buyouts and governance using firm-level data throughout the next decade, which included publication in special issues spanning economics, management and entrepreneurship in *Academy of Management Journal* (Hoskisson et al., 2000), *Journal of Business Venturing*, *Journal of Comparative Economics* (Estrin and Wright, 1999) and *Journal of Management Studies* (Wright et al., 2005). Because this research program had a strong policy as well as research focus, we were able to generate funding from research councils but also national and international agencies such as EBRD, OECD, ILO, DFID, etc., with production of the EBRD Technical Note on Management and Employee Buyouts in Central and Eastern Europe being a key policy document outcome.

As the economies of CEE began to develop, our research interest turned towards China, facilitated by connecting up with Hui Liu who was a colleague of Trevor Buck's by now at Loughborough University.

We obtained modest funding from the British Council to conduct a preliminary survey of returnee entrepreneurs in an environment where there were no archival data and where there was considerable sensitivity regarding answering such questionnaires. Because the study was focused on science parks, some of which were associated with universities, connections could be made with the work on academic entrepreneurship in progress at the time to analyze resource dimensions of locations decisions (Wright et al., 2008b).

Our subsequent work in China was facilitated by the availability of firm-level archival data sets that identified returnee entrepreneurs enabling us to explore their exporting activity (Filatotchev et al., 2010) as well as spillover effects on ventures created by local entrepreneurs (Liu et al., 2010, 2011;).

As the topic has matured, attention is evolving to address the dark side, or challenges faced by returnee entrepreneurs in returning home. A particular issue concerns overcoming the problems of deterioration of local networks because of having been abroad such that returnees become outsiders. This work is also being extended to other contexts where returnee entrepreneurs are important, but somewhat different from China, notably India.

Still on the road, heading for another joint

My research has evolved over the past three decades to explore the dimensions of entrepreneurial ownership mobility in terms of organizational and geographical mobility. As I have indicated, all four of the aspects of entrepreneurial ownership mobility have continuing research agendas. A strong contextual thread has run through all aspects of my work. This has potentially important research and policy implications because the drivers and impact vary according to the heterogeneity of ventures and the contexts in which they operate.

Increasing attention to the importance of exploring the contextual influences on entrepreneurship ownership mobility is recognizing that the complexities of context go way beyond institutional aspects at the country level, nor are they static (Zahra and Wright, 2011). This clearly applies to institutional regulations that may influence the nature of cross-border VC and PE activity (Meuleman and Wright, 2011) and the ownership of IP by academic scientists (Fini et al., 2015). The re-emergence of state involvement in enterprises (Grosman et al., 2015; Wood and Wright, 2015) doesn't simply bring things full circle, but opens up new potential research avenues regarding implications for entrepreneurial ownership mobility. Changing context also relates to the emergence of new forms of microfinancing to fund new ventures (Bruton et al., 2015), which have different abilities to provide support for entrepreneurs and time horizons before they need to exit.

What lessons have I learned over the evolution of my research? Alertness to opportunities for new research projects is particularly important. But adaptability is also key to sustain a research program. Although it wasn't a deliberate strategy at the outset, seeing the possibilities for making connections between apparently different domains and phenomena has been important to opening up new areas. This oftentimes involved reaching back to make connections with work carried out some years previously.

I hope that I have conveyed that a constant theme in the evolution of my research has been the interaction with practice. This has helped create a virtuous circle by throwing up new questions that could not have been gleaned from the literature but which in turn have created opportunities for research funding. The important challenge has been connecting the new ideas and new phenomena to the literature, in order to avoid the danger of descending into 'train spotting'.

Building and rebuilding collaborative teams is important to realizing research opportunities. Collaborative teams bring new conceptual and methodological expertise. One shouldn't be afraid to go outside one's comfort zone in both these respects. Hence my work has adopted and developed a variety of conceptual lenses, as well as utilizing both quantitative and qualitative methods. In new emerging areas I have found qualitative case studies to be important in getting to understand the issues. Questionnaire surveys are increasingly challenging, both in terms of response rates and because of their cross-sectional nature. However, they do enable questions to be addressed that cannot be addressed by archival data sets constructed for a different purpose even if those data sets exist which in new areas they likely do not.

But finally, and above all, I didn't pursue any topic unless I found it interesting.

Notes

1 At the time in the United Kingdom it was possible to be recruited to a faculty position without having a PhD.

2 Collecting the data by calling the firms funding buyouts also established important contacts, which then enabled us to conduct our initial survey.

3 We frequently kept one step ahead of practice in building the database to take account of new developments. The funders were explicit that we focus on building a database only on UK management buyouts, so when management buyins began to emerge, these data had to be collected clandestinely, until, of course, the day came when they asked us for data on management buyins and similarly by incorporating other countries.

4 I have explored the stock market effects of this ownership mobility from private entrepreneurial ownership to crossing the threshold to public ownership both in respect of MBOs but also with respect to VC-backed firms in collaboration with Ranko Jelic, Igor Filatotchev and Salim Chahine, among others (Jelic et al., 2005; Zhou et al, 2014; Bruton et al., 2010).

5 Work on family firm buyouts opened up a more general family firm research agenda for me, which has involved exploration of the determinants of survival of family firms (Wilson et al., 2013), contextual influences on family firm behaviour (Wright et al., 2014) and innovation in family firms (Chrisman et al., 2015; Miller et al., 2015).

6 A similar conversation led to a survey for Deloitte's valuation department on the valuation methods used by VC firms. We were able to turn this into an academic article and then by building collaborative links with colleagues in Europe and the United States, notably Sophie Manigart and Harry Sapienza, we were able to develop a series of articles on differences across European countries, eventually extending it to countries in Asia to provide broader contextual comparisons (e.g., Manigart et al., 2002). Having developed these collaborative links, it was a short step to utilize them subsequently to undertake comparative work on VC syndication (Manigart et al., 2006) building on work developed for Andy Lockett's PhD dissertation for which I had been supervisor (Wright and Lockett, 2003).

References

Amess, K., Stiebale, J. and Wright, M. 2016. The Impact of Private Equity on Firms' Patenting Activity, *European Economic Review*, 86, 147–160.

Amess, K. and Wright, M. 2007. The Wage and Employment Effects of Leveraged Buyouts in the UK, *International Journal of Economics and Business*, 14(2), 179–195.

Arnfield, R., Chiplin, B., Jarrett, M. and Wright, M. (eds.) 1981. *Management Buy-outs: Corporate Trend for the '80's?* Proceedings of the first National Conference on Management Buy-outs, University of Nottingham Industrial and Business Liaison Office.

Autio, E., Kenney, M., Mustar, P., Siegel, D. and Wright, M. 2014. Entrepreneurial Innovation Ecosystems and Context, *Research Policy*, 43(7), 1097–1108.

Baerts, C., Meuleman, M., DeBruyne, M. and Wright, M. 2016. Portfolio Entrepreneurship and Resource Orchestration. *Strategic Entrepreneurship Journal*, forthcoming

Bruton, G., Filatotchev, I., Chahine, S. and Wright, M. 2010. Governance, Ownership Structure and Performance of IPO Firms: The Impact of Different Types of Private Equity Investors and Institutional Environments, *Strategic Management Journal*, 31, 491–509,

Bruton, G., Khavul, S., Siegel, D. and Wright, M. 2015. New Financial Alternatives in Seeding Entrepreneurship: Microfinance, Crowdfunding, and Peer-to-peer Innovations, *Entrepreneurship Theory and Practice*, 39(1), 9–26.

Chapple, W., Lockett, A., Siegel, D. S. and Wright, M. 2005, Assessing the Relative Performance of University Technology Transfer Offices in the U.K.: Parametric and Non-Parametric Evidence, *Research Policy*, 34(3), 369–384.

Chiplin, B. and Wright, M. 1987. *The Logic of Mergers*. IEA Hobart Paper No 197, April.

Chiplin, B. and Wright, M. 1980. Divestment and Structural Change in UK Industry. *National Westminster Bank Quarterly Review*, 42–51.

Chrisman, J., Chua, J., De Massis, A., Frattini, F. and Wright, M. 2015. The Ability and Willingness Paradox in Family Firm Innovation. *Journal of Product Innovation Management,* 32(3), 310–318.

Clarysse, B., Wright, M., Lockett, A. and Mustar, P. 2007. Academic Spin-offs, Formal Technology Transfer and Capital Raising, *Industrial and Corporate Change*, 16, 609–640.

Clarysse, B., Wright, M., Lockett, A., van de Elde, E. and Vohora, A. 2005. Spinning Out New Ventures: A Typology of Incubation Strategies from European Research Institutions, *Journal of Business Venturing*, 20(2), 183–216.

Estrin, S. and Wright, M. 1999. Corporate Governance in the Former Soviet Union: An Overview of the Issues, *Journal of Comparative Economics*, 27: 398–342.

Filatotchev, I., Liu, X., Buck, T. and Wright, M. 2010. The Export Orientation and Export Performance of High-Technology SMEs in Emerging Markets: The Effects of Knowledge Transfer by Returnee Entrepreneurs, *Journal of International Business Studies*, 40(6), 1005–1021.

Fini, R., Fu, K., Mathisen, M., Rasmussen, E., and Wright, M. 2015. Institutional determinants of university spin-off quantity and quality: A longitudinal, multi-level, cross-country study. Paper presented at the Academy of Management, Vancouver, August.

Franklin, S., Wright, M. and Lockett, A. 2001. Academic and Surrogate Entrepreneurs and University Spin-out Companies, *Journal of Technology Transfer*, 26(1–2), 127–41.

Gilligan, J. and Wright, M. 2014. *Private Equity Demystified, 3rd edition*, London: ICAEW.

Grimaldi, R., Kenney, M., Siegel, D. and Wright, M. 2011. Bayh-Dole 30 Years On: Reassessing Academic Entrepreneurship. *Research Policy*, 40, 1045–1057.

Grosman, A., Okhmatovskiy, I. and Wright, M. 2015. State Control and Corporate Governance in Transition Economies: 25 Years on from 1989, *Corporate Governance-International Review*, 24(3), 200–221.

Harris, R., Siegel, D. and Wright, M. 2005. Productivity of UK MBOs, *Review of Economics and Statistics*, 87, 148–153.

Hawley, F. 1907. *Enterprise and the Productive Process*. New York: G Putnam's Sons.

Hoskisson, R., Eden, L., Lau, C-M. and Wright, M. 2000. Strategies in Emerging Markets, *Academy of Management Journal*, 43(3), 249–267.

Howorth, C., Westhead, P. and Wright, M. 2004. Buyouts, Information Asymmetry and the Family-Management Dyad, *Journal of Business Venturing*, 19, 509–534.

Jelic, R., Saadouni, B. and Wright, M. 2005. The Performance of Private to Public MBOs: The Role of Venture Capital. *Journal of Business Finance and Accounting*, 32(3-4), 643–681.

Jensen, M. 1986. Agency Costs of Free Cash Flow, Corporate Finance, and Takeovers. *American Economic Review*, 76, 323–329.

Karsai, J. and Wright, M. 1994. Accountability, Governance and Management Buy-outs in Hungary, *Europe-Asia Studies* (formerly Soviet Studies), 46(6), 997–1016.

Link, A., Siegel, D. and Wright, M. 2015. *The Chicago Handbook of Technology Transfer and Academic Entrepreneurship*, Chicago, IL: Chicago University Press.

Liu, X., Lu, J., Filatotchev, I., Buck, T. and Wright, M. 2010. Returnee Entrepreneurs, Knowledge Spillovers and Innovation in High-Tech Firms in Emerging Economies, *Journal of International Business Studies*, 41(7), 1183–1197.

Liu, X., Wright, M., Lu, J., Dai, O. and Filatotchev, I. 2011. Human Mobility, Global Networks and International Knowledge Spillovers: Evidence from High-tech Small and Medium Enterprises in an Emerging Market, *Strategic Entrepreneurship Journal*, 4(4), 340–355.

Lockett, A. and Wright, M. 2005. Resources, Capabilities, Risk Capital and the Creation of University Spin-Out Companies. *Research Policy*, 34, 1043–1057.

Lockett, A., Wright, M. and Franklin, S. 2003. Technology Transfer and Universities' Spin-out Strategies, *Small Business Economics*, 20, 185–201.

Manigart, S., De Waele, K., Wright, M., Robbie, K., Desbrières, P., Sapienza, H. J., et al. 2002. Determinants of Required Return in Venture Capital Investments: A Five-country Study, *Journal of Business Venturing*, 17(4), 291–312.

Manigart, S., Lockett, A., Meuleman, M., Wright, M., Landström, H., Bruining, H., et al. 2006. Venture Capitalists' Decision to Syndicate, *Entrepreneurship Theory and Practice*, 30(2), 131–153.

Meuleman, M. and Wright, M. 2011. Cross-border Private Equity Syndication: Institutional Context and Learning, *Journal of Business Venturing*, 26: 35-48.

Meuleman, M., Wright, M., Amess, K. and Scholes, L. 2009. Agency, Strategic Entrepreneurship and the Performance of Private Equity Backed Buyouts, *Entrepreneurship Theory and Practice*, 33, 213–240.

Miller, D., Wright, M., Lebreton-Miller, I. and Scholes, L. 2015. Resources and Innovation in Family Businesses: The Janus-Face of Family Socio-emotional Preferences. *California Management Review*, 58, 20–40.

Mueller, C., Westhead, P. and Wright, M. 2012. Formal Venture Capital Acquisition: Can Experienced Entrepreneurs Compensate for the Spatial Proximity Benefits of 'Star Universities'? *Environment and Planning A*, 44(2), 281–296.

O'Brien, D., Howe, W., Wright, M. and O'Brien, R. 1979. *Competition Policy Profitability and Growth*, London: MacMillan.

Pauwels, C., Clarysse, B., Wright, M. and Van Hove, J. 2015. Understanding a New Generation Incubation Model: The Accelerator, *Technovation*, DOI: 10.1016/j.technovation.2015.09.003.

Robbie, K. and Wright, M. 1996. *Management Buy-ins: Entrepreneurs, Active Investors and Corporate Restructuring*, Studies in Finance Series, Manchester: MUP.

Robson, P.J.A., Akuetteh, C.K., Stone, I., Westhead, P. and Wright, M. (2013). Credit-Rationing and Entrepreneurial Experience: Evidence from a Resource Deficit Context. *Entrepreneurship and Regional Development*, 25(5-6), 349–370.

Robson, P.J.A., Akuetteh, C.K., Westhead, P. and Wright M. (2012b). Innovative Opportunity Pursuit, Human Capital and Business Ownership Experience in an Emerging Region: Evidence from Ghana. *Small Business Economics,* 39(3), 603–625.

Siegel, D. and Wright, M. 2015. Academic Entrepreneurship: Time for a Rethink? *British Journal of Management*, 26, 582–595.

Thompson, S. and Wright M. 1986. Vertical Disintegration and the Life-Cycle of Industries and Firms. *Managerial and Decision Economics*, 7, 141–144.

Thompson, S. and Wright, M. 1987. 'Markets to Hierarchies and Back Again: The Implications of Management Buyouts for Factor Supply', Journal of Economic Studies, 14: 3-24.

Thompson, S., Wright, M. and Robbie, K. 1990. Management Buy-outs and Privatisation: Organisational Form and Incentive Issues. *Fiscal Studies*, 11(3), 71–88.

Ucbasaran, D., Westhead, P. and Wright, M. 2008. Opportunity Identification and Pursuit: Does an Entrepreneur's Human Capital Matter? *Small Business Economics*, 30(2), 153–173.

Ucbasaran, D., Westhead, P. and Wright, M. 2009. The Extent and Nature of Opportunity Identification by Experienced Entrepreneurs. *Journal of Business Venturing*, 24, 99–115.

Ucbasaran, D., Westhead, P., Wright, M. and Flores, M. 2010. The Nature of Entrepreneurial Experience, Business Failure and Comparative Optimism. *Journal of Business Venturing*, 25(6), 541–555.

Vohora, A., Wright, M. and Lockett, A. 2004. Critical Junctures in Spin-outs from Universities, *Research Policy*, 33, 147–175.

Wennberg, K., Wiklund, J. and Wright, M. 2011. The Effectiveness of University Knowledge Spillovers: Performance Differences between University Spinoffs and Corporate Spinoffs, *Research Policy*, 40, 1128–1143.

Wervaal, E., Bruining, H. and Wright, M. 2013. Entrepreneurial and Administrative Management and Private Equity Positions in Management Buy-Outs, *Small Business Economics*, 40, 591–605.

Westhead, P. and Wright, M. 1998. Novice, Portfolio and Serial Entrepreneurs: Are they Different?, *Journal of Business Venturing*, 13(3), 173–204.

Wilson, N. and Wright, M. 2013. Private Equity, Buyouts and Insolvency Risk. *Journal of Business Finance and Accounting*, 40, 949–990.

Wilson, N., Wright, M., Siegel, D. and Scholes, L. 2012. Private Equity Portfolio Company Performance during the Global Recession, *Journal of Corporate Finance*, 18, 193–205.

Wood, G. and Wright, M. 2015. Corporations and New Statism: Trends and Research Priorities, *Academy of Management Perspectives*, 29, 271–286.

Wright, M. 1979. Inflation Accounting in the Nationalised Industries: A Survey and Appraisal, *Accounting and Business Research*, 10(37), 65–73.

Wright, M. 1980. Real Rates of Return on Capital: Some Estimates for British Gas, *Journal of Business Finance and Accounting*, 7(1), 89–103.

Wright, M. 1986. The Make-Buy Decision and Managing Markets: The Case of Management Buy-outs, *Journal of Management Studies*, 23(4), 443-464.

Wright, M., Clarysse, B., Mustar, P. and Lockett, A. 2007. *Academic Entrepreneurship in Europe*, Cheltenham: Edward Elgar.

Wright, M. and Coyne, J. 1985. *Management Buyouts*. Beckenham: Croom Helm.

Wright, M., Coyne, J. and Lockley, H. 1984. Trade Unions and Management Buy-outs Dispelling the Myths, *Industrial Relations Journal*, 15, 45–52.

Wright, M., Filatotchev, I., Buck, T. and Robbie, K. 1994. Accountability and Efficiency in Privatisation by Buy-out in CEE, *Financial Accountability and Management*, 10, 195–214.

Wright, M., Hoskisson, R., Busenitz, L. and Dial, J. 2000. Privatization and Entrepreneurship: The Upside of Management Buy-outs, *Academy of Management Review*, 25(3), 591–601.

Wright, M., Liu, X., Buck, T. and Filatotchev, I. 2008. Returnee Entrepreneur Characteristics, Science Park Location Choice and Performance: An Analysis of High Technology SMEs in China, *Entrepreneurship Theory and Practice*, 32(1), 131–156.

Wright, M. and Lockett, A. 2003. The Structure and Management of Alliances: Syndication in the Venture Capital Industry, *Journal of Management Studies*, 40(8), 2073–2102.

Wright, M., Robbie, K. and Ennew, C. 1997a. Venture Capitalists and Serial Entrepreneurs, *Journal of Business Venturing*, 12(3), 227–249.

Wright, M. and Sharma, P. 2013. Sustaining a Publications Career. *Family Business Review*, 26, 323–332.

Wright, M., Thompson, S. and Robbie, K. 1992. Venture Capital and Management-Led Leveraged Buy-outs. *Journal of Business Venturing*, 7, : 47–71.

Wright, M., Thompson, S. and Robbie, K. 1993. Financial Control in Privatisation by Management Buy-out, *Financial, Accountability and Management* 9(2), 75–99.

Wright, M., Thompson, S., Robbie, K. and Wong, P. 1995. Management Buy-outs in the Short and Long Term, *Journal of Business Finance and Accounting* 22, 461–482.

Wright, M., Thompson, S., Starkey, K. and Robbie, K. 1994. Longevity and the Life-Cycle of Management Buy-outs, *Strategic Management Journal*, 15(3), 215–228.

Wright, M., Wieser, O. and Robbie, K. 1997b. Austrian Buy-outs from the Public Sector, *Annals of Public and Cooperative Economics* 68(4), 689–712.

Zahra, S. and Wright, M. 2011. Entrepreneurship's Next Act, *Academy of Management Perspectives*, 25, 67–83.

22

Researching entrepreneurship at the intersection

Reflections on three decades of research

Shaker A. Zahra

Introduction

From the beginning, I have sought to connect strategy and entrepreneurship, especially in global high-technology industries. Extending over three decades, my research has taken many detours only to arrive where I started as a freshman at Al-Azhar University in Cairo, Egypt. There I was first introduced to the themes of globalism, technology, and entrepreneurship – terms that were vaguely mentioned in my classes but rarely discussed with seriousness. Today, these terms are widely accepted globally, as well as debated by serious scholars, insightful managers and entrepreneurs, and informed policy makers in advanced and emerging economies.

In this chapter, I will reflect on the evolution of some of the key ideas in my research, trace their origins and highlight their implications. I will review key themes from my research over the past thirty years, factors that shaped my scholarship, and key lessons learned. As such, this chapter is not a well organized or tidy presentation of the evolution of my research agenda per se because my program of research has never been that well planned or systematic. I have often followed my intuition and went where I thought interesting ideas were to be discovered. My research has also evolved from the feedback I have received from the broader marketplace of ideas, my failures and successes, and, most important, the countless collaborators I have had around the globe. How this work will fare over time and what contribution it makes is entirely up to others' evaluation and judgment.[1] Consequently, I will only provide background information as to the factors that were behind the ideas I have offered and the articles I have produced. Likewise, I will highlight some of the key decisions and choices I have made and how they collectively shaped my findings.

Learning about entrepreneurship

My introduction to entrepreneurship was in my first economics course in Egypt. The textbook we used included three poorly written chapters on entrepreneurship, globalism and the role of technology in economic development. Written in arcane Arabic and poorly translated from English references, we could only sense that these were topics that had received attention outside our national borders. They appeared ad hoc and almost irrelevant; it was hard to see advanced technology overtaking poorly run, conservative government–owned enterprises that dominated ailing Egypt's economy. And the government did everything it could to discourage creativity and entrepreneurialism. Access to the international community was both controlled and limited. My economics professor was trained in Edinburgh University, whereas all other economics professors on the faculty were trained in Soviet institutions, and thus capitalism was not highly valued then in our department or Egypt; neither was entrepreneurship. Getting a job, any job, with a government agency was the ultimate secret of success and security.

As a student, I worked in a small, family-owned travel agency in Cairo. The company focused on serving the U.S. upper-middle-class traveler while visiting Egypt and other parts of the Middle East. There I met some of the truly most interesting, intelligent, hardworking, motivated, and entrepreneurial people. The owner, a former engineer, expected us (even the newest of us) to come up with solutions – not problems. The smallness of the company, physical proximity of space, quick rotations among jobs, and the constant feedback from colleagues all stimulated individual and group creativity and entrepreneurship. It was also easy for a novice like me to apply what I was studying at the university in my job and be rewarded for doing so. My more senior and experienced colleagues taught me new things every day. We came up with new programs, ways of doing things, and tried new things (and dropped failing ones) almost at the speed of light. Then came the point when my colleagues who have learned a great deal on their jobs and taught me so much decided to move on to create their own hugely successful travel businesses. I opted for an academic career and later moved to the United States.

Nearly twenty-five years after taking my first economics course, as I was reviewing my slides for a panel presentation in Sweden, I realized then that I had spent most of my career trying to connect the three areas of entrepreneurship, technology, and globalization. My work has been almost always at the intersection of these topics and their crucial implications for the firms and their managers and strategies. The intersection of these ideas has proven to be a wonderful place to find and develop my own intellectual space, offering an endless supply of fresh ideas, data, and collaborators who took me to places I had never even imagined. To be sure, some of these travels proved to be a mirage. Despite all the care exercised, I could not have foreseen that these journeys were fruitless. But I learned much from them and from my collaborations. These painful and frequent failures, too, were part of my journey, taking me to new issues and new experiences. I tried what I learned in the travel agency by exploring as many new things and be ready to alter course. I found out that this was an expensive strategy and the academic market place has very little tolerance for people who are "unfocused". Some of my collaborators discontinued their work with me in favor of more managed and narrowly defined research programs. I have never blamed them for making these decisions; most remain good friends.

Before shifting my focus to the study of entrepreneurship, I spent over a decade doing research in strategy studying the governance of large publicly held corporations (Pearce and Zahra, 1991; Zahra and Pearce, 1989) and technology strategy (George, Zahra and Wood, 2002; Haeussler, Patzelt and Zahra, 2012; Kelley, Ali and Zahra, 2013; Zahra, 1996a, 1996b; Zahra and Covin, 1993; Zahra and Das, 1993).[2] This research highlights the role of governance in inducing innovation and other value-creating activities (Zahra, 1996c). Parallel to this research, I began collecting data from large companies about their innovative and entrepreneurial activities. My work began with the belief that forces within a company – especially senior management – were crucial to promoting innovation. This belief was driven by the recognition that U.S. companies had fallen behind their Japanese, Korean, and other countries' companies in creating new technology and penetrating new markets around the globe. U.S. companies at the time had become complacent and bureaucratic, failing in technology commercialization. Although this premise was widely accepted, I found that managers were eager to introduce and lead change. In particular, middle managers held the real power when it came to strategic change, renewal, and entrepreneurship. Strategic change is embedded in the organizational culture.

Understandably, a related belief that had guided my early research was the crucial value of organizational culture (Zahra, 1991, 1995; Zahra and Fescina, 1991). Writings about organizational culture at the time when I began my work were abundant, despite recognition of the elusive nature of the concept. These writings, however, pointed to the need for cultural change to bring about innovation and induce entrepreneurship, especially at the firm level of analysis (Block and MacMillan, 1993). My work and early field interviews also reaffirmed the crucial role middle managers play in making large-scale corporate cultural changes. This is one point I regret not taking more seriously in my research program. Middle managers are the center of gravity in many companies (Hornsby, Kuratko and Zahra, 2002), even after the severe reorganizations and restructurings that have occurred and the redefinition that took place of these managers' roles because of radically changing technology.

One of my first decisions was to focus on firm-level entrepreneurial activities because of their importance for organizational survival and performance. Equally important, entrepreneurship scholars were then (and are still) busy importing concepts and constructs from psychology to explain who the entrepreneur is and what he (she) does. As I contemplated my path, I was struck by the contradictory and fragmented findings that that body of research has produced.[3] I could not see how I might add to this body of work and therefore intuitively focused on the firm-level of analysis, a choice that was consistent with my early strategy work. This focus proved to be both an opportunity and a great challenge. Studying firm-level entrepreneurship allowed me to apply many of the insights I have learned from studying and teaching strategy, applying its theories and analytical models. On the other hand, some refused to accept this ("my") work as entrepreneurship (and, of course, strategy scholars did not see this work as strategy). This did not matter much because I thought my work connects two important areas that needed to engage in a substantive dialog. Corporate entrepreneurship (CE) provided this important bridge.

Research at the intersection

My research has been primarily at the intersection of four disciplines, both conceptually and empirically. It connects international business, strategy, technology, and entrepreneurship. This focus has been driven by my training and broad interests. It has also been shaped more by the changing nature of global competition and corporate practice. My fieldwork and executive education experiences have given me a different set of eyes on research that matters.

I have studied CE and connected it with strategic change and renewal, international entrepreneurship, and linked innovation to strategy and later entrepreneurship. Although strategic change is an overall encompassing activity, it also serves as an independent dimension of CE. I have studied family firm internationalization (Zahra, 2003) and innovation (Zahra, 2005a) and linked governance and entrepreneurship (Chahine, Flatotchev and Zahra, 2011; Mahnke, Venzin and Zahra, 2007; Mustakallio, Autio and Zahra, 2002; Zahra, 1996b; Zahra and Flatotchev, 2004; Zahra, Wright and Flatotchev, 2009). In all of these instances, I have found research at the intersection exciting, offering me a unique space to explore different new issues, integrate knowledge across boundaries, arbitrage research opportunities and methods, borrow and apply new theories, and export findings from one area to other fields.

I have also written and debated the merits and challenges of doing research at the intersection, especially in theory building (Zahra, 2015; Zahra and Newey, 2010). The challenges encountered in theory building, data collection, and empirical testing in this type of research are enormous but the rewards far exceed the difficulties. Creative work requires infusion of ideas across knowledge boundaries and translating them differently. It also requires interactive expertise – the facility to communicate across different knowledge domains. Such interactive expertise develops as one gains mastery of and insights into other disciplines to the point of being able to communicate well with specialists. Working with colleagues at the intersection offers an important means to learn and use this expertise. The process does not necessarily become easier over time – it becomes better understood and risks become easier to estimate and work around.

Focus on corporate entrepreneurship

Initially, my research on CE sought to bring clarity to the domain of this important construct. It attempted to articulate, relate and test its constituent dimensions (Dess et al., 2003; Zahra, 1991, 1993a, b, 1996b; Zahra and Covin, 1995; Zahra and Garvis, 2000; Zahra and Hayton, 2008; Zahra, Neubaum and Huse, 2000; Zahra, Nielsen and Bogner, 1999), building especially on the work of Danny Miller (1983). I paid attention to entrepreneurial orientation (EO), which remains a popular concept in the literature today. I thought that EO was useful in understanding a company's disposition toward entrepreneurship. As I saw it, EO had both formal and informal activities. A large number of papers have been published since then about EO. Yet, over time I have found it more meaningful to move away from "disposition" and instead examine the behaviors or actions (initiatives) that companies and their managers actually use to instill entrepreneurship. Actions are more easily documented, observed, and measured. Further, there are countless actions that make up the mosaic of a firm's entrepreneurship, which makes it difficult to capture all these actions. But these actions are much more meaningful than dispositions and perceptions, even though some of my early work reports strong positive correlations between EO perceptions and actions.

As my research agenda developed, I abandoned EO and focused more on entrepreneurial capability to account for the fact that not all actions firms take are meaningful in affecting entrepreneurship. Capability refers to skills and mastery beyond normal or average levels – and this qualitative difference has implications for a company's performance. An organizational capability is multidimensional, as presented elsewhere (Abdel-Gawad et al., 2013; Zahra and Nielsen, 2002). I agree that there is a subset of organizational capabilities that are distinctively related to entrepreneurship and that we need more research that explicates the types and nature of those capabilities.

My focus on capabilities was a natural fit with the growing literature on dynamic capabilities, a vast body of work that had nonetheless overlooked entrepreneurial companies (Newey and Zahra, 2009; Zahra et al., 2006). My concern centered on explicating the nature of these capabilities in entrepreneurial (Abdel-Gawad et al., 2013; Zahra et al., 2006; Zahra, van de Velde and Larrañeta, 2007) and dynamic settings (Zahra, 2005a; Zahra and George, 2002 a, b), and their implications for firm performance (Sapienza et al., 2006).

Diversity, variety and context

Context has played a key role in my decisions as to what to study and how to study it (Zahra, 2007a, b; Zahra, 2014; Zahra and Wright, 2011). Earlier in my career, I worked in academic departments that – like the rest of the field – viewed entrepreneurship as lacking intellectual substance and legitimacy. Attentive to these concerns, I pursued strategic management research with an occasional paper on entrepreneurship. Lack of support and limited resources led me to seek opportunities to connect with companies and trade associations and gain access to data. I frequently traded consulting opportunities for help in data collection. The extreme variability in the faculty composition of the departments where I worked left room for a focused conversation, pushing me to travel abroad and take part in multiple research projects as a way of learning.

My move in 2002 to Babson College took me to an entirely new world with great resources and well-established connections that enhanced my learning. My move three years later to the Carlson School at the University of Minnesota was driven by the disciplined and strong research focus where I found myself with some of the most talented colleagues in the field. This move encouraged me to collaborate and learn. I attended doctoral seminars throughout the university in theory building and econometrics, among others. This, along with changes already in my own research project and the field itself, encouraged me to rethink the nature of my research and its contribution.

I have studied different strands of entrepreneurship, looked into a variety of entrepreneurial companies by exploring different contexts and settings. I have also made use of very different research methods and theories. My research has also made good use of my co-authors' connections, data, native understanding of research sites, and skills. Variations in these inputs have produced a number of studies that have raised different questions about the nature of entrepreneurship and the entrepreneurial act.

My studies included corporate, social, international, and technological entrepreneurship. I have examined multiple dimensions of each, with a focus on their implications for performance – especially in an international setting. I have studied corporate and independent ventures, clarifying the implications of their origins for performance and strategic choices (e.g., technological strategies). I have also studied family firms' internationalization and entrepreneurial activities. In conducting these studies, I have used U.S., British, Swedish, Finnish, Danish, French, German, Australian, and other countries' data. This has led one of my colleagues (Susan Hill, 2015) to observe that:

> [W]ithin each of the varieties you've researched, my impression is that you have sought to ask 'big questions' about each variety. You have not taken casual extant understandings of the varieties of entrepreneurship of interest to you for granted, but endeavored to push understanding thereof by asking 'big' questions about the nature of each variety, its strategic dynamics, and its practical importance ('relevance' I guess . . .). The last two I see as fairly strongly aligned with your strategy lens; the first strikes as being somewhat akin to the work of a taxonomist in terms of identifying the genealogy of species. To illustrate this a bit further, when I think of your CE work, what comes immediately to mind is (a) that you differentiated between a variety of forms CE can take that had been lumped together in previous work ('what actually is CE?'), (b) that you tried to specify points of strategic divergence and commonality between corporate and independent forms of venturing ('does CV actually differ from independent venturing?'); and (c) that you pushed investigation of the strategic implications/relevance of CE to firms ('does CE actually matter to its target audience?').

Variety is a core concept in my research where I see entrepreneurship as creating and perpetuating variety in organizational forms, missions, and structures (Zahra and Wright, 2011). Entrepreneurs use varied raw material to create very different firms that do different things.[4] There is a difference between counting the number of companies (or individual entrepreneurs) for statistical analysis and recognizing this variety in explaining entrepreneurial phenomena. There are obvious similarities across types of ventures in the activities entrepreneurs undertake, as observed in the literature. Yet, there are profound differences in the *quality of the mind* that underlies creating a Microsoft and Google versus starting a new travel agency, for example. These companies require different financing, organizational, and strategic models. They also have very different implications for their communities and society. Which societies produce Apple, Microsoft, Google, Intel, and Facebook? How many companies should a society develop to create an Apple? How many Microsofts are needed to keep the industry vibrant and dynamic? How can we structure the relationships between such large companies and very young small ventures? What kinds of ecosystems are conducive to sustaining new venture creation while inducing symbiotic relationships between these ventures and well established companies? These are a few of the questions that have come to mind as I think about variety in studying entrepreneurship. Companies need also to enrich their strategic repertoire through exploration and exploitation (Uotila et al., 2009) that enhance their strategic variety (Larrañeta, Zahra and Galán, 2012).

Throughout my career, I have given special attention to the context of my research (Zahra, 2007b; Zahra and Wright, 2011; Zahra, Wright and Abdel-Gawad, 2014). For example, I have reframed the debate on the origins of entrepreneurial opportunities by examining CE in high-technology companies, logically showing that there is a dynamic and virtuous cycle between discovery and creation. I have also explored different types of young, dynamic, and vibrant industries such as telecommunications, biotechnology, consumer electronics, software, and video games. Likewise, I have studied more mature, even declining, industries. My research has also included some of the world's largest companies and multinationals as well as younger and even nascent firms. I have paid attention to the structures of these industries, particularly the forces that shape their competitive environments and their implications for entrepreneurship (Zahra, 1991, 2003. I have further studied the relationships that develop among companies within those industries (Maula, Keil and Zahra, 2013; Zahra, Maula and Keil, 2005; Zahra, Nash and Bickford, 1995). In studying these relationships, I have used theories derived from organizational theory, organizational economics, industrial economics, and sociology. My coauthors have been especially helpful in introducing me to some of these theories as we translated them for use in our research.

I worry that some researchers avoid exploring context by simply incorporating statistical control variables in their analyses; these controls are essential for rigorous analyses. But they should not mean that we ignore the context. Context, for example, can tell us why psychological ownership matters differently in family firms and independently owned new ventures. If we are examining the role of different capabilities in new venture survival, timing of their internationalization should be incorporated into our theories about these relationships. Similarly, studying social ventures' business models in emerging markets should require us to reflect on the characteristics of these economies and incorporate this into our research designs and analyses. Likewise, the growing research on networks among new ventures (or between new ventures and well-established companies) would benefit from considering spatial and temporal dimensions that influence the formation and maturation of these relationships.

Diversity in my research was also manifested in the way I collected data. I used mail (and email) surveys, interviews, large-scale secondary databases, and a combination of these approaches. I have also used case studies, which I have always admired but have had little skill in doing. But, here too, my coauthors proved to be a great source of inspiration and learning. Their insights allowed us to consider some of the effects of spatial, temporal, hierarchical forces that influenced the relationships we examined (Zahra, 1991; Zahra, 2010; Zahra, Abdel-Gawad and Tsang, 2011; Zahra and Covin, 1995; Zahra, Wright and Abdel-Gawad, 2014). The use of case studies also proved to be useful in exploring cross-level influences of sociopolitical forces within companies on entrepreneurial activities (Newey & Zahra, 2009).

I have also paid attention to the role of intraorganizational context in influencing entrepreneurial outcomes such as technology commercialization (Zahra and Nielsen, 2002) and opportunity exploitation (Foss, Lyngsie and Zahra, 2013, 2015). My research suggests that organizational designs are essential to successful CE and other entrepreneurial activities. Along with my earlier research on the role of culture and knowledge sharing (Van de Ven and Zahra, 2016), this research shows that the degree of centralization, formality, organicity, and communication have serious implications for CE, consistent with the literature (Burgelman, 1983; Miller, 1983)

Despite the variety of evidence of my attention to setting and context, a key limitation of my work is the lack of systematic recognition of time and its implications for the relationships being examined. Perhaps because my early work relied heavily on mail surveys, incorporating time (beyond logical order effects) in the analyses was difficult. Even though this is a common characteristic of much of the early work in the strategy and entrepreneurship fields, the structure of these relationships over time remains unclear. The recent application of econometric modeling would have been useful in uncovering the longitudinal effects of CE on performance (Zahra, 1991, 1996b) or the moderating effect of the environment on performance (Zahra, 1993a; Zahra and Covin, 1995), for example.

I have learned three lessons from considering context in my work. First, context matters in profound ways in shaping the questions to be asked and to whom and how they are asked. It matters also in choosing the kinds of variables we study and the explanations we offer. Nuanced explanations are possible from understanding and incorporating the context, supporting the "engaged scholarship" lens. Second, theory and context should be finely connected, understanding that theories inform our explorations and that context enriches theoretical explanations (Zahra, Newey and Li, 2014). Third, as stated elsewhere (Zahra et al., 2013; Zahra and Wright, 2011), entrepreneurship research will make increasingly significant progress by paying greater attention to context – whether this research is qualitative or quantitative.

International and internationalization

From its earliest beginnings, my research has recognized and exploited internationalization as a driving force of entrepreneurial activities (Carr et al., 2010; George, Wiklund and Zahra, 2005; George and Zahra, 2002; Hayton, George and Zahra, 2002; Li and Zahra, 2012; Mudambi and Zahra, 2007; Sapienza, Autio, George and Zahra, 2006). It adopted a broad view of internationalization, one that embodies not only transactions and business activities across international borders but also the beliefs, attitudes, cognitions, and dispositions to pursue entrepreneurship (Zahra, Abdel-Gawad and Tsang, 2011). The movement of people across national borders is part of this definition. This broad view of internationalization has proved to be profitable, giving me a unique territory in which I have understood and studied entrepreneurship. This work has shown that entrepreneurship drives internationalization that, in turn, fuels entrepreneurship (Zahra, 2015). Further, this cycle produces important and new knowledge that has important consequences for the evolution of the firm and its strategic moves (Zahra, 2005a; Zahra and Garvis, 2000; Zahra and Hayton, 2008; Zahra, Ireland and Hitt, 2000; Zahra, Neubaum and Naldi, 2007). This makes learning to create, absorb, and exploit new knowledge an important managerial task as well as a serious challenge (Zahra, Abdel-Gawad and Tsang, 2011).

Internationalization was not only a "context" in my research; it has been a key source of incredibly rich raw material from which I have drawn inspiration. Colleagues and coauthors who have lived outside the United States proved to be a key source of nuanced knowledge about the role of national cultures, institutions, and the internationalization process itself, improving my understanding of entrepreneurial activities on a global scale. My early work at Jonkoping International Business School (JIBS) in Sweden was particularly useful in making great connections to coauthors and data sources. In its earlier years, JIBS was a great melting pot of ideas – a great hub of leading scholars from all over studying entrepreneurship. Although most faculty and visiting scholars focused on the individual level of the analysis, I learned a great deal about entrepreneurship from my discussions and attending visiting faculty members' seminars. It was remarkable to see and appreciate the diversity of views on what entrepreneurship is – a topic that I still find complicated to explain even today. A short stay at Stockholm School of Economics (SSE) also introduced me to a myriad of other people studying entrepreneurship from different perspectives. Visits to several universities outside the United States have also educated me about the diverse views people hold regarding internationalization and entrepreneurship. These diverse views have enriched my understanding of the role of internationalization vis-a-vis entrepreneurship.

Some of my colleagues were focused on the born global phenomenon, an important topic that has received considerable attention in the literature (for a review, Zahra, 2005a). My interest was broader, however, as I saw born global firms as a fairly small segment of "international entrepreneurship" that could occur in large established companies, established SMEs, or born global new ventures (Zahra, 1993a, 2005a). Though some continue to study born global firms as a distinct phenomenon, it is gratifying to see the evolution of thinking on the topic to adopt the broad view I held from the start.

With my interest in internationalization, it was natural to study the role of knowledge and learning within entrepreneurial activities (Sapienza et al., 2006; Zahra, 2005a; Zahra et al., 2000; Zahra, Ireland, Gutierrez and Hitt, 2000; Zahra, Nielsen and Bogner, 1999). Companies use different entrepreneurial approaches to internationalize, build their market positions, promote their brands, take advantage of local resources and knowledge, and build connections to local companies and institutions. They also exhibit varying levels of creativity in conceptualizing their value and supply. These activities promote learning and knowledge creation. My work with Ireland and Hitt (2000) has looked into technological learning by new ventures using different modes of entry into foreign markets. This work has also linked technological learning to financial performance.

I have also examined how new ventures, whose absorptive capacity is typically limited, are able to learn about culturally distant markets. This work was motivated by the observation that new ventures often "skip" stages in the traditional internationalization process and enter markets that are as culturally distant from their home markets (e.g., French-born global firms going into China). It also was motivated by the proposition that new ventures going abroad have advantages of their own in terms of their learning, that is, the "learning advantage of newness" hypothesis (Sapienza et al., 2006). My work, using data from U.S., Swedish, and French companies entering Chinese markets, shows systematic differences in how these companies learn from and about these markets (Zahra, 2005a).

Recently, I began to explore knowledge and innovation networks and how they contribute to entrepreneurship (Zahra and Nasimbam, 2011). This interest stemmed from the diversity of the co-authorship network involving many colleagues located around the globe. This diversity has offered me a basis to do different types of research. I reasoned that relationships within this network are likely to mirror those discussed in the broader business networks' literature. Business networks typically involve multiple players with different types and levels of expertise, skills, incentives, and powers. In a global economy where knowledge creation is widely dispersed, understanding the dynamics of knowledge accumulation, absorption, conversion, and exploitation is crucial.

In studying knowledge and innovation networks, my work highlights the impact of context on the types of knowledge being created and how it is converted to applications and multiple other uses (Zahra et al., 2007). Therefore, I examined the absorption of this knowledge (Zahra and George, 2002a) as well as its conversion (Zahra, 2015; Zahra et al., 2007). Currently, we know more about knowledge absorption than conversion. Many appear to assume that once knowledge is acquired and shared, it becomes easy to use and commercially exploited (Zahra et al., 2015; Zahra, Neubaum and Larraneta, 2007). Therefore, my research highlights a need for a knowledge conversion function where acquired knowledge is processed and transformed into bundles that give meaning to ideas that can become the basis for new products, goods, services, and business models. Studying knowledge conversion would allow us to better understand why some companies and entrepreneurs are able extract more value from knowledge than others. It can also draw attention to knowledge recombination and how they develop and are later used. In turn, this requires reconsideration of the various organizational and managerial processes and decisions associated with those creative activities that pervade the development of these knowledge combinations. Further, examining conversion invariably requires attention to the process of knowledge integration, an increasingly critical organizational skill.

Expanding boundaries

Earlier in my career, I saw a big shift from a focus on smaller companies to the study of new firm creation as the defining foundation of entrepreneurship. This shift resulted in a large body of research grounded in psychology about new venture founders and their characteristics. I saw a growing emphasis on understanding organizational emergence and related imprinting and other cohort effects. Organization theories were also used to study top management teams and their effects on new venture performance. The governance of young companies was also examined in more detail (Zahra, 2015). Likewise, over the past three decades, researchers continued to give venture financing and funding considerable thought and attention. Venture finance and resource assembly are important issues, but they should be studied also in context as well as in relation to other types of resources companies need such as knowledge and social capital.

The focus on new venture creation has led nearly two decades later to the opportunity perspective that has come to dominate thinking and theorizing about entrepreneurship. Despite its polarity, I have never been a strong believer in the exclusivity of this view as a definition of entrepreneurship (Zahra and Dess, 2001). It limits the span of attention by failing to recognize the nature and sequence of the entrepreneurial process. Opportunities are recognized *after* the fact, because of discovery and creation. Still, it has become fashionable to invoke the opportunity perspective in conceptualizing new venture creation. This research has also tended to overlook the processes and activities entrepreneurs undertake – which usually show the diversity and the uniqueness of the entrepreneurial acts associated with each activity.

The boundaries of the field have changed again by the growing body of research on corporate entrepreneurship, an area that earlier some saw as lying outside the traditional domain of the field. But existing companies do create new ventures, and people working for incumbent companies routinely engage in entrepreneurial activities. Young entrepreneurial companies themselves are sometimes the product of spin-offs by large companies and established family businesses. Successful entrepreneurial ventures also grow into new fields and spin off some of their operations, perpetuating the entrepreneurial act of creation.

It is not surprising that some early CE research has shown great similarities in the entrepreneurial act between corporate and independent entrepreneurs – despite the understandable differences in contexts, actors and motivations. These findings have encouraged both the AOM entrepreneurship division and Babson conference to incorporate CE in their definition of the field and annual conference programs – and other organizations quickly followed their lead. This has legitimized CE research, promoting the integration of multiple insights from strategy, organizational theory and organizational behavior, and economics. This integration has led to a richer variety of questions being explored and methods being used.

The changing boundaries of the field, which I have just described, reflect the maturity, success, and diversity of research being conducted in the field. As such, they give the opportunity to re-examine our assumptions and theories about entrepreneurship. They also provide a forum to conduct innovative research at the disciplinary intersection. They challenge us to re-examine our research questions and their theoretical and practical relevance. As with other disciplines, research in entrepreneurship remains loosely connected, and conversations are limited to a few individuals within given, and often, very narrow domains (Gartner, Davidsson and Zahra, 2006; Schildt, Zahra and Sillanpää, 2006).

I have been a persistent and passionate advocate of keeping entrepreneurship connected to the field of strategy and other disciplines.[5] This is where entrepreneurship can infuse new thinking into entrepreneurial phenomena and other disciplines as well. Fields flourish when they stop worrying about their own domain and identities and are willing to engage in a fruitful dialog with other disciplines. Entrepreneurship as a field should retain open borders that welcome newcomers from anywhere, regardless of their ideological and disciplinary beliefs or methodological tastes. Doing otherwise (e.g., strongly adopting a particular view of what appropriate research is) risks a serious decline of the creativity and rigor of research over time.

The addition of CE and related concepts such as absorptive capacity and capabilities has broadened the definition of the domain of entrepreneurship while adding realism about the locus of these activities. Larger and established companies have been on the forefront of innovation, partly because they have hired and retained entrepreneurial people. Some have also developed entrepreneurial cultures to promote innovation and CE, the lifeblood of these companies competing in dynamic markets. Many of these companies have been engaged in corporate venturing activities to sustain growth through innovation and market entry. I cannot imagine a field that does not recognize both individual and firm-level (corporate) entrepreneurship. There are rich opportunities to study how individual variables shape CE. There is also the opportunity to explore the micro-foundations of entrepreneurial action both corporate and individual.

Another expansion was the introduction of social entrepreneurship (SE) into my research over the past few years (Zahra, 2010, 2011, 2014, 2015; Zahra et al., 2008, 2009; Zahra et al., 2014; Zahra, Newey and Li, 2014). My work to date has been conceptual, aiming to gain more clarity about the concept and its usefulness. It had sought to define SE relate it to social innovation, present a typology of different social entrepreneurs, and link SE to internationalization. In doing so, I have focused on both independent and corporate SE (Zahra et al., 2014). Throughout these efforts, I have attempted to ground my discussion of SE in established theories to ensure clarity and usefulness of the concepts being discussed.

My interest in SE stems from concern with moral and social responsibilities organizations and individuals have toward society. As an undergraduate student, I studied management at Al-Azhar University (Islam's leading university) where I received a heavy dose of theological training that instilled a sense of moral and social responsibility. Perhaps this is the reason I have shown interest in corporate social responsibility issues (Neubaum and Zahra, 2006; Surroca, Tribo and Zahra, 2013) and the debates surrounding them. It is natural, therefore, for me to probe SE and the social role of entrepreneurship (Zahra and Wright, 2016).

I have studied entrepreneurship in family firms – an area that is beginning to attract scholarly attention. I have examined ways in which entrepreneurship flourishes in these companies and the role of family variables in inducing and sustaining entrepreneurship (Zahra et al., 2008; Zahra, Hayton and Salvato, 2004). I have investigated how these firms contribute to the development and growth of new ventures (Zahra, 2010) and the symbiotic relationships that exist between these new firms and established family firms. I have also studied the internationalization of these firms as an example of the entrepreneurial activities that occur in these firms (Zahra, 2003).

Similarly, I have focused on knowledge sharing and learning and their implications for family firms (Zahra, 2012; Zahra, Neubaum and Naldi, 2007), drawing attention to the contribution family characteristics play in determining important organizational outcomes.

In studying family firms, I have used ideas I developed when studying CE such as venturing and knowledge creation through entrepreneurship. I have also paid great attention to the unique and rich context of family firms such as family involvement, family conflicts vs. cohesion, and transgenerational transfer of knowledge and learning (Zahra and Sharma, 2004) as well as how this context shapes managers' decisions. My work also contributes to the growing discussion on innovation – especially social innovation – by these firms. Likewise, I have connected my interest in technology and internationalization with the study of family firms (Zahra, 2005a). As with other aspects of my research, I have applied different theories to understand the relationships being studied.

The bulk of my research has been conducted in the context of advanced economies, mostly in high-technology global industries. But two-thirds of the world population live in poorer and emerging economies. My work on family firms and SE in particular has paid increasing attention to emerging economies, hoping to gain greater clarity about the forms of entrepreneurship (especially informal activities) in those countries. Family firms and SMEs also are the backbone of these economies, and I am cognizant of this fact as I explore new research avenues.

Entrepreneurship as knowledge

Definitions of entrepreneurship abound in the literature, encompassing opportunity (Shane, 2012) and effectuation (Sarasvathy, 2001) and bricolage (Baker and Nelson, 2005), among others. One of the findings from my research has been the recognition of entrepreneurship as knowledge – a source of different knowledge that results in heterogeneous opportunities that breed variety (for a review, see Zahra, 2015). This knowledge emerges from the discoveries made in the entrepreneurial activities undertaken by individuals or groups (Zahra, Nielsen and Bogner, 1999). It results also from flashes of creativity and insight as well as accidental discoveries. Such knowledge should be captured, absorbed, and shared to be useful through conversion to products, goods, technologies, business models, etc.

Given the popular belief in the literature that entrepreneurship results from combining and recombining different types, I studied knowledge absorption and integration. Researching absorptive capacity has been a turning point in my research (Zahra and George, 2002a, 2002b). Some see this research far removed from entrepreneurship, and I disagree. Knowledge fuels entrepreneurship and entrepreneurship generates different types of knowledge (Zahra, 2015). Understanding the factors that affect knowledge accumulation, sharing, and exploitation is therefore intimately connected to entrepreneurship. Absorptive capacity refers to the firm's prior knowledge that serves as a foundation for discovery and creation of entrepreneurial opportunities. This might explain why certain discoveries (or innovations) occur only in particular companies. These discoveries are made because of the talent, skill, and creativity of the firm's human capital that takes advantage of the firm's absorptive capacity to bring in new knowledge that is combined to create novelty and variety. Considering absorptive capacity enables us to think how internal and external knowledge are combined to create such opportunities. How productive knowledge combinations are identified and exploited remains an elusive phenomenon that researchers have yet to examine systematically.

Following my work, other researchers have developed measures and ways to capture absorptive capacity. Others have linked it to different organizational outcomes such as innovation, opportunity recognition and even organizational performance. What is amazing, however, is that limited attention has been given to the development of absorptive capacity in new ventures which typically have limited organizational memory but need to learn fast from others in order to survive and succeed. This knowledge is useful for capability building and competencies that enable successful competition. If new ventures indeed have learning advantages over established companies (Sapienza et al., 2006), we need to study how these advantages enable them to compete by evolving capabilities. How do new ventures learn about their markets? How do they accumulate this learning? How do they exploit the knowledge gained from this learning? What types of knowledge are being created as the firm operates or builds new capabilities? How do these firms choose the capabilities being built? How do they sequence them? These are some of the issues that require study. Born global companies is one such unique setting in which we can study such issues.

The invisible college and idea factory

Empiricism is the core of American research tradition. Naturally, as a child of this tradition, my early research was primarily empirical and large scale. In particular, conducting my own research on CE altered me to the fact that companies and careers rise and fall based on the quality of ideas. In executive education sessions, I heard from my students how managers create forums in which ideas develop and flourish. Companies also often buy promising innovations developed elsewhere. They also recruit and attract rare talents.

Knowing about the value of idea creation was one of the most important early lessons of my career: How managers surround themselves with people with ideas – especially those with radically new ideas. I found my part-time MBA and executive MBA classes to be an important source of fresh knowledge about corporate practices. Other in-house executive education sessions did the same thing. Working with PhD students around the globe was another useful source of fresh ideas for my research. Collaborating with colleagues also provided me with countless research ideas. Visiting scholars were also helpful in this regard. Former students who ended up in consulting companies were an especially useful conduit of information – with a ceaseless supply of ideas. I visited companies and leading innovation centers in and outside the United States and was stunned to see how ideas are born, incubated, and cared for.

I have been fortunate to be part of small research groups at JIBS and later Helsinki University of Technology (Aalto University), where I have learned a great deal about how to promote collaboration and keep a small group productive and innovative. In both cases, the group leaders were especially adept at bringing our diversity into focus, allowing us to canvass as many ideas as possible and then pick one or very few for systematic analysis. One of these leaders referred to what we have a done as "operating an idea factory". To me, there was something paradoxical about having an "idea factory" – factories typically perform well structured activities whereas creative ideas are rarely structured. But I got the key point and learned the importance of allowing ideas to flow without barriers and then putting some of them to use in a fairly disciplined way. Over time, I created my own "idea factory" which is virtual, global, disorganized, widely dispersed, and inhabited by a wide mix of different people with different and often discordant views and styles. This is probably one reason for the wide range of topics and ideas I have explored in my research over the years.

One of the most frequent questions I have received from other researchers is: How can I come up with ideas for my research? This is a puzzling question, one I find impossible to understand because ideas are available in abundance. However, good ones are shaped and crafted by closeness to the phenomenon, managers, and entrepreneurs – becoming an active conversant in global innovation or knowledge networks that permeates our world. Following one's intuition is essential – fields develop by a majority of people in an area pursuing known questions and a few others who see things many others do not yet see. The gift of foresight is almost never normally distributed in academic fields. Like artists of a different type, we sketch, draw, create, and fight for our ideas – things take their place, slowly and with thoughtful imagination. We need time to think, reflect, and theorize about things to come. But I think we need to be surprised at the discovery that the simplest of our thoughts, and ideas could be powerful engines of our imagination, creativity, research, and writing. Having an "idea factory" is the beginning of all of this.

Lessons and moving forward

In many ways, my own career and research program mirrored what companies often do to remain relevant and productive: strategic reorientation, new business development, and new market entry. As a field, entrepreneurship has developed in significant ways that are sometimes hard to explain, let alone foresee scholarly impact. This makes reinvention essential to staying alive and productive. As the field continues to change, there is no dearth of topics to study and make a worthwhile contribution. But to stay at the core of the discipline, a new sort of craftsmanship is needed – one that could benefit greatly from the insights gained from doing research at the intersection as I have done. Three decades of research have taught me that journeys of discovery have their own logic, and no well-drawn plans or maps can fully guide them. Indeed, a map (plan) might be dangerously dysfunctional, keeping one on schedule only to arrive at the wrong destination. Interactions with colleagues, students, and managers, as well as a sense of adventure, are better in defining the right destination. Thus, I have learned the virtue of being open to surprises and flights of fancy.

Another important lesson is the value of collaborations, the key source of inspiration and progress in my career. Collaborations, although challenging at times, are major sources of knowledge and resources. They are also a great source of personal, emotional, and social growth. My work has improved because of the quality of my collaborators; so has my life. The diversity of views, personalities, nationalities, and styles has all added much needed and appreciated breadth and depth to my writing and my life.

As the field relies more and more on archival data, we need to remain connected to the phenomenon, the research sites, and the actors (people) we study. Visits to science parks, talking to entrepreneurs, consulting with venture capitalists, watching new business plan pitches, and physically being part of the landscape that defines the research subject are all essential to grounding one's thinking and interpretations. Entrepreneurs and managers are very insightful (and often delightful) people – they are a rich source of ideas that deserve study. Some of these things are not directly described in my work but I know (with certainty) they have shaped my work and defined what I saw and how I studied it.

Scientific fields are a complex mixture of competing views, well-developed paradigms, and emerging ideas. The cacophony of these differences should be welcomed because it provides the intellectual space where we individually find our respective niches. This cacophony gave me the opportunity to examine multiple emerging ideas as well as a few established ones. Rather than attempting to reduce or fight that noise, I was lucky to recognize that it is the sound of new ideas trying to express themselves. I have come to accept that new ideas have their own distinct sounds – just as we see in different and emerging music genres. Thus, as someone who loves classical music, I have come also to respect metal, country, folk, and rap music. I feel the same thing about ideas. We cannot have only country or classic music – the same with the growth of our field. We should welcome, support, and celebrate the birth of new ideas because they keep us and the field young.

Conclusion

From the beginning, my research has connected strategy, entrepreneurship, and internationalization, especially in high-technology industries. It has focused on firm-level issues, consistent with my interests and my prior strategy research. Collaboration with a large number of co-authors around the globe has greatly influenced the range of issues, methods, and theories I have explored and the contexts within which I have conducted this research. I have been eager to examine emerging issues intersecting different areas. My research program has been loosely organized to capitalize on the growth of our young field. This has given me a more accepting, eclectic, and broad view of entrepreneurship while allowing me to contribute by researching at the intersection of several disciplines.

Acknowledgements

To Judy Sena and my coauthors who taught me a great deal. I am grateful for the suggestions of Sondos Abdel Gawad, Neda Bahman, Cristina Bettinelli, Garry Bruton, Susan Hill, Maria Teresa Bolivar Ramos, Harry Sapienza, Mike Wright, and Patricia H. Zahra.

Notes

1 I refer readers to one review of my work by Audretsch (2015). I have also reviewed one of my research streams in Zahra (2015), outlining my views on entrepreneurship as knowledge.

2 I believe that the strategy–entrepreneurship nexus is one of the most important research arenas. Research can inform us of the emergence of strategic initiatives and how strategies can constrain or induce entrepreneurial activities. As a result, I have maintained the need not to separate the two fields (Zahra and Dess, 2001) and instead promote research on the intersection of these two sister fields (Zahra, 2015).

3 Later, when I worked with Jonkoping International Business School (JIBS) faculty in Sweden on the Panel Study of Entrepreneurial Dynamics (PSED), I learned more about that body of literature but I was (still) unable to shake off multiple other explanations of the findings that have been left unexamined. This was troubling because I could not understand from these studies how individual variables could influence firm-level decisions. Early in my affiliation with JIBS I examined PSED-Sweden and spent time looking into the U.S. results to draw inferences about new venture creation. This experience was useful when I later joined the Global Entrepreneurship Monitor (GEM) representing a professional family firm foundation. Many of the GEM measures were developed in the PSED project. These experiences were important as I looked into independent and corporate ventures in a series of studies in several industries. I remained focused on the different strategic actions new ventures took, without delving into the psychological background of their founders and leaders.

4 When Ghent University granted me an honorary PhD degree, Mirjam Knockaert and Tom Vanucker made a similar observation:

> For us, however, the key word that sums up his research is 'diversity'. Diversity in research topics, whereby he was one of the first to explore the field of entrepreneurship, and was one of the founders of entrepreneurship as a research domain, in which he also involved the domains of strategy, technology and internationalisation. Diversity as well, in the methodologies he uses in his studies, in which he seamlessly combines qualitative and quantitative research, interviews and databases. Diversity in his study objects, involving entrepreneurs, investors and organisations in more than 18 different countries. Not to mention diversity in the group of people he works with, including both young PhD students and people who, like himself, are among the top in their field of research. His studies follow current trends wherever possible, as is clear from his current research activities focusing on crowdfunding, social media and radical innovation. . . .

5 In their explanation for granting me honorary PhDs, both Stockholm School of Economics and Gent University took note of my work at the intersection and how it has connected different disciplines. Equally

noteworthy, both the Stockholm School of Economics and Global Award citation highlight the effect of this work on other social sciences and business disciplines. Thus, my work has built on concepts, theories, and methods from different disciplines, but (hopefully) it has also given back to these disciplines.

References

Abdel-Gawad, S., Zahra, S., Svegiova, S. & Sapienza, H. Entrepreneurial Capability. *Journal of Leadership & Organization Studies*, 2013, *20*: 394–407.

Audretsch, D.B. & Shaker A. Zahra: Pioneering Entrepreneurship Scholar. *Small Business Economics*, 2015, *44*(4): 721–725.

Baker, T. & Nelson, R.E. Creating Something from Nothing: Resource Construction through Entrepreneurial Bricolage. *Administrative Science Quarterly*, 2005, *50*(3): 329–366.

Block Z. & MacMillan I.C. *Corporate Venturing: Creating New Businesses within the Firm*. Boston, MA: Harvard Business School Press, 1993.

Burgelman R.A. A Process Model of Internal Corporate Venturing in a Diversified Major Firm. *Administrative Science Quarterly*, 1983, *28*: 223–244.

Carr, J.K., Haggard, S., Hmieleski, K. & Zahra, S. A Study of the Moderating Effects of Firm Age at Internationalization on Firm Survival and Short-Term Growth. *Strategic Entrepreneurship Journal*, 2010, *4*: 183–192.

Chahine, S., Flatotchev, I. & Zahra, S. Building Perceived Quality of Founder-involved IPO Firms: Founders' Effects on Board Selection and Stock Market Performance. *Entrepreneurship: Theory & Practice*, 2011, *35*: 319–335.

Dess, G., Ireland, D., Zahra, S., Floyd, S., Janney, J. & Lane, P. Emerging Issues in Corporate Entrepreneurship. *Journal of Management* [Special issue], 2003, *29*: 351–378.

Foss, N., Lyngsie, J. & Zahra, S. The Role of External Knowledge Sources and Organizational Design in the Process of Exploiting Strategic Opportunities. *Strategic Management Journal*, 2013, *34*: 1453–1471.

Foss, N., Lyngsie, J., & Zahra, S. Organizational design requirements of entrepreneurship: the roles of decentralization and formalization for opportunity discovery and exploitation. *Strategic Organization*, 2015, *13*(1): 32–60.

Gartner, W., Davidsson, P. & Zahra, S. Are you Talking to Me?: The Nature of Community in Entrepreneurship Scholarship. *Entrepreneurship: Theory & Practice*, 2006, *30*(3): 321–331.

George, G., Wiklund, J. & Zahra, S. Ownership and Internationalization of Small Firms. *Journal of Management*, 2005, *31*(2): 210–233.

George, G. & Zahra, S. Culture and Its Consequences for Entrepreneurship. *Entrepreneurship: Theory & Practice*, 2002, *26*(4): 5–8.

George, G., Zahra, S. & Wood, D. The Effects of Business–University Alliances on Innovative Output and Financial Performance: A Study of Publicly Traded Biotechnology Companies. *Journal of Business Venturing*, 2002, *17*(6): 557–590.

Haeussler, C., Patzelt, H. & Zahra, S. Strategic Alliances and Product Development in High Technology New Firms: The Moderating Effect of Technological Capabilities. *Journal of Business Venturing*, 2012, *27*: 217–233.

Hayton, J., George, G. & Zahra, S. National Culture and Entrepreneurship: A Review of Behavioral Research. *Entrepreneurship: Theory & Practice*, 2002, *26*(4): 33–52.

Hill, S. Personal communication, May, 2015.

Hornsby, J., Kuratko, D. & Zahra, S. Middle Managers' Perceptions of the Internal Environment for Corporate Entrepreneurship: Assessing a Measurement Scale. *Journal of Business of Business Venturing*, 2002, *17*(3): 253–273.

Kelley, D., Ali, A. & Zahra, S. Where do Breakthroughs Come From? Characteristics of High Potential Inventions. *Journal of Product Innovation Management*, 2013, *30*: 1212–1226.

Larrañeta, B., Zahra, S. & Galán, J.L. Enriching New Ventures' Strategic Variety through External Knowledge. *Journal of Business Venturing*, 2012, *27*: 401–413.

Larrañeta, B., Zahra, S. & Galán, J.L. The Effect of Strategic Variety and Origin on New Venture Performance. *Strategic Management Journal*, 2014, *35*(5): 761–772.

Li, Y. & Zahra, S. Institutions, Culture, and Venture Capital Activity: A Cross-Country Analysis. *Journal of Business Venturing*, 2012, *27*: 95–111.

Mahnke, V., Venzin, M. & Zahra, S. Governing Entrepreneurial Opportunity Recognition in MNEs: Aligning Interests and Cognition under Uncertainty. *Journal of Management Studies* [Special Issue], 2007, *44*: 1278–1298.

Miller D. The Correlates of Entrepreneurship in Three Types of Firms. *Management Science*, 1983, *29*: 770–791.

Mudambi, R. & Zahra, S. The Survival of International New Ventures. *Journal of International Business Studies*, 2007, *38*: 333–352.

Mustakallio, M., Autio, E. & Zahra, S. Relational and Contractual Governance in Family Firms: Effects on Strategic Decision Making. *Family Business Review*, 2002, *15*(3): 205–222.

Neubaum, D. & Zahra, S. Institutional Ownership and Corporate Social Performance: The Moderating Effect of Investment Horizons, Activism, and Coordination. *Journal of Management*, 2006, *32*: 108–131.

Newey, L. & Zahra, L. The Evolving Firm: How Dynamic and Operating Firms Interact to Enable Entrepreneurship. *British Journal of Management*, 2009, 20(special issue): 81–100.

Pearce, J. & Zahra, S. Relative Powers of CEOs and Board of Directors: Associations with Corporate Performance. *Strategic Management Journal*, 1991, *12*: 135–153.

Sapienza, H., Autio, E., George, G. & Zahra, S. The Effect of Early Internationalization on Firm Profitability and Growth. A*cademy of Management Review*, 2006, *31*(4): 914–933.

Sarasvathy, S. Causation and Effectuation: Toward a Theoretical Shift from Economic Inevitability to Entrepreneurial Contingency. *Academy of Management Review*, 2001, *26*(2): 243–264.

Schildt, H.A., Zahra, S. & Sillanpää, A. Scholarly Communities in Entrepreneurship Research: A Co-citation Analysis. *Entrepreneurship: Theory & Practice*, 2006, *30*(3): 399–415.

Shane, S. Reflections on the 2010 Decade Award: Delivering on the Promise of Entrepreneurship as a Field of Research. *Academy of Management Review*, 2012, *37*(1): 10.

Surroca, J., Tribo, J. & Zahra, S. Stakeholder Pressure on MNEs and the Transfer of Socially Irresponsible Practices to Subsidiaries. *Academy of Management Journal*, 2013, *56*: 549–572.

Uotila, J., Maula, M., Keil, T. & Zahra, S. Exploration, Exploitation and Firm Performance: Analysis of S&P 500 Corporations. *Strategic Management Journal*, 2009, *30*: 221–231.

Van de Ven, A. & Zahra, S. Knowledge Complexity, Boundary Objects, and Innovation. In Fredrik Tell, Christian Berggren, Stefano Brusoni & Andrew Van de Ven, editors. *Managing Knowledge Integration across Boundaries*. Oxford, UK: Oxford University Press, 2016.

Zahra, S. Predictors and Financial Outcomes of Corporate Entrepreneurship: An Exploratory Study. *Journal of Business Venturing*, 1991, *6*(4): 259–285.

Zahra, S. A Conceptual Model of Entrepreneurship as Firm Behavior: A Critique and Extension. *Entrepreneurship Theory and Practice*, 1993a, *14*(4): 5–21.

Zahra, S. Environment, Corporate Entrepreneurship and Financial Performance: A Taxonomic Approach. *Journal of Business Venturing*, 1993b, *8*: 319–340.

Zahra, S. Corporate Entrepreneurship and Company Performance: The Case of Management Leveraged Buyouts. *Journal of Business Venturing*, 1995, *10*(3): 225–247.

Zahra, S. Technology Strategy and Company Performance: Examining the Moderating Effect of the Competitive Environment. *Journal of Business Venturing*, 1996a, *11*(3): 189–219.

Zahra, S. Technology Strategy and Performance: A Study of Corporate-sponsored and Independent Biotechnology Ventures. *Journal of Business Venturing*, 1996b, *11*(4): 289–321.

Zahra, S. Governance, Ownership and Corporate Entrepreneurship among the *Fortune 500*: The Moderating Impact of Industry Technological Opportunities. *Academy of Management Journal*, 1996c, *39*: 1713–1735.

Zahra, S. International Expansion of US Manufacturing Family Business: The Effect of Ownership and Involvement. *Journal of Business Venturing*, 2003, *18*(4): 495–511.

Zahra, S. Entrepreneurial Risk Taking in Family Firms. *Family Business Review*, 2005a, *18*(1): 23–40.

Zahra, S. A Theory on International New Ventures: A Decade of Research. *Journal of International Business Studies*, 2005b, *36*(1): 20–28.

Zahra, S. An Embeddedness Framing of Governance and Opportunism: Towards A Cross-Nationally Accommodating Theory of Agency – A Critique And Extension. *Journal of Organizational Behavior*, 2007a, *28*(1): 69–73.

Zahra, S. Contextualizing Theory Building in Entrepreneurship Research. *Journal of Business Venturing*, 2007b, *22*(3): 443–452.

Zahra, S. The Virtuous Cycle of Discovery and Creation of Entrepreneurial Opportunities. *Strategic Entrepreneurship Journal*, 2008, *2*: 243–257.

Zahra, S. Harvesting Family Firms' Organizational Social Capital: A Relational Perspective. *Journal of Management Studies* [Special Issue], 2010, *47*(2): 345–366.

Zahra, S. Organizational Learning and Entrepreneurship in Family Firms: Exploring the Moderating Effect of Ownership and Cohesion. *Small Business Economics*, 2012, *38*(1): 51–65.

Zahra, S. Public and Corporate Governance and Young Global Entrepreneurial Firms. *Corporate Governance: An International Review*, 2014, *22*(2): 77–83.

Zahra, S. Corporate Entrepreneurship as Knowledge Creation and Conversion: The Role of Entrepreneurial Hubs. *Small Business Economics*, 2015, *44*: 727–735.

Zahra, S., Abdel-Gawad, S. & Tsang E. Emerging Multinationals Venturing into Developed Economies: Implications for Learning and Entrepreneurial Capability. *Journal of Management Inquiry*, 2011, *20*: 323–330.

Zahra, S. & Bogner, W. Technology Strategy and Software New Venture Performance: The Moderating Effect of the Competitive Environment. *Journal of Business Venturing*, 2000, *15*(2): 135–173.

Zahra, S. & Covin, J. Business Strategy, Technology Policy and Firm Performance. *Strategic Management Journal*, 1993, *14*: 451–478.

Zahra, S. & Covin, J. Contextual Influences on the Corporate Entrepreneurship–Company Performance Relationship in Established Firms: A Longitudinal Analysis. *Journal of Business Venturing*, 1995, *10*(1): 43–58.

Zahra, S. & Das, S. Innovation Strategy and Financial Performance in Manufacturing Companies: An Empirical Analysis. *Production and Operations Management*, 1993, *2*(1): 15–37.

Zahra, S. & Dess, G. Defining Entrepreneurship as a Scholarly Field. *Academy of Management Review*, 2001, *26*: 8–10. (Dialogue section).

Zahra, S. & Fescina, M. Will Leveraged Buyouts Kill U.S. Corporate Research & Development? *Academy of Management Executive*, 1991, *5*(4): 7–21.

Zahra, S. & Flatotchev, I. Governing the Entrepreneurial Firm: A Knowledge Based View. *Journal of Management Studies*, 2004, *41*(5): 885–898.

Zahra, S. & Garvis, D. International Corporate Entrepreneurship and Company Performance: The Moderating Effect of International Environmental Hostility. *Journal of Business Venturing*, 2000, *15*: 469–492.

Zahra, S., Gedajlovic, E., Neubaum, D. & Shulman, J. A Typology of Social Entrepreneurs: Motives, Search Processes and Ethical Challenges. *Journal of Business Venturing*, 2009, *24*(5): 519–532.

Zahra, S. & George, G. Absorptive Capacity: A Review, Reconceptualization and Extension. *Academy of Management Review*, 2002a, *27*(2): 185–203.

Zahra, S. & George, G. Net-enabled Business Innovation Cycle and the Evolution of Dynamic Capabilities. *Information Systems Research*, 2002b, *13*(2): 147–150.

Zahra, S. & Hayton, J. The Effect of International Venturing on Firm Performance: The Moderating Influence of Absorptive Capacity. *Journal of Business Venturing*, 2008, *23*: 195–220.

Zahra, S., Hayton, J., Neubaum, D., Dibrell, C. & Craig, J. Culture of Family Commitment and Strategic Flexibility: The Moderating Effect of Stewardship. *Entrepreneurship: Theory & Practice*, 2008, *32*(6): 1035–1054.

Zahra, S. Hayton, J. & Salvato, C. Entrepreneurship in Family vs. Non-Family Firms: A Resource-Based Analysis of the Effect of Organizational Culture. *Entrepreneurship: Theory & Practice*, 2004, *28*(4): 363–381.

Zahra, S., Ireland, D., Gutierrez, I. & Hitt. Privatization and Entrepreneurial Transformation: A Review and Research Agenda. *Academy of Management Review*, 2000, *25*(3): 509–524.

Zahra, S., Ireland, D. R. & Hitt, M. International Expansion by New Venture Firms: International Diversity, Mode of Market Entry, Technological Learning and Performance. *Academy of Management Journal*, 2000, *43*: 925–950.

Zahra, S., Labaki, R., Abdel-Gawad, S. & Sciascia, S. Family Firms and Social Innovation. In L. Melin, M. Nordqvist & P. Sharma, editors. *Handbook of Family Business Research*. New York, NY: Sage, 2013, 442–459.

Zahra, S., Maula, M. & Keil, T. Building Technological Capabilities: Strategic and Industry Determinants of New Ventures' Inward Licensing. *European Management Review*, 2005, *2*: 154–166.

Zahra, S., Nash, S. & Bickford, D. Transforming Technological Pioneering into Competitive Advantage. *Academy of Management Executive*, 1995, *9*(1): 17–31.

Zahra, S. & Nasimbam, S. Entrepreneurship in Global Innovation Networks. *AMS Review*, 2011, *1*(1): 4–17.

Zahra, S., Neubaum, D. O. & Huse, M. Entrepreneurship in Medium-Size Companies: Exploring the Effects of Ownership and Governance Systems. *Journal of Management*, 2000, *26*(5): 947–976.

Zahra, S., Neubaum, D. & Larrañeta, B. Knowledge Sharing and Technological Capabilities: The Moderating Role of Family Involvement. *Journal of Business Research*, 2007, *60*: 1070–1079.

Zahra, S., Neubaum, D. & Naldi, L. The Effects of Ownership and Governance on SMEs' International Knowledge-based Resources. *Small Business Economics*, 2007, *29*: 309–327.

Zahra S. A. & Newey, L. R. Maximizing the Impact of Organization Science: Theory-Building at the Intersection of Disciplines and/or Fields. *Journal of Management Studies*, 2009, *46*(6): 1059–1075.

Zahra, S. Newey, L. & Li, Y. On the Frontiers: The Implications of Social Entrepreneurship for International Entrepreneurship. *Entrepreneurship: Theory & Practice*, 2014, *38*(1): 137–158.

Zahra, S. & Nielsen, A. P. Sources of Capabilities, Integration and Technology Commercialization. *Strategic Management Journal*, 2002, *23*: 377–398.

Zahra, S., Nielsen, A. & Bogner, W. Corporate Entrepreneurship, Knowledge and Competence Development. *Entrepreneurship: Theory & Practice*, 1999, *23*(3): 169–189.

Zahra, S. & Pearce, J. Boards of Directors and Corporate Financial Performance: A Review and Integrative Model. *Journal of Management*, 1989, *15*(2): 291–334.

Zahra, S., Rawhouser, H., Bhawe. N., Neubaum, D. & Hayton, J. Globalization of Social Entrepreneurship. *Strategic Entrepreneurship Journal*, 2008, *2*: 117–131.

Zahra, S., Sapienza, H. & Davidsson, P. Entrepreneurship and Dynamic Capabilities: A Review, Model and Research Agenda. *Journal of Management Studies*, 2006, *43*(4): 917–955.

Zahra, S. & Sharma, P. Family Business Research: A Strategic Reflection. *Family Business Review*, 2004, *17*(4): 331–346.

Zahra, S., van deVelde, E. & Larrañeta, B. Knowledge Conversion Capability and the Performance of Corporate and University Spin-Offs. *Industrial & Corporate Change*, 2007, 16: 569–608.

Zahra, S. & Wright, M. Entrepreneurship's Next Act. *Academy of Management Perspectives*, 2011, *25*(4): 67–83.

Zahra, S. & Wright, M. Rethinking the Social Role of Entrepreneurship. *Journal of Management Studies*, 2016, *53*(4): 610–629.

Zahra, S., Wright, M. & Abdel-Gawad, S. Contextualization and the Advancement of Entrepreneurship Research. *International Small Business Journal*, 2014, 32(5): 479–500.

Zahra, S., Wright, M. & Flatotchev, I. How do Threshold Firms Sustain Corporate Entrepreneurship? The Role of Boards and Absorptive Capacity. *Journal of Business Venturing*, 2009, *24*(3): 248–260.

Index

first-level managers 157–9
Fisher, G. 163
Fitz Roy, F. 37
flexibility 60, 111, 162
Florida, R. 6, 65
Florida International University 154, 163
footwear industry 174
Ford Foundation 17
formalization 108
Foss, K. 104
Foss, N. N. 101–15, 147–50, 264
foundations 8, 10, 30, 268
founder-owners 82
Franklin, S. 251
Fraunhofer Institute for Systems and Innovation
  Research (ISI) 119
Freeman, J. 20–1
free markets 7
free trade 7
Free University of Amsterdam 187
Frid, C. 139
Friedman, M. 34, 102
Friedrich Schiller University (Jena) 123
Fritsch, M. 116–29
Fuller, T. 223

Garrett, R. P. 163
Garrison, R. 146
Gartner, W. B. 29, 78–9, 81, 86n6, 108, 130–45,
  225–7, 268
Gates, B. 8, 39
Gates Foundation 10
Gatewood, B. 136, 138–40, 221
Gavron, B. 57
gazelles 80
gender 24, 27, 42–3, 48, 50–1, 109, 189, 202–3,
  222, 226
General Electric 205
general equilibrium theory 5
genes 182, 189–91
geographic proximity 7, 36
geography of innovation 6, 36
George, G. 224
George Mason University 7
Georgetown University 138, 141
German Federal Ministry of Economics 217
German Research Foundation (DFG) 124, 223
German reunification 124
German Social Insurance Statistics 118–19
German State Company for Technical Assistance
  (GTZ) 214
Germany 3, 7, 33, 39, 65, 116–22, 124–5, 126nn14,
  15, 186, 214, 216–17, 221, 226
Geroski, P. 33–5
Gibb, A. 215
Gibrat's law 188
global economy 7, 162, 266

Global Entrepreneurship and Development Index
  (GEDI) 7
Global Entrepreneurship Monitor (GEM) 7, 59, 79,
  109–10, 187, 219, 272n3
global financial crisis 11, 61, 80
globalization 10, 39, 205, 260
Goldsby, M. G. 156, 161, 163
Google Scholar 69, 75–6, 79, 86n4, 187
Gordon, G. 16
government-owned enterprises 259
Graf von der Schulenburg, J. M. 37
Gras, D. 97
Great Depression 9
Greene, P. 79, 120, 136, 221
grief 161
Griliches, Z. 34–5
Grilo, I. 188
Groenen, P. 189
Grove, A. 93
Gruss, P. 37

Habermas, J. 4
habitual entrepreneurs 250–1
Hall, T. 25
Haltiwanger, J. 77, 110, 126
Handbook of Entrepreneurship and Economic Growth
  (Thurik and Carree) 187
Hannan, M. 18–21, 173
Harding, R. 59
Hart, B. 37
Hart, M. 221
Harvard Business Review 189
Harvard University 172
Hayek, F. A. 102–3, 105, 107, 112n2, 117, 146–7,
  151nn1, 2
Hazlitt, H. 102, 146
health care system 19
Hébert, B. 167, 169, 170nn2–4
Heilbroner, R. 4
Helsinki University of Technology (Aalto
  University) 270
Herron, L. 138
Hessels, J. 192
Hewlett Packard 93
Hicks, J. 4, 54
high-density areas 117, 123
higher education institutions 214
high growth firms 47, 81
high-tech 6, 25, 38, 173, 259, 269, 272
high-wage employment 212
Hill, S. 185, 263, 272
history 6, 9, 14, 53–4, 68, 70n5, 74, 80, 94–5, 97,
  103, 119, 130, 136, 140, 167–8, 172, 208, 211,
  213, 219, 226
Hodgetts, R. M. 154, 163
Hofer, C. 141
Holtham, G. 57